Regatta 1879

Probably – H.R.H. Yacht – Formosa

R.N. Training Brig.

Dolphin – G.W.R. ferry – at the Spithead Pontoon, 1869

St Saviours Church – 1372

New Inn, 1736, Castle Inn, 1774, Castle Hotel, 1841, Royal Castle Hotel, 1902, – on New Quay

Hauley – R.D.S.B. Co's new screw tug 1878

END PAPER PHOTOGRAPHS COURTESY OF GRAHAM WEATHERLY

The CHRONICLES *of* DARTMOUTH

AN HISTORICAL YEARLY LOG
1854-1954

Mr Robert Cranford, founder in 1854 of The Dartmouth Chronicle.
*He was the conscience of Dartmouth, a disciple of the truth and lover
of the town, Mayor in 1872, a strong regatta advocate, an ardent
supporter of the South Embankment Scheme, and a champion of
retaining old Dartmouth buildings.*

DARTMOUTH TOWN COUNCIL

The CHRONICLES of DARTMOUTH

AN HISTORICAL YEARLY LOG
1854-1954

Don Collinson

in association with
𝔗𝔥𝔢 𝔇𝔞𝔯𝔱𝔪𝔬𝔲𝔱𝔥 ℭ𝔥𝔯𝔬𝔫𝔦𝔠𝔩𝔢

Richard
Webb

AUTHOR'S DEDICATION

To my wife Kathleen, our dear daughter Donna, her partner Dan and my grandson Jasper.

Don Collinson

PUBLISHER'S DEDICATION

*To Gilly, my wife for her love and support and in tribute to my late parents
and the three generations of my family who have lived in Dartmouth.*

Richard Webb

Text copyright © 2000 Donna J. Collinson
Typography and design © 2000 G. B. Webb
The Dartmouth Chronicle title and extracts © 2000 South Hams Newspapers Ltd.

The right to Don Collinson to be identified as the Author of the work has been asserted by him in
accordance with the Copyright, Designs and Patents Act 1988.

First published in 2000 by Richard Webb, Dartmouth

Designed by Laurence Daeche, Anonymous Design Company, 9 Colleton Crescent, Exeter EX2 4DG
Edited by Sue Viccars and Mary Edwards
Pre-edited and word-processed by Neil and Jean Baxter
Indexed by Michael Forder

ACKNOWLEDGEMENT

Full and grateful acknowledgement is given to the directors of
The Dartmouth Chronicle and South Hams Newspapers Limited for the use of
source material and extracts from their archives.

British Library Cataloguing in Publication Data
A catalogue record for this book is available from the British Library
ISBN 0 9536361 00
Printed and bound in Great Britain by Short Run Press, Exeter
Set in 10/12 New Aster

G. B. Webb trading as Richard Webb, Publisher

Richard Webb, Publisher
9 Duke Street, Dartmouth, Devon TQ6 9PY
England

CONTENTS

The Newman Family

1442 to the present day

A unique early photograph of the Newman barquentine Retriever *entering Harbour Breton, Newfoundland in full sail in 1887.*   SIR GEOFFREY NEWMAN

Since 1442, the Newmans have been dominant in Dartmouth as merchant venturers, and their ships, regularly sailed from Dartmouth to Newfoundland taking with them saleable commodities before joining in the dried salt-cod trade. By 1654 they owned estates in St John's, Newfoundland, and in Oporto, Portugal. Intially bartering was the main business. Salt and wine from Portugal were exchanged for the codfish of Newfoundland. It was then discovered that the port wine having undergone this journey had greatly improved and consequently it was in much demand in England.

In the eighteenth century, during the wars with France and Spain, Richard and Robert Newman, fitted out in Dartmouth the *St Nicholas, Richard and Robert* and *Tygress* as privateers, with 'letters of marque'. By the spring of 1788, over 150 vessels were able to leave Dartmouth for the Newfoundland fisheries, with over 3,000 men, and 300 boys aboard. However, the later Napoleonic wars hampered trade and by 1807 Portugal was occupied, so business temporarily switched to Oman, Muscat, Zanzibar and Madagascar, to continue trading in ebony and ivory.

After the wars the Newmans renewed their Newfoundland trade, but this time in partnership with other successful trading families. They gradually replaced the older vessels with a fleet of fine locally built brigantines, *Velocity, Harrier, Chanticleer, Talbot, Beagle, Terrier* and *Retriever*. By 1900, the trade was over and the remaining fleet was sold.

In 1774, Thomas Newman of Dartmouth married Sarah Page in Oporto. Their son Robert William, became High Sheriff of Devon and Exeter's Member of Parliament and in 1836, was knighted for public service. The second Baronet, Sir Robert Lydston, a Captain in the Grenadier Guards, fell at the Battle of Inkerman. He was succeeded by his brother Sir Lydston and on his death in 1892 the baronetcy passed to his eldest son Robert Hunt Stapylton Dudley Lydston. As M.P. for Exeter from 1918 to 1931 he was then raised to the peerage as Baron Mamhead. He never married, and on his death in 1945, the peerage became extinct, but the baronetcy devolved to his cousin Sir Ralph Alured, father of the present sixth baronet, Sir Geoffrey Robert Newman.

Like the second baronet, Sir Geoffrey served in the Grenadier Guards. He now manages the Blackpool and Start Estate which includes the family business at Blackpool Sands. This Estate has helped protect some of South Devon's finest heritage coast, a coastline which has little changed from the time that Newman ships used to sail past on their way to distant ports.

FOREWORD

When invited to write a foreword to this book I was expecting to be shown a dry historical record. However, having worked with Don Collinson on other historical projects and having appreciated his devoted interest in all matters to do with the Dart, I should have known better. Don has written an outstanding portrayal of everyday life around the Dart, interspersed with fascinating photographs and incredible accounts of the characters and industry which have made this port so famous. My family has been associated with the Dart for some 600 years, the most prosperous time being during the mid 19th century. Don has captured those vibrant times and led us with the help of the archives of the *Dartmouth Chronicle* through the eventful 100 year period that finally ended in peace and new hope after the uncertainties of both World Wars.

SOUTH HAMS NEWSPAPERS

SIR GEOFFREY NEWMAN

The Retriever *owned by Newman Hunt & Co., unloading a cargo of port at Newman Co. trading plantation at Harbour Breton, Newfoundland.*

Sir Geoffrey Newman, Bt

PREFACE

The haven of the Dart is, to many, like 'Jupiter among the gods', second to none, and Dartmouth is the jewel in the crown. Historically Dartmouth is well documented academically by three excellent books, but its older neighbour, Kingswear, merits only a few pages in the 1954 *Transactions of the Devonshire Association*. Although the regattas have been well recorded, the commercial life of the harbour has received little attention. Therefore this book, whilst not an in-depth research, seeks in the first chapter to redress the paucity of recorded Kingswear history, with a short résumé of its neglected past, followed by a chapter on the development of yachting in the harbour: The first two chapters embrace events until 1854, when Robert Cranford published the first edition of the *Dartmouth Chronicle*, so ending the area's isolation from local, national, and worldwide news and events, and establishing the point from which our story proceeds in a yearly format.

It is from the outstanding journalistic talent contained in those early volumes that pearls from the past have been abstracted, collated and linked together on an annual basis, and with numerous local and related photographs, most previously unpublished, to present a kaleidoscope of everyday life and events in both the harbour and the communities on either side of the river.

The story features the Harbour Commission; shipping and coaling trade; mail and river steamers; the three ferries; the railway; North and South Embankments; mansions; local regattas and yacht clubs that have eventually transformed Kingswear and Dartmouth from a rail terminal and thriving commercial port to a yachting centre and major tourist venue.

Don Collinson, Kingswear, 2000

Richard Webb, the publisher of this book and Don Collinson, the author celebrating Don's 80th birthday on 8th September 1999

CHAPTER 1

Kingswear—Port of the Pilgrims

1170 to 1850

FROM POVERTY TO PROSPERITY

Kingswear is exceptionally well situated at Kittery Point on the River Dart, Queen Victoria's 'English Rhine'. Its southern aspect enjoys a Madeira like climate with maximum sunshine, and its surroundings are 'Turneresque'. It boasts a steam railway terminus, with adjacent wharfs and quays, a lighthouse and Daymark, three separate river ferries, three marinas, a royal yacht club, a twelfth-century church, three castles, and numerous handsome mansions set in beautiful coastal countryside. It is also a prime yachting site with several marinas. The delightful town of Dartmouth is on the opposite shore, with the towns of Brixham, Paignton and Torquay a few miles away.

Geographically its position is outstanding; it clings precipitously to a promontory on the southern tip of the Brixham peninsula at the confluence of the sea and the broad deep River Dart, an ideal safe anchorage and yachting centre. The peninsula, which the town of Brixham to the north shares with Kingswear, is formed by an isthmus one-and-a-half miles wide from Galmpton Creek on the Dart to Broadsands in Torbay. It is five miles long by two miles wide at the extreme, containing over 7,000 acres of rich fertile land on a coastal plateau 583 feet above sea-level. Apart from Brixham and Kingswear the peninsula is sparsely populated, with some ancient farms and quality residences. It is encompassed by 22 miles of exceptionally beautiful coastline, largely owned by the National Trust with numerous secluded coves and beaches to welcome visiting yachtspeople.

Brixham Cross, the meeting place of the roads from Noss, Galmpton, Brixham and Kingswear is on the crest at Hillhead forming a natural division of the peninsula, with Brixham to the north and east, and Kingswear to the south and west. From earliest times access to Kingswear has been restricted to one major approach road, Slappers Hill gently falling two miles from Hillhead to Waterhead Creek, continuing alongside the creek and river to the church, the Royal Dart Hotel, and the lower car and passenger ferries to Dartmouth. There is a secondary approach via the Toll House halfway down Slappers Hill but turning into Boohay Road passing Nethway House, Boohay, and Mount Ridley before either proceeding on to Kingswear Castle or descending Church Hill to the Lower Ferry. Also from Hillhead, Bridge Road falls tangentially for two miles to meet the Higher Ferry at Noss, a mile up the river from Kingswear.

Until 1974 Kingswear was a tiny enclave of about 100 acres, roughly triangular in plan, starting from the end of Waterhead Creek and continuing down the middle of the creek to Kittery Point, there turning 90 degrees seaward along the shoreline to just past Kittery lighthouse, here to about face 135 degrees, climbing at one in seven to the old fort, the Redoubt, on the hilltop 383 feet above sea level, then falling sharply down to intersect with its start point, Waterhead Mill, at the head of the creek.

THE THREE FERRIES

The River Dart formed an obvious barrier to travellers. Kingswear, conveniently close to Torbay, had a natural embarkation point for a short crossing at Kittery Point, so from time immemorial a ferry was established for travellers and pilgrims, followed by a church, priory and inn to serve their needs.

The earliest surviving records show that in 1365 the Close Rolls transferred lands, rents, services and Kingswear ferry from Martin de Fishacre to the powerful Cary

NEW COMMUNICATION OVER THE DART

Castle Inn, Dartmouth, 3 Oct 1829.

In consequence of notices given under the sanctions of the Right Hon. Earl Morley, a numerous and highly respectable meeting took place on Saturday last, in the large room at the Castle Hotel for the purpose of receiving a report from Messrs Rendell and Foulstone upon the plans suggested for accomplishing this most desirable object.

Soon after twelve o'clock, a letter was read from the Noble Earl, stating that having been attacked suddenly by the gout, he was sorry to be prevented attending the Meeting the object of which he very much desired to see carried into effect. His Lordship also expressed a hope that should another Meeting take place upon the subject, he should be able to attend.

J H Seale, Esq. Having expressed his regret at the absence of his noble friend Lord Morley, begged to propose that George Stanley Carey of Follaton, be requested to take the chair. Mr Cary having acquiesced, briefly stated that his course, he believed, was to call upon the Engineer, Mr. Rendell, for the statement he had prepared upon the subject for which the Meeting was called.

Mr. Rendell then read to the Meeting a Report of which the following is the substance. He alluded to the notorious inadequacy of the present ferry across the Dart, to afford the public that accommodation, which the improved state of the roads through the South coast of the county imperiously demands; the establishment of a better means of passing would also materially promote the particular interest of Dartmouth and its neighbourhood. (The Bridge proposed is a floating Bridge; the shape of which and its capabilities will be better understood by a reference to the engraving which we have sub-joined. By a reference also to the above engraving of the River it will be seen that the proposed course of the Bridge is from Lower Noss to Lower Sand-Quay.) This, continued Mr R., though sufficiently removed from the anchorage ground of the Harbour to prevent inconvenience to the Bridge, or injury to the navigation, is within a few hundred yards of the town. Here the river is at low water about 800 feet wide, and at high water about 1200. The currents are very moderate, the situation sheltered, and the shores well adapted to the formation of proper landing places. Two plans were exhibited by the Engineer, one of which will be found more particularly described by the engraving already referred to, the other having for its execution an endless chain, the lower part of which passing through brass collars fixed at the bottom of the River, would be worked machinery on the shore. This latter plan involving more expense than the former was left out of view by the Meeting, and therefore the Engineer confined himself to the plan first mentioned. He stated that the cost of making the bridge, erecting piers, chain, & c. would be £2550. That the total required capital to pay the expense of an application to Parliament, to form approaches to the Bridge from the Turnpike Road leading to Torquay, Brixham, &c. about a mile and a half in length and the requisite approach on the Dartmouth side

would be £5200. The proposed road on the East side of the Harbour would shorten the distance from Dartmouth to Torquay and Paignton, at least a mile and a half, besides cutting off that tremendous hill at Kingswear. The annual expense of the Bridge is estimated at £235 which includes £60 to be paid to Mr. Luttrell as compensation for the deterioration of the present ferry at Kingswear. To meet this expense and to defray the interest upon the capital, it is expected that the tolls will produce an annual income of £625 per annum, thus leaving a surplus of £205. 10s as a balance to be applied as the shareholders may determine.

W J Clark, Esq. Of Buckland Tout Saints, Kingsbridge, then moved the resolution, for which see advertisement.

Dr. Puddicombe stated to the Meeting from Mr Elton, who had formerly opposed the erection of a Bridge at Greenway, that he should not throw any impediments in the way of the proposed plan, though it would materially affect his ferry at Dittisham.

J B Smith, Esq. Congratulated his fellow townsmen upon the respectability and the unanimity of the Meeting, and he trusted that though the worthy Chairman now saw what he may call the nakedness of the land, that this Meeting would be a grand cause of enabling the town of Dartmouth to enjoy all the benefits of its local and physical advantages. He congratulated the Meeting on the apparent facility of carrying the proposed plan into execution; but he thought it would be the wisest and best course if before they took any decided steps, the plan should be laid by a Committee which the Meeting would then appoint, before the Corporation of Dartmouth, and the legal advisors of the Duchy of Cornwall (Applause). He could contemplate no objection to the plan, but others may, and to prevent if possible any disappointment in carrying this magnificent plan into execution, he hoped that before anything was done, that a Committee from that Meeting would lay the fullest possible statement of the case before the above authorities, previous to any expense being incurred.

Col. Seale observed that the resolution now before the Meeting could only be considered as a basis upon which the plan may proceed.

W Hockin, Esq. agreed entirely with the sentiments expressed by Mr. Smith with regard to the parties alluded to. He remembered very well expression of Governor Holdsworth at Kingsbridge when canvassing for Mr. Bastard, 'they talk of doing much for Mr. Bastard in the North of Devon, let them come and see what we are doing in the South.' Perhaps at the next Meeting they may hope to see their representative, but he hoped, if the corporation had any objection to the plan so manifestly for the interest of the town at large, that they would come forward and openly state their objections; and not lay back until everything was prepared, and all the time and money necessary for the preliminaries were expended and then come forward with an opposition which may have the effect of delaying, at least, this most important and beneficial measure.

The Rev. R. Holdsworth came forward, and stated that he thought it irrelevant alluding to the Corporation and his brother, under present circumstances. With respect to the Corporation, the Mayor of Dartmouth had not, he believed, been advised of the present Meeting.

The observations of the Rev. Gentleman led to some explanations on the part of Mr. Smith, C. Seale, and Mr. Rendell, from which it appeared that Mr. Governor Holdsworth had been always favourable to the accomplishment of the object proposed by the Meeting, the cause of his not drawing back was not however explained. The Committee, for which see also advertisement, being appointed, the Meeting adjourned as therein specified.

The fullness of the Meeting was a very strong proof of the anxiety which is felt by the public general towards the measure.

****

The following figure will enable our readers to form a tolerably correct idea of the machine intended to be used in this new communication:-

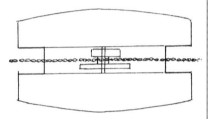

It represents a twin-boat united by a steam-engine, which turns a wheel over which the chain represented in the cut passes, and as the chain is fixed to both sides of the shore, the Bridge is propelled backwards or forwards as the chains may require. The platform of the boat will not be much raised above the water mark, and the whole length being 15 feet, will enable carriages and horses to come from the road immediately upon the Bridge; there will be a parapet on each side of the boat four feet high, and as the ends, are of course made to swing for the purpose of adapting themselves to the state of the tide, they will also turn up, when the Bridge is passing to prevent accident from horses or other cattle. The steam engine is estimated to be of six horse power, and the passage will not exceed six minutes upon an average.

We feel ourselves justifies in adding that the success of this work must have a great influence upon the prosperity and convenience of a considerable part of this county, and upon Dartmouth in particular, which has of late begun to experience a little of the improving spirit of the age; the new road to Totnes and Kingsbridge is a great improvement, and the NEW MARKET PLACE recently erected adds very materially to the convenience of the inhabitants; we must not omit to state, that the accommodation at the Castle Hotel, for families or individuals, cannot be exceeded by any Inn in the West of England.

3 Oct 1829 Report of the general meeting held at the Castle Inn, called to promote a scheme to bridge the Dart, prior to the formation of the Floating Bridge Company.

KEITH PERKINS

Left: *From Collins Quay showing the Three Ferries; Squire Luttrell's horse- and rowing-ferries, and Sir Henry Paul Seale's* Floating Bridge, *circa 1832.*
Tom Casey

Right: *Sir Henry Paul Seale's* Floating Bridge *No. 2 chain-ferry at Sandquay: traction-propelled by horses, sometimes blind and reportedly ill-treated.*
Tom Casey

family. In 1544 Thomas Gales held the Manor of Kingswear with the ferry rights on payment of a yearly tithe. The next owners in the seventeenth century were the Mallocks and Holways, and passage money was due from neighbouring villages. Then the Fownes family became the owners of Nethway and most of Kingswear, with its Manor and the Plume of Feathers Inn (Royal Dart Hotel), to which at some stage the rights for running the ferry had been transferred. Apart from the slip alongside the inn, another small slip, Collins Quay by Kittery, was occasionally used, and for a short period in the early nineteenth century a ferry appears to have operated from the old Passage House Inn at Hoodown. However, the Fownes Luttrells remained responsible for maintaining a rowing ferry and small horse boat operated by long sweeps until 1865, when they were acquired by the railway company.

In 1828 a second crossing up the river became a prerequisite to complete the toll road link between Exeter and Plymouth, so Colonel John Seale of Mount Boone, with the Earl of Morley, commissioned the eminent Plymouth engineers James Meadows Rendel and John Foulston, whose first proposal was a suspension bridge from Dittisham to Greenway. This project had to be abandoned because of fierce opposition from Edward Elton (owner of the Greenway Estate) and the small Dittisham ferry. The impasse was resolved with a novel scheme for a steam-propelled chain ferry lower down the river between Sandquay and Rock Point, which evoked strong opposition from Governor Holdsworth, whose family controlled Dartmouth and had a feud with the Seales. Alternatives, both probably moved by Holdsworth, were suggested: a steam-crossing between Hoodown Passage House Inn and Spithead, or a high-level bridge from St Barnabas's new church to Kingswear. Eventually a company was formed by Colonel J Seale and others to promote the *Floating Bridge* scheme from his lands at Sandquay, a Parliamentary bill was obtained and work commenced. This resulted in a new two mile long road being cut from Rock Point to Brixham Cross with the grand opening two years later in August 1831. Although much appreciated by inhabitants and travellers alike, the *Floating Bridge* was never a commercial success, incurring a penalty payment of £60 per annum to Mr Luttrell, owner of the Lower Ferry, as compensation for the loss of revenue from the Post Office mails. After four years the chain ferry was converted from steam propulsion to horse traction by treadmill, and continued to operate for a further twenty years until the *Floating Bridge* sank in a storm at the Sandquay mooring, causing serious inconvenience to local traders and others. In 1856 a new ferry was provided and since then various *Floating Bridge* replacements, lower ferries and the later railway ferry have continued to give good service to the present day.

KINGSWEAR CHURCH
When Kingswear was a market town,
Dartmouth was a furzy down.

Left: Kingswear 1799. A Girton etching showing the old low-roofed church, the white three-gabled Manor House of the Gale family, the Trust Rooms, Kittery Court, the Plume of Feathers Inn and the ferry.
TOM CASEY

Right:
In 1845 the old church was demolished and rebuilt except for the tower, and the abutting Gripes House was removed in 1860. Drawing by Governor Arthur Howe Holdsworth.
BRIGADIER W HINE-HAYCOCK

So states a couplet on a 1309 Papal Bull, once held in the parish chest. There is some truth in this old adage, for a church symbolises a town's importance, and Kingswear's twelfth-century stone church of St Thomas à Becket was constructed on land owned by the Norman Northumberland de Vescy family several decades before Dartmouth's first stone church, St Clements, was built in 1200 at Townstal a mile above town.

Archaeological evidence shows that the Brixham peninsula was sparsely but continuously occupied from the last Ice Age, through Stone, Bronze and Iron Ages, to AD57 when the Romans occupied Britain, until their departure in the fourth century. In August 1886 the *Chronicle* reported the find, of a second century Roman coin in the garden of The Beacon, Kingswear, inscribed V T Commodius (AD180) with the spread eagle on the reverse. After two centuries of the Dark Ages the Angles, Saxons and Jutes arrived, followed in 705 by the main body of Saxons who formed settlements in Kingswear, Kingston, Galmpton and Coleton. Marauding Danes, however, forced the settlers to take refuge on higher ground at Townstal, Boohay, and Hillhead.

After the Norman invasion William of Normandy created the *Domesday Book*, recording all Saxon property and holdings which he gave as rewards to his Norman followers. To Judhael he gave Totnes and the Brixham peninsula, but not Kingswear and Kingston, which went to the de Vescys. The Normans quickly realized the importance of Dartmouth's harbour in serving their estates in France and it was used as an assembly port for pilgrimages. On 23 May 1147, 164 ships left for the second crusade. They called at Oporto where the King of Portugal persuaded them to take part in the siege of Lisbon, when after seventeen weeks the city was recaptured from the Moors . Few ships proceeded on, and in 1190 King Richard assembled a further hundred ships in Dartmouth, destined for the third crusade to the Holy Land.

The Normans attempted to subdue the Welsh and the Scots, and after their 1196 victory over King Malcolm of Scotland, Yvo de Vescy secured Alnwick, Northumberland, and erected a massive border fortification in Alnwick Castle. The family also had estates in Normandy, which is perhaps why they retained Kingswear, with Kingston Vescy. Kingswear church was built into the hillside, possibly on the site of a Saxon church, 50 feet above the water, and a priory and inn were also constructed. Kittery Point was a natural river-crossing near the sea, and it became the embarkation point for pilgrims going to the shrine of St James of Compostela, and for those pilgrims disembarking to visit Canterbury. Conflict retained the de Vescys in Northumberland, and in 1170 Willelmus de Vescy gave half of his Kingswear estate to Totnes Priory. Four years later Alnwick Castle successfully withstood siege by King William of Scotland, although in nearby Warkworth 300 English people taking refuge in the church, were massacred. In 1196 Walterus de Vescy gave the remaining half of the Kingswear land to Torre Abbey, the family retaining possession of Alnwick until 1297.

The new owners of Alnwick were the Anglo-Norman Percy family, and only three of the Earls (including 'Hotspur') were not killed in battle, murdered, shot or left to die in the Tower. The male line died out with the 11th Earl and his only daughter married the Duke of Somerset, their son being made Duke of Northumberland in 1766. The above union thus restored the ties between Kingswear and Northumberland, for a later Duke of Somerset was for fifteen years Commodore of the Royal Dart Yacht Club (1905-1920).

The oldest relic in Kingswear Church, apart from the font, is the stone coffin lid of Brother Philip, 1280, devoid of its brass insertions but inscribed around the edges, 'You who pray for the soul of Philip shall have thirty days' pardon as a reward'.

By the nineteenth century the church ceased to be a chapel of ease to Brixham and in 1837 a separate parish was created and the Reverend John Smart was appointed rector. In 1845 Edward Appleton, architect, was appointed to rebuild the church (except for the old tower) at a cost of £1,574. The church walls were partly pulled down to hillside level and the new building erected just inside the remaining portions of the old walls, which then acted as retaining walls to the hillside. The new walls were heightened, and the eaves' level raised, making the ridges level with the top of the old tower, as they are today.

Kingswear old church interior, prior to rebuilding in 1845-1847. Drawing by Governor Arthur Howe Holdsworth
KINGSWEAR CHURCH

SHIPBUILDING

The village expanded from the church, northwards creekwise to Wood Lane, thus creating Fore and Higher Streets (East Town), and southwards along the Kittery foreshore to Ravenswell, (1657), creating Lower Street (South Town).

East of Kittery Point, adjacent to Waterhead Creek and approximately halfway up Fore Street, stood Kingswear's shipyard, sheltered from the winds and tide race. From earliest times some shipbuilding must have been carried out in Kingswear*, but few records exist before the 1786 Act (26, Geo III, cap 60), which created the Merchant Shipping Registers. Unfortunately, of the eighteenth century Dart Customs Registers, only 1789, 1791 and 1792 remain.

For Kingswear, however, there is a record in 1784 of the construction by an unknown builder of the 14-ton sloop *Good Intent*. The nineteenth century Customs Registers from 1816 to 1820 list W Matthews building three sloops, average 40 tons, the *Clio, Catherine* and *Rose Bank*, and a two masted schooner, 87 tons, *Lovely Cruizer*. The next entry is for Henry Nichols building from 1840 to 1846 an 11-ton cutter *Albatross*, five sloops average 30 tons: *Start, Flora, Jane Burrow, Neriad* and *Swift* and three schooners of 95, 99, and 107 tons, the *Saucy Lass, Fear Not,* and *Trial*. Finally, Edward Alford built three sloops from 1855 to 1863, averaging 40 tons, *Sultana, Lady Churston,* and *William and Sarah,* and the 154-ton schooner *Mizpah*.

In 1864 the shipyard was obliterated under the tracks of the new locomotive terminus, and although the railway company constructed a small alternative yard at Hoodown Point, no serious shipbuilding was recorded on the eastern shoreline until 1890, when Simpson, Strickland & Co decamped from Sandquay and established a major shipyard and engineering works at Noss, expanding to become a national firm, which Philip & Son took over in 1918.

KITTERY, MAINE USA

Meanwhile, Dartmouth's growth outstripped Kingswear's, though at Kittery a complex of merchants' houses, tofts, palaces and quays developed into a thriving waterside community, engaged in the Newfoundland fisheries, Portuguese wine and salt trades (and smuggling: Jack Rattenbury, Parson Peter, Jim Davis, Nancy Tallon, and others).

*Taken from a compilation by the master nautical researcher, the late Grahame Farr, and given to Dartmouth historian, the late Percy Russell, who later passed same to the Brixham historian, the late John Horsley, who carried out further extensive research.

During Thomas Gale's occupation of the Manor of Kingswear he disposed of certain quayside properties to some of the incoming merchants, such as Alexander Shapleigh (1578), Richard Kelly (1587), William Rowe (1617), and the Champernownes. The Shapleighs and the Champernownes were related in business and by family, and shared adjacent properties on Kittery shore; the quay, south of Collins Quay (now Kittery Garden Cottage), belonged to the Shapleighs, and the neighbouring wharf (the Royal Dart Yacht Club and Longford) to the Champernownes. The Champernownes held a seventy-year lease on the old castle (Godmerock) and grounds in 1591.

By 1636 consensus believes the two families combined to open a settlement in New England. Francis Champernowne, twenty-two-year-old second son of Arthur Champernowne of Dartington, was funded to a sum of £1,118 by mortgaging their Godmerock and Kittery properties. He sailed in the *Benediction* for the Americas, where the Champernownes and Shapleighs established a settlement in Maine, at the mouth of the River Piscataqua, also on the mainland and on an island opposite New Hampshire. The mainland was named Godmerock, the houses Kittery and Greenway, the island Dartington, while another holding, Shapleigh, was established nearby. Kittery is the oldest township in Maine, and there is a Kittery Society whose members occasionally make pilgrimages to Kingswear.

CASTLES, MANSIONS, AND LOCAL PERSONALITIES

Three Castles guarded Kingswear: between 1499 and 1503 the harbour defences were strengthened, and opposite the recently built Dartmouth Castle (1488-95), Kingswear Castle was erected, a strong square tower with embrasures for ordnance pieces. Before the present fifteenth century castle, the much older natural defensive fortification may have been partly Saxon. Prior to the dissolution of the monasteries in 1539, the castle possibly belonged to the Mohuns, early owners of Tormohun, Torquay (and coincidentally of Dunster Castle, later in 1376 the home of the Luttrells of East Quantoxhead, Somerset,) and in 1747 to Henry Fownes of Nethway, Kingswear.

Further downriver, at Silver Cove, are the remains of the third castle, Godmerock Castle (a fortified house), below which a chain was made fast to a pierced natural rock formation and stretched across the harbour in times of war. Godmerock also had links to Dunster Castle, for after 1747 Henry Fownes owned both castles and the lineage of his mother (Anne, née Maddock) traces back to the sixteenth century to one Reginald de Mohun, a descendant of the original Mohuns, builders of Dunster Castle. The castles participated in the later Civil War, along with a stone-faced star-shaped bastion, Fort Redoubt, built on Mount Ridley by the Royalists under Sir Henry Carey. Unfortunately the fort was mainly obliterated in 1882 during the construction of the mansion, The Redoubt.

NETHWAY MANOR AND ESTATE

The Coles were the first owners of Nethway, a large estate comprising Hoodown, Croftland, Boohay (Leitewigston), Kingston Vescy, Coleton and Brownstone. The original manor house was built about 1380 in the reign of Richard II and was owned by William Cole, succeeded by John Cole.

The Hodys Sir William Hody, Chief Baron of the Exchequer, was the next owner through his marriage in 1440 to John Coles's daughter. During his stewardship he allowed the old chapel of Holy Trinity on Down End Point to fall into ruin. This, built 525 feet above sea-level, had served a dual purpose as church and landmark for mariners at sea, and was not replaced until four centuries later when Dartmouth Harbour Commission built the present 80-foot high hollow Daymark. All traces of the earlier chapel have vanished although the font was used as a pig trough, then later as an urn for flowers in the garden of Boohay Farm, from whence it was retrieved in the eighteenth century and returned to Kingswear church to resume its rightful duty.

By 1662 the 400-acre Brownstone part of the estate had been acquired by the Hayne family. Nine years later on 23 July 1671 the heirs of Sir William Hody at Nethway entertained and accommodated the 'merry monarch', King Charles II, Dartmouth's first yachtsman, who was returning to London by coach after arriving in Dartmouth in his yacht *Cleveland* on the previous day. In 1696 John Hody began building the present commodious mansion, and two years later, with the house still incomplete, he sold the whole estate to John Fownes.

The Fownes/Fownes Luttrells When John Fownes of Plympton Priory bought the Nethway Estates, according to Luttrell deeds it comprised: 'two messuages, six cottages, six farms, seven gardens, three orchards, one grain mill, one fulling mill, one windmill, 300 acres of arable, 140 acres pasture, 40 acres of woodland, 150 acres of furze and heathland, Nethway House, Hoodown, Waterhead, etc'.

He completed the mansion then extended his local holdings, acquiring Kingswear Manor in 1717 from the Gale family, and Barnes House (Kittery House) and garden from Thomas Aylwyn and Mary Harson. Six years later he bought the site and ruins of a house from Susan Shapleigh, thus now owning both the previous Champernowne and Shapleigh properties. His influence increased in 1731 when his daughter Elizabeth married John Seale, of Mount Boone, Dartmouth. John Fownes died in that year and John Fownes II succeeded him, but only survived until 1735.

Two grandsons were next in line: Henry Fownes inherited Nethway House and estate, his younger brother Thomas acquired the Kittery properties. Henry Fownes (1723-1780) inherited the larger portion of the estate, Nethway House, numerous farms and Kingswear properties, and in 1747 married Margaret, only child and heiress of the Luttrells of Dunster Castle, Somerset, thus acquiring a castle, over 15,000 acres, and the ancestral name of Luttrell, which he combined with Fownes to continue the lineage. The family had increased wealth and influence, and they raised six sons and four daughters; the second son John Fownes Luttrell (1752-1816) inherited in turn and sired five sons: John, Henry, Francis, Alexander and Thomas: and four daughters. The two elder boys never married, while Colonel Francis Fownes Luttrell had five sons and four daughters. The family resided principally at Dunster Castle and until 1832 represented as MPs the nearby town of Minehead, but retained the Kingswear Estate, though Nethway House was allowed to deteriorate.

After the death of John Fownes Luttrell in 1816, his eldest son John inherited and continued to add to the estate, acquiring for a short period the fine mansion Greenway House, former home of Sir Humphrey Gilbert, and increased the moiety of Kingswear and Nethway Manor with Galmpton Manor. He also joined Charles Seale Hayne on the board of the Dartmouth & Torbay Railway Company, for as owner of a large tract of land likely to be required by the company, he stood to gain from sales and increased land values. In January 1857 he died and Henry inherited, and until his death in 1867 further improved Kingswear by cutting Lower and Higher Contour Roads and building the waterworks. The third son, Colonel Francis Fownes Luttrell, had predeceased him, so the estate passed to the colonel's son George Fownes Luttrell, who built the new Kingswear School, but in 1874 he

Left: Kingswear Castle, 1491-1502. A joint harbour fortification with Dartmouth Castle – the first to be built to accommodate artillery. It was restored and extended in 1855 as a residence for Charles Seale Hayne, the owner. AUTHOR'S COLLECTION

Right: Nethway House. The original house was built around 1380 by William Cole but rebuilt in 1696 by John Hody. In 1698 it was purchased by John Fownes, who, after marriage, later added the name Luttrell to continue the lineage. The house and eventual 2,000-acre-estate remained in the family possession until 1874-1875 when it was sold to the Llewellyn family. COLIN SMART

offered for sale the whole 1,752-acre estate, which included most of Kingswear; thus after 176 years the Fownes Luttrells relinquished their domination of the area.

The Llewellyns Unsold at the Luttrells' great sale, Nethway House and a large acreage was bought by Llewellyn Llewellyn in 1875 for £22,000, and shortly after he became a sponsor and a prime mover in the building of the Royal Dart Yacht Club's new riverside headquarters and Nethway School (now Dragon House). The family retained ownership until well into the next century.

KITTERY COURT

Left: Brookhill Mansion, built in 1825, home of Governor A H Holdsworth and the Rev. Robert Holdsworth; in 1820 the latter built the first Brookhill, which was destroyed by a landslip. Two servants were killed while the owners were at a church service.

Mrs Dob Shelley

Thomas Fownes determined on obtaining the remaining properties in the Kittery complex to create a gentleman's waterside residence with lawns and gardens encompassed by sea walls. Until the nineteenth century further purchases were made of six holdings and land, resulting in the demolition of the warren of old merchants' houses, stores and quays and the building of Kittery Court around 1760. He was appointed Rector of Brixham, and died in the early nineteenth century; his son Henry George Fownes inherited and Kittery remained in the family's possession until around 1828.

The next occupier was John Browne Smith, of Dartmouth, but in the 1840s it became the property of the influential Kingswear family, the Roopes of Blacklers (Carlton Lodge), where Lieutenant General Benjamin Roope lived with his two sisters, Sarah and Mary. In 1841, Sarah Roope generously endowed the Trusthouses as a Sunday School room and five dwellings for the needy. She died in 1868, and Kittery Court passed to George Roope, who remained until the 1890s. Then followed Mr Teague for some years, whose family had earlier been in the wine trade with the Roope family. The next occupier was Mr Cross, a director of Simpson, Strickland & Co, who invented an improved three/four crank expansion engine, and his brother became Admiral Cross. In 1912 Archibald Hine-Haycock became owner and it remained in the family until the later 1980s when the property was sold and purchased by Dr and Mrs Warner from Canada, the present owners.

BROOKHILL

Right: Kittery Court, originally Barnes House, was converted around 1760 by Thomas Fownes who demolished the warren of old merchants' houses and quays and built the encompassing sea walls to create a gentleman's residence, gardens and small estate.

Dr Warner

This lovely house was for many years the home of Robert Holdsworth vicar of Townstal, and Arthur Howe Holdsworth, eighteen years MP for Dartmouth, twice Mayor of Dartmouth, and last Governor of Dartmouth Castle. They came from a long line of merchants who had virtually controlled Dartmouth for 300 years, and their family seat was at Widecombe House, Stokenham, with a town house, Mount Galpin, at Dartmouth. Early in the nineteenth century they purchased, probably from the Luttrells, Mouth Farm Kingswear, on the shoreline at Silver Cove, and built a commodious mansion, Brookhill. Unfortunately a geological fault caused a landslip which seriously damaged the house and killed two servants and the property was rebuilt in 1825 further up the hillside. The salubrious climate encouraged gardens of tropical splendour, increased by the purchase of the adjacent Godmerock Castle and grounds. In creating the garden, the skeleton of a huge man was discovered around which Arthur Howe

Holdsworth moulded the story, *The grave of the unknown*, passed down for generations. Mr Holdsworth implanted his own grand personality on the house, with the establishment of the superb memorial room, the walls covered with fine carved panelling (supposedly similar to that once in the demolished house of Thomas Newcomen, Dartmouth). There was also an elaborate fibrous plastered ceiling moulded into intricate panels which, like the walls, contained countless small replicas of the coats of arms of the principal families of Devon. The room also contained a splendid carved fireplace, again reputed to have come from Thomas Newcomen's house (there are several claimants to Newcomen's fireplace). The *pièce de résistance* was a fibrous plaster moulded chimneypiece of Shadrach, Meshach and Abednego, surrounded by angels in the fiery furnace. It is reputed to have been removed from the Greenway home of Sir Humphrey Gilbert by Roope Harris Roope, a former occupant, then acquired by Mr Holdsworth, but fortunately it is now back at Greenway House (later the home of Agatha Christie).

In the mid 1840s Mr Holdsworth moved nearer to Kingswear, building The Beacon, and Brookhill passed to Mr Davenport, who sold it on to William Johnston Neale, a popular author of the time. It was twice visited by royalty during this time, once by the ex-Emperor of France, Napoleon III. The next occupant was Mrs Augustus Packe, followed in 1879 by the Wilkins family, gold bullion dealers of London who loved the house, later purchasing Fountain Violet Farm and Godmeroc; the Brookhill gardens became quite famous. Mr Wilkins was also well known for his charitable work, later buying and saving Gallants Bower. Brookhill was sold in 1946 to Mr Sanderson, to become the Fountain Violet Country Club. It was next purchased by Mr and Mrs Shelley, who sold it in 1964 to a firm of developers who split up the property into the present group of flatlets.

THE BEACON

In 1845 Governor Holdsworth purchased from the Fownes Luttrells several acres of land nearer Kingswear at the junction of Beacon Road and Castle Road. Just above the 1864 lighthouse which he had advocated in his 1841 report to the Admiralty, he built another spacious mansion, which he named The Beacon. He lived there until his death in 1860.

Governor Holdsworth was a controversial, charismatic and far-sighted man, who, among his many achievements,, should have the credit for ending Dartmouth's geographical isolation. In 1815 he obtained from Parliament the Dartmouth Improvement Act which between 1823 and 1828 resulted in the infilling of the Mill Pool to create a much-needed central area on which to build the market and the New Road, which rose 350 feet to join the old Modbury-to-Dartmouth Road at Townstal. He then promoted the Kingsbridge/Torcross/Dartmouth Turnpike Trust which built the first section of road from Dartmouth to Stoke Fleming. The remaining Stoke Fleming-Torcross section was not completed until 1855, again at his instigation. He was also a principal motivator of the Torquay/Paignton/ Kingswear Trust's western road link to Dartmouth.

In 1837 Governor Holdsworth formed the River Dart Steam Navigation Company, and with his *Dart* instigated the first steamboat service to Totnes. However, the formation and intrusion of rival companies with the Paul Pry and later *Volante* and *Undine* proved the service to be uneconomic for more than one steamboat, and all were withdrawn a few years later. This was repeated in 1856 when he sponsored the *Royal Dartmouth* against Captain Moody's *Dart* and Charles Seale Hayne's *Louisa*. After Governor Holdsworth's death W Froude purchased the *Royal Dartmouth*.

In 1840 he successfully petitioned the Lords of the Admiralty for Dartmouth to replace Falmouth as packet station, but he was defeated by the chicanery of Plymouth politicians. In 1853 he was promoter of the unsuccessful Dartmouth Railway Company's scheme to bring railway communication to Dartmouth, and in 1856 became a major shareholder in Charles Seale Hayne's Dartmouth & Torbay Railway Company, which opened in 1864.

This last event, four years after his death, marked the fruition of his endeavours to link the landlocked 'Haven of the Dart' with the hinterland by Road, River and Rail, 'the three Rs'.

BROWNSTONE

This 400-acre former part of the Nethway Estate, acquired by the Hayne family in 1662, occupies an exceptional position at the mouth of the Dart, and was composed of the two major farms, Higher and Lower Brownstone, Kingswear Castle and an 86 acre rabbit warren.

It remained in the ownership of the family for 241 years until the death of Charles Seale Hayne (1832–1903), when it was sold. During his lifetime on the estate, the latter had restored Kingswear Castle as a local address, laid out the roads and built several commodious mansions. He was, like his older neighbour Governor Holdsworth, a mentor of Dartmouth, and over a period of thirty-one years, in spite of often petty and vitriolic opposition (which in 1885 caused him to abandon the area to pursue a political career) he secured, for the 'Haven of the Dart', the following impressive achievements.

In 1854 he financed Captain Moody's *Dart* so reviving the defunct Totnes steamboat service; in 1855 he restored Kingswear Castle. In 1856 he sponsored the building of the Dartmouth Lighthouse. From 1857 to 1864 he promoted and created the Dartmouth & Torbay Railway. In 1858 he introduced the first steam tug *Pilot*. In 1859 he started the Dartmouth Steam Packet Company. In 1863 he formed the Dartmouth Harbour Commission to build Kingswear's wharfs, quays and so on. In 1864 he built Kingswear's Lighthouse and the Daymark. In 1865 he commissioned the PS *Eclair* for the cross-channel service, and the PS *Perseverance* river ferry. In 1866 he created the Dartmouth & Kingswear Hotel Company (Castle Hotel and Dart Yacht Club Hotel); in 1867 he replaced *Perseverance* with PS *Dolphin;* finally he promoted the building of Dartmouth's 'jewel in the crown', the Embankment.

KINGSWEAR MANOR

Up to the dissolution of the monasteries Kingswear had, through Torre Abbey, strong monastic connections in the church, Priory and the Manor of Kingswear. In 1544 a grant was made to Thomas Gale of Crediton and of the Manor of Kingswear of: 'a house, curtilage, garden, stables, cellars and six parcels of land, four of which lay above town around the archery butts,' (now Beacon Lane).

The Manor, a substantial three-gabled property, faced the church alongside Butt Steps (now Alma Steps) and is shown in early paintings. Thomas Gale, then his widow and later heiresses resided there until 1717 when it was purchased by John Fownes of nearby Nethway House, but in the next century it was allowed to fall into disrepair.

Left: Butt Steps (renamed Alma Steps during the Crimean war), then leading to the archery butts in Beacon Lane. The right-hand houses are the rear of the old houses lining The Square, Lower Slip, and arch by Avis's Shipyard.
BRIGADIER W HINE-HAYCOCK

Right: 1856, Lower Street, now Priory Street, showing houses and the first arch that led to the old Kittery waterside complex of Elizabethan merchants' houses, warehouses, and wharfs; all were demolished later to create Thomas Luttrell's Kittery Court, The Square and The Priory.
BRIGADIER W HINE-HAYCOCK

The Rt Hon Charles Seale Hayne's Remarkable Achievements in Dartmouth & Kingswear
1854-1885

Restored Kingswear Castle 1855

Dartmouth & Torbay Railway 1857/64

Dartmouth Harbour Commission 1863

Dartmouth Lighthouse 1856

CHARLES SEALE HAYNE
1833–1903

Dartmouth & Kingswear Hotel Co 1866

Dartmouth Steam Packet Co 1857

Cross-Channel Packet Eclair 1866

First Steam Tug Pilot 1858

Seale Hayne Agricultural College 1912

Railway Ferry Dolphin 1869

Kingswear Daymark 1863

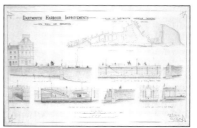

Dartmouth Embankment Scheme 1879/85

OTHER MANSIONS

The delightful Kittery foreshore was the location of several other major properties. Prominent among these was Ravenswell (1651), home of the smuggling *Parson Peter* in A E Norway's book of that name. Close by in Clockhouse Gardens is Yarrow Bank, a pretty castellated house (1833), built by Robert Newman of the powerful Dartmouth family on land leased from James Somerset and John Yarde Fownes of Kittery Court, feoffees of the church lands. Other substantial dwellings are Kingswear Lodge (1847), Lincoln House (Toft Quay: 1850), and Riversea (1857).

THE ONGOING FUTURE

By the mid-eighteenth century the fortunes of the harbour had begun to improve, principally due to the endeavours of a son of Dartmouth, Thomas Newcomen. His early experiments in steam were later developed into the steam engine, steamship and locomotives, heralding the Industrial Revolution. Steam's potential was recognized and it was to revitalise Dartmouth's dormant entrepreneurial spirit, resulting in the establishment of coaling depots in 1855 for the increasing numbers of calling steamships, regular steamboat services to Totnes, connection with the advancing nationwide railway network, and later in general harbour improvements.

Meanwhile the wealth generated by Britain's developing empire, world influence and commercial strength, combined with improving communications, underwrote the ever-growing sport of yachting, with the general recognition of Dartmouth harbour as a prime centre. Its unique position and beauty began to attract more and more visiting yachtspeople who in turn contributed to the local economy, and an influx of wealthy gentlemen, many of whom settled in Dartmouth and Kingswear to shape the progress and destiny of the area's future. From that period, commercial growth, development and yachting went hand in hand.

1856 Lower Street (now Priory Street) showing the second and third archways spanning the road leading to the old Kittery complex (now Kittery Court). The nearest arch was an extension from the present RDYC steward's cottage (now the oldest remaining Kittery property, apart from Ravenswell). The furthest segmental archway with outside staircase was the old schoolroom, superseded in 1869 when squire Luttrell provided the means to erect the present school in Wood Lane. The house on the left (the blacksmith's) and the arches were demolished in 1875 to build The Priory, while the Elizabethan houses on the right were removed in 1885/1887 to build Priory Cottages, now called Longford.

B<small>RIGADIER</small> W H<small>INE</small>-H<small>AYCOCK</small>

CHAPTER 2

Early Yachting on the Dart

1671 to 1850

A ROYAL BAPTISM

Inaugural yachting events are normally launched by prominent personalities or persons of high rank, and they don't come higher than the king of the realm. Dartmouth was particularly fortunate in that it was no less than the 'merry monarch' King Charles II who established the town as a premier yachting centre on his visit in 1671 aboard the royal yacht *Cleveland*. Eleven years previously, when returning from Holland to reoccupy the throne of England, the Dutch authorities placed a yacht at his disposal and he was so impressed by her design, elegance and performance that he stated his intention to construct a similar vessel in England. Such was his enthusiasm that the burghers of Amsterdam purchased the Dutch East India Company's latest yacht *Mary* and generously presented it to him, fostering his interest in yachting. During his twenty-four-year reign Charles II commissioned one royal yacht per year and indulged in racing, often against his brother the Duke of York and the nobility.

In 1671, on a visit from Portsmouth to Plymouth to inspect the new citadel, the King set the precedent for down-Channel voyages, travelling in the newly built yacht *Cleveland*, 'designed by Sir Anthony Deane, cutter rigged, 54 feet by 20 feet by a depth of eight feet, 120 tons, carrying six light guns and twenty crew'.

At Yarmouth, on the Isle of Wight he was joined by his brother James (later James II) in the yacht *Catherine*. The fleet of six small warships and seven yachts made Plymouth without mishap, to be fêted by the nobility, local dignitaries and townspeople. On returning, contrary winds off Lyme Regis caused the fleet to turn back to Dartmouth harbour. The King landed and was entertained by the mayoralty in the magnificent panelled room of the recently rebuilt Butterwalk (now the local museum). The King stayed the night at Nethway House, Kingswear, having established the potential of Dartmouth as a yachting centre.

THE FIRST CLUBS

Yachting remained a sport for royalty, nobility and gentry until 1720 when the Water Club of Cork was formed in Ireland, later to become the Royal Cork Yacht Club. In 1773 the Starcross Yacht Club was formed in Devon, a small club still in existence today. In 1775 the Cumberland Sailing Society was formed with the Duke of

1671. King Charles II's royal yacht Cleveland, *the first yacht to enter the port of Dartmouth presaging it as a future yachting haven.*

DARTMOUTH MUSEUM

Cumberland as its president, which eventually became the Royal Thames Yacht Club.

In London in 1815 a grand gathering of premier noblemen and some forty influential gentlemen, with a common love for Cowes, Isle of Wight, met and formed 'The Yacht Club'. By 1817 the Prince Regent and his two brothers had joined, and on the Prince's accession to the throne in 1820, the club became the first 'royal' yacht club, later the Royal Yacht Squadron (RYS).

By the early nineteenth century, with the end of the Napoleonic Wars and the advent of the Industrial Revolution, the pattern of life, steadfast for centuries, was changing. Modes of travel rapidly diversified, due to the canal system, turnpike roads and later the rail network. The therapeutic values of the seaside were now recognized, particularly by more affluent members of society who rented or erected desirable waterside residences and indulged in the ever-increasing sport of yachting. Southampton's broad waters, close to London, became a popular venue, with Cowes the focal point.

THE REGATTAS BEGIN

Areas naturally suitable for sailing and racing due to their territorial or geographical position began to develop. The Dartmouth area is that served by the local pilotage service, Hope's Nose to Start Point. As yachting gathered momentum the *Exeter Flying Post* reported that during 1800 to 1802 boat races were held on the River Exe in front of Powderham Castle. The 1802 race was over a six mile course and contested by fifteen yachts for prizes valued at £35, given by the Viscount Courtenay. Then followed a lull until 1807 when Teignmouth organized sailing matches. In 1811 Torquay organized boat races and these events were advertised as annual. By 1813, both towns described these annual events as regattas, the first in south Devon, and they have continued until the present day.

In 1819 the Start Bay Regatta was held, initiated by Governor A H Holdsworth of Stokenham and Dartmouth. It was a tremendous success, with over 3,000 people attending, and a ball was held until 5am.

In 1822 Dartmouth held its first regatta, with yachts from the Royal Yacht Club, Cowes, racing; the *Exeter and Plymouth Gazette* reported as follows:

> *The Regatta gave the highest gratification to numerous visitors. The situation is particularly adapted for an exhibition of this sort. The hills around the roadstead where the yachts assembled to start for prizes, formed a natural theatre and presented to those on the water the appearance of thousands of people in galleries. The setting of the harbour was very beautiful, with the fine yachts from Cowes and other parts of the coast.*

The format of this regatta was repeated until 1827, when, surprisingly, it ceased until 1834, possibly as a result of bitter rivalry between Governor Holdsworth and Colonel Seale. The altercation between these leading figures stemmed from Colonel Seale's wanting to bridge the Dart with a suspension bridge or a steam-powered floating bridge from Sandquay, while Governor Holdsworth favoured supplementing Mr Luttrell's horse ferry with a bridge to Kingswear or a steam bridge from Spithead to the Old Passage House Inn, Kingswear.

Left: 1843. Queen Victoria aboard the first steam yacht Victoria and Albert I *visited Dartmouth and received a civic welcome; in the royal barge she explored the River Dart which she called her 'English Rhine'.*

DARTMOUTH CHRONICLE

Right: 1856. Queen Victoria aboard her second steam yacht Victoria and Albert II *revisited Dartmouth on regatta day and granted Dartmouth the honour of adding the title 'Royal' to all future regattas.*

W T LAWSON/W M THOMPSON

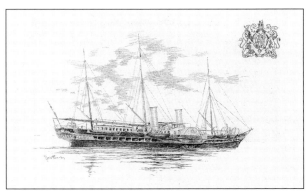

In July 1828 Dartmouth was again honoured by royalty, the Duke of Clarence, the Lord High Admiral, in HMY *Royal Sovereign* accompanied by HM *Cutter Arrow*. *Royal Sovereign* was a full rigged yacht, (278ton, 96ft x 25ft 6in). Landing at the New Ground steps he was met by Governor Holdsworth and Captain Bastard RN MP, and was entertained at Governor Holdsworth's home, Mount Galpin. An immense number of townspeople were allowed aboard the *Royal Sovereign* and later treated to a pyrotechnic display. The visit lasted four days, and Clarence Street and Hill were named after him.

There was still no regatta by 1831 but there was great rejoicing in Dartmouth for the opening of Colonel John Seale's Floating Steam Bridge from Sandquay to Rock Point, Noss.

Dartmouth's first official regatta was held in 1834, and included a race for sailing lighters and six-oared craft. It became the official starting date from which all future regattas were numbered. The pattern thereafter remained the same, and in 1836 the six-oared pilot boat race was won by *Dove*, built at St Mawes in 1820. That same boat, now belonging to the Newquay Sailing Club, survived to participate in the 1994 regatta. Little concession was made to yacht racing, though it was on the increase; indeed only the 1839 regatta included a race for sailing boats, and it was not until 1853 that races for sailing vessels became an annual event. During that fourteen-year period it is uncertain whether any regattas were held, as for eleven of those years there are no newspaper reports.

In 1843 the *Exeter Flying Post* reported another royal visit, that of young Queen Victoria in her steam yacht *Victoria and Albert I* with HMS *Black Eagle* and the steam frigate *Prometheus*. The yacht had been built that year as a single-funnelled two-masted wooden steam-driven paddler, 1,034 tons, 200ft long with a beam of 33ft. The Queen was received by Sir John Seale, his son Henry Paul Seale, and the Mayor. Later she boarded the royal barge and proceeded upriver, which she named 'The English Rhine', returning in the afternoon to leave for Plymouth.

The regattas continued intermittently but without races for sailing craft. However, by mid-century there were twenty yacht clubs around England that had received a royal warrant. The Royal Western Yacht Club, Plymouth, was established in 1827, but the premier club was the Royal Yacht Squadron (RYS), which dominated the British yachting scene from its headquarters at the Gloucester Hotel, West Cowes on the Isle of Wight, with almost 200 members and with over 100 yachts, most over 100 tons.

THE AMERICA'S CUP

Yachting became an international activity, particularly popular across the Atlantic in the cities of New York and Boston, which possessed the two essential ingredients: a suitable environment, and men of wealth with leisure and influence.

In 1844 George L Schuyler and John C Stevens, with seven other rich and powerful men, met in the saloon aboard the 25-ton schooner yacht *Gimcrack*, (designed and built by George Steers), where they founded America's first and most wealthy and influential yacht club, the New York Yacht Club (NYYC). This had far-reaching consequences, not only in America but also in England, where Dartmouth had a part to play.

By the mid-nineteenth century Great Britain was at the height of her power; the wealth created by her great empire and the Industrial Revolution was to be paraded before the world at the Great Exhibition of 1851, and yachting was to feature in the celebrations through the regatta at Cowes. In the autumn of 1850 an English merchant had written to his New York counterpart suggesting they should participate in the celebrations at the 1851 Cowes Regatta, racing one of their famous New York pilot boats against the fast English schooners.

This epistle was shown to G L Schuyler and John C Stevens, then Commodore of the New York Yacht Club, sparking their enthusiasm and imagination to build a vessel finer and faster than any of their existing pilot boats to become their national champion. Their confidence lay in the fact that they had the services of a brilliant young builder and designer, George Steers, son of Henry Steers, a Dartmouth born shipwright who had emigrated to America in 1819 with his wife and children. A consortium of six wealthy men agreed to take shares in the new vessel and wrote out the extraordinary terms of the building proposal for shipbuilder Mr Brown's signature, as follows:

New York, November 15th 1850.

To George L Schuyler, Esq

Dear Sir,   I propose to build for you a yacht of not less than 140 tons custom-house measurement on the following terms. The yacht to be built in the best manner, coppered, rigged, equipped with joiners' work, cabin and kitchen furniture, table furniture, water closets, etc, etc, ready for sea – you are to designate the plan of the interior of the vessel and select the furniture. The model, plan and rig of the vessel to be entirely at my discretion, it being understood however that she is to be a strong sea going vessel, and rigged for ocean sailing. For the vessel complete and ready for sea you are to pay me $30,000 upon the following conditions: when the vessel is ready, she is to be placed at the disposal of Mr Hamilton Wilkes, Esq, as umpire, who, after making such trials as are satisfactory to him for the space of twenty days, shall decide whether or not she is faster than any vessel in the United States brought to compete with her.
The expense of the trials to be borne by you.
If it is decided by the umpire that she is not faster than every vessel brought against her, it shall not be binding upon you to accept or pay for her at all. In addition to this, if the umpire decides that she is faster than any vessel in the United States, you are to have the right, instead of accepting her at that time, to send her to England, match her against anything else her size built there, and if beaten still to reject her altogether.
The expense of the voyage out and home to be borne by you.
The test of speed in England will be decided by any mode acceptable to you and consented to you in writing.

Respectfully yours,

W H Brown.

Work started but the completion date was exceeded, leaving little time for trials. No engagements were arranged in England; she had to compete for national pride and such honour and prizes as were available.

Assured of a warm welcome by Earl Wilton, Commodore of the RYS, the finest schooner ever built in *America* sailed for England on 21 June 1851, with a crew of thirteen. Captain Dick Brown was master and three of the Steers family were aboard: George Steers, designer and supervisor; James R Steers, shipbuilder, and Dartmouth-born; and fifteen-year-old Henry Steers.

The superior quality of *America* was proved when, off Cowes, she met the newest and fastest English cutter, *Laverock*, which turned into a race which *America* won easily by a third of a mile. This caused consternation, particularly when the Americans offered a challenge through the RYS to race any craft of suitable size for any wager, but sadly the challenge remained unanswered, much to British embarrassment.

THE FAMOUS RACE

As no challenger emerged, the *America* entered for the RYS Cup race on Friday 22 August 1851, watched by Queen Victoria on the royal yacht *Victoria and Albert II*. The race has been chronicled many times; the *America* romped home twenty to twenty-three minutes (records differ) ahead of her nearest rival *Aurora*. The famous exchange between Queen Victoria and her signal master on the deck says it all:

'Say, signal master, are the yachts in sight?'
'Yes, may it please your Majesty.'

'Which is first?'
'The America*'*
'Which is second?'
'Ach, your Majesty, there is no second.'

Later a similar theme was used by Daniel Webster, the founder of Webster's Dictionary, who was educated at Dartmouth College, New Hampshire, when announcing America's famous victory. He broke off his address to a large audience in the House of Representatives to say 'Like Jupiter among the gods *America* is first, and there is no second'.

There is no denying the *America*'s famous victory, but a statement in Douglas Phillips-Birt's History of Yachting is of considerable interest:

> *Some twenty-three minutes after the* America *(records of the times differ) her closest rival, the little cutter* Aurora, *followed her over the line.* Aurora *was 47 tons compared with the* America's *140 tons, and but for the fact that time allowance had been waived for the race she would have been the winner by a handsome margin. She might have even won on elapsed time, for owing to muddled race instructions the* Aurora *and several other English yachts, sailed a longer course.*

This most famous yacht race ever to have been sailed was, as a sailing contest, unsatisfactory. When the band on shore played 'Yankee Doodle Dandy' as the American schooner crossed the line, it was applauding unquestionably the best yacht among the nine schooners and cutters that had raced that day round the island, but under the prevailing conditions it was chance, accident and bad organisation that produced so appropriate a result. Luck converted the Royal Yacht Squadron Cup into the best known of all yachting trophies, the America's Cup. But it was another nineteen years before the cup re-entered history, and many more before it became famous.

Britain regained some pride and dignity six days after the race when the great engineer Robert Stephenson, designer and builder of the locomotive *Rocket*, took up the Americans' challenge for a wager of £100. He had a new 100-ton schooner *Titania*, built by John Scott Russell, who later in 1856 built Governor A H Holdsworth's tiny 42-ton paddle-steamer the *Dartmouth* and in 1857 Brunel's 22,500-ton *Great Eastern*, five times larger than any ship in the world. The *America* won easily by seven miles. But Dartmouth associations continued, for Robert Stephenson was a friend of another great engineer George Parker Bidder, owner of the 68-ton *Mayfly*, and who, with Stephenson, attended Dartmouth's 1858 Regatta in *Titania II*. This led to Mr Bidder's later purchase of and residence in Ravensbury. In 1859 Isambard Kingdom Brunel, engineer to the unfinished Dartmouth & Torbay Railway, and his friend Robert Stephenson, both died. Robert Pearson Brereton, Brunel's chief engineer, took over. His nephew, George Robert Stephenson, inherited Stephenson's business and in 1866 he visited Dartmouth with G P Bidder, R P Brereton and Colonel C Manby, secretary of the Institute of Civil Engineers; they all became founder members of the Dart Yacht Club (DYC).

Left: 1851. Queen Victoria with the Prince Consort aboard the America, *which had won the RYS cup race, being introduced to Mr John Stevens, Commodore of the New York Yacht Club accompanied by Colonel James Hamilton and Lord Alfred Paget (later a Royal Dart Yacht Club member).*
W H Lawson/
W M Thompson

Right: 22 August 1851, Cowes. The schooner yacht America *coming up to the start line at the start of the RYS cup race.*
W H Lawson/
W M Thompson

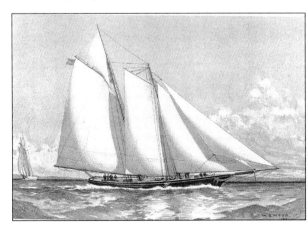

After the August race against *Titania* NYYC Commodore John Stevens, with the cup and national pride intact, was anxious to return home to receive a hero's welcome. With the approval of the consortium, he sold the *America* for £5,000 to Lord John Blanquiere, who promptly issued a challenge for the *America* to take on any boat in England. There were no takers and four years later he disposed of her to Lord Templeton. He raced her for a year then laid her up at Cowes until 1859, when she was dry docked at Northfleet, Gravesend. During the lay up she was found to have extensive dry rot, so his lordship sold her for scrap value to the yard owner, who to his credit restored her to her former glory, with oak framing and teak planking. In 1860 he sold her to Mr H E Ducie, who renamed her *Camilla* but raced her for only one year.

In April 1861, ten years after her arrival in England, the *America* once again crossed the Atlantic and returned home, but this time to Savannah, having been purchased by an unknown Confederate agent. She was renamed *Memphis* and armed to become a blockade runner and despatch vessel for the Confederate Navy. Her turn of speed ensured her survival even when pursued by the fast screw frigate USS *Warbash*, for she outsailed them all. However in 1862, when the gunboat USS *Ottawa* navigated the St John River to capture Jacksonville, the masts and spars of a sunken schooner proved to be those of the *Memphis*, so Commander T H Stevens forfeited the prize money on the condition that she was raised, repaired and renamed *America* for use as a practice vessel for cadet training at the Naval Academy, Annapolis.

She remained there until 1870 when she was de-commissioned and offered for sale by auction. She was purchased by General Buller, who had her repaired and raced her on many occasions. In 1880 and again in 1885 she was practically rebuilt and continued racing, and he offered her to the New York Yacht Club (an offer they refused) as a test boat against contenders hoping to be chosen to defend American honour in the forthcoming 1885 America's Cup challenge by either Sir Richard Sutton, RYS, in *Genesta* or Lt Henn, RDYC, in *Galatea*. Unfortunately *Galatea* had a ballasting problem and was unable to attend and compete until 1886. Sadly both attempts failed. The *America* remained with General Buller until well into the next century. This legendary yacht continued racing under various owners until finally returning to Annapolis, (named after King James's daughter Anne) and she was destroyed in a snowstorm in a boatyard in 1945. For almost ninety-five glorious years she was a fitting tribute to the genius of a son of Dartmouth, George Steers.

A yachtsman's dream is recorded as follows:

> *Before the* America *sailed for England Mr Stevens acquired from the sellers of the late Mr Bingham of Philadelphia, father of the wife of the late English Minister to the United States, Lord Ashburton, two dozen bottles of Madeira over half a century old, with which it was proposed to drink the health of her Majesty. Before sailing the commodore's wife concealed the wine in a secret place in the vessel, but failed to inform him so that when he sold her, the wine without his knowledge went with her. He discovered the mistake on his return home, and immediately wrote to Lord de B. (the new owner of the* America*) saying that he would look in a certain hidden locker in the* America *and he would find some wine (worth double the price of her) and made a present of it to him.*

> *W T Lawson and W M Thomsons'* History of the America's Cup

DESIGNER OF THE *AMERICA*

The *America* was a lucky ship, defying superstition about Friday and the number thirteen. Henry Steers told a meeting of the Seawanhaka Yacht Club that the *America* carried thirteen men, her first day in English waters was a Friday, the cup was voted as a trophy at a meeting of the RYS on a Friday (9 May 1851) and won on a Friday (22 August 1851), while engraved on the cup are the names of the thirteen vessels defeated by the *America*. He and George Steers, the designer and builder of *America*, were two of thirteen children of a Dartmouth man.

In 1907 controversy arose in the *Dartmouth Chronicle* when E W H Holdsworth requested information on the American and Dartmouth Steers' families. After several contradictory letters the matter was finally resolved with the following letter, from J R Steers, New York:

Sir,
Your letter to the Dartmouth Chronicle *requested information concerning my uncle, George Steers, so herewith is a short account of him and his work.*

As a boy I frequently heard in the family that my father, James R Steers, and my uncle, Henry T Steers, were born in Dartmouth, England, and that my uncles George and Philip Steers, were born at Washington DC. That my grandfather, Henry Steers, was also born in Dartmouth. He learned the trade of shipbuilder there, and became a 'quarterman' (a kind of foreman) in the English Government dockyard at Plymouth. He came to America before 1820 and took a position in the Washington Navy Yard. He built the frigate Brandywine, *which brought Lafayette to America on his first visit after the Revolution. He afterwards came to New York and built the dry dock at the foot of 10th Street, on the East River, the first of its kind in America.*

George Steers formed a partnership with a Mr Hathorne, and their shipyard was in Williamstown, afterwards annexed to Brooklyn and now a part of New York. There my uncle designed and built many yachts and pilot boats. Among the former were the Syren, Cygnet, Una, Julia: *all fast, and winners in their classes. Among the latter were the* Mary Taylor *(built for Dick Brown, who sailed the America when she won the cup),* Hagstaff, Neilson, George Steers, Moses Taylor, *and others. The last two were built at New York. In 1850-51 my uncle designed and built the* America. *She was built in the shipyard of William H Brown, at the foot of 12th Street and East River. In 1854 Congress passed a bill to construct six steam frigates, and George Steers was designated as special naval constructor of the* Niagara *at the Brooklyn Navy yard. I became his clerk and served with him from the fall of 1854 until the fall of 1856, when he died from the effects of injuries received in jumping from his carriage while his horses were running away. His age was then thirty-six years.*

While he was building the Niagara: *he, with my father, was building the* Adriatic *for the Collins line of steamers, in their shipyard at the bottom of 7th Street and East River. George Steers designed both ships and built that famous sailer the 'Sunny South'. George and Henry Steers also went to a place near Rochester, NY and built two large steamers for use on Lake Ontario. George Steers also superintended the construction of the new* Atlantic. *He may, with my father, have visited their sister Ann at Dartmouth in 1851, when they went to England in the* America, *but my father and my brother-in-law, Mr George C Lake, did visit my aunt Ann in Dartmouth in 1880. My Uncle George had then been dead twenty-four years*

Mr George Steers, son of Henry Steers Dartmouth

Lines of the American schooner America *designed by George Steers and captained by Dick Brown, who with three men from Dartmouth in the crew of thirteen, crossed the Atlantic to win the Cowes RYS Cup race in 1850.*
BOTH
W T LAWSON/
W M THOMPSON.

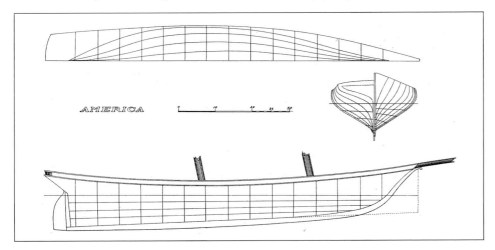

The Dartmouth Chronicle *1854*

Mr Robert Cranford, founder of The Dartmouth Chronicle.

NEW LOCAL PUBLICATION

Just Published and will continued Monthly

THE DARTMOUTH CHRONICLE

MONTHLY RECORDER & GENERAL ADVERTISER

No.1	JANUARY 1854	PRICE 1d.

The advent of the Dartmouth Periodical will no doubt be looked upon by many of our readers with no small surprise: but thanks to the enterprising spirit of the age, the means of producing and continuing our little paper are placed within easy reach, with but a comparatively trifling amount of uncertainty.

We earnestly hope in the outset, that none will be found to discourage this attempt; or criticise too severely the first effort of this kind that has ever been made in Dartmouth. Let all remember that "great events from little causes spring," and if those among our townsmen who are willing and able, will come cordially forward, and each, to the best of ability, assist our earnest endeavours, we have little doubt but that this unpretending sheet may grow with coming years into a much more important organ of general instruction and information.

The first ever issue of The Dartmouth Chronicle

CHAPTER 3

The Formative Years

1850 to 1863

THE BIRTH OF THE CHRONICLE

1850 marked a turning point in the fortunes of Dartmouth, for after the depression following the Napoleonic Wars and the decline of the Newfoundland, trade the fruits of the Industrial Revolution at last reached the town. For centuries communication with the hinterland was mainly via the harbour for the town was poorly served by roads. However, the advancing nationwide rail network had reached Totnes by 1847, Torquay by 1848, and by 1850, small steamers began to call to replenish bunker coals.

1854 News was sparse, newspapers in Dartmouth were at a premium, read many times by many, and odd copies of *The Times* that arrived were hired out for months after publication date. So in late 1850 Robert Cranford formed the *Dartmouth Advertiser* and there was jubilation in 1854, when he published the first issue of the *Dartmouth Chronicle*. It was issued monthly, price 'twopence', and in 1871 became a weekly newspaper. Publication continued and today as the *Chronicle* it is part of a newspaper group that covers the whole of the South Hams.

The first issue was well received and contained the illuminating report from The *Western Flying Post* headed, Extract of a letter from Dartmouth, April 7th 1788:

> *Within the past 24 hours a fleet of nearly 50 vessels has left the port for St Johns, Newfoundland. The whole Dartmouth fleet this season will amount to a full 150 vessels, and will carry 300 youngsters, part of the 3,000 men engaged in the fisheries. The Newfoundland trade with England and Ireland will employ in the boat and bank fisheries and those engaged on the Labrador coast, in taking seals and salmon, combined with the seamen on the vessels to carry the catch to foreign markets, upwards of 10,000 men.*

It also reported an interesting proposal mooted by the council the householders should not only be reasonable for the cleanliness of the area within their ownership, but, also, any path, road, lane or highway abutting their premises (which was strongly resisted).

Regatta 1854 included a race for sailing barges, a race for sailing boats, and four rowing events. Sailing barges had participated only twice since the official start of regattas, in 1834 and 1842, but they continued to race from 1854 until 1869. Sailing-boat races had been held in 1834, 1839, 1847, 1853 and 1854 and continued thereafter. However, during that twenty-one year period there are eleven years for which there is no collaborative evidence that regattas were held in the harbour at all.

The year closed with the launch of the Missionary Vessel, the *Allen Gardiner* from Mr Kelly's Sandquay yard. The Reverend G P Despard blessed her and all who sailed in her on her mission to the save the benighted tribes of South America.

Also there was and interesting advert, as follows:

> 'How to win a Lover', *Mr Watson sends free directions to enable Ladies or Gentlemen win the devoted affections of the opposite sex. The process is simple, captivating and enthralling and all may be married irrespective of age, appearance, or position, while the most fickle, or cold hearted, must bow to its attractions. Young or old,*

peer or princess, as well as the peasant are alike, subject to its influence; and last, it can be arranged with such ease and delicacy that disclosure is impossible.

Write, Mr Watson, Robert Street, Strand, London, enclosing 12 stamps, and receive particulars.

1855

The January edition of the Chronicle contained the news of the death in the Crimea of Sir Robert Newman BT, of Mamhead and included a sad letter from his batman illustrating the privations suffered by all ranks:

I was with my poor master in all engagements, at night we shared the same blanket. No tongue can describe the horrors of Inkerman, it took me eight hours to find him among the dead, he was riddled with shot and had five bayonet wounds. I took him eight miles to Balaklava, to his brother, where we buried him in the churchyard.

This evoked the following letter:

I regret that no effort has been made by this port, with which his family is so intimately connected, to perpetuate his valued memory and unflinching courage. They should build a pillar or obelisk, high on the eastern shore of the harbour entrance, to be seen from Start and Torbay, and so call down the thanks of many a weary mariner.

In the seventeenth century there had been a seamark on Downe End Point, the tower of Holy Trinity Chapel, which Sir William Hody of Nethway had allowed to fall into ruins. Regrettably the above proposal, and one made in 1861 by Mr Studdy to erect a two hundred foot granite tower to the memory of Governor Holdsworth, both failed. It was not until 1863 that the Dart Harbour Commission (DHC) erected the present Daymark.

The star of 1855 was Captain John Moody, who bought the steamboat *Dart* and reinstated the defunct Totnes service. He purchased Charles Vincent's house-coal business and started the first Dartmouth Coal Bunkering Depot to supply calling steamships. The *Chronicle* was emphasizing the need for a powerful tug, and the wealthy Governor Holdsworth was complaining bitterly about the steamer's regular failure to meet the Totnes train and threatening to establish a rival service. This so alarmed Captain Moody that he offered to buy a suitable tug if the competing riverboat scheme was abandoned, as two services would not be viable. Governor Holdsworth refused and ordered the new steamer *Dartmouth* from Scott Russell's yard. This forced Captain Moody to form a new company and, with financial support from Charles Seale Hayne, he ordered the *Louisa* from Langley's yard. His finances were overstretched and he was forced to dispose of his fledgeling bunkering business to his manager, Mr Ashford Junior, who retained it until 1862, when he sold it to Mr Hingston who in turn sold his hulks in 1888 to the Channel Coaling Company.

Regatta 1855 was much improved, with a race for sailing barges and sailing boats, and seven rowing events. The Grand Challenge Cup for £20 was the highest prize south of the Thames and it was awarded to *Lightning* after protest, as the crew of *Black Joke* had hurled verbal abuse at the committee boat. This year saw the first appearance of the indomitable Mr Chalker, doyen of the next twenty-eight regattas, who introduced the famous Alfresco Ball, attended by over 2,000 people on the New Ground. Dancing went on until 2am to the light of flaming tar barrels, which turned the participants into black and white minstrels. He also organized duck hunts, donkey races and foot hurdling.

In September, after twenty-four years' service, the *Floating Bridge* sank at its Sandquay moorings, causing serious inconvenience to Dartmouth traders. At Paradise Point, Warfleet, Paradise Fort was demolished to build a new house -

Paradise (renamed Ravensbury in 1860) - home to many prominent Dartmouth residents. Five skeletons of sailors from a Dutch ship, who had died from the plague in 1774, were discovered on the site. The two principal hotels also changed hands. Thomas Cox retired from Kingswear's Plume of Feathers Inn and was replaced by Philip Sandover from the Castle Hotel in Dartmouth, which was, in turn, taken over by Dominic Stone from the Crown Hotel in Weymouth.

1856

was a charismatic year which started quietly with Brookhill in Kingswear at last finding a caring owner, W Johnstoun Neale. In August a positive plethora of events took place, as follows:

2 August Sir H P Seale's new Bath House for ladies and gentlemen opened near Dartmouth Castle.

4 August The SS *England*, 1,159 tons, arrived in the harbour. She was owned by William Shaw Lindsay, MP and shipowner, who had secured the Government mail contract to the Cape Colonies and Calcutta and had chosen Dartmouth as a mail station.

5 August A celebratory dinner was provided at the Castle Hotel, the principal guest being Mr Lindsay who was met at Totnes by the Viscount Courtenay and conveyed downriver in a six-oared gig to Dartmouth to receive a nineteen-gun salute. He promised his liners would remain for the full five-year contract. Then followed a ball which ended at 5am with the band marching around the town.

6 August The SS *England* weighed anchor and with the Blue Peter at the fore steamed out of harbour saluted by the castle guns.

10 August Mr Holdsworth's new paddle-steamer the *Dartmouth* arrived for service on the Totnes run.

11 August Queen Victoria with Prince Albert and the royal family arrived aboard the royal yacht *Victoria and Albert II*, mainly because of stormy weather in the Channel, accompanied by ten escort vessels. The royal yacht was virtually new, built at Pembroke as a wooden two-funnelled three-masted paddler of 2,470 tons, 300ft x 40ft. She anchored off the New Ground, whilst the bells of St Saviours pealed a merry welcome. The royal party then intimated they wished to go upriver, and Prince Albert, the Prince of Wales and their retinue left in Mr Holdsworth's newly arrived steamboat *Dartmouth* and sailed to within sight of Totnes. On returning they met Her Majesty, the Princess Royal and ladies-in-waiting in the royal barge at Dittisham, all expressing their

1856. Queen Victoria on her visit to Dartmouth in the Victoria and Albert II *being received by Lady Seale and Sir Henry Paul Seale, the Mayor, and Corporation prior to a tour of Dartmouth and a visit to Mount Boone. The meeting was on the New Ground (an artificial island created in 1684) connected to the New Quay (1584) by a bridge alongside Plumleigh Conduit. The latter (demolished 1868) was owned by Dominic Stone (Castle Hotel) who re-erected the ball finial (1874) over the gateway to his new home, The Priory, Kingswear.*

EXETER UNIVERSITY
LIBRARY

delight at the beauties of the river. Thereafter the *Dartmouth* awarded herself the unofficial title 'Royal' flying the white ensign, which Customs requested she cease, but the practice continued, although the flag was defaced with a small piece of red braid sewn in one corner. The Queen came ashore to be received by the Mayor and Corporation, and after a brief tour of Dartmouth visited Mount Boone, home of Sir Henry and Lady Seale. Later illuminations were lit and the Queen ordered the fleet to do the same. Mr Cranford printed a regatta programme on white satin, and Her Majesty showed her appreciation by awarding a prize of £25 for the regatta. Regrettably they departed early the following morning, regatta day, but not before awarding the port the honour of adding the prefix 'Royal' to all future regattas, although no royal warrant was ever issued.

12 August **Regatta 1856** was something of an anticlimax after the heady events of the day before. Mr Seale Hayne laid the foundation stone for the new lighthouse by St Petrox church, to guide the mailboats into port. Sadly the look-outs found they were unable to signal from the turret to the Bayard's Cove pilots because St Petrox church spire completely blocked their line of vision. This was later remedied by simply removing the spire. It was also discovered that the lighthouse was sited on the wrong side of the harbour, a fact recognized by Governor Holdsworth in his report to the Admiralty in 1841, and caused a new lighthouse to be built by the Dartmouth Harbour Commission (DHC) in 1864 on the Kingswear shore.

19 August John Browne Smith of Kittery Court reopened the Nethway Slate Quarries and Hoodown Quay for business after many years of closure.

20 August Mr Seale Hayne with Captain Moody acquired Mr Alford's old Coombe Shipyard, to repair their river steamboats and create a foundry to carry out limited iron ship repairs.

23 August was the zenith of this frantic month. A notice appeared in the *Chronicle* from Mr Seale Hayne and seventy-seven prominent citizens asking the Mayor to convene a public meeting to request railway communication to Dartmouth. This was to become the source of Dartmouth's future prosperity.

30 August Mr Seale Hayne and Captain Moody's new steamboat *Louisa*, (named after Mr Hayne's mother), arrived, sadly too late for the royal celebrations.

August 1856 hosted a unique conglomeration of events, yet there was still more to come. In October, Sir H P Seale, who had been served with a mandamus by aggrieved users, launched a new replacement *Floating Bridge* at Mr Kelly's yard. The *Chronicle* published a full-column prospectus for the Dartmouth & Torbay Railway Company, chairman Mr Seale Hayne. A bill was presented: the line was to cost £120,000 and be six-and-a-half miles long, with Smith and Knight the contractors, and Isambard Kingdom Brunel the engineer.

1857

1857 brought news of the death of John Fownes Luttrell, of Dunster Castle and Nethway, Lord of Kingswear Manor with a 2,000 acre estate. Dartmouth celebrated the arrival of the electric telegraph to be stationed on the New Ground. Parliament was dissolved and an election called, and the ebullient Mr Seale Hayne was selected as Liberal candidate. The standing Conservative MP stood down, and Mr Lindsay, also a Conservative MP and owner of the shipping line using the port, introduced his own candidate, Mr Caird, a Scot, intimating that if he were not elected, the steamers would be withdrawn. This veiled threat, and the lack of support from his uncle, the Conservative Sir H P Seale, resulted in Mr Hayne's defeat by thirty-three votes. A few months later the Chronicle announced to universal dismay that after barely one year's operation the Government was cancelling Mr Lindsay's contract and seeking new tenders. His vessels were underpowered and penalties for late delivery were causing financial problems.

In his disappointment Mr Seale Hayne engaged in developing his 400 acre Brownstone Estate, Kingswear. He commissioned a Torquay architect to produce plans for fifty villas and for cutting a new road to Nethway Cross. He had some satisfaction when in July the Dartmouth & Torbay Railway Bill received royal assent.

Regatta 1857 was one day only, and among the participating yachts were *Zera* owned by the Earl of Wilton, Commodore of the RYS during the Cowes 1851 Regatta when the *America* won the coveted America's Cup, and also *Mayfly* owned by George Parker Bidder, who was later to become a resident, a founder member and Vice Commodore of the Royal Dart Yacht Club.

The year closed with two maritime events. Firstly, Vincent & Hingston announced that two steam coasters, the *Clifton* and *Pioneer*, would call every thirty-six hours on a circular route from London to Bristol. Secondly, the Caledonian Steam Towing Company, London, announced that it would station a tug in Dartmouth for a trial period. Both schemes failed within the year, mainly through insufficient usage.

THE BIRTH OF THE RAILWAY

1858 Since the beginning of the railway era the inhabitants of Dartmouth had hoped for closer links with the hinterland. On 21 January the ceremonial 'cutting of the first sod' took place in a field near Torre station. It was a brilliant day and steamboats conveyed Dartmouth's Mayor and Corporation to Torquay harbour to join an immense concourse assembled there. The principal guest was the local MP Lawrence Palk, whose family owned most of Torquay. Charles Seale Hayne opened the proceedings with the following speech outlining the objectives of the railway:

1. *To open up Dartmouth Harbour to trade and the large steamers of the present day.*
2. *To develop the traffic from the increasing Port of Brixham.*
3. *To place the harbour of the River Dart within reach of visitors from Torquay and Paignton, with the erection of a station at Livermead for improved accommodation of Torquay inhabitants.*
4. *To create a scheme offering ample returns on capital invested, benefiting all.*

Then Mr Margery, engineer, handed to Mr Palk a plan of the line, while Mr Knight, the contractor, presented a handsome mahogany wheelbarrow and polished ornamental steel spade with which the honourable member turned the first sod, wheeling it a short distance. The military fired a feu de joie, the band played the national anthem and three hearty cheers were given. The other dignitaries also turned the ceremonial sod, but Mr Woolacombe, chairman of the SDR broke the handle of the ornamental spade and in his address said he 'hoped the circumstances would not be considered a bad omen for the undertaking'. He felt satisfied they would soon replace the beautiful spade, more ornamental than useful, and bring the railway to a successful determination' There was an uncanny irony in this event, for

Left: Dartmouth's first and only public bath house, built in 1856, south of Warfleet Creek by Sir Henry Paul Seale. An ahead-of-its-time project sited too far from town to succeed.
DARTMOUTH MUSEUM

Right: Warfleet Mill, built by Governor A H Holdsworth in 1819, at the head of Warfleet Creek as a paper mill and powered by the largest water wheel (demolished 1872) west of Bristol. It later became a grist mill, then an engineering works then a brewery, and finally a pottery. The adjacent viaduct was designed by George Parker Bidder and funded by him and three other neighbours.
H HUTCHINGS

1858. Possibly Governor Holdsworth owner of the Royal Dartmouth *boarding at Totnes having just refused a government offer to purchase her for Dr Livingstone's exploration of the River Zambesi.*

TOTNES MUSEUM

***Right:** George Parker Bidder, a Moretonhampstead -born boy genius (known as the 'calculating-boy') and later one of Britain's foremost engineers, responsible for many major projects in the United Kingdom and abroad. He was also colleague and friend of Isambard Kingdom Brunel and George Stephenson.*

E F CLARK

the line well exceeded the contract both in terms of time and money. Finally Sir H P Seale thanked the principal guests, and they all retired to a large marquee to consume bumpers of champagne.

A procession, led by the band, was followed by the navvies (with barrows and spades), civic dignitaries, directors, shareholders, the Rifle Corps and a line of handsome carriages with the ladies at the rear. The cavalcade, over a mile, long halted at the Union Inn where 250 gentlemen sat down to a dinner which a contemporary described as a 'sumptuous repast'. Finally Governor Holdsworth concluded the festivities with an apposite speech, reported thus:

> *the long years had taught him, and he hoped Dartmouth, that after the Newfoundland trade, they must not look to shipping alone to bring them prosperity. Both mistakenly had assumed that the establishment of Dartmouth as a Packet Station would restore its maritime importance, but it was not so. They should look to the success and growth of Torquay as a watering place, so why not Dartmouth.*

[Sound advice 140 years ago.]

Regatta 1858 The harbour was again honoured by the return of the eminent engineer George Parker Bidder in his schooner *Mayfly*, this time accompanied by another famous engineer, Robert Stephenson, in his schooner *Titania II*. Later Stephenson, in poor health, sailed his yacht to Egypt to meet his friend Isambard Kingdom Brunel, also unwell and who, among numerous other projects, was engineer to the Dartmouth & Torbay Railway. These two great men met on Christmas Day 1858 at the Hotel d'Orient in Cairo and dined together for the last time, for by October 1859 both were dead.

The bitter rivalry between the two steamboat companies continued and interest was aroused when the *Chronicle* announced that the builder of the *Dartmouth*, John Scott Russell, offered on behalf of the Government to repurchase her for £2,500 for Dr Livingstone's exploration of the Zambezi River. There was surprise when Governor Holdsworth refused the offer, as it was well in excess of the original purchase price.

Captain Moody in Shields purchased the tug *British Hero,* renaming her *Pilot*; while H Follett returned and restarted shipbuilding in his old Silver Street yard. Meanwhile problems beset the railway project, as local landowners, who had originally with true public spirit agreed to accept agricultural valuation, let avarice surface and demanded exorbitant prices. This meant expensive court proceedings that reduced the claims, but resulted in over expenditure and delay.

1859 commenced with Governor Holdsworth's home, The Beacon, being offered for sale or let, while Sir Henry Paul Seale's bold enterprise, the public baths (now Rosebank) on the shore adjacent to Dartmouth Castle, were offered for sale after only two years' operation. They were built by H Roberts of Dartmouth and comprised two storeys, a basement with three gentlemen's private rooms, and four ladies' rooms over, with the latest plumbing units from Exeter. Bathing took place in two small inlets, one either side of the house. The distance from the town was a major factor in the failure of this precocious venture.

During this period Henry Fownes Luttrell, the new squire of Dunster Castle and Nethway, who owned the Hoodown land, realized it had great potential value, since the railway's terminus was scheduled to be at Noss Point. He engaged London architect G Vulliamy to prepare plans to develop the area. The proposal was for seventy-four villas on the wooded hillside alongside the river, and an esplanade from Noss to Kingswear. If the railway had stopped at Noss Point, Kingswear could have possibly rivalled Dartmouth as a visitors' resort, for Kingswear's foreshore has one priceless extra asset - sunshine all day.

In April another by-election occurred when the Dartmouth MP Mr Caird resigned. Mr Seale Hayne was once again selected as Liberal candidate to contest the Conservative Sir T Herbert. Then Mr Sketchley appeared and, keen to be a Liberal MP, offered to purchase £3,000 of Dartmouth & Torbay Railway shares if he was allowed to stand. Consequently Mr Seale Hayne stood down and Mr Sketchley entered the lists, where he was not only Liberal in his politics but with his personal fortune as well. He was elected, but was accused by Sir T Herbert of bribery, and another election ensued, which was won by a different Conservative candidate, James Dunn.

The bitter rivalry between the two steamboat companies continued unabated and what should have been a pleasant river trip became a trial of endurance, as this abridged *Chronicle* letter shows:

> *How long is this miserable war of our river steamboats to continue? All concerned are injured by it, let them imitate the cats in the saw pit, who fought until there was nothing left but two tails, and a little bit of fleece; the whole town suffers from their rivalry. Visitors arriving at Totnes become objects of fierce strife, their baggage carried aboard one boat, while they are got aboard another, then - volleys of oaths - shaking of fists - all but actual fighting. The boats start, but instead of the quiet enjoyment of the beauties of the river, it becomes a race, and in the case of nervous people, the fear of an explosion or collision. Visitors then resolve their first visit to Dartmouth will be their last. By amalgamation the traffic on the river would be remunerative and give greater accommodation, plying hours that would meet the wants of the inhabitant and visiting public. Arrangement should be made so that one liberal company could carry out both the river traffic and the towing of ships.*
> *PAX VOBISCUM*

Charles Seale Hayne proposed a compromise to end the two and a half years of rivalry and issued a prospectus inviting amalgamation in a new company, the Dartmouth Steam Packet Company Ltd, but regrettably Governor Holdsworth refused to join the new company, causing much anger in the town. Captain Moody sold his remaining shares in *Louisa* and *Pilot* for £2,500 to Mr Seale Hayne, who was appointed chairman of the new company. Captain Moody returned to Goole.

Regatta 1859 had only a small number of events.

By 1 August the railway had reached Paignton, though well behind schedule, but on 15 September the engineer to the railway, Isambard Kingdom Brunel, died. He was a great genius and universally mourned. In December responsibility for the line was taken over by his principal assistant Robert Pearson Brereton, who was later to take a major part in the affairs of the harbour and yacht club.

1860
January should have been a time for celebration in Dartmouth for it was the original completion date for the railway, but it was only just approaching Brixham Road (Churston), leaving a further two-and-a-half miles to complete to reach its terminus at the Floating Bridge.

In Kingswear subscribers had raised sufficient money for the first public clock in the area to be placed on Kingswear church tower, it was to be big enough to be seen across the harbour. A London speculator, Mr Davies, appeared with a proposal to convert Brookhill at a cost of £40,000 into the Winter Palace and Yacht Hotel, half the size of the Great Western Hotel, Paddington. He coerced the Mayor to convene a meeting at the Guildhall, where he outlined his scheme and launched a prospectus, but made little progress.

In Dartmouth, the authorities announced that they intended to improve the town's fortifications. Two new batteries would be erected on the old sites. The lower battery would be casemented and made bombproof with three guns facing the sea, and one howitzer covering the entrance, while the upper battery would be open with two guns and a guardroom connected to the magazine and battery below. Nearby the late Mr Fox's newly completed Paradise was purchased by the eminent engineer George Parker Bidder, who promptly renamed it Ravensbury and called in Dartmouth builder Mr Lidstone to make alterations, including a new billiard wing.

Regatta 1860 The Challenge prize for four-oared gigs was increased to £50 and for the first time was run in heats. The *Chronicle* reported that over 2,000 people had attended the regatta.

In November news was received of the death of Dartmouth's standing MP, the Conservative James Dunn, on a liner in the Red Sea. This presented a third opportunity for Charles Seale Hayne to stand as Liberal candidate. After a hard-fought contest he lost to his Conservative opponent John Hardy, by only two votes. However Dartmouth was able to retain the services of Mr Seale Hayne for many years, a man dedicated to improving the area.

1861
started with the new MP Mr Hardy, presenting the town with a fine Negretti & Zambra barometer for mounting on Bayards Quay for the benefit of pilots and fishermen (a similar one is found there today).

On 14 March the railway finally reached Brixham Road station (Churston), but rejoicing was muted due to the fact that, on the same day, the House of Lords rejected the company's Deviation Bill to resite the Floating Bridge terminus at Greenway, though the section to raise limited extra capital was approved; without extra capital the railway would have to terminate at Brixham Road. The bill was the brainchild of Mr Seale Hayne who had learned that a Parliamentary Bill was to be submitted to construct the 'Plymouth & South Hams Railway' from Plympton, through Modbury and Kingsbridge to Dartmouth, and he realized that this scheme could have great financial potential for both companies.

From his Kingswear Castle address he penned an eight page copperplate circular to his board to the following effect:

*as the original terminus was to be sited at Maypool, if they resited
the current Floating Bridge terminus with a high-level station at
Greenway it could result in a £50/60,000 saving and might
encourage the P & S H Co to bridge the Dart and connect to theirs,
to the mutual benefit of all. He stated that the current ceiling of
£120,000 was insufficient to complete the line to the* Floating
Bridge *terminal, and the total cost would exceed £200,000.
However he said that no blame could be attached to their late
engineer Mr Brunel, for he had been reluctant to accept the original
low estimate. He also said that in abandoning the remaining two-
and-a-half mile section to the* Floating Bridge *in favour of a high
level station at Greenway they would save not only on track but an
expensive tunnel, two viaducts and the Railway Ferry. He felt Mr
Harvey, the owner of Greenway House, would object, so they might
have to purchase the whole estate, but the house could be converted
into a hotel.*

[an understatement, as the line would run within 22 yards of his
mansion]

Thereupon, with the support of his board but without consulting
shareholders, Mr Brereton was instructed to prepare plans for Parliamentary
approval for the high-level Greenway terminus with a zigzag rail
communication to the riverside. Shareholders were informed at the AGM of 7
February, which reconvened on 5 April, when the result was known. News of
the rejection of the deviation scheme caused general dismay, both to the
company and to Dartmouth, for apart from the cost, it had wasted several
months' work, and severe financial problems remained.

In April that grand old man, Arthur Howe Holdsworth, the last Governor of
Dartmouth Castle, died. He and his family had played a prominent part in
Dartmouth's affairs, and he had resided in Kingswear for the last forty-one years.

Regatta 1861 This was the first regatta to be held over two days. It was
extended because of the weather, and yacht races were held outside the
harbour for the first time since 1820. Then Kingswear's annual regatta
followed, held in Waterhead Creek. There were prizes for sailing boats, four-

*Paradise, built by
J E Fox in 1855
on the site of
Paradise Fort
damaged in the
Civil War. It was
purchased in
1860 by G P
Bidder who
renamed it
Ravensbury. The
present owner has
renamed it
Paradise Point.*
D A GERRARD

George Philip, who came to Dartmouth in 1858 and founded Philip & Son Ltd at Sandquay's Middle Yard in 1865.
PHILIP & SON LTD

oared gigs, two-oared boats by women, two-oared boats by lads, a sculling match, gig and punt race, a duck hunt race, rural sports and donkey racing, and a dance was held in Princes Square.

The year ended with Mr Kelly, after seven years at Sandquay, closing his business due to pecuniary difficulties. This calamity was due to Colonel Holditch failing to honour his commitments and leaving a large barque, the *Prince Arthur*, on his hands. Later Mr Kelly's nephew Robert Moore, chief clerk and surveyor, recommended shipbuilding on the adjacent derelict Higher Sandquay yard. The yard foreman George Philip, who came to Dartmouth in 1858 to take Mr Mansfield's job at the yard, left to commence shipbuilding with Mr Couch, taking over Andrew Alford's old Coombe yard from the Steamboat Company, while John Holman of Topsham took over Mr Kelly's vacant Sandquay yard.

1862 started with a fire aboard the Dutch barque *Maleyer* so she was beached at Noss and holes pierced in her bows and sides, but the fire in her cargo still raged above water-level and through her decks, engulfing the whole ship till her masts and yards fell overboard and she burned to the water-line. Flames illuminated the night sky and the fire was watched by large crowds.

In Kingswear Mr Levitt Prinsep took Mr Holdsworth's old home The Beacon, whilst in Dartmouth two major events occurred. The first, sponsored by Captains Cleland and Arkwright, Sir H P Seale and Mr Bidder, was a viaduct and new road at Warfleet bypassing the existing tortuous road. The other was the announcement of the council's open competition to builders and others to improve Dartmouth's chronic road system in order to accommodate the anticipated extra traffic and trade the railway would generate. The successful scheme submitted by Mr Bell, engineer, resulted in building a new road which involved the demolition of property, including the home of Dartmouth's most famous son - Thomas Newcomen - after whom the road was named. The rejected scheme was by Mr Roberts, and was an embankment project which later formed the basis of Samuel Lake's South Embankment scheme.

Regatta 1862 The Navy participated for the first time, sending HMS *Colossus* and two training brigs.

Since the railway's arrival in March 1861 at Brixham Road, (Churston), communication was maintained by steamer to Greenway Quay, then by omnibus to Churston. There was also a service from Kingswear and Dartmouth, via the *Floating Bridge*. However, Mr Harvey objected to the use of Greenway Quay for passengers and took legal action, which resulted in an out-of-court settlement for its continued use, a result which pleased neither party. Because of financial restrictions the railway made no further progress, though siren voices in Brixham called for the terminus to be sited there, to which the answer was: 'Yes, if you pay for it'. Captain Bulley resigned from the railway board and was replaced by Mr W Froude, a brilliant researcher and a wealthy man. Then at the ninth AGM the chairman reported that a Parliamentary bill had been submitted for a new share issue, a loan and extra time to complete the line. Therefore, new plans had been prepared to extend the railway to Hoodown Point, and preliminary investigations had been made to establish the best site for a station building at Dartmouth. Sir H P Seale resigned to be replaced by Mr Knight, the railway contractor and major shareholder. In July the bill received royal assent to raise moneys to the value of £52,500 and loans of £10,900, which was on top of the approved and unused money obtained in the 1861 Deviation Bill. Tenders were obtained, the old contract terminated, and a new contract placed for an October start with Blinkhorn & Atkinson Ltd to continue the line from Brixham Road to Hoodown Point. There were still insufficient funds, however, to construct the necessary wharfs, quays, and sidings alongside the new terminus, or for a deep water jetty for a cross-channel service.

THE DARTMOUTH HARBOUR COMMISSION
Bureaucracy pays a dividend

At long last in September 1862 the railway directors were rewarded with a little good fortune, receiving an unexpected enquiry from the powerful East India & London Shipping Company Ltd. The Government contract for the Cape & Colony Mails, held by the Plymouth-based Union Line, was approaching renewal date and new tenders were being sought. The company was interested in using Dartmouth as its mailing port, as this abridged October *Chronicle* reports:

> *A party of gentlemen, including the Chairman, Directors, and Brokers visiting the port to ascertain its suitability as a mail port, were met by Mr Seale Hayne, and Directors. In the Steam Tug* Pilot *the party proceeded three miles seaward to view the harbour entrance. Then in the* Louisa *steamed upriver to Totnes, returning to Kingswear Castle to be entertained by Mr Seale Hayne, and the following morning the* Pilot *conveyed them to Torquay, for London.*

During their visit the gentlemen visitors imparted invaluable advice that the creation of a Harbour Commission would entitle them access to Government loans and grants to progress the port facilities. A letter followed from the chairman Mr R Pelly to Mr Seale Hayne, outlining the facilities required if their tender was to be successful:

A) *A distinguishing mark on the North side of the Harbour on the high land, and the whitening of a portion of the Mew Stone.*
B) *A fourth order Dioptic light on the Kingswear shore visible at the distance of eight miles and the present red light on St Petrox to be maintained and improved.*
C) *The Pin Rock to be buoyed or possibly removed.*
D) *Six large warping buoys wanted, four North shore and two South and a more powerful Steam Tug.*
E) *A 400 ft Jetty with a depth alongside of 24 ft at low water springs, connected to a Pier with a Store Room, Office and a Coal Depot ashore or afloat.*

Regrettably, although the East India & London Shipping Company Ltd's tender was the lowest, the contract was awarded again to the Union Line, after suspected political intervention by Plymouth MPs. However, Dartmouth had gained invaluable advice to create a Harbour Commission and gain Government loans and grants. The board instantly complied and by November the Dartmouth Harbour Improvement Bill appeared in the *Chronicle* with all the above requirements and others to create port-side facilities alongside the railway terminus as follows (briefly):

> *(Incorporation of Commissioners) - Power to construct piers, lighthouses, and other works, and otherwise improve the harbour; to take lands and the present lighthouse, tolls and dues; to levy tolls; to lease, sell, or amalgamate to, or with, the Corporation of Dartmouth, or the Dartmouth & Torbay Railway Company.*

It received royal assent in the following year, giving Dart Harbour Commission (DHC) permission to borrow £14,000 to implement the harbour works and appoint eleven commissioners, as follows: C S Hayne (chairman), W Froude, G Knight, Sir H P Seale, G P Bidder, J Belfield, G Carew Hunt and G F Luttrell, plus three appointed by the Board of Trade.

Left: 1863 HMS
Britannia IV, *a*
Crimean war
veteran and still
full-rigged, shown
shortly after her
arrival in the
River Dart for use
as a training ship,
moored off
Sandquay. This
was before the
arrival of the
railway.
R JONES/R TUCKER/
DARTMOUTH MUSEUM

Right: 1870.
HMS Britannia V
and HMS
Hindustan
moored at
Sandquay and
linked by a
covered gantry.
The cadets are
manning the
foremast of HMS
Britannia.
DAVE GRIFFITHS/
ROY BARNES.

1863
Work on the railway continued and it arrived at last at Hoodown Point, but a decision had been made to continue the line over Waterhead Creek to a terminus adjacent to the Plume of Feathers Inn.

In Dartmouth Sir Henry Paul Seale sold a part of his large Gallants Bower Estate, Lower Wick, Dyer's Hill, Pinhay, Milton and Ford, a total of 500 acres, for £38,000 to Hugh Muir, London and Glasgow. Regrettably Mr Holman decided to cease trading only two years after taking over Mr Kelly's bankrupt Sandquay business.

Regatta 1863 Bad weather predominated - there was a race for sailing barges, one for sailing boats and three for rowing boats. Only 46 craft attended

BRITANNIA ARRIVES

In August the harbour was inspected by the Lords of the Admiralty in the steam yacht *Enchantress*, followed by a visit from Captain Powell, commander of HMS *Britannia*. The Devonport steam tug *Prospero* with No 9 mooring lump, the lighter *Hamoaze* and a party of riggers arrived, and sank close to Old Mill Creek four 5-ton anchors in five fathoms of water, each with 70 fathoms of cable, sufficient to moor a large vessel 'all fours'. Then, to great joy, on a bright and clear day, 30 September, the *Britannia*, in the tow of the steam sloop *Geyser* and the tug *Prospero*, arrived on an ebb tide at the harbour entrance. Watched by large cheering crowds, she was towed through the narrows between the castles to her prepared moorings off Sandquay. Here further large crowds were assembled, and all the church bells rang as she took the anchorage that was to be the berth of a ship bearing the name *Britannia* for the next fifty-three years. She was joined, in more ways than one, in 1864 by a two-rater - the *Hindustan* - to provide extra accommodation. The *Britannia* was later found to be inadequate and unhealthy, so in 1869 she was replaced by a three-decker the *Prince of Wales*. The latter was unfinished and had never been to sea, so was fitted out as a training ship, and renamed *Britannia*. Both vessels remained at Dartmouth until 1905 when the shore-based naval training college was completed. The *Hindustan* left and the *Britannia* remained until 1916.

Renaissance on the Harbour

1864 to 1874

EUPHORIA IN DARTMOUTH

1864

Firstly, peace returned. After bitter years of rivalry between the owners of *Louisa* and *Royal Dartmouth*, the latter had been purchased by William Froude for his experiments into ship stability. His election to the DHC, Dartmouth & Torbay Railway, and Steam Packet Company contributed to harmony. The Steam Packet Company, devoid of competition, only operated one vessel giving improved service and profitability; so it placed a £1,800 order for a new paddle-steamer *Newcomen*, similar to the *Louisa* but larger; Lewis & Stockwell of London were to provide the hull, whilst Bolton & Watts of Birmingham were to supply the 20hp engine.

The Dartmouth & Torbay Railway Company decided to extend the line to Kingswear and purchased land from Mr Luttrell, namely Hoodown Ferry House, shipyard, granary, Plume of Feathers Inn, slipway and ferry rights. Work commenced and soon the primitive waterline beauty of the Kingswear shoreline disappeared under rough treatment from the pick and shovel. While the construction of the 492-foot tunnel, 500-foot stone viaduct, two timber viaducts and embankments proceeded apace, the shipyard disappeared under the station built by Call & Pethick, Plymouth. Then the Board purchased a powerful double-ended paddle-steamer, aptly renamed *Perseverance*, and fitted out by Lewis & Stockwell. Dartmouth station was sited centrally at Spithead and both sides would be served by landing pontoons linked to shore with hinged covered gantries. Earlier Sir H P Seale had realized that there were insufficient funds to buy his ferry, and facing competition from the railway ferry, he obtained an injunction stopping the railway from crossing the *Floating Bridge* road. The 1858 Railway Act contained clauses enabling it to purchase the Floating Bridge, so Sir H P Seale had been granted a board seat and £2,000 to ensure co-operation; to avoid expensive litigation a compromise was reached, Sir H P Seale received a further £150 and withdrew the injunction forbidding any ferry within three miles of the Floating Bridge, while The Dartmouth & Torbay Railway Company surrendered their right to purchase the *Floating Bridge*.

Then the DHC applied to the Public Works Loan Commissioners for £14,000 to develop harbourside facilities as follows:

> *Discontinue St Petrox light and construct a new lighthouse on the Kingswear shore, with a Dioptic 4th Order light with an 11 mile range.*
>
> *Erect a Day Beacon 80ft high 500ft above sea level at Froward Point, on the Eastern Shore.*
>
> *The Pin Rock to be removed or reduced by blasting to 4/5 fathoms below low water spring tides.*
>
> *Construct alongside the railway terminus a Quay having 21ft at water spring tides, 16ft at neap tides, 6ft at low water spring tides, also a Warehouse and Fish Shed.*
>
> *A Deep water Jetty carried to 21ft at low waters spring tides.*
>
> *To Buoy and mark obstructions, passage and fairway.*
>
> *To make and charge Tolls, Dues, and By-laws.*

Approval was obtained and orders placed with Blinkhorn & Atkinson Ltd at £105 for the lighthouse and £523 for the Daymark.

1864. Kingswear Lighthouse; in December Mr Thomas McQuire was appointed the first lighthouse keeper at ten shillings (50p) per week.

DAVID SOUTHWICK

Meanwhile the conversion of the railway ferry was proving difficult; it was £600 to £800 over estimate, and would be unfinished at the opening ceremony. In June the *Newcomen* arrived, but was soon withdrawn because passengers were annoyed by falling pieces of calcinated soot; her funnel was lengthened by six feet and an awning fitted over her afterdeck. Work continued preparing primitive station facilities, only a platform and a booking office. The morning of 10 August dawned bright and clear as a special train left Brixham Road station carrying directors and other dignitaries and arrived at Kingswear station around noon. Here, they boarded the *Newcomen* to be received on the New Ground, Dartmouth, by the Mayor, Sir H P Seale, and the Corporation amid cheers from hundreds of spectators. After welcoming speeches they paraded to luncheon and further speeches; Mr Seale Hayne closed by referring to a weakness in the Railway Act, with lawsuits costly to Paignton. The following extract is abridged from the *Torquay Directory*:

> *in regard to the promotion of small railways they had an undue share of provoking difficulties. Unfortunately the hardship is that the cumbrous machinery necessary for legalising a small line is as for a large line. An Act had now been introduced to remedy this evil. He did not desire in all cases compulsory possession of land; but when intelligent men sanctioned by a district determined that a particular line of railway was the best, the less difficult the legislature the better for the country. However they now could contemplate the advantages likely to accrue from the Torbay & Dartmouth Railway.*

Regatta 1864 had barge and rowing races, and a race from Dartmouth to Ryde for schooners of the Royal Victoria Yacht Club. Fourteen craft participated weighing from 40 to 216 tons.

The *Chronicle* reported that Mr Seale Hayne had purchased Dartmouth's Castle Hotel for £3,500, and had split his Brownstone Estate into two farms, Higher and Lower Brownstone, the latter having a new farmhouse built for £600 by Mr Silly, Dartmouth.
The *Chronicle* reported:

> *The railway ferry* Perseverance *has arrived, but difficulty is found in working her, arising from her unusual construction, which gives the prevailing winds considerable power on her high sided hull, and interferes with the facility of movement so necessary on a steam ferry.*

This year closed with the completion of Kingswear's station, the Daymark and the lighthouse, whose light was to shine over a revitalized harbour for another 120 years.

1865

The DHC placed further orders with the railway contractors, Blinkhorn & Atkinson, for wharfs, quays, warehouse, fish shed, weighbridge and a deep water jetty, and Tathams were ordered to remove the Pin Rock down to five fathoms below low water spring tides. As the harbour was no longer a port of free entry, a series of tolls, dues and charges were introduced to cover operating costs and the repayment of loans. A new slip and small shipyard were also built at Hoodown Point and leased to Mr Alford. George Philip ended his partnership with Mr Couch and leased the vacant Middle Sandquay yard, thus creating the famous firm Philip & Son Ltd. The Steam Packet Company then launched two share issues totalling £25,000 to purchase from Kirkpatrick & McIntyre, Port Glasgow a two-funnelled cross-channel paddle-steamer (368 tons, 185ft x 90ft x 9ft) with 106hp diagonal oscillating engines to ply between Dartmouth, the Channel Islands and St Malo. Called *Eclair* she arrived in June, running two trips a week in summer and one in winter, and was fully tested in November, leaving Jersey in a violent storm when no other vessels ventured out of harbour.

Regatta 1865 had a race for sailing barges and several races for sailing and rowing boats in the harbour.

Trouble began with the *Perseverance* requiring repairs to her machinery and boilers at Plymouth and resulted in the *Louisa* standing in.

The small riverside village of Kingswear was now transformed into a thriving commercial centre, with six trains a day serving the terminus and dockside facilities and cross-channel services. There was also a growing national awareness of the area's latent potential, with its natural beauty, healthy situation and superb position as a yachting centre; this resulted in a new and vibrant community, and an influx of people with independent means who commissioned the building of several substantial villas. On his Brownstone Estate Mr Seale Hayne began to erect Penang Villa (The Grange), Castella (Kingswear Court), Sea View Villa (The White House), Start Bay Villa (Pinewoods) and Warren Cottage. Mr Davies, the London developer, resurrected his 1860 scheme to buy Brookhill and convert it to a hotel; this time he formed a company and leased Brookhill for use as a boarding house; then he absconded with the capital raised!

Later the *Chronicle* reported that Mr Luttrell was cutting a new road from Mount Ridley Road through Kingswear Wood, gradually descending to join the Turnpike Road, as the trustees had agreed to re-route it behind the water-mill to connect with the new Higher Contour Road. The old short and narrow secondary road out of Kingswear, from the Wood Lane/Fore Street junction, which passed behind the new Chapel Cottages before turning 90 degrees to join the Brixham Road, was

Below: This old lithograph of Tom Thumb was found in Dartmouth. He was only 12 years old, 25 inches tall and only 15lbs in weight, and performed in the music halls as Napoleon Bonaparte. In 1867, in violent storms, he crossed from St Malo to Dartmouth, in the PS Eclair *and stayed at the Royal Castle Hotel, and wrote expressing his admiration for the ship's sailing ability, 'She walked the waters, like a thing of life'.*
P T BARNUM

Left: 1866. Pilot *early in the great storm rendered assistance; for months after she salvaged wrecked vessels.*
ALAN KITTRIDGE

Right: 1866. The horrific scene at Brixham breakwater – wrecked ships the morning after the great storm.
DARTMOUTH MUSEUM

Left: 1865. Kingswear's centuries-old Plume of Feathers Inn
R KELLAND/ G THOMAS

Right: The front cover of a later descriptive brochure of the Royal Dart Hotel (1881)
JIM THORPE

abandoned and a new road, Lower Contour Road, was cut from the Wood Lane/Fore Street junction to intersect with the new Higher Contour Road and Turnpike Road.

Mr Luttrell had also commissioned Edward Appleton to build at the head of Waterhead Creek a brass and iron foundry, Chapel Cottages and a waterworks to serve the village and its new developments.

1866 started in evil mood with the French smack *Augusta* going aground off Broadsands; *Pilot* was soon in attendance but the only way she could make contact was by sending out a small dog with 70 fathoms of light line for the hawser to be hauled aboard; the dog then rescued a crewman who had fallen overboard. Robbed of her prize the sea then really showed her might, for at sunset on 10 January hurricane force winds struck a fleet of seventy-nine merchant and fishing vessels sheltering in Torbay. Only eleven rode out the storm and over 100 lives were lost; eight boats driven ashore were recovered, several were sold where they lay. Many vessels could have made Brixham harbour but trawlers obstructed the entrance. The tug *Pilot* was busy for months on salvage, providing her best ever yearly returns.

In the harbour at Kingswear the goods shed and customs house were completed, the sidings laid, the wharf extended, a jetty turntable and rails laid, a grid iron and a steam crane from Applebys introduced. However the Dartmouth & Torbay Railway Company still had financial problems and negotiated with the South Devon Railway (SDR) for amalgamation. They agreed to lease the line and the SDR Act 1866 obtained royal assent in June; the Dartmouth & Torbay Railway Company thus lost its independence but gained monetary security against liabilities of over £200,000. Mr Seale Hayne was given a seat on the board.

Charles Seale Hayne determined to profit from the port's potential by providing quality hotel facilities: he already owned the Castle Hotel in Dartmouth, and he formed the Dartmouth & Kingswear Hotel Company Ltd with Dominic Stone and Henry Studdy as directors. They acquired a seventy-five year lease on Kingswear's Plume of Feathers Inn from the railway company, who retained the ferry rights which were

 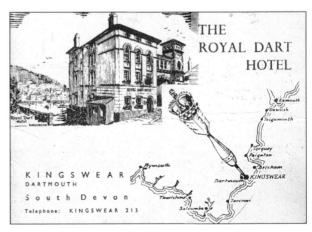

leased to Thomas Avis senior, boatbuilder and postmaster adjacent to the Lower Ferry. The Dartmouth & Kingswear Hotel Company Ltd then transformed the inn on a tight budget, making cosmetic alterations to the existing doors and windows; they removed the roof and built a further two storeys, some of the work was timber framed with lathe and plaster cover; they added an adjacent four-storeyed wing with a clock tower linked to the existing building by a wide archway which gave access to the quays and ferry gantry; the property was ideal, being adjacent to the railway station, the deep water pier and both the lower and railway ferries. The architect was Mr Gribble of Torquay and the contractors Call & Pethick of Plymouth, builders of Kingswear station. It was built in Italianate style and had every facility. The basement had the tap with parlours, larders, cellars and conveniences; the ground floor had a spacious entrance hall with encaustic tiles, sitting rooms, kitchens, butler's pantry and scullery; the first floor had a handsome bar with adjoining parlour plus coffee and club rooms with bay windows and balconies with river views, smoking rooms, private sitting-rooms and cloakrooms. There were two separate staircases, the one for visitors was very handsome. The top floor had eight single and double bedrooms overlooking the river. The hotel opened on 10 August 1866 and Mr Seale Hayne held a private party attended by many eminent Devon people. This was to become the Dart Yacht Club Hotel.

FORMATION OF THE DART YACHT CLUB

June 1866. The first page of the membership book of the Dart Yacht Club, (later the Royal Dart Yacht Club, 1872) with the names of many famous founding members including; 1 Henry Studdy, marine inventor 7 Arthur Holdsworth, Dartmouth worthy 8 R Newman and 9 G Hunt, Newfoundland traders 10 Admiral Sheringham, oceanographer 12 Thomas Woolacombe, Chairman, South Devon Railway 19 Sir Henry Paul Seale, Dartmouth landowner 21 George R Stephenson, nephew of Robert Stephenson 24 Robert P Bretherton, Brunel's deputy and successor 25 George P Bidder, engineer and mathmatician 26 Charles Manby, Founder of the Institute of Civil Engineers.

Henry Studdy,
Commodore,
1866-1904,
founding member
of the Royal Dart
Yacht Club, .
ROYAL DART YACHT CLUB

Henry Studdy of Waddeton Court began canvassing friends' opinions as to the feasibility of forming a local yacht club. On 8 June he chaired a meeting of seven potential members at the Castle Hotel and said that thirty-three people had intimated they would join; it was resolved that:

> *A yacht club be formed in Dartmouth by the gentlemen present and named 'Dart Yacht Club'. The club be constituted by and consist of members, whether bona fide owners of yachts or otherwise to be elected. The entrance fee would be 10/6d and annual subscription one guinea.*

William Smith, a Dartmouth solicitor, was appointed honorary secretary, the rules prepared and an Admiralty warrant sought. On 15 June Mr Studdy was appointed Commodore, a position he held for thirty-eight years, and he reported that the Yacht Club Hotel had offered two rooms facing the river, furnished and with attendance, at £25 a year. This was accepted, not surprisingly, as the hotel was already called the Yacht Club Hotel; Mr Studdy lived nearby and was a director of the hotel company. The club opened and determined from the outset to obtain the 'Royal' prefix to enable members to carry the crown on their ensign and burgee. At the first AGM in June 1867 George Parker Bidder, Ravensbury, was elected Vice Commodore. The membership book lists thirty founding members, a 'Who's Who' of local gentry and national well-known personalities, covering a wide field of activities.

Regatta 1866 The Dart Yacht Club changed the format of regattas, with yachting playing an increasing part. The Town Committee ran the usual sailing and rowing races, including one for ten-oared cutters from HMS *Britannia* and one for four-oared coastguard cutters. The Town Plate had prizes of £50, £20 and £10 and was won by *Son of the Thames*. The second day, races were run outside the river and controlled by the yacht club from the tug *Pilot* – two races of two rounds, 15 miles each, around the Eastern Blackstone and a markboat in Start Bay. The race was for DYC members only, for yachts not over 25 tons, and had eight starters. It was won by Mr Turner's *Electra* (£25), the Rev E T Seymour's *Lone Star* came second (£10). The allcomer's race, prize £10, was won by Captain Whitbread's *Queen*.

The year closed with a *Chronicle* report that the Rev E T Seymour was building a new house named Riversea in Kingswear and selling Warfleet House, possibly because Warfleet Mill, opposite his property was to be turned into a brewery.

1867 started in a low key, though not at Kingswear Quay, where in two months several vessels berthed, two with coals for Torquay, two with china clay, one with Haytor granite, a Dutch schooner with sugar for Bristol and another with oats from Ireland.

Mr Avis, had replaced the old rowing boats with new, and faced competition from *Perseverance*, so he ordered from White's yard at Cowes the first Lower Ferry steam launch to power the new railway horse and passenger float. When he collected the steam launch he had to run for shelter into Weymouth harbour and struck an unmarked rock, causing extensive damage. She eventually arrived by rail and was named *Pioneer*; 30ft x 7ft x 2ft 11in with a high-pressure engine and a four-bladed screw propeller, she was capable of carrying thirty passengers.

Regatta 1867 had a new trawler race, with a prize of £30; there were nine starters and it was won by *Dart* (37 tons).

The year ended with the death of Mr Henry Fownes Luttrell, who was succeeded by his nephew George Henry Fownes Luttrell.

1868 In February the Steam Packet Company announced that the much-loved *Eclair* was no longer viable, and it was to dispose of her for £5,500 to D'Oyly & Rimson Ltd for service in the Bristol Channel, where she remained until 1877 when she was sold on to the Thames Steamboat Company.

Chennals of Totnes commenced a river service with the 142-foot *Alexander*, renamed the *William and Thomas*, but to the relief of the Dartmouth company a series of disasters caused her withdrawal. Sunday trips failed through lack of support, while the boat, badly handled or unmanageable, twice smashed her paddle boxes, grounded several times, gouged out riverside rocks, ran into other vessels and, finally, when loaded with passengers, backed instead of going forward then went forwards instead of reversing; this so alarmed the passengers that they demanded to disembark and make their own way back.

Regatta 1868 had a new event for the *Mosquito* fleet of sailing boats not exceeding 18 feet, with fourteen starters. The main club race was for the handsome silver Luttrell Cup. This race is commemorated in the present RDYC clubroom's magnificent oil-painting given by Mr Kensington, one of the contestants, as listed below:

Emmett	28 tons	Yawl	Mr Levett-Prinsep
Luna	25 tons	Cutter	Mr Daniell
Queen	15 tons	Cutter	Capt Whitbread
Una	15 tons	Cutter	Mr Kensington
Isabel	15 tons	Cutter	Mr Freake
Wild Duck	20 tons	Yawl	Mr Studdy
Quiver	12 tons	Cutter	Capt Chamberlayne
Gondola	50 tons	Cutter	Lt Studdy

The event was won by Mr Levett-Prinsep of The Beacon, Kingswear.

Captain Chamberlayne, owner of *Quiver*, was one of the few survivors of the charge of the Light Brigade immortalized in Tennyson's poem; he died two years after this regatta and was buried at St Petrox church. His obituary stated that he entered the Army as cornet in the 18th Light Dragoons, and he distinguished himself by his courage in that fatal charge at Balaklava, riding up to the enemy's guns on the right hand of Lord Cardigan at the front of his regiment. On fighting his way out with the few gallant comrades remaining, his favourite charger, Pimento, was shot three times before it fell. Captain Chamberlayne was seen within range of the Russian batteries, the ground ploughed up by shot and shell, coolly removing the saddle and holsters and walking to the rising ground where what remained of the gallant 600 had re-formed. He was received with a burst of hearty cheering. Captain Chamberlayne was so loved by his troop that, on his retirement, each man donated a day's pay, and presented him with a handsome inscribed and chased silver snuffbox.

Another yacht club member attending the regatta in his yacht *Red Gauntlet* was Edward Langtry, later husband of the beautiful 'Jersey Lily'. Mr Langtry's attendance at several regattas gives credence to the rumours that Mrs Langtry, mistress of the Prince of Wales, made clandestine incognito visits with her royal escort to local mansions, among them Warfleet House and Riversea, both then owned by the wealthy Rev E T Seymour. Also, in residence at Brookhill was a friend of the Prince, Thomas Freake, who later inherited Warfleet House and built the adjacent Warfleet Lodge in 1882. This splendid castellated residence's only connection to the house was by an elevated gallery; the lodge contained magnificent carved panelling and fireplaces, gunroom, billiardroom and ballroom and superb private apartments with stained glass windows containing the royal coat of arms. In the adjacent Warfleet Creek was a large thatched boathouse where the Prince's yacht was sometimes berthed.

Property moves closed the year: William Smith, solicitor, moved into Park Hill, Lieutenant Studdy moved into Warfleet House, and Henry Bridson bought nearby Higher Wilderness, and renamed it Derwent Lodge. In Newcomen Road the newly built Roman Catholic church of St John the Baptist opened; the building was of a pleasant compact design by London architect, Mr Anson, and the services attracted sizeable congregations. At Greenway Mr Harvey purchased an extra 700 acres and engaged Mr Farley of Kingswear to re-lay roads and build rows of cottages for his tenants. After 700 years Kingswear acquired a second place of worship when the Wesleyans, who had used a cottage for fifty-eight years, constructed a small Gothic-style chapel to hold 150 people on Wood Lane; it was instigated by Mr Patten, the stationmaster, and designed by Mr Roberts of Dartmouth.

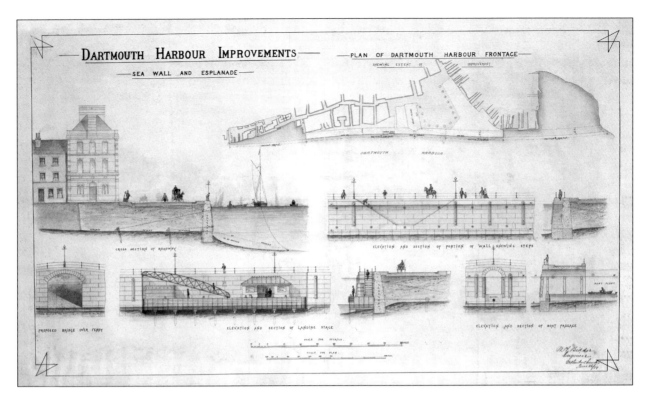

In 1879, Samuel Lake commissioned, from the late G P Bidder's Westminster office a scheme to reline Dartmouth's silting waterfront with an esplanade. It received Town Council and D H C approval for funding, and they then applied for a Parliamentry Bill. This was bitterly contested by F C Simpson and his anti Embankment committee. However G P Bidder II, the D H C's Counsel with Lake as a principal participant secured final approval in the House of Lords and Royal Assent for Dartmouth's jewel in the crown, the South Embankment.

DARTMOUTH MUSEUM

1869 introduced Samuel Lake who played a major part in the affairs of Dartmouth; at ten he had shipped aboard a schooner from Dartmouth, served in a foreign navy and then was contracted for the Government in Calcutta. There he displayed great bravery, and saved the lives of 450 Muslim pilgrims who were returning from Mecca aboard the barque *Diamond*. In 1866 Samuel Lake returned home with £10,000 or more, married Mary Knowling Ford, raised four children and engaged in commercial enterprises. He was presented with the Albert Medal for his bravery by Sir Henry Paul Seale. With a partner from Bombay, James Armeson, and Captain Twyman, he built up a fleet of twenty sailing trawlers. For the crews, he built Coombe Terrace Cottages, the first houses in the country to be made from poured concrete. He participated in the formation of the Torbay & Dart Paint Co Ltd, and was also involved in the Sandquay brickworks and various local quarries. He was a town councillor but moved to London, and contracted to build Milford Haven, and later, Felixstowe Docks. He was fascinated by promotional schemes and was involved in Brunel's *Great Eastern*, met royalty, owned Castle Hall, Milford Haven (once home of Nelson's Lady Emma Hamilton), and a large steam yacht, but he overreached himself and finally became bankrupt. His main achievement in Dartmouth was the father of the Embankment and the bunkering trade.

THE FIRST STEAM TRAWLERS

In late 1868 Mr Lake had purchased from Liverpool the 40 foot tug *Thistle* to assist the trawlers in light winds. With Kingswear's self-taught engineer George Kingdon, he modified her machinery and fitted a larger screw propeller which vastly improved her performance and enabled them to experiment with steam trawling ten years before Newcastle claimed to have done. This experiment secured the interest and financial support of George Parker Bidder, Ravensbury, who designed and financed the first prototype trawler *Florence*. She was London built, 46 feet long, wood on iron frames and brought round by Samuel Lake, but she proved too small and was soon converted back to sail.

On 1 April, the Government ordered the registration, numbering and lettering of fishing boats, and all boats exceeding 15 feet had to bear the first and last letter of their port of registration. Locally this was Dartmouth, not Brixham, whose large fishing fleet was obliged to bear, the letters 'DH' until 1902, giving free publicity to their rival port.

Samuel Lake *1845-1887*
...a Courageous and Generous Entrepreneur, with a Long Record of Achievements

1870 Coombe Terrace, the first pre-formed poured-concrete houses in this country and where Lake's family resided until 1920.

DARTMOUTH MUSEUM

Samuel Lake, was the original contractor for what are today, the two largest dock complexes in the UK. Milford Haven Dock, 1879, now part of the oil terminal and Felixstowe Dock, 1881, now part of the container terminal. Mrs Lake and daughter Bhimee shown sitting on the right.

FELIXSTOWE DOCK AND RAILWAY COMPANYT

Samuel Lake's shipyard at Castle Pill, Milford Haven, showing his newly completed rail swing bridge, with one trawler on the stocks, and three completed nearby.

LESLIE JONES

The evolution of the 1867/73 Bidder/Lake Dartmouth experimental steam trawlers, culminating in 1882/83 at Lake's Castle Iron & Steel Works, Milford Haven, in what were probably the first five practical working steam trawlers in the country. They were built under the supervision of W E Redway, manager, and John Houston, yard foreman, both ex-Dartmouth Sandquay builders. The Birda, *the last for F J Sellick, was on the stocks at the time of Mr Lake's bankruptcy, and was completed later.*

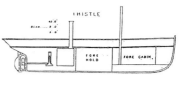

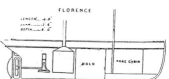

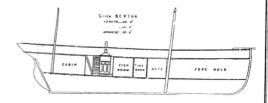

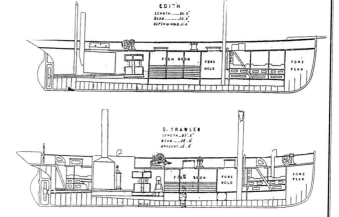

MARINE ENGINEER - 1883 BY PERMISSION OF THE BRITISH LIBRARY

The railway ferry Dolphin *(built in 1869 at Harveys, Hayle) with Captain Thorne at the wheel arriving at Kingswear pontoon.*
G THOMAS

The *Perseverance*, suffering constant breakdown and costly repairs, ran out of steam whilst crossing to Dartmouth; she collided with and sank a lighter, causing legal action. So the SDR decided to stop persevering with *Perseverance* and ordered from Harveys, Hayle, a new vessel fitted with her overhauled boiler and engine and named *Dolphin* (someone must have had a sense of humour to compare her with the graceful dolphin!). She was of similar construction, steered from both ends, but with larger deck accommodation, her bulwarks carried out amidships to her outer sponson line thus enabling her to carry 361 passengers.

In July Sir Henry Paul Seale's Norton Downey Estate (Townstal), 840 acres of farms, houses and building land was auctioned in London and later in the Castle Hotel, but was unsold. The latter hotel acquired a new and commodious billiard room, measuring 32ft x 13ft and panelled in pitch pine, with the ceiling divided into beautifully decorated panels. It was announced that Bayards Cove Castle had been leased for conversion to a private residence (fortunately not acted upon).

The first *Britannia* was decommissioned after only six years and towed away by the tug *Scotia* and sloop *Buzzard*. She was replaced on 17 August by the wooden three-decker *Prince of Wales*, 3,994 tons, built at Portsmouth as a screw-line battleship but never commissioned. She was renamed *Britannia*, and remained on the river until 1916.

Regatta 1869 had the usual races but, surprisingly, the trawler race was abandoned after only two years. The fireworks were set off from the attending naval brigs and yachts.

The Steam Packet Company ordered from Harveys, Hayle, a new tug which was launched by Miss Alice Vincent with these delightful words: *'Beautiful vessel! On this the day of your launch I name thee* Guide! *Go forth on thy destined element and be prosperous. Save ships in peril; assist those requiring aid; and guide all to a haven of safety, or forward them on successful voyages'.*

After eleven years, W Follett closed his Silver Street shipyard.

In November Mr Bidder and Mr Lake headed the poll and were elected councillors. Mr Armeson terminated his four-year partnership with Mr Lake, the latter retaining the quarries and some trawlers, and Mr Armeson the Sandquay brickworks; his five trawlers were placed for auction at the Marine Tavern (now Hope Cottage on the Dartmouth Lower Ferry Slip with Fortuna moulded on the plastered wall). Mr Armeson then moved his building business to his Kingswear home Mount Agra (he had taken refuge at Agra Fort during the Indian Mutiny) which was built above the village with Sandquay bricks stamped 'Armeson'.

1870Mr Armeson purchased and demolished old buildings in Kingswear's square and built the present three-storey block of houses and shops, then he built Agra Villas in Brixham Road; also under construction on Church Hill were Owensville (Kingswear House), Claremont (Colonsay), Mount Ridley, Ridley House and Eastney. The old school, located over the third arch in Priory Street, was totally inadequate, so a sizeable school and teacher's residence was erected next to the Wesleyan chapel. At nearby Galmpton a small Congregational church and school were built and the Manor Inn was opened.

In February the brigantine *Eureka* with coals from Newcastle ran up on the Froward Rocks; three crew were drowned and the survivors climbed the cliffs to Brownstone Farm. Later the Brixham schooner , in ballast from Fécamp, lost her mainsail in a gale, then dragged her anchors by Dartmouth Castle and the tug *Guide* was unable to close; the six crew took to the boat, but capsized a mere three yards from shore, and five men were drowned. The sixth was saved by Mr Crocker, landlord of the Royal Oak (Bayards Restaurant). With two vessels and eight lives lost in two weeks the call for rocket apparatus and a lifeboat for Dartmouth was raised again.

Mr Bidder progressed his experiments in steam trawling, ordering from Mr Moore of Sandquay another prototype, *Bertha*, a 66ft x 16ft x 10ft schooner with engines from Stephenson's Newcastle yard. She was built according to a new principle of iron plating on a wood frame to alleviate strain, but she operated for only one year before conversion to a sailing ketch.

Regatta 1870 The Dart Yacht Club ran an extra race, Dartmouth to Torquay and back, for a water-colour given by Mr Bridson. In the harbour there were seventy-five sailing boats and six steam yachts.

In this year HMS *Captain* was lost. She was a revolutionary armoured turret ship with only eight feet of freeboard and a full rig of sail. She had been the brainchild of Captain Cowper Coles, who developed her from his experiences with gun-mounted rafts in the Crimea. The protégé of Mr Childers, First Lord of the Admiralty, Captain Cowper Coles engaged in bitter controversy with the Chief Constructor of the Navy, Mr Reed, who doubted the ship's stability and designed a similar vessel, HMS *Monarch* with 14 feet of freeboard. To manifest his confidence in Captain Cowper Cole's vessel, Mr Childers transferred his midshipman son Leonard (possibly a *Britannia* cadet) from HMS *Monarch* to HMS *Captain*, which capsized during a storm off Spain on 7 September 1870, causing the death of young Childers and 500 other unfortunate men. As a result of this tragic accident the Admiralty formed a Committee of Naval Construction to advise on naval architecture, and included two senior Dart Yacht Club members, George Parker Bidder (Ravensbury), and William Froude (Chelston Cross, Torquay). In October Mr Ashford, who three or four years previously had let his middle Sandquay yard to Alex Philip, rented his two remaining Sandquay yards (one either side) to Mr Redway, an Exmouth shipbuilder. This

Kingswear station, quays and Eclair *Pier. The picture shows Fore Street widened and the Embankment rebuilt by the railway company from Wood Lane to Higher Street; also the ferry, possibly the* Perseverance *(1864 - 1869), and the Wesleyan Chapel (1869 - 1970).*

ERIC BOVEY

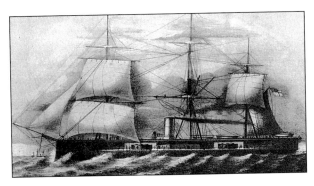 

Left: 'Shifting Main Topsail Yard After Being Sprung Going About in Mid Channel May 14th 1870' – HMS Captain, *double-turreted, double-screwed, full-rigged and ironclad. The captain was H T Burgoyne VC. Eleven weeks later she capsized with the loss of 500 men, only four months after her launch.*

AUTHOR'S COLLECTION

Right: 1870 - 1885. The Admiralty appointed a committee of warship design which included two RDYC members, G P Bidder and William Froude, who were experimenting with model hulls made in Kingswear from a launch on the Dart. Then Sir Edward Reed, Chief Navy Constructor secured from the Admiralty a £2,000 contribution for Mr Froude (the foremost authority who had worked for Brunel on the Great Eastern *and the Atmospheric Railway) to carry out further research. He constructed in his garden at Chelston Cross, Torquay, a semi-recessed water testing tank (278ft x 30ft x 10ft) and the delicate measuring instruments needed to test ship model hulls in the tank. The photo shows either his son R E Froude, or Kingswear's George Kingdon. The experiments continue today in premises at Haslar, Portsmouth.* JOHN PIKE

resulted in eight years of bitter rivalry between the two firms. The Totnes competition hired *Annie* (45ft) for winter service, but unluckily the river froze over for two miles below Totnes and she sustained serious bow and engine damage whilst smashing through the ice, and was withdrawn. Finally Mr Hingston, the Danish vice-consul, bought the damaged Danish barque *Happy* as a standing coal hulk for the growing bunker trade. In 1869 Mr Armeson had recognized the potential of a permanent floating coal hulk, and purchased the *Marinus*, wrecked in 1867 at Berry Head. Towed to Dartmouth and laid up, he converted her to a hulk and stationed her by Hoodown Point, but she broke loose to sit on the rocks by Gunfield. Because of numerous business ventures with Mr Lake, some unsuccessful, Mr Armeson failed to exploit an opportunity that was to become the mainstay of Dartmouth for eighty years.

THE CASTLE LINERS

1871 The new year brought rejoicing in Dartmouth for, after fourteen years, the port was to become a mailing station again. This justified all the risk, outlay and effort Mr Seale Hayne and fellow directors had put into the railway, harbour and hotel company. The initiative for the enterprise belonged to George Payne, shipbroker, who undertook all the risk, issued a prospectus and formed the Cape & Natal Steam Navigation Co. It was to ply monthly to the Cape and colonies with private mail, passengers and freight, calling at Madeira and St Helena, taking thirty days under steam. The service would receive no annual Government grant and would compete against the Government subsidized Union Steamship Company's Royal Mail Line service from Southampton.

The *Chronicle*, a weekly, reported the inaugural dinner on 6 February at the Castle Hotel. The Mayor and local dignitaries attended to entertain Mr Payne and his directors, who announced that they had ordered four new ships. On 10 February the chartered SS *Gambia* with forty passengers and 900 tons of cargo aboard proudly sailed into the harbour to moor alongside Kingswear jetty. Here Edward Marsh Turner, the appointed company agent, saw her off for the Cape and Natal.

A monthly service ensued using the following chartered vessels: *Beethoven, Lumsdin, Westenhope, Sweden, Carolana, Warrior, Sprite, Cella, Marc-Antony, Medway* and *Thames*. The *Westenhope* was wrecked at Port Elizabeth, as was the *Gambia*. Mr Payne approached a friend, Donald Currie, and chartered the *Iceland* and the *Gothland* to continue the service. Then Lake & Co formed the Dartmouth, Plymouth & Torbay Steamship Trading Co Ltd, purchasing a small screw-steamer *Maud* for a twice weekly service to those ports, yet though well patronized, the company was wound up only eleven months later and the *Maud* went to Liverpool. Mr Avis purchased another steam launch, *Picnic*, licensed to carry fifty passengers for ferry or river trips. To local consternation, the demolition of the Ship-in-Dock Inn was announced, but it was rebuilt further back, improving the entrance to Clarence Street and Ridge Hill.

On a more humane level Thomas Short, a builder working at Kingswear Castle lost his life rescuing a servant girl from the sea; a visitor who witnessed the brave deed was so moved that he commissioned and paid for a fine marble plaque in Kingswear church.

Regatta 1871 The *Chronicle* published a letter from 'a sea nymph' chiding the Mayor for non-attendance at the ball. In the harbour were eighty-seven sailing boats and nine steam yachts. There was also a great bell-ringing match which Blackawton won, although it was claimed the supposedly 'independent' judges knew when this team was ringing. One pickpocket was sentenced to two months on the treadmill.

In September the *Chronicle* reported:

> *The ex-Emperor Napoleon III arrived at Kingswear by train with Prince Murat and physician Dr Couneau. After luncheon at the DYC Hotel they proceeded to Brookhill, where Mrs Neale showed the party over the house and grounds. Then while standing on the Kingswear jetty he dropped his gold headed stick into the Dart. Its head was a French golden eagle with a golden ball in its mouth. A Mr Bartlett dived seven times and found the stick and restored it to the Imperial Hotel, Torquay, where Count Pierrefond gave him the Emperor's photograph for bringing the French eagle above water.*

Later aboard Mr Bridson's 150-ton yacht *Derwent* in Torquay his Imperial Majesty graciously accepted honorary membership of the DYC.

After many disagreements with the SDR and the chairman Mr Woolacombe, Mr Seale Hayne resigned from the board, leaving Dartmouth with no representation.

Dartmouth was then chosen as a port of call for the Red Ball Line, trading between London, Barbados and Demerara with the following boats to call:

1871	*Penelope*	995 tons	1868	*Astarte*	1400 tons
1871	*Calliope*	1123 tons	Bldg	*Bacchante*	2000 tons
1870	*Volante*	995 tons	Bldg	*Daphne*	2400 tons
1869	*Evadne*	1400 tons	Bldg	*Thisbe*	1800 tons

1873. The Donald Currie & Co. vessel, the SS Florence *in The Bight. This was her only Dartmouth visit prior to sailing to establish a joint coastal mail service between Cape Town and Natal with the Union Steam Ship Co.*

KATHLEEN DAVIES/E WIDDICOMBE

In 1876 the company was restructured as the Castle Mail Packet Co Ltd and this picture shows a liner, possibly the Garth Castle, *moored at the packet buoys during the annual regatta.*

MAJOR D MALLOY

The Bidder/Lake partnership then ordered the third prototype steam trawler from Philips' yard. Finally on Christmas Eve the *Floating Bridge*, which had been leaking for some time, sank at her moorings. This raised fears for the chargehand sleeping aboard, but fortunately he had spent the night ashore! The *Floating Bridge* was brought up some days later.

1872 There was gloom that Dartmouth might, as in 1857, lose the mail service. In February Mr Payne informed Donald Currie that he could no longer charter his two boats, and suggested that he should continue the service himself, which fortunately he did, with Mr Payne acting as his broker. Mr Payne's company held an Emergency General Meeting, the directors recommended that the company should be wound up:

> *The company they had ordered four new vessels from (only* Marc Antony *delivered) A McMillan & Son Glasgow had offered to liquidate their liabilities, paying each shareholder 10/- in the £ on the capital paid up and taking over all the assets.*

This resolution was accepted and a liquidator was appointed.

Mr Currie continued with his own two boats on a fortnightly basis and also chartered others. The *Dover Castle* was to be the first Castle liner sailing in April, but she was replaced by the chartered *Westmorland* until October when the *Walmer Castle* (Dartmouth, Bordeaux, Cape Town) became the first of the fortnightly Donald Currie Liners from Dartmouth to the Cape and colonies. Donald Currie Liners continued for the next twenty years, and became affectionately known as the 'Dartmouth boats'.

On the domestic front, Kingswear church received a new organ constructed by Bryceson & Co London and costing £130 which was raised by voluntary subscription and a grant from Rev and Miss Seymour, Riversea. In Dartmouth the Rev Priestly Foster and parishioners of St Saviours were in dispute over rented pews, reduced services, lock-outs, and Roman practices; parishioners showed their displeasure by 'crossing the Jordan' in Mr Avis's Picnic to listen to powerful services from the Rev J Smart and sing gusty hymns to Kingswear's new organ.

On the seventeen-year-old *Floating Bridge* one of the chains broke, stranding it midstream loaded with cattle, which had to swim ashore.

The third Bidder/ Lake experimental trawler Edith *after alterations in 1873, moored abreast Philips' yard. After acquisition by Lake she was lengthened, widened and re-masted to become a general carrier. J Houston, Philips' foreman during conversion, later joined Redways as foreman, and in 1881 both he and E Redway moved to Milford Haven as foreman and yard manager respectively of Lake's Castle, Iron & Steel Works. With experience previously gained at Dartmouth, they recommenced building steam trawlers.*

E F Clark

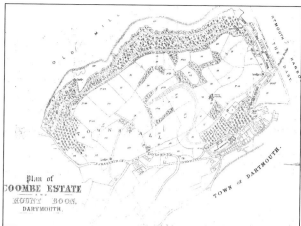

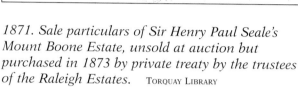

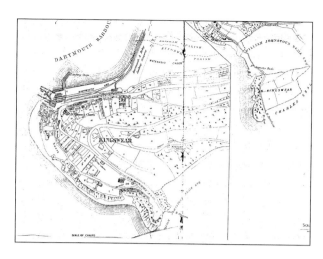

1871. Sale particulars of Sir Henry Paul Seale's Mount Boone Estate, unsold at auction but purchased in 1873 by private treaty by the trustees of the Raleigh Estates. TORQUAY LIBRARY

1874. Sale particulars of George Fownes Luttrell's Nethway and Kingswear Estate. Partly sold at auction, the remainder was sold in separate lots at later dates. BRIGADIER W HINE-HAYCOCK

A royal yacht club was achieved when, after six years of effort, perseverance was rewarded with the long-coveted accolade: the right to add the prefix 'Royal' to the DYC and adorn the ensign and burgee with the symbolic crown. The club, now named the Royal Dart Yacht Club (RDYC), recorded the receipt of the royal warrant in the minute book and a special tribute was paid to two founder members, Mr Bidder and Lt Col Charles Manby, secretary of the Civil Engineers Institute, for their efforts in achieving the royal warrant. The club celebrated by issuing further regatta trophies, one was a magnificent silver parcel gilt tankard, illustrating the German legend 'The Wild Huntsman', value £100 with £30 added; the cup needed to be won twice in succession to secure ownership. There was also a silver parcel gilt claret jug in the Collins style valued at £40 for cutters and yawls, not exceeding 40 tons, belonging to any royal or recognized club. Both beautiful prizes were from London & Ryder, New Bond Street.

Regatta 1872 In the harbour were 122 sailing boats, five steam yachts, five training brigs, and a miniature steamer known as the *Holmes Patent,* with 'brilliant lights acting as the propeller power'.

The Dartmouth Mutual Marine Association faced heavy damages when the schooner *Alarm* sank and filled with sand, restricting navigation on the River Parrett. Unable to salvage her, Mr Lake proposed the use of litho-fracture/nitro-glycerine for the first time in Britain, but nobody would transport the volatile material, so Mr Lake did it himself. Hundreds of people lined the banks to watch a series of controlled explosions which blew the schooner 60 feet above the waters and cleared the fairway.

Finally, the Bidder/Lake third steam trawler *Edith* (87ft 6in x 20ft x 11ft 6in, 85 tons), was launched at Philips' yard with a steam capstan, and a lifting, self-coupling propeller device designed by Mr Lake. Her boilers had to be fitted at Totnes as Dartmouth's crane had insufficient lift. Her trials, with the Earl Vane aboard, were satisfactory and her catches good, for without wind she could sail close inshore, make port and never be becalmed. But prejudice and the Devon Share System ensured the failure of this venture which was ten years ahead of its time. In spite of all *Edith's* advantages, including being able to carry to a fishing port or to London six times the load of a sailing trawler, the system would only allow her two shares out of ten, so the unequal terms forced her to join the North Sea fleet, merely as a fish carrier.

1873 In January after 150 years in the family, Sir H P Seale's 2,000-acre estate, including the mansion, shipyards, Floating Bridge Inn and ageing higher ferry had been acquired by the Raleigh Estates Trustees for over £100,000 (the heir being only two years old). The Seale family retired to their Norton Estate.

Above: *Belmont, Ridge Hill, former home of the Codner family, Dartmouth mayors and merchants. The elegant furnishings include columns in Ashburton marble, fine doors and a splendid staircase. In 1873 it was renamed Combecote on becoming the home of Francis Charles Simpson, wealthy founder of the yacht and engineering company Simpson & Denisons, later Simpson & Strickland Co Ltd. According to the 1891 catalogue, it was in a small shed in the garden that the first Kingdon compound engine and boiler was assembled for marketing and installation. Between 1879 and 1917 this became the bedrock of the company's growth and prosperity, first at Kings Quay, then Sandquay and finally at a major shipbuilding and engineering works complex built on the east side of the Dart at Noss. In its heyday it employed around 300 to 400 Dartmouth and local men.*

DARTMOUTH MUSEUM

The Dart Boat Sailing Club (DBSC)was created to encourage small boat racing. Mr Bridson moved to Warfleet House, and newcomer Francis Charles Simpson, later to play a major part in Dartmouth, took over Derwent Lodge. Together with Samuel Lake, George Whitaker, an artist of merit, and others, they met at the Castle Hotel and formed an open boat sailing club. There were no small boat sailing clubs in the South West, only a few yacht clubs. The Dart Boat Sailing Club was formed, with Mr Lake as Captain, Mr Simpson as Lieutenant, and twenty-nine enrolled members. Henry Bridson, Rear Commodore RDYC was President, with his son, Andrew Hugh, a member. The subscriptions were low, 5s (25p) per annum, with no entrance fee, to encourage sailing; rules were drawn up and a burgee set, navy blue with a silver dart and two balls. Using his knowledge gained in India, Mr Lake engaged Mr Redway to build him two boats based on the felucca and caique, the *Problem* and the *Q.E.D.* His winning of races caused controversy; it was claimed that *Q.E.D.* could not fail to win on handicap with a waterline measurement less than boats smaller overall. Mr Redway claimed that beam versus depth challenged boat building systems. However, Mr Lake's entrepreneurial activities caused a change and Mr Simpson became Captain of the DBSC.

Regatta 1873 began with a contretemps with autocratic Torquay trying to dictate regatta dates. The dates suggested met none of Dartmouth's criteria, including tide times, with he result that Thursday and Friday were approved. The outstanding feature was the appalling weather which caused an extension to three days, while the RDYC day had hardly a breath of wind and racing was postponed to the Saturday. The new DBSC held its first year's races in the Range, the RDYC donating £5 to the prize money. The regatta ball was voted the best event of a regatta dominated by rain. However, the *Chronicle* reported a happy story relating to Mr Batterskill, Dartmouth china and glass merchant, who with his beloved small dog crossed by ferry to catch the train for a holiday in Newton Abbot; unfortunately the dog was lost in Newton Abbot and after three days Mr Batterskill was forced to return without it. A few days later however the dog returned and had made its own way over 16 miles, and according to Mr Avis, Lower Ferry operator, without paying the penny fare for the ferry crossing!

Then came the first mention of Father Ignatius, an Anglican monk with a mesmeric talent to hold large audiences spellbound. He had built a monastery, Llanthony Abbey, in the wild Black Mountains in Wales, and was travelling the country preaching and raising funds to set up chantries, some to be located in South Devon.

As Mr Lake's endeavours to make Dartmouth a fishing port had proved unremunerative, he reluctantly disposed of his trawlers and became the sole owner of the *Edith*. She was returned to Philips' yard to be adapted as a general carrier, lengthened 25ft and spread amidships 2ft making her 120ft overall, capable of carrying 200 tons, but retaining the same engines, originally in *Bertha*.

1874
SS *Edith*, in her new role as a general carrier, arrived from Calstock, with 200 tons of firebricks from the Dimson Estate Fire Clay Company, which Mr Lake also managed. They were to be used in building the Dart Ochre, Umber, Oxide of Iron & Silicate Works, Dartmouth, on land at Coombe

SV Sly Boots *1868 built at Philips, a two-masted barquentine of 189 tons, 104ft x 25ft x 13ft for J Tolman & Co for the Newfoundland and coasting trade.*

Lt Cdr P D Holden

Martin Taylor

owned by Mr Lake. A new company was formed, the Torbay & Dart Paint Company Ltd, the directors being Sir George Elliot, G P Bidder, T L Eastlake and others. They also acquired the Wolston Torbay Iron Paint Works at Brixham and the Sea Mills Iron Mines at Stoke Gabriel.

In May the DHC transferred offices from Newton Abbot to William Smith's Cromwell House in Fairfax Place, Dartmouth, and Mr Smith took over as clerk from Alex Lloyd. Then Mr Armeson died and in Kingswear Mount Agra was offered for sale, together with Agra Villas and the shops in the square. Riversea was also sold by Rev E T Seymour to Captain Toms. At Brownstone, Warren Cottage and the 86-acre rabbit warren were offered for sale. In Dartmouth Mr Simpson sold Derwent Lodge to Mr Edward Marsh Turner, Donald Currie's shipping agent, and bought Belmont, Clarence Hill, renaming it Combecote. Barely a year after the disposal of the Mount Boone Estates, George Fownes Luttrell decided, after 176 years of family ownership, to auction his entire estate of 1,750 acres, which included most of Kingswear. This decision may have been taken to raise extra finance to pay for extensive renovation carried out at Dunster Castle by Anthony Slavin from 1869 to 1872. Mr Fownes's choice of this eminent architect coincidentally relates back to Kingswear, for Mr Slavin's very first commission in 1826 was the rebuilding of Mamhead, the seat of Sir Robert Newman, head of a powerful family of Dartmouth and Kingswear merchants. Anthony Stavin's greatest project was the remodelling of Alnwick Castle between 1854 and 1865 for the Duke of Northumberland. Alnwick was the ancestral home of Williamus de Vescy, the original twelfth century owner of Kingswear. Kittery Court, former home of the late Thomas Fownes, was not included in the sale for in 1828 it had been sold to Lt General Benjamin Roope and his two sisters Sarah and Maria. At the auction lots 85-87, six dwelling houses and foreshore (Longford House) made £725 from Mr Avis, a resident tenant. Lots 88-92, four dwelling houses, carpenter's and blacksmith's shops, the old archway schoolroom, foreshore and the houses and gardens down Alma Steps, made £890 from Dominic Stone. The latter then obtained permission from the Board of Trade to enclose part of the foreshore by Collins Quay with a sea wall,

Left: Dunster Castle, home of the Fownes Luttrells, who for over 150 years also owned the manors of Kingswear and Galmpton, and the 2,000 acre Nethway Estate. At the time of William the Conqueror the castle was the seat of the Mohans but in 1376 it was acquired by the Luttrells, who in 1617 built the present mansion within the castle walls. Later support for the Royalist cause in the civil war evoked a penance, the destruction of the curtain walls, but the mansion survived. Then in 1747 Margaret, an only child, married her second cousin Henry Fownes of Kingswear, who adopted the surname Luttrell to continue the lineage and used his fortune to further improve the house. In 1869 George Fownes Luttrell commissioned Anthony Slavin to completely renovate the mansion, which today is owned by the National Trust. National Trust

creating a fill area for rubble from the demolished properties, and enlarging his site. He also erected The Priory, where many traces of monastic buildings had been discovered, and built the high stone encircling wall, with its fine archway, crowned by the ball finial from Dartmouth's Plumleigh conduit, (purchased on the demolition in 1868). But sadly two extremes prevailed: on the one hand was the fine lifestyle of Kittery Court's mansion and grounds, the pretentious RDYC Hotel for prosperous guests of the Castle Liners to the Cape, and the wealthy Royal Dart Yacht Club society with fine yachts; and on the other hand, between Kittery and the hotel, was a ghetto of semi-derelict and overcrowded properties where dozens lived in abject squalor and poverty. This sad state of affairs is highlighted in the *Chronicle* article abridged below:

> *An inquest was held at the RDYC Hotel on John Waymouth, aged seventy-three, found hanging outside his bedroom door…The jury viewed the body lying in a bedroom 6 feet square containing two beds, situated over two flights of narrow stairs. The property is a nest of tenements at the end of which is a closet used by about twenty persons, smelling very badly being unsupplied with water…Mrs Ann Harvey said 'John Waymouth was my father…He lived with Mother and received parish pay 2/- [10p] and a loaf. My mother works two days a week for 1/- [5p] per day from one place and 10d [4p] from the other. That was all they had to live on.'*

Regatta 1874 saw the participation of the Marquis of Ailsa's successful *Bloodhound*.

Finally the old turnpike road system was abolished, the trust disbanded, any remaining money was distributed and future responsibility placed with the local authorities. In the harbour steam began to dominate, for no longer did fleets of sail leave annually for the Newfoundland fishing grounds. The salt-cod business, established in the early eighteenth century, never recovered after the Napoleonic Wars and was in decline, with only a few vessels of the Newman, Hunt & Co and Hudson Bay Companies still engaged in the trade.

THE NEWFOUNDLAND TRADE

After the Napoleonic Wars trade in Dartmouth was at a low ebb, the only employment being provided by wealthy local families, the Newmans, Hunts, Henlys, Roopes and Teagues, and a few local shipowners, all engaged in the dried salt-cod trade with Newfoundland. The fleet sailed in the spring, returning in the fall via the Mediterranean ports with wines for the English market, the brigs then wintered in Old Mill Creek. These vessels were mainly built at Hardness in shipyards abutting Silver Street (Undercliffe), and later Sandquay, but by the 1870s the trade was mainly over. Fortunately it was replaced by the bunkering trade.

SV Retriever 1876 built at Philips, a three-masted brigantine of 216 tons, 117 ft x 23 ft x 14 ft for Newman, Hunt & Co for the Newfoundland trade.

GEORGE PHILIP

CHAPTER 5

Progress vs Petulance

1875 to 1887

BLACK DIAMONDS IN THE HARBOUR

1875 The three-quarters benchmark of the nineteenth century heralded an escalation in Dartmouth's prosperity, largely due to Samuel Lake. He knew Mr Bidder's friend and business associate Sir George Elliot, an ex-pit boy who had obtained a knighthood and owned the multinational Powell Duffryn Colliery Group. Sir George frequently visited the regattas, sometimes as a steward, and noticed the increasing bunkering trade. Through Samuel Lake, he would have met the ambitious George Collins, aged twenty-three, who arrived in Dartmouth in 1860 and later established a ship brokering business on Customs House Quay and became the agent for Mr Hingston, owner of Dartmouth's only coal bunkering business. In 1875 the Powell Duffryn Group registered the company G H Collins & Co Ltd with Mr Collins as their managing agent, to compete in the growing bunkering trade. Within a decade this encouraged several companies to station hulks in Dartmouth to share in the growing lucrative trade that was to become the port's staple industry into the twentieth century, employing at its height 300 to 400 men.

The Admiralty, despite opposition, determined on Dartmouth for their naval college and appointed a committee to secure a site, which took twenty-five years!

Dominic Stone became sole owner of the Dartmouth and Kingswear hotels and Mr Appleton embarked on improving them both. To create further bedrooms at the Castle Hotel, the public bars were removed to a converted stable building at the rear and connected by a covered archway thrown across the dividing lane. The new bars were called The Shades, a handsome bar and spirits engines to the casks were installed in a grand room measuring 30ft x 20ft, gaslit with pitch pine panelling. The RDYC Hotel also underwent improvements. Both upgraded hotels were offered for sale and Mr Stone retired to his property, The Priory. Later both hotels were purchased by H C Collier.

Llewellyn Llewellyn bought Kingswear's Nethway House and Estate, unsold at auction, and engaged Edward Appleton to restore the house and develop the estate. Harry Seaton ordered from Mr Nichols a 65ft tug named *Lily* to compete with the *Guide* and *Pilot*, and commissioned Mr Appleton to build a pleasant detached villa on Beacon Road, Hilo Villa (Two Guns).

The *Chronicle* reported the following event, which had undertones of a comedy film, but could have been very serious:

> *A passenger train with seven carriages was travelling between Torre and Torquay, when to avoid a minor accident the driver put the train into reverse, then with the fireman abandoned the train. It then ran backwards gathering speed to 60 mph and through Paignton alarming passengers. Aboard were two Dartmouth railway men, Mr Harley and Purcell, who realising something was wrong, one climbed onto the roof and made his way to the engine and shut off steam, while the other clambered along footboards applying the carriage brakes and succeeded in halting the train just before Churston, before the downward stretch to the tunnel and Kingswear terminus.*

This brave action prevented an horrific accident and loss of life, and with money raised from a subscription list the heroes received silver watches and £25 each; the driver was dismissed and the fireman demoted.

Left: 1880. Two steamers coaling on the River Dart at standing hulks, (left) R Hingston's hulk Happy, *(right) G H Collins' hulk* Monarch.
AUTHOR'S COLLECTION

Right: 1876. Floating Bridge *No. 3, purchased by the new owners, Raleigh Estates from Willoughbys, the Plymouth shipbuilders.*
TOM CASEY

Regatta 1875 included a launch race for the training brigs. The newspapers reported a sad accident involving the tender *Alberta* with Queen Victoria aboard: steaming at 17 knots in poor visibility, she collided and cut in half the 120-ton yacht *Mistletoe*, three lives were lost. *Mistletoe* was built in 1860 at Nichols Yard, Kings Quay, Dartmouth.

Finally Mr Hingston, who had lost his agent and faced severe competition from a national colliery group, retaliated by applying to the DHC for extra moorings and a concession of a halfpenny per ton on steamers calling for the coals; both were granted.

1876 established the pattern of future trading between the competing coaling companies – 'dog eat dog' – for Mr Collins, now managing agent for the Powell Duffryn Group, also applied for 'permission to moor a large hulk *Monarch* 1,180 tons (over twice the size of Mr Hingston's *Happy*), and a 3d (11/2p) rebate on vessels calling Dartmouth for coaling only'. With extra revenue in mind the Commission agreed, as follows: The commissioners will allow a rebate of threepence per ton on all coal taken by any vessel from the said hulk towards payment of the ordinary dues to which such vessel would be liable and to the full extent of such dues. This gave the DHC much improved returns, for several ships would not take the full quota, leaving the balance to pay. Also the Board of Trade under the 1863 Act agreed to increase the maximum dues allowed from 2d (1p) to 3d (11/2p) per ton, and a levy of 2s 6d (121/2p) per hulk was introduced. In February the 1,180-ton *Monarch* arrived from Plymouth for G H Collins & Co to serve as a standing hulk off the Coombe Mud.

In February another momentous event occurred when the SDR, which had acquired the line from Dartmouth & Torbay Railway in 1866, in turn reached agreement that the Great Western Railway (GWR) would work the line for a period of 999 years.

The new *Floating Bridge* arrived for the Raleigh Estates from Willoughbys, Plymouth, replacing Sir H P Seale's dilapidated twenty-year-old ferry which they had acquired on purchase of the estate in 1873.

In Dartmouth the Hudson Bay Co Ltd took over the lower floors of the Newman Building (now DHNA) for the storage of salmon, cod, furs, oil etc brought from Labrador by *Kyoshk*. All five of Newman, Hunt & Co's handsome Newfoundland vessels: *Chanticleer, Terrier, Talbot, Retriever* and *Beagle* were in harbour. The shipyards were busy and Mr Hodge and Mr Houston commenced shipbuilding, the former building crack racing yachts opposite the Floating Bridge Inn, the latter building trawlers at Coombe, while Mr Avis disposed of Alford's 1864 replacement yard at Hoodown, Kingswear.

Regatta 1876 The RDYC presented a new Kingswear Cup, value 20 guineas, and the DBSC raced on the third day. The new Yacht Racing Association rules applied to over 150 yachts in the harbour, while for the first time a regatta gun was fired at 08 00hrs on the two regatta days.

The lovely Gunfield House, Warfleet, with two and a half acres, was sold by Mr Fotheringham. After being vacant for eighteen years the Warfleet Brewery, built in 1819 by Governor Holdsworth as a paper-mill, resumed operations for the third time as a brewery under Maddock & Symons. Also for the first time Dartmouth had a roller-skating rink measuring 70ft x 40ft with oak floors and gaslit, but it soon went bankrupt.

Finally Samuel Lake again showed utter disregard for his life, when, during a crossing of the *Dolphin* to Kingswear, a passenger tried to leap ashore during berthing and fell in the water. Without even discarding his heavy overcoat, Mr Lake plunged in and supported him until help arrived.

1877 started with the demise of the old Dartmouth Steam Packet Co; profitability had been declining since 1872, when Charles Vincent, secretary, fell off the Royal Dartmouth's sponsons onto the drydock stone pitching and died. Voluntary liquidation was decided and the entire fleet, stores, hulk and premises were offered for sale, but the reserve price was not reached. At an EGM in January William Smith, chairman, offered £2,850 for the entire unit, including debts of £850, paying shareholders 3s 2d in the pound; this was accepted. A new company, the Dartmouth & Torbay Steam Packet Co, was formed with William Smith chairman and J R Tolman managing owner, with offices at Cromwell House, Fairfax Place, Dartmouth.

This time the name 'Torbay' was incorporated into the title, for the new board was associated with the GWR, who, since 1876, had worked the South Devon Railway, which included the Dartmouth & Torbay Railway. In February a twenty-five-year lease was negotiated to manage the latter's railway ferry *Dolphin*, and to provide a relief steamer on breakdown and overhaul. The tug *Guide* was sold to Milford Haven and an order placed with Harveys of Hayle for a new screw tug, 61ft x 32ft, named *Hauley*. The name *Hauley* has remained associated with Dartmouth to the present day, for altogether eight other tugs used mainly to propel the Lower Ferry horse- and later all car-floats, have borne the name: *Hauley I* Casey & Heal, 1909; *Hauley II* and *III* Peters & Heseltine, 1931 and 1932; *Hauley IV* General Estates Ltd, 1933; *Hauley V* and *VI* Dartmouth Corporation, 1954 and 1957; *Hauley VII* and *VIII* South Hams District Council, 1995 and 1996.

The inefficiency of the port's pilotage system was causing concern, and some influential townspeople were asked to canvass the Elder Brethren of Trinity House for a meeting, which took place at the Castle Hotel; a committee including the Mayor, DHC and other principals attended with Mr Lake chairman and Mr Collins, secretary. Three senior members of Trinity House heard Mr Lake, and the harbourmaster read a list of steamers calling for pilots without success, and pressed for the pilots to be increased from six to fourteen, with a pilot boat on station for twenty-four hours, rather than the present twelve, and for the local subcommittee of the pilotage to be increased from three to five. Trinity House's members agreed the number of pilots be increased as trade demanded, a 60-ton cutter be kept on the range, and the subcommittee be increased.

WHO CALLS THE FERRYMAN?

In June a notice appeared in the *Chronicle* as follows:

> *Messrs Casey will take possession from Monday next of the Lower Ferry, and in lieu of the usual rowing boats run a steam launch taking passengers to and from all trains during winter and summer. A steam launch is now in the course of construction (*Forester*) to be put on the service, thus affording better accommodation.*

Thomas Avis, operator since 1865, had run an all-weather service every day of the year, as well as a boatbuilding business and excursions in his launch *Picnic*. He extended his activities with William Owens, engineer, to develop a special screw vessel, *Water Lily*, fitted with capacious water tanks and powerful pumps to supply fresh water to calling steamships anchored in midstream; so he surrendered his lease to GWR, who negotiated a five-year-lease with William and Adam Casey, from an old-established Kingswear family, who gave good service for fifty years.

Top left: John William Casey who operated the ferry with his brother George Adam Casey until 1901 when Tom Casey took over until 1925.

Top right: The original ledger setting out costs and disbursements for the first week's operation, including the purchase of the steam launch Blanche *and two rowing boats.*

Bottom left: The front page of the Lower Ferry 1877 lease with the South Devon Railway Co.

ALL AUTHOR'S COLLECTION

Regatta 1877 A third sailing race was introduced for open sailing boats used for pleasure only; it had five starters and was won by Captain Sheen of the Marine Tavern in *Mona*. There was a remarkable fireworks display by Paines Fireworks, and a new attraction was the lighting of coloured fires on the hills around Dartmouth. There were 118 yachts, including eleven steam yachts, in harbour, as well as two training brigs and a German corvette.

1878 In early March HRH Prince of Wales with his sons attended Philips' yard to launch the 165-foot brigantine *Albert Victor*. Within the month Philip & Son went into liquidation owing £4,847 with only £936 security, the creditors receiving two shillings in the pound. The arrangements made allowed them to continue in business, hopefully to return to profit and pay creditors. In

July H Nichols, shipbuilder, ceased trading and the yard was offered for sale. Then a great fire occurred in Redway's yard destroying the trawler Ben Venue, stores, machinery and tools valued at £7,000, and forced it to close. Finally John Houston, a recently started shipbuilder at Coombe, was declared bankrupt. Severe hardship resulted, though the wheelwrights found employment fitting out several showman and gypsy vans, in polished mahogany, with fine carvings and gilding.

In Kingswear, the church, though over 700 years old, lacked interior embellishments, stained-glass windows, carvings, furnishings, etc. It had been mainly rebuilt in 1845-47 by architect Edward Appleton, who, in 1878 as church warden, determined to correct this. As a director of the Watcombe Terra-Cotta Clay Co, Torquay, (established in 1869 as a venture with the commendable object of providing local employment rather than profit for the directors), Edward Appleton paid for a specially designed wall tiled reredos panel, as abridged from the *Chronicle*:

> *It is a wall lining of tiles from the floor to the underside of the east window the full width of the chancel. The centre compartment forms a panel, a copy of Leonardo da Vinci's picture* The Last Supper *with side panels of Alpha and Omega and bordered by white and blue with vine leaf decoration.*

The tiles were by the Watcombe imperishable frescal process and the artist Arthur Mumford. As the only important example of this type of work it is both valuable and rare.

The subcommittee of pilotage, responding to the coaling agents, obtained permission for future vessels to take only pilotage inwards.

1878. The unusual and neglected 122 year old Watcombe Terra-Cotta Clay Company's tiled reredos in Kingswear church, a copy of Leonardo da Vinci's painting The Last Supper. *Hidden for many years behind a curtain, in 1996, the author brought it to the attention of the Torquay Pottery Collectors Society who declared it a major find, the only one in the country, and mounted a symposium attended by over 300 worldwide members to examine the reredos.*
KINGSWEAR CHURCH/AUTHOR/G VANSTONE

Left: 1878. The royal galley with Prince Albert Victor, Duke of Cumberland, in the bow and Prince George, Duke of York, coxswain, landing at Sandquay.
DAVE GRIFFITHS/ROY BARNES

Right: Shore-based fully-rigged scaled-down training ship at Sandquay, dressed overall by cadets.
DAVE GRIFFITHS/ROY BARNES

Regatta 1878 This was the last one at which the RDYC awarded gold medals. The *Jullana*, a 127-foot yawl, won the RDYC Challenge Cup outright after two successive wins. This magnificent silver parcel gilt tankard was much admired. All members regretted that in 1872 they had not imposed harsher terms for its retention. The loss of this principal prize was mainly due to the member William Froude, who had developed theories revolutionizing hull design. At Paignton, then at Chelston Cross, Torquay, with Admiralty help, William Froude experimented with scale model ships in testing tanks, applying science to new fields of study – skin friction, oscillation and stability on ships' hulls – tests which were later applied to warships and steamships. Mr Bentall, an agricultural implements engineer, incorporated Mr Froude's principles, (that is extreme length with minimal wetted water contact) and the sternpost set well forward, on the yacht *Jullana*.

Dominic Stone died at The Priory, Kingswear, and George Parker Bidder died at Ravensbury. In October the RNLI concluded that the increasing number of steamships calling for coals warranted the stationing of a lifeboat in Dartmouth; the donor was Miss Maud Hargreaves of Esher. Built by Wolfe & Son of Poplar, London, it was a ten-oared intermediate 33ft x 8ft 2in vessel which was both self-righting and discharging; she arrived by rail at Kingswear, and was launched with Captain Lewis and the harbourmaster in command. His crew pulled around the harbour, and passing Sandquay saved a twelve-year-old boy who had fallen into deep water and who was safely hauled aboard to the cheers of the crowd. The official launching ceremony took place on a beflagged New Ground, Mrs Hockin breaking the traditional bottle and naming the boat *Maud Hargreaves*. She slid fully manned down the slipway to show her capabilities, capsizing, righting, and discharging in a few minutes. During Dartmouth's twenty-year period as a lifeboat station the crew performed no outstanding rescues nor saved any life, and was once severely criticized for incompetence and inefficiency.

The schooner *Comet*, on passage from Sligo to London laden with oats, pulled in with a split mainsail and broken foregaff and anchored close to Mill Bay Cove, Kingswear Castle. The tug *Hauley* warned it was a dangerous position but she refused towage. Trying to get away later and setting the mainsail, she missed stays and was driven towards the shore; her anchor failed to hold and attempts to secure her by *Hauley* failed. She broke up on the rocks, and the crew scrambled ashore to the safety of Higher Brownstone farmhouse.

1879 The *Chronicle* reported that Mr Lake was updating Mr Robert's 1862 scheme for embanking Dartmouth waterfront: at his own expense he had commissioned Mr Bidder's office to draw up plans for an embankment from Bayards Cove to Coombe, which the town council approved and passed to the DHC for consideration.

The Rev Joseph Lyne, Father Ignatius, returned to increase his local following and purchased the Chantry, Slapton, to form the 'Priory of St Scholasticus', his Church of England order of Benedictine monks. He brought with him seven female adherents, three sisters of mercy, two secular sisters and two schoolmistresses, startling the whole village. His meetings attracted large and sometimes vociferous crowds to listen to his mesmeric preaching. The people of Slapton accepted him with open arms and the vicar asked him to preach to his congregation, which caused a sensation.

Kingswear's Wesleyan chapel acquired its own minister, the Rev C E Jolliffe. A gold-bullion dealer, Mr Wilkins, bought Brookhill from Mrs Augusta Packe for £6,000. Both men took an active part in local affairs, particularly the very wealthy Mr Wilkins, who supported the cottage hospital and purchased Gallants Bower, securing it from development. The *Chronicle* also reported that whilst several other towns shared the illustrious name Dartmouth, a small township in Otago, New Zealand, was named Kingswear.

In Dartmouth 2,000 people watched the *Dublin Castle* depart with the 60th Rifles for the Zulu War in South Africa, and in May Sir Garnet Wolesey and his staff left the harbour to take civil and military command in South Africa.

In April after twenty years' service *Pilot* was sold to Wards of Teignmouth. She was to replace *Sensation*, which had been damaged on Kingswear Castle rocks.

Newspapers reported events relating to the Prince of Wales, and indirectly to Dartmouth: during the regatta in Jersey, Mrs Langtry's home port, a seaman was lost off *Hildegarde* whilst racing. The Prince directed that the widow should receive £24 per annum from his personal income, plus a guinea at Christmas and Easter, and her four children's education should be provided for. *Enchantress* arrived with Lords of the Admiralty to join the Prince of Wales for the laying of the foundation stone for the new Eddystone lighthouse. It was designed and built by Sir James Douglass, whose family lived at Gramercy Tower, Dartmouth, and whose family members are buried in St Petrox churchyard. The Prince then visited Dunster Castle, Somerset, home of George Fownes Luttrell, lately owner of Kingswear Estates, for stag hunting on Exmoor. Five magnificent hunters were despatched from Windsor, creating much local excitement, as the last royal visit to Exmoor had been in 1645.

Regatta 1879 was visited by royalty. As the two princes (Prince Albert Victor and Prince George) had completed their two years aboard *Britannia*, the royal party joined *Hildegarde* and *Formosa*. Mr Avis's launch *Picnic* was put at the disposal of the Prince of Wales, who graciously accepted honorary membership of the RDYC. Regatta had such severe weather, however, that some yachts failed to arrive. Mr Wheeler won the Kingswear Cup for the second time outright, and it was not replaced.

In November Mr Learmouth, master of Llewellyn Llewellyn's yacht *Star of the West*, drowned *en route* for Gibraltar in a gale; he fell overboard and, in spite of immediate action a long search failed to find him. For many years he had been master of Mr Bridson's 150-ton schooner yacht *Derwent*.

The Steamboat Company ordered a new iron paddle-steamer *Berry Castle* (108ft x 14ft x 7ft) from Polyblanks, newly established in Waterhead Foundry; this was the first Dart-built iron steamship and a 120-foot long shed was erected at the creek end for working under cover. In December the keel was ceremonially laid with three long wrought-iron keel pieces riveted together by the directors, the red-hot rivets passed from the forge by young Master Clare.

Left: Sir James Douglass, builder of the Eddystone Lighthouse 1878 - 1882.

Mike Holgate

Right: Gramercy Tower, long-established home of the Douglass family.

Tom Casey

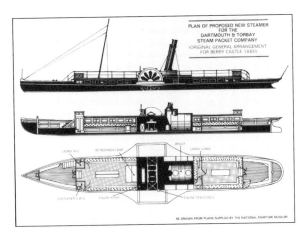

Left: Redrawn
plans of the 1881
paddle-steamer
Berry Castle. *Hull
and engines from
Messrs Polyblank,
Kingswear Creek,
superstructure and
fittings, Messrs
Philip, Sandquay.*
ALAN KITTRIDGE

Right: Master and
crew aboard the
Berry Castle *on
the Dart.*
TOM WILLIAMS/DAVE
GRIFFITHS

1880 marked the start of another progressive decade. Eli Fleet, a Kingswear fisherman, trawled up a six-foot elephant tusk off Brookhill, which came from a privateer burned at anchor 200 years previously.

In April the Rev John Smart, Kingswear's much-loved vicar since 1836, died at his vicarage, Ravenswell, and his parishioners presented to the church a beautiful three-light stained-glass window as a memorial. The Rev Walker assumed office in October.

At Warfleet, on a difficult site, Maddocks & Symon engineers commissioned from Kelly's ex-foreman, Mr Mansfield, a 63 foot schooner, *Mayflower*. Mr Wilkins of Brookhill bought Godmerock Castle and grounds from Mr Luttrell.

At Clarence Hill, Mr Simpson who had previously opened a small engineering works to develop his protégé George Kingdon's 'patent compound engine and boiler', using hulls supplied by Hodge's yard, established in 1876 opposite the Floating Bridge Inn. He formed a company, Simpson & Denison, to market them in waterside premises. Later, in the adjacent vacant Nichols' shipyard at Kings Quay Mr Simpson began to build his own launches, even though the proposed Embankment scheme would isolate his works.

Mr Hingston, competing with the powerful Powell Duffryn Group, became agent for Nixon's Steam Coal Company. Fox of Plymouth also had a standing hulk at Coombe, and both Mr Collins and Mr Fox produced lavish brochures extolling Dartmouth harbour and claiming the largest floating depots in the Channel.

In July Polyblank's new iron paddle-steamer *Berry Castle* was ready. Launchings were commonplace, but this was exceptional; she was at the head of a shallow creek and had to be navigated under a viaduct offering little headroom or width, as the *Chronicle* reported:

> *Messrs Casey attended with their launches* Forester *and* Blanche, *horse and rowing boats, while private boats and* Royal Dartmouth *arrived crowded, others coming by rail and coach. Every vantage point on hills and fields was occupied, including hundreds in the yard, in all 3,000 people attended. On a raised red carpeted platform were Sir Henry and Lady Seale and leading inhabitants. She was certified for 350 passengers and cost £3,000, 112ft x 14ft x 7ft and fitted with two compound, highpressure, surface condensing, oscillating engines. She had two saloons and a refreshment bar, the after saloon was furnished in mahogany, with maple and gold mouldings, the cushions and curtains in Utrecht velvet. The decklights were decorated with representations of Berry Castle while on the bows and the stern were carved and gilded mouldings and scrolls, bearing the Arms of Dartmouth, the hull black with a gold streak.*

Lady Seale wished 'success to the *Berry Castle*', broke the bottle, and the first Dart iron-built steamship slid down the slipway to great cheers. Then, with difficulty, she was guided under the railway viaduct and floated to Philips' Sandquay yard where the superstructure above deck level was fitted. In September the *Chronicle* reported 'the rapacity of creditors has brought up this excellent firm, with liabilities of £7,000 yet with assets of £11,000 and caused unemployment for over 100 men'.

Regatta 1880 The Prince of Wales arrived in *Formosa*, but two incidents marred this visit. *Formosa*, his 110ft cutter, was leading the over-41 ton race when the race was, perhaps undiplomatically, cancelled. A quayside stroll by the Prince was curtailed by the over-exuberance of the public, necessitating a hasty retreat to the Castle Hotel. News also arrived that ex-Vice Commodore H Bridson had died in Madeira; in his memory his brother, Vice Commodore T R Bridson, presented the RDYC with two magnificent inscribed brass cannons.

A NEW CLUBHOUSE

In October two wealthy RDYC members, Vice Commodore T R Bridson and Llewellyn Llewellyn, purchased The Priory and the recently cleared area adjacent to Collins Quay from the executors of the late Dominic Stone's estate and offered to construct a new clubhouse. An EGM was called and their generous offer accepted. Member Mr Appleton was nominated architect, and a contract for £1,100 was awarded to Mr Fordham, Ashburton. The site was cleared except for the Steward's Cottage, the only part of old Kittery remaining today, and the present brick premises were erected. The filled area behind the new sea-wall became garden, and The Priory gardens were made into a tennis court.

DHC asked Mr Brereton for costings for Mr Lake's Embankment scheme, to include dredging the harbour to 25-foot low spring tides. Mr Simpson, a sizeable employer whose works would be isolated by the scheme, mounted vigorous opposition, enlisting support from others similarly placed and from yacht owners concerned by a proposed yacht tax. In November with three supporters, Mr Simpson stood for election to the town council, but somehow five names appeared on the nomination paper and it was declared void.

The year was notable for other rebuilding works: the old Assembly Rooms at the end of the Butterwalk were demolished; they were in a poor state of repair, so bad that Sir Henry Paul Seale, Mayor, in 1877 requested attending members of the public not to stamp their feet as vibration could be dangerous. They were replaced by Parade House, a neo-classical four-storey building (now NatWest Bank). Mr Cranford engaged Kingswear's Mr Appleton to design in Elizabethan style three shops of three storeys opposite his premises in Fairfax Place; the road was widened and the existing dilapidated 1620 buildings demolished. Jasper Bartlett's earlier premises, 1587, Borough Stores (now Boots), on the corner of The Quay and Smith Street, were rebuilt at the same time.

1881 started quietly. The Gunfield, empty for some four years, was sold to the Tew family of Bath, who became leading local figures. With the Newfoundland trade almost over, the Hudson Bay Co vacated the Newman Buildings, Oxford Slip (DHNA), a prime waterside property which was promptly taken by Mr Collins' bunkering company. In Kingswear, Lt Col Toms, JP and GWR member of the DHC, brought his work home by constructing a magistrates' room onto his splendid house, Riversea. In June Bellamy & Co, Plymouth agents for the

Left: Copy of the original 1880 sketch by Kingswear and Torquay architect and club member Edward Appleton of the proposed new Royal Dart Yacht Club clubhouse for the sponsors, Vice Commodore T R Bridson, Llewellyn Llewellyn, and the management committee.
ROYAL DART YACHT CLUB

Right: Early ornate Royal Dart Yacht Club membership certificate.
ROYAL DART YACHT CLUB

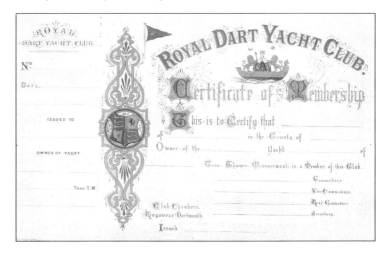

Dowlais Steam & Iron Coal Co, applied to the DHC and received permission to moor a hulk and share in the growing bunkering trade. This meant further rearrangement of the coaling lines, with Mr Collins' Monarch being moved to the eastern shore.

Regatta 1881 saw the ball held in the new RDYC clubhouse in celebration of its official opening, and over 200 titled and eminent people attended. It was hoped that the Prince of Wales would be present, as he had attended the last two regattas. It was rumoured, probably falsely, that the sailing committee's unpopular decision the previous year to abandon the over 41-ton race while his cutter *Formosa* was leading and their refusal to surrender the prize when claimed, incurred the Prince's displeasure. All previous contestants had been informed the race would be rerun, but only one, *Samoena*, came to sail over and claim the prize. Bad weather caused a day's postponement; when the police tried to shut down the stallholders as their licences had expired, there was a near riot until the Mayor issued an extension. The Dart Boat Sailing Club had to run their races the following Saturday. The water purity of the River Dart was illustrated by a report of too many otters; a three-foot male strolled into the bar of the Royal Dart Hotel and retreated hastily when efforts were made to contain him.

THE SOUTH EMBANKMENT SCHEME

During the year the Embankment saga began to dominate local affairs, and continued to do so for several years. In February a public meeting was held with Mr Smith, DHC clerk, supported by previous plans, ie Mr Rendell's (1832), Mr Roberts' (1858), Mr Lake's (1879) and the latest, Mr Brereton's. Mr Smith outlined the project, gave approximate costs, and said it would be in two sections. The southern would be financed by the DHC and funded by a levy on incoming house coal, not bunker coal, and a tax on yachts; the northern would be financed by the town council and funded by a charge added on to the rates. In each case the townspeople paid and the yachtsmen objected on principle. Mr Simpson, realized that the scheme would not go away and his Silver Street yard would be truncated, began to campaign hard, and formed an anti-Embankment group including Mr Collins, who wanted any money expended to be used for dredging the harbour to expand the bunkering trade. Once again this group tried for election to the town council; once again five names were entered on the nomination paper and the election declared void. This blatant strategy, (possibly instigated by the town clerk Mr Hockin, a strong Embankment supporter,) was contested at law and a re-election ordered for the following April. Mr Simpson, alarmed at the possible implementation of the scheme, hedged his bets and transferred his works to Mr Redway's vacant Sandquay shipyard. The Dartmouth Harbour Improvement Bill was prepared, published, pontificated on and presented to Parliament; it became a prime example of progress versus petulance.

1882 Dartmouth's growing importance as the principal bunkering station in the English Channel encouraged several shipping lines to make it a port of call. Ships, bound for the four quarters of the world, graced its waters and from Dartmouth it was possible to embark for many exotic locations, as follows: 'Donald

Currie Lines to Lisbon, Madeira, St Helena, Cape Town; Ellard King Line to Natal direct; Smith & Co to Jamaica; Scrutton, Son & Co to Demerara, Surinam, Berbice, Barbados, Trinidad, Grenada, St Lucia, Dominica, St Kitts and Nevis; Kosmos Line, Hamburg, to Monte Video, Punta Arena, Port Stanley, Falkland Islands and Valparaiso.' Increasing prosperity had its drawbacks, however, such as the sometimes sustained day-and-night whistling of steamers for boats and pilots.

Mr Hingston, founder of Dartmouth Coaling with his 300-ton hulk *Happy,* was overtaken by Collins' *Monarch* (1,180 tons), and Fox's *Prince Arthur* (1,500 tons) and *Bellamy* (1,600 tons), but fortune intervened as it had with *Happy* in 1870. In May SS *Bayswater* collided with the Norwegian barque *Prodomo* in fog off Start Point, and when settling she was picked up by the tug *Hauley* and towed to Dartmouth, sinking in Lighthouse Cove, Kingswear. A salvage firm was engaged and a series of misadventures resulted in her being raised and sinking again five times. When she was finally offered for sale by rival Mr Collins, Norwegian consul Mr Hingston purchased her for use as a hulk, using a nominee to conceal his true identity from the other coaling companies, and thus levelled the score.

On an ebb tide the SS *Winston*, cutting too close between the Kingswear shore and the moored *Warwick Castle*, caught her keel on the Kittery shoal and, losing leeway, crashed amidships into the liner crushing two workboats and a boatman and causing considerable damage. *Winston*, with a curved bow, was mainly undamaged but the liner *Warwick Castle* began taking water, so all the boats were lowered and passengers were ordered ashore to stay at the Castle, Dart and other hotels. With extra pumps and temporary repairs the water was contained, so *Warwick Castle* returned to London and the *Dunrobin Castle* was promptly dispatched to embark the passengers for the Cape.

On the deaths of Miss Roope and Mr Harvey, Kittery Court and Greenway were sold, the latter bought by Mr Bolitho of Cornwall. In Kingswear three splendid mansions were erected: Bryndart for Mrs Barnes; Butts Hill (Inverdart) over the old archery butts for Mr Baker QC (GWR and DHC); and The Redoubt over Sir Henry Cary's Redoubt Fort for Mr Wansey, Bristol solicitor. At Higher Sandquay Robert Moore ceased shipbuilding after twenty years and the Admiralty took over the yard for *Britannia*.

Regatta 1882 There was a new race for steam launches not exceeding 30 feet, the RDYC held four races and the DBSC six.

The dominant feature of the year was the Embankment issue, with many letters for and against the scheme appearing in the *Chronicle*. In April Mr Simpson's group of four stood for the election to council for the third time and this time they succeeded, but, unable to form a majority they filed a petition against the Harbour Bill progressing through to the House of Lords. Their case failed to convince their Lordships and the bill, minus the tax on yachts, was passed and royal assent received. Recognizing that some discontent existed in the town, the bill stipulated town council approval for the northern section to be passed by a two-thirds majority. By now the scheme had been costed at £30,000, construction being £24,000, dredging and legal fees £3,000 each, and

Left: 1879. Simpson & Denisons Co's engineering works on Clarence Hill; the steam launches are at the newly acquired part of the former H Nichols Kings Quay shipyard.
G THOMAS

Right: Simpson, Strickland & Co's fitting shop at Noss Works assembling small Kingdon patent compound engines and boilers.
DARTMOUTH MUSEUM

tenders received below budget. Mr P Hockin, town clerk, - aware that majority support for the scheme would be lost if Mr Simpson's supporters were successful in the November election - obtained approval, by eight votes to six, for payment by the council of £10,000 to £13,000 for the northern section of the Embankment scheme. The Corporation seal was attached and passed to a delighted DHC who promptly placed the £24,000 order with Thomas & Thomas, Newport, and work commenced.

As anticipated, Mr Simpson's supporters were successful in November but were too late to stop the scheme. They elected Mr Simpson Mayor and formed an anti-Embankment committee. Mr Collins, in four short lines, dismissed Percy Hockin, town clerk for twenty-one years.

1883 Preliminary work started on the Embankment, but the principal topic of conversation was the bankruptcy of Samuel Lake, whose fatal fascination for financial ventures proved his downfall. In 1879 he recklessly tendered to complete the building of Milford Haven docks in seven months for £80,000, extended three years later to £192,000; he then over extended himself by contracting in 1881 to construct Felixstowe docks for £100,000. He was well liked in Dartmouth, and his wife and family resided in Coombe Villa, Coombe Terrace, which they owned. Concern was expressed for Edward Redway who after the great fire of 1881 went to Milford to manage Lake's Castle Iron & Steel Works and there continued the development of the steam trawler.

Rumours circulated that Bellamys, established 1882, was to cease trading and Mr Collins was taking over. In March Mr Collins announced that he had acquired the SS *Prince Waldemar* with a full cargo of coal, and with Bellamys' 1,600-ton hulk under tow by the tug *Scotia*, they were to leave for Portland where he would establish another competing coaling depot.

At Warfleet, Sir Charles James Freake, (a London developer who had amassed a fortune from building property in Kensington), and who in 1880 had purchased Warfleet House, embarked on a substantial rebuilding programme. It was to demolish the existing adjacent coach house and stables, and build on the same site Warfleet Lodge to provide extra accommodation. It was connected to the main house by an elevated gallery.

On completion, the locals declared, 'it was fit for a king' which in some ways was true, for Sir Charles was a personal friend of Edward, Prince of Wales, and it is said that the Prince and Lillie Langtry occasionally stayed there. The main property, Warfleet House was built in the 1860s by the Rev G T Seymour, who in 1866 built and moved to Riversea, Kingswear. Then came Lt Studdy until 1873, followed by Mr Henry Bridson, Vice Commodore of the R.D.Y.C. who died in Madiera in 1880. Sir Charles's son Thomas Freake, who since 1868 had resided in Kingswear (Brookhill, and the Beacon) then took residence, and after Sir Charles died in 1884, he assumed the title and the family remained there until 1933. It was then purchased by a local entrepreneur and benefactor Mr Finch Ingram, who gave Warfleet Quay and Kilns to Dartmouth Corporation and later sold the estate to the millionaire shipping magnate Mr Vernon MacAndrew, another Vice Commodore of the R.D.Y.C.

The castellated Warfleet Lodge built in 1883, by Sir Charles James Freake as an annex to Warfleet House and an occasional secluded rendezvous for Edward VII, Prince of Wales and Lillie Langtry.

G Bush, Michael Bennett & Co

On a similar scale, Mayor Simpson purchased from Lord Churston a large acreage on the eastern shore including Noss Point and Maypool. He engaged Mr Fulford, Exeter architect of Butts Hill, Kingswear, to build, the imposing Maypool House, high above the river, for £4,500. The purplish stone was quarried locally, the quoins were red sandstone, cut from egg-shaped boulders dating from the ice age and found in the fields. It was the first house locally to have a cavity wall, stone faced externally with a half-brick internal skin as protection against damp. The main feature was the central hall open to the roof, with a huge lantern light (a belvedere) and a circular gallery where, it was rumoured, Mayor Simpson later had a powerful telescope mounted to watch his works at Noss. At this time Kingswear's nearby water-mill ceased trading and two roads collapsed – 80 yards of Fore Street fell, demolishing the engine shed, and Beacon Road, adjacent to the lighthouse, slid onto the beach. Both roads were rebuilt.

Regatta 1883 There were no special half-century celebrations, just the usual sailing and rowing events; the RDYC races were decimated by bad weather, though the DBSC raced in the harbour. Sadly Charles Chalker died after thirty-six years dedicated to the regatta, including founding the alfresco ball and rural sports.

The Embankment dispute festered on, Mr Simpson and his anti-Embankment team obstructing whenever possible, but the contractor made steady progress. Preliminary work was completed, foundations laid and sea walls started, barges were built and dredging proceeded. The DHC negotiated two loans, £15,000 from the Rock Life Assurance at 4½ per cent and £11,000 from the Rational Sick & Burial Assurance. The new town clerk, Osmonius Smart Bartlett, later jailed for embezzlement, instigated legal action to reverse the old council's right to fund the northern section, but the legal action and the subsequent appeal were lost. Mr Simpson still refused to pay, while the GWR also went to court and won their action against moving their pontoon, resulting in a seven-foot to ten-foot gap which remained in the Embankment until the station building in 1889.

Finally the Steam Packet Company's steamboats, usually laid up for the winter, were kept running, awaiting the arrival of their new 58-foot screw launch *Dart* which had been built to meet competition from a rival Totnes company running *Dainty* built by Simpson & Denison, with Kingdon engine and boiler.

1884 started badly for the DHC when the SS *Triumph* (1,797 tons) under pilotage struck the Homestone Rock due to a misplaced buoy, and taking water, was run up on the Kingswear beach for repairs (an omen of trouble ahead). Misfortune also hit the Haytor Mining Company who, three years previously, had reopened the Haytor Iron Mines and established their office in The Square, Kingswear, freighting the ore by rail to Kingswear quays for onward transmission. The business prospered and in 1883 they built in Glasgow two fully equipped vessels both of 500 tons capacity, the SS *Kingswear* and the SS *Dartmouth*, to ship the ores from Kingswear and other working ports. Unfortunately four months later the SS *Dartmouth* vanished without trace, and being under insured, the business failed and was wound up.

Left: The superb oak staircase and magnificent stained-glass window with the royal coat of arms and those of the Freake family. The newel post griffin, the staircase sentinel, must have many a tale to tell.
G Bush/G Thomas

Right: This unique and intricately carved walk-in fireplace portrays the Freake family coats of arms, foliage, carved beams and cornice, and took over three years to create
G Bush, Michael Bennett & Co

Left: *WAR ... The 1854 Sebastopol cannon, which spread death and carnage amongst the lancers of Captain Chamberlayne's 18th Light Dragoons. They were part of the gallant 600 in the charge of the Light Brigade into the Valley of Death. The cannon stands against the snow in Chamberlayne's home town of Dartmouth, a silent sentinel on the Embankment, while local children battle over a game of marbles.*
TOM CASEY

Right: *AND PEACE ... The quizzical looks of these children begs the question, 'Are they really tunnelling into the vaults of the Naval Bank?' (now the NatWest Bank) in Parade House, Dartmouth.*
TOM CASEY

At the same time Polyblank's shipyard, formerly the Old Brass Foundry and empty some three years, was taken by George Mitchelmore, owner of the former Dartmouth Steam Laundry. His previous property was The Malt House, South Town, but it had been completely destroyed by fire, leaving his main clients, the cadets at the Britannia Naval College, seriously short of a change of clothing. Speed was paramount, and within two months the buildings were refurbished and equipped with the latest laundry machinery and reopened as the Dartmouth & Kingswear Steam Laundry.

Kingswear church, like other harbourside churches, had only a small churchyard, and for centuries had accommodated not only its own parishioners but also the casualties of the harbour. Goods recovered from the sea and handed to the Customs attracted a reward of one-third of their value, but the recovery of a body, an unpleasant task, attracted a reward of only 1s (5p), and the loss of a day's pay to attend the inquest. As maximum capacity had been reached, a Burial Board was formed and an acre-and-a-half at the junction of the Brixham Road and the new road purchased for £250. Mr Appleton produced plans and a new cemetery and a lodge costing £285 were erected by Mr Windsor, Dartmouth.

Regatta 1884 had fine weather. Two exceptional yachts participated, both already flying many winning flags – the *Irex* and *Genesta*. Both were to star in the 1887 Jubilee races, and the latter *Genesta*, owned by Sir Richard Sutton, had challenged unsuccessfully for the America's Cup.

News then arrived of an horrific incident involving a local man, Captain Dudley, who had served with Eli Fleet, Kingswear fisherman, and later commanded Sir Charles Strickland's yacht *Myrtle*. At the previous regatta aboard Mr Thompson's yacht *Terpsichore*, Mr West had contacted Captain Dudley to deliver his yacht *Mignonette* to Sydney, New South Wales, details from the *Chronicle*, as abridged below:

> *The three men and a boy set sail for Australia and in a storm foundered, launching a small punt with just two tins of preserved turnips. On this meagre fare and a turtle they caught they existed for twenty days, then in the desperation of starvation they slew the boy, quenching their thirst with his blood, devouring his liver, heart, and some flesh before being picked up by the brigantine* Montezuma *and landed at Falmouth. After a protracted trial they were found guilty* [but pardoned a few years later].

Mr Simpson and Mr Turner had been elected on to the DHC board as town council representatives intent on retarding the Embankment scheme if possible. But Mr Turner turned and became an ardent supporter of the Embankment scheme, while Mr Simpson was disqualified at the year's end, much to the relief of Mr Seale Hayne and the board. During this period he was, with other anti-Embankment members of the clique, re-elected to the council to employ every opportunity to obstruct; but, in spite of all their efforts, work continued apace.

1885

The January Customs returns for 1884 confirmed fears that Mr Collins' new Portland Depot was reducing the number of steamships calling for bunker coals at Dartmouth – 591 vessels in 1884 against 779 in 1883, a shortfall of 188 ships – but there was a shipping depression and many vessels, including two from Donald Currie's Castle Line, were laid up in major ports.

The newspapers were full of the bizarre details of the failure to hang John Lee; formerly known as 'Boots' at the Royal Dart Hotel, he took employment with a Babbacombe lady whom he was accused of murdering. He was found guilty and sentenced to hang, but the scaffold trap failed to answer three times and the sentence was commuted to life imprisonment. On release he returned to stay with a relative, a Dartmouth publican. He then married and set up as a newsagent in London, later emigrating to America.

In July the Steam Packet Company sold the faithful *Newcomen* to French owners in Bordeaux on the River Gironde, and she was renamed *Courrier de Langionan* after a small town on the river.

Regatta 1885 *The Times* reported 'an ugly tumble of sea' in which *Marjorie*, an 85-ton cutter, broke her mainmast six feet above the deck, her crew were thrown overboard, but all were saved. The Embankment proved a tremendous success; instead of being crowded on the New Ground, hundreds of spectators watched in comfort the five training brigs, 32 steam yachts and 146 schooners, yawls and cutters attending.

For the DHC, 1885 proved memorable for several reasons, for, in spite of the council's intransigence and refusal to honour its monetary commitments, the North Embankment was continuing at the board's expense, while the unnecessary legislation costs were also growing.

Mr Seale Hayne, anxious to concentrate on his longtime ambition to become an MP, and disillusioned by the petulant and spiteful opposition, sent the following abridged letter of resignation to the DHC (which said it all):

> *Gentlemen, I regret it is necessary to resign from the board, as owing to increasing engagements I cannot give that constant attendance on your committee; or accept responsibility for decisions based on conferences in which I am unable to take part. I quit with much regret as I was mainly instrumental in its foundation and occupied your chair from the beginning. The good results are the harbour is now frequented by a larger class of vessels, and as the early completion of the Embankment is now assured my resignation will in no way prejudice that undertaking, which will do for the town of Dartmouth a benefit equal to that which our other works have done for the Port.*

Left: 1884. John Lee, 20, Abbotskerswell-born formerly 'Boots' at the Royal Dart Hotel then porter at the railway terminus, Kingswear. He was later convicted of brutally murdering his 70 year-old employer Miss Emma Ann Keyes at her home, The Glen, Babbacombe.
JOHN PIKE

Right: 1885. A horrendous scene depicting the hooded Lee's attempted execution at Exeter Jail when the trap failed to drop three times, thus resulting in his sentence being commuted to life imprisonment, of which he served 22 years.
JOHN PIKE

THE BABBICOMBE MURDER- SHOCKING SCENES ON THE SCAFFOLD!

Left: 1870. This composite picture shows the area between Spithead and the lower slipway, developed over the centuries by Dartmouth merchants as continuous riverside warehousing to service their sea-borne trade, and enable sailing vessels at high water to berth, take the ground and discharge. However, the increasing size of sailing vessels and steamers forced them to lay off and anchor, and made the need for an Embankment imperative.

R TUCKER

Right: The Harbour Commission's Embankment was completed in 1885 after bitter opposition from a small group in public office acting for their own self-interest. This busy picture shows the barquentine Jane Kilquor, *a brigantine, a ketch and sloops moored alongside the northern section.*

G WEATHERLY

My family has for generations held property in the borough and having been actively engaged my whole life in promoting various enterprises for its benefit, I have felt deeply the unnecessary acrimonious character of the opposition to our present work, although it has been chiefly by gentlemen whose connection with Dartmouth is of very recent date. My regret is the greater because expenditure upon law, which this opposition has involved, adds to the charges upon the local rates and harbour dues; and throws burden on trades and labour, and establishes a unique exemption from local charges in favour of the rich.

Wishing you prosperity and success, I remain, Gentlemen,

Yours faithfully, C Seale Hayne.

His departure was a bitter disappointment, but the DHC appointed Sir Henry Paul Seale, his uncle and a founder, to continue the Seale dynasty for a further ten years.

By midsummer the contractors had requested final payment, but due to the board's chronic cash problems, they were offered (as others were) bonds in lieu of cash. The commissioners were forced to take legal action against the Corporation for the outstanding £13,000. They were only able to make partial payments to the insurance companies, and the cumulative result was that costs built up to the extent that the solicitors of the parties reluctantly advised that a receiver should be appointed.

1886 was the nadir, as 1882 was the zenith, for the DHC, for, on 29 January, a receiver was appointed; coincidently (or was it?) the receiver was none other than Charles Seale Hayne, who, in the previous November, had been elected MP for Ashburton, so at least they had a friend in court.

Bunkering returns for 1885 still showed a decline in steamships calling, but on a much reduced scale compared with the massive shortfall of 188 steamers in 1884. It was, however, sufficient to cause the coaling agents to review their commitments and institute change. Fox & Son withdrew as agents for Cwmaman Coaling Co to concentrate on their shipping and consular interests, leaving Cwmaman to take direct control in new offices two doors further down (possibly Hingston's old offices), adjacent to the seaman's mission. The newcomer, Thomas Wilton, a canny Geordie, would play a major part in the town's affairs for the next thirty-eight years. Richard Hingston, an 1862 founder, having sold his premises, decided to withdraw and offered for sale his hulks *Prodomo* (467 tons), *Happy* (284 tons), *Eldre* (150 tons), barge *Brothers* (40 tons), and the lifeboat *May*, but there were no takers, so the business carried on for a further two years.

Tragedy occurred when the Steam Packet Company's newly arrived *Dartmouth Castle*, (100ft x 13ft x 6ft 3in), was returning at full speed from Totnes. A group of men installing electric lighting in Mr Singer's mansions at Redworth and Bowden House were larking about in the bows when one fell overboard under the threshing paddle wheels and, in spite of a thorough search, his severely lacerated body was not found for some days.

Regatta 1886 included a sailing barge race for the first time since 1868. There was also wrestling after many years' absence, and the newspapers reported that this regatta was one of the most successful ever.

In Kingswear a group of gentlemen members of the RDYC entered into negotiation with Mr Roope, owner of the adjacent Kittery Court, for him to surrender a small strip of land and the Coach House to allow Collins Quay to be increased in width from eight and a half feet to 22 feet. This would result in the only wide deep-water public slip in the area; in exchange the village would surrender a right of way, from Kittery Stairs, through Mr Roope's garden, and a small length of Priory Street.

1887started with the report of the death of Samuel Lake in Marseilles, four hours after the arrival of his wife and daughters. A man of energy, practical ability, independent spirit and charisma, among his many achievements were the development of the steam trawler, permanent prefabricated poured concrete housing (Coombe Terrace 1870, Milford Haven 1881) and the fostering of the bunkering trade and South Embankment scheme. In July the *Chronicle* reported that the Swedish Government had awarded him posthumously their highest honour, the Gold Bravery Medal. This was his third award for bravery, after the Gold Albert Medal (1866) and the RNLI Vellum (1880). He lost his life at the comparatively young age of forty-five from a fever contracted whilst saving the crew of the Swedish barque *Ida*, wrecked on the coast of Corsica, where he was engaged in supervising the mining of copper and silver. The columnist thoughtfully concluded that there should be a civilian VC worded not 'for valour' but 'for humanity'.

A positive galaxy of house-building then began in Kingswear. Jubilee Orchard and Spittis Park Terraces were built for artisans engaged on the railways, quays and coaling. Fir Mount and The Pines were built for the managers and Nethway School was built for 100 children (cost £285). The gentry, attracted by the area's beauty and pleasant climate, had built The Vicarage on Church Hill (cost £800) for Rev Walker, Oversteps at Waterhead (cost £500) for Mr Llewellyn, Castella at Waterhead (cost £400) for Mr Ambrose, and The Cottage (now Longford) which is more a mansion than a cottage, at Kittery Point for Mr Wilkins.

On both sides of the river preparations were under way to celebrate Queen Victoria's Jubilee. Kingswear settled on a village club, although it took a further two years to evolve, and then only due to the generosity of the oft-maligned gentry, Mr Llewellyn and Mr Bridson buying a 30ft x 17ft corrugated-iron building and giving the ground above The Priory's tennis court. It was nicknamed 'The Iron House', failed two years later through lack of support and became The Priory Billiard Room.

Dartmouth held a public meeting and approved a proposal by the Mayor to create the Dartmouth Cottage Hospital. A committee was formed of the four local practitioners and premises acquired (Morocco House) adjacent to the Customs House, Bayards Quay. Sir H P Seale presented a large and handsome marble drinking fountain for the New Ground gardens but it remained without water for two years. After brass band ceremonies on 21 June, the cottage hospital and drinking fountain were duly opened.

Left: Kingswear Steam Laundry, Waterhead Creek. Built as Popes Brass & Iron Foundry 1866 - 1873 it then became Polyblank's Shipbuilders and Engineers from 1874 to 1881, and Mitchelmore's Steam Laundry, 1883 to 1971.
AUTHOR'S COLLECTION

Right: Local staff at work in the ironing and drying department.
DARTMOUTH CHRONICLE

Left: The Dartmouth & Torbay Steam Packet Co's iron-screw harbour tug Hauley *(1877/1898) 32GT 61ft x 14ft*

JOHN PIKE

Right: Iron paddle river steamer Dartmouth Castle *(1885/1907) 59GT 100ft x 13ft. She and* Hauley *were built by Harvey, Hayle, Cornwall.*

JOHN PIKE

In mid-May the Navy started the Jubilee celebrations when twenty-four torpedo boat destroyers, dead slow in two divisions and led by the 19-knot HMS *Rattlesnake*, steamed into the harbour and remained for several days. The officers of the naval colleges combined and presented Her Majesty with two magnificent three-foot long silver models (900oz) of *Britannia* and *Victoria*.

In lighter vein, a group of prominent young gentlemen hired the tug *Hauley*, sailed for the Spithead Review and steamed up and down between the lines of anchored warships, to the amusement of their crews, singing lustily to an organette bolted to *Hauley's* deck.

Regatta 1887 One yacht participating was the 95-ton cutter *Ilex*, owned by Mr Jamieson, club member, and considered the fastest boat afloat. She had earlier in the year in the RYS *Jubilee* long-distance race Cowes/Cherbourg/Eddystone/Cowes beaten twenty-nine British and foreign competitors for the prize of £300. A yachting 'first' in this celebration year took place in June when the Royal Thames Yacht Club organized a race around Britain and, arranged through club member Sir Donald Currie, the hire of a Castle Liner *Northam Castle* to accompany the yachts, which called at sixteen ports including Dartmouth. Several RDYC members joined the cruise for the last leg of the race to the Isle of Wight, then to the finish at Dover.

After ten years the original ten-oared lifeboat *Maud Hargreaves* was replaced by a new twelve-oared lifeboat *Henry and Amanda Shaw*, (34ft x 8ft), London-built and with the new water ballasting.

Ravensbury, sold by Mr Bidder's widow in 1884 to Mr E H Whinfield, was let to General Valentine Baker Pasha, brother of the well-known explorer Sir James Baker. The general's only daughter Miss M S Baker, originally living at Riversea, Kingswear, bought Ravensbury in 1889, but later became Lady Carden of Tipperary. Strangely the famous General, had once as a Lieutenant Colonel been discharged for indecent assault for kissing a lady (how things have changed!).

Finally, Mr Simpson's partnership with the Denisons ended with the formation of Simpson, Strickland & Co; Strickland, a Bridlington relative and youngest son of Sir Charles Strickland, was married to a daughter of the famous engine and boat designer, Sir William Thorneycroft.

Model of the Henry and Amanda Shaw, *given to the RNLI by the donors on launching in 1887. Dartmouth's second and last lifeboat. Sold 1896*

G THOMAS

DARTMOUTH MUSEUM

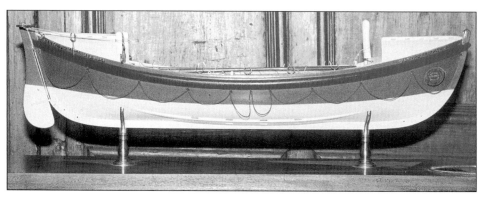

Coal becomes King

1888 to 1900

NEW CAPTAINS OF INDUSTRY

1888 On New Year's Day, the Seamen's Mission, operational in Dartmouth since 1876, moved to new premises on Bayards Quay, (paid for by a subscriber). Progress elsewhere in Dartmouth was faltering. The DHC was bankrupt due to the SS *Triumph* disaster and ongoing legal costs incurred by the town council's refusal to fund their contribution to the Embankment scheme. The number of steamships calling for bunker coals was declining; two coaling agents, Mr Bellamy and Mr Fox, had withdrawn, and Mr Hingston was in the process of doing so as trade was slipping away to rival Portland. In April the verdict was given against the DHC in their action against the town council, and a month was given for appeal, which was duly lodged.

In July the *Chronicle* reported the following:

> *The SS* Armellia *Malta to London is at Kingswear Quay (usually busy with coal imports for Torquay and district) discharging 500 tons of 'valonia' (for tanners at Bristol). It has also over 100 'zingina' (gypsies) aboard, Greek, Turkish, and Romanian bound for Philadelphia. Though they have money they are of abject and dirty appearance and have persistent mendicant habits. The women and children are almost nude, passing their time begging from prominent Dartmouth and Kingswear residents, who are distributing cakes and sweets to them, while Kingswear's PC Lock is keeping good order, stopping fights and the men's habit of beating the women. Also aboard, for Baroness de Falba, at present on her yacht* Chazalia *in the harbour, is a 7-foot long 'ram' from Pyra, Asia Minor, for breeding on her estates at Chudleigh.*

Regatta 1888 There were the usual races and a Dartmouth/Portsmouth race. Another event was a model yacht race and a boxing tournament.

Fortune then smiled on the hard-pressed DHC when Jasper Bartlett (a prosperous and progressive Dartmouth merchant, owner of the brewery and several licensed properties) formed a new company, the Channel Coaling Company Ltd, with himself

Left: The Britannia and Jasper Bartlett's newly formed Channel Coaling Co's two standing hulks, Happy 264 tons, and Prodomo 468 tons, two shifting hulks and two steamers calling for bunkers, moored up and awaiting the close of the regatta.

AUTHOR'S COLLECTION

Right: The newly completed embankment and visiting yachts, dressed overall for the regatta, with the Hudson Bay Co Ltd flying their house flag on their offices. The RDSC Ltd tug Nimble is moored nearby.

G WEATHERLY

1889 regatta with a broad guage locomotive approaching Hoodown Point, where Messrs Collins & Co Ltd (Coaling Agents) intended to manufacture coal briquettes from coal slack stored in the massive 1500 ton J M Reed *moored nearby. Their original hulk* Monarch *and other companies' condemned hulks lie abandoned on the Ballast Cove shoreline.*

as managing director, in the hope of arresting the decline in the bunkering trade. He bought some of Mr Hingston's hulks, took over his agency for Nixon's Steam Navigation Coals, and applied for a mooring space. The delighted DHC immediately revised its mooring plan, convened a meeting with Collins & Cwmaman Coal Company and instructed them to remoor their hulks, at their own expense, in different positions to accommodate the new company. Meetings and action took a mere five days, in contrast to the dealings with the GWR who, almost thirty years after the Dartmouth & Torbay Railway Bill, and after years of procrastination, had finally reached agreement with both the town council and the DHC and settled on the first of their two submitted plans i.e. Dartmouth railway station to be sited at Spithead. DHC's good fortune was short lived, however, for on 18 December the court of appeal decided by two to one against them, to the delight of Mr Simpson and his anti-Embankmenteers. The DHC's only recourse would be to the House of Lords, but, being in receivership and having incurred heavy legal expenditure, the creditors were reluctant to risk further outgoings. The DHC's solicitors, Batten & Parfitt, received instructions to negotiate and seek a compromise with the town council.

1889 Mr Hayne, in residence at Kingswear Castle, entertained the Prime Minister, Mr Gladstone. There was much building on both sides of the river. In Kingswear large extensions commenced on two mansions on the Brownstone estate, Sea View Villa (Kingscliffe/White House) and Start Bay Villa (Coombeside/Pinewoods); the Dartmouth & Kingswear Steam Laundry erected six adjacent cottages for the workers, and Mr Casey was building the first two houses at the top of Wood Lane.

After years of procrastination the sloop *Ida* arrived off the Embankment with a crane and materials for Mr Jenkins, the Plymouth contractor, to start the new railway station.

In Dartmouth's council, heated debate raged over a scheme to position the new post office in the Butterwalk instead of on the Embankment. The proposal involved demolishing a large part of the Butterwalk and replacing it with a 36-foot high three-storey plain brick building with no ornamentation; surprisingly a group of local businessmen attended to support the motion, but much to his credit (considering his obsessive opposition to the Embankment), the Mayor, Mr Simpson, strongly opposed the move, saying: 'Once we start pulling down part of the Butterwalk the rest will surely follow and in later years we shall be branded vandals, and I can say I did my best to preserve a great rarity and did not aid in its replacement by a plain brick building as can be seen in any modern city.'

The Charmed Life of the Butterwalk *1888-1945*

Above: *Venetian Dartmouth*
The original and later bombed, but restored old Butterwalk, faced other predators besides some councillors, and acts of war, - Rising Tides.

DARTMOUTH MUSEUM/DAVE GRIFFITHS

1888 Councillor Voisey, 'The Butterwalk is no ornament and as such old rubbish should be removed to accommodate the new Post Office.'

1888 Mayor Simpson, 'Once we start to demolish part of the Butterwalk, in later years we shall be branded vandals.'

1889 The new Post Office was sited in the first new building on the Embankment, the Raleigh Temperance Hotel.

1909 A Butterwalk lessee sells to a Midland person a magnificent carved fireplace illustrating the Judgement of Solomon with twelve life-sized figures of the apostles.

1912 The Town Council fails to support a scheme by the 'Newcomen Memorial' to restore the Butterwalk for the Burgesses of Dartmouth.

1913 Councillor Scammel, lessee, proposes to sell the King Charles II fireplace and panelling (Museum) to a non-resident.

1914 The Town Council takes counsel's advice and aborts the sale.

1942 The Butterwalk is seriously damaged in an air raid by German aircraft.

1943 The Ministry of Works (MoW) commissions a survey to establish the extent of the damage.

1943 Councillor Scardfield states, 'it is suffering from acute old age and decay and is beyond repair as it would cost thousands and should not be entertained'.

1943 Town Council debates and decides to demolish the Butterwalk.

1943 The MoW refuses the council permission to demolish the Butterwalk.

1944 Councillor Oke says, 'It is slum property and should be pulled down.'

1945 The MoW thwarts the town council (to its disgust) by making the Butterwalk a listed building, to be restored later for future generations to enjoy.

The Raleigh Temperance Hotel and new Post Office.

Councillor Voisey replied, 'The property we propose to remove is in no way an ornament to Dartmouth, and in the interest of securing a central site *such old rubbish should be removed*. I hope the Post Office will not take the destruction of the old building into account, and for myself, I would *like the whole building removed and set back and new buildings erected to improve the locality*.'

Fortunately the scheme did not materialize, leaving the Butterwalk to face possible demolition several decades later by like-minded councillors and from acts of war.

In June the first imposing building was opened on the Embankment's wide esplanade, the Raleigh Temperance Hotel, costing £1,800, and a few months later the ground floor was converted to accommodate the new Post Office. This was quickly followed by a neat two-storey office block for Edward Marsh Turner, Shipping Agent (now Somerfield).

Regatta 1889 had a new Grand Challenge Cup for coxed fours in two heats and a boxing tournament. In the RDYC races the America's Cup contender *Valkyrie* won her contest.

Affairs of the harbour dominated thereafter: bunkering had declined since Mr Collins had transferred his main effort to his Portland depot in 1883, but trade was now boosted by the great London Dock strike. Freight increased by 1s 6d (7½p) per ton, and many ships that normally coaled in London queued to bunker in the harbour. One, the *Grantally Castle*, took 850 tons, causing a shortage and demand so acute that even expensive house coals were used, and the companies' chartered colliers ran flat out to keep up supplies. The DHC was concerned at the deteriorating condition of some of the older hulks and insisted that Mr Collins' *Monarch* and Mr Bartlett's *Happy* (once Mr Hingston's) be replaced after thirty years' service; the *Happy* gained a year's reprieve, while Mr Collins beached *Monarch* at Ballast Cove and offered her for sale, replacing her with *Prince Henry*. Philips, privy to information that the Government were seeking a hulk to test their latest 'brunner torpedo', bought *Monarch* for £5, carried out some minor repairs and sold her to the Government for £300, much to Mr Collins' chagrin.

Mr Collins, however, patented a process to fabricate moulded fuel briquettes. He obtained permission to moor the *J M Reed*, a 1,500-ton open flat barge, to store the small coals alongside a modest building erected to manufacture these at Hoodown Point, Kingswear. The local inhabitants complained bitterly, as they were already awakened from 4am by the whistling of steamers and trains, and bothered by the noise and dust from the railway, quayside cranes, collier trade and loading and discharging of hulks. They were supported by the local and visiting yachtsmen who, proud of their yachts, did not relish a veneer of coal-dust. Fortunately the scheme made little headway, languished and died.

Kingswear's crowded quays, illustrating the urgent need for enlargement. The clipper-bowed trader is alongside the Eclair *Pier, and a collier and ketch are being unloaded by a steam-crane into broad-gauge wagons.*

Eric Bovey

October 1890. The Dunottar Castle *(5,625 tons) the latest, largest and fastest of Sir Donald Currie's Castle Liners. After twenty years, Dartmouth once again is about to lose its status as a mail station for the Cape and Colonies.*
DAVE GRIFFITHS

1890 The new decade did not start well for the town council: the Mayor, Mr Simpson, had received some acclaim for resisting the move to demolish the Butterwalk, but was now severely criticized, along with his fellow councillors, for failing to save another of Dartmouth's treasures, the 'Spithead Pavings'. This was an elaborate example of the paviour's art, the main feature being a large compass with all points shown and centrally dated 1679. The surrounding areas were laid out as a Dutch garden, with a maze of paths and flowerbeds, covering the whole of Spithead Quay.

THE START BAY YACHT CLUB

Some RDYC Dartmouth members had, for many years, tried to resite the club in Dartmouth, and in late 1889 a small group of gentlemen met at the Castle Hotel under the chairmanship of A H Bridson, strongly supported by F C Simpson, Rear Commodore RDYC. Their object was to form a Dartmouth Yacht Club for 20-raters and unders, and agreement was reached to form the Start Bay Yacht Club (SBYC) with an annual subscription of one guinea, the burgee to be a white cross on a red ground, with the Dartmouth coat of arms in the centre. Officers were: Mr Simpson, Vice Commodore; Mr Bridson, Rear Commodore and Hayne Smith, Secretary. Two upper rooms were taken in Mr Turner's recently erected Embankment offices. Mr Simpson's position as Rear Commodore, RDYC, became untenable; several senior members were close friends of Mr Seale Hayne, and Embankment supporters, and relationships turned from difficult to vitriolic. In three months there were two special meetings at which a Rear Commodore was elected twice, and resigned twice, due to intervention by Mr Simpson. Eventually Sir Thomas Freake took the position. There was some light relief, however, when the RDYC was notified of the formation of a Manchester Yacht Club, whose only proximity to the sea was 36 miles away via the projected Manchester Ship Canal! The indomitable Mr Simpson then purchased from Lord Churston a further 25 acres near his home at Maypool on the eastern shore, to develop Noss Point as a yacht building and engineering works, which later became the main works on the river.

In Kingswear W F Owens began building a substantial semi-detached mansion (Baytrees/Baytrees House) behind Owensville, the first all-brick houses built locally to use cavity walling. Nearby Mr Fitzherbert's 1860 property The Cottage (Dunheved) caught fire while he was developing film and burned to the ground. Mr Casey had a good business running his launches *Blanche* and *Forester* to Nelson Steps for sightseers to view the ruins.

Regatta 1890 This year had an extra town race for dinghies, while the RDYC over 30 ton race was won by the 62-ton *Yarana* beating the 102ft cutter *Thistle*, the unsuccessful 1889 America's Cup contender. Also racing was another later contestant, the Earl of Dunraven's *Valkyrie I*. On the third day the Start Bay Yacht Club held their first two races, and the DBSC ran three races with the newly formed 'Minima Club' participating.

In October, before admiring crowds, Sir Donald Currie's latest liner, the magnificent two-funnelled *Dunnottar Castle*, (5,625 tons), which was built to compete against the rival Southampton-based Union Line's *Scot*, left on a shakedown voyage to Cape Town (no hint of the wind of change).

Finally in Kingswear Colonel Toms presented the village with a fine recessed drinking fountain, situated in the square, to mark his twenty-fifth wedding anniversary. Nearby, Churston Golf Club was founded.

1891
Coaling returns for the previous year illustrated the remarkable revival of the bunkering trade since 1888 when Jasper Bartlett had formed his new company. A total of 1,168 vessels coaled in 1890, against 881 in 1889, an increase of 267, with an average 24 more ships per month, of which Channel Coaling bunkered over 70 per cent. Mr Bartlett's main advantage was that as managing director he could make instant decisions without recourse to a head office. His success triggered a chain reaction and motivated the other coaling agents. On 1 January Mr Collins issued a pamphlet stating that he was sole owner of the firm G H Collins & Co Ltd and no longer acting as managing agent for the Powell Duffryn Group; after fifteen years based on Bayards Cove, and an ardent anti-Embankmenteer, he swallowed his pride and moved offices to his stores in the Newman Building (Oxford House/DHNA) on the much-abused South Embankment, where palatial offices had been prepared over his partner's, J E Turner's, coal depot. This activated Mr Bartlett to move from his current offices in Newcomen Road to Mr Hingston's old premises (possibly once Cwmaman's) on Bayards Quay. The chain reaction continued and a few months later Mr Wilton, to participate in the bunkering bonanza, resigned as agent for Cwmaman Coaling Company, and the previous agents Fox, Son & Co Ltd, reassumed command. According to DHC minutes Mr Wilton obtained permission to moor a hulk and barges in the harbour. By October 1892 the firm Wilton & Co appeared and by January 1893 had become Renwick & Wilton Co Ltd. Mr Wilton had previously established some wholesale gas and coal outlets; in tandem with Mr Renwick, Torquay coaling factor, he competed against Whiteway & Ball and other companies to supply local gasworks and commercial concerns with coals imported over the Kingswear wharfs. For some time he had campaigned for the GWR to increase Kingswear's quays and cranage to accommodate two steamers, as his chartered vessels SS *Sinbad* and SS *Sabrina* often incurred demurrage waiting a week or more for a berth.

Over two years had elapsed since the DHC agreed to seek a compromise with the town council over the South Embankment scheme, and, as there had been no further response, the commissioners had decided to proceed with an appeal to the House of Lords. The town council, anxious not to lose or incur further legal expenditure, developed their previous March settlement proposals, which were broadly accepted by the DHC's legal advisers, formalized and presented for acceptance on 4 March 1891. The offer was meagre: £3,000, being £2,000 for the Embankment, £600 for legal costs and £400 reserve; so Dartmouth Corporation had received two-and-a-half acres and the Embankment costing £30,000 for 10 per cent of its value. Ironically in the same year, anti-Embankmenteer Mayor Simpson was replaced by William Smith, solicitor, former DHC Secretary and personal friend of Charles Seale Hayne.

On 5 June the *Roslin Castle* sailed and on 12 June the *Chronicle* editorial ran 'Welcome the coming; speed the parting guest'.

Then the unthinkable happened; *The Times* reported that the next departure of the *Dunnottar Castle* on 20 June would be from Southampton. The shadow of 1857 loomed again, for, after twenty years, the graceful Donald Currie liners were to withdraw and Dartmouth was once again to lose its status as a mailing port. The reason given was that the Cape Government wanted a Saturday sailing, and Her Majesty's Post Office after making up the Australian, Indian and China mails on the Friday could not simultaneously accommodate the South African mails for Westcountry dispatch. So Southampton, closer to London, became the port of departure.

Regatta 1891 was normal, but it was noticeable that the smaller and the cruising yachts were gaining momentum; the cruiser owners arranged a race to Plymouth with eight starters on the Monday after regatta.

There was much curiosity at the arrival of the SS *Rossia*, (2,022 tons) from St Petersburg for bunkers at Fox's hulk *Prince Arthur*. SS *Rossia* had ninety-one female convicts aboard, some with children, with sentences in Siberia ranging from five to twenty-five years for murder, poisoning, arson and firing a whole village. They were bound for Vladivostok, calling at Nagasaki, and it was no surprise to learn weeks later that the transport was burnt out in Port Said, as the ladies were not keen to proceed.

In the harbour, electricity was installed on the *Hindustan*; the generators placed on board caused so much noise and vibration that study was impossible and many cadets became ill until the generators were moved ashore.

Finally a meeting was convened to hear a report on the Dartmouth lifeboat. It did not make good reading; there had been no practice in bad weather, it had failed to answer a call because a crew could not be mustered, and it was considered by the RNLI to be the worst branch in the country; it must improve or be withdrawn.

1892 started with this report in the *Chronicle*: 'In 1891 the Dartmouth Fire Brigade received 51 false call outs which meant men being called from home and work, horses being harnessed to the engine, steam raised, and often travelling to no avail'.

In February Captain R Cleland, eighty-two, twice Mayor of Dartmouth, died. He came to Dartmouth in 1853 and bought Rock Hill, a mansion which has since been demolished adjacent to Warfleet House. He had the distinction of commanding Cunard's first transatlantic wooden paddle-steamer *Britannia*, (1,156 tons), and twice received inscribed silver salvers from grateful passengers for his superb seamanship when crossing the Atlantic in appalling weather.

A current Dartmouth 'institution', Cundells, was founded when G B Cundell took over the Royal Dart Grocery, a wine, spirit and grocery store on the quay.

In April, some twelve months after the Castle Liners had departed, it was announced that the British & Colonial Steam Navigation Co Ltd (Bucknell Bros) liners for South Africa would call at Dartmouth, and E M Turner would be the local agent. The fleet list included *Afrikaaner, Mashona, Kaffir, Zulu, Transvaal,*

1892. Kingswear terminus' railtrack being reduced from broad to standard gauge to comply with the GWR's decision to standardise its lines to comply with those throughout the rest of the country.
JOHN PIKE

Basuto, Ponda, Bloemfontein and *Monica*. The *Afrikaaner*, (4,100 tons) arrived two weeks later to pick up mails and was coaled in The Bight by Channel Coaling Company's collier SS *Llandaff*. However, this was countered by Collins, agents to the Kosmos Line to the Falklands, receiving notice that they were to cease calling at Dartmouth and were to depart direct from Tilbury.

In pursuance of their policy to change from broad to narrow gauge to standardize with the rest of the system, GWR gave notice that it was to commence the Kingswear section on 27 May. The work was completed in the incredibly short period of three days, by two separate gangs, one starting from Churston, one from Kingswear. The gangs were fortified by vast quantities of oatmeal, with which gruel was made, to sustain them during the long hours worked. Fortunately the weather was perfect.

Regatta 1892 The Town Committee ran four sailing and ten rowing events, while the RDYC ran six races, the SBYC five with three abandoned, and the DBSC raced on the Monday.

As the year closed, news was received that the man who had done so much for Dartmouth, Charles Seale Hayne, had been rewarded with the position of Postmaster General at a salary of £24,128 per annum. Both Mr Seale Hayne and Mr Gladstone were Old Etonians, but his post would have been earned on merit, and not as the following doggerel by an ex-headmaster suggests:

> *The doors are always left ajar*
> *and the Hall of Fame is always full*
> *Some came through the door marked push*
> *but* most *through the door marked <u>pull</u>.*

1893

started with a front-page advertisement in the *Chronicle* for an interesting sale of antiques on the Embankment, the principal item was the roof of St Saviours church, removed in 1888.

DHC received the settlement for the Embankment, but another £221 legal charges had been incurred and the town council was forced to borrow £3,000 to settle.

Considerable activity was taking placing on both sides of the river. In Kingswear the change to narrow gauge track meant that there was now room to carry out long-needed improvements, widening and roofing over the platforms, building a new weighbridge, signalbox and sidings at Hoodown, and infilling part of Waterhead Creek for more sidings. Renwick & Wilton Co Ltd's success in obtaining the two-year contract to supply Torquay Gas Works with 26,000 tons of coal per annum would further congest the already overcrowded quays. In Dartmouth there were several new developments; eight years after the infilling of the 'blessed pool' a much wanted new road (Mayors Avenue) was constructed. Mrs Spittal dealt with infilling by securing the patent for side-fixing corsets! On the Embankment/Spithead corner Mr Way's imposing York House was opened. The SBYC promptly vacated the first floor of Mr Turner's nearby shipping offices (which were taken by the Dartmouth & Torbay Steam Packet Co), and took possession of prestigious new quarters on the first floor of York House. Also, moves were afoot to secure a plot on the Embankment and build a new cottage hospital, while after several years of searching, the Port Sanitary Authority acquired the ex-Mersey ferry *Mayfly*, (728 tons), to establish a floating isolation hospital for infectious diseases. She was built in 1863, for 155 passengers, and had saloons, promenade decks and double plating, and was to be moored by the *Floating Bridge*. *Mayfly* cost £700 out of an allowance of £1,000, which left £300 for towage and conversion by Philips.

Regatta 1893 introduced the really big cutters to club races, 141 to 162 tons; the Prince of Wales withdrew his *Britannia*, (151 tons) out of respect for the death of his uncle, the Duke of Saxe-Coburg-Gotha.

Glenorley (Kingswear Court), adjacent to the castle, was totally destroyed by fire. As Kingswear had no fire engine it took three hours of strenuous effort for the Dartmouth fire engine to arrive and carry out the last rites over the remains of a once beautiful mansion.

THE *THEKLA* TRAGEDY

This was reported in the *Chronicle* and abridged below:

> The German ship Thekla *was short of provisions and hove to off the harbour while the pilot cutter* Gwendoline *put pilot Crocker aboard. Ashore Fox & Co, German consul, prepared their gig commanded by George Macey, manager, with oarsmen James Stevens, John Collins, and George and Edward Lester. The weather was very stormy and deteriorating so Mr Coursens, CCC Ltd, begged Mr Macey to hire a tug. However they continued and on completing endeavoured to return pilot Crocker to the cutter but in the wild sea the gig was thrown onto her bowsprit and overturned throwing all into the raging sea. Only pilot Crocker was hauled aboard the cutter, while pilots Kelland and Gurney launched the cutter's boat and searched for several hours for their comrades in vain. Pilot Maycock with the exhausted Crocker aboard managed to sail the cutter back to the range, meeting pilot Wright who took over from Crocker. They*

1894. Totnes Castle *built for the Dartmouth & Torbay Steam-Packet Co by Philips on her trials off Sandquay. Moored behind is the converted Mersey ferry* Mayfly, *the Port Sanitary Authority's hospital ship for visiting seamen with contagious diseases.*
DAVE GRIFFITHS/ROY BARNES

then sailed the Gwendoline *back with the broken gig suspended from the bowsprit, which brought down the topmast and fittings. The Dartmouth lifeboat with coxswain Pillar was launched and searched for several hours without success. Later pilots Kelland and Gurney were found exhausted where they had landed near Blackpool Sands.*

Then another tragedy occurred, the *Chronicle* reporting as follows:

Mr A Trimen (26) was staying at Mr Percy Hockin's daughter's home, 2 Alma Steps, Kingswear. He left for the Daymark but it seems he went to nearby Newfoundland Cove and did not return in the evening. The following day pilots landing on the beach found clothes, compass, walking stick and a clock. On leaving they observed something strange under the water, which when the tide receded they found was a body attired in diving dress of peculiar construction. The head was a square tin box with a valve in front which was unscrewed and off and the tube connecting the helmet to the air cylinder was broken. The helmet weighed one hundredweight and it appears he fell forward while conducting the experiment at high tide and drowned alone on that lonely beach.

HMS Britannia's *sail/steam tenders. The first was HMS* Dapper *succeeded as follows:*

Left: *HMS* Racer *1893 (in full sail during a training period). She was replaced in 1905 by HMS* Espiegle *which was relieved in 1910 by HMS* Pomone *which left in 1922; HMS* Sturgeon *came in 1919 and was replaced in 1925 by HMS* Forres *until 1930.*

Right: *HMS* Wave *(1882) is acting as mark boat for the race for twelve-oared cutters during regatta.*

R BARNES/DARTMOUTH MUSEUM

Renwick & Wilton Co Ltd agreed to act as agents for the Little Western Steamship Co Ltd, to call in Dartmouth *en route* from London to Plymouth and Bristol. Simpson, Strickland & Co completed their move to Noss; they now had a 25-ton crane, two 68ft and 25ft fitting shops, forges, sawmills, joiners' shops, building and engine sheds and a handsome new main office with three bays,and a drawing block (architect Mr Appleton). Ninety men were employed locally and many were ferried over daily from Dartmouth.

1894 Exactly forty years since its foundation, the *Dartmouth Chronicle* became the *Dartmouth & South Hams Chronicle*, but the founder and editor Robert Cranford continued the same high standard of journalism and fairness when reporting local events. Behind his Fairfax Place offices and alongside York House on the Embankment, he erected a heavily timbered two storey flat-roofed building (now the Carved Angel) of two shops with offices over; the latter were promptly occupied by Renwick & Wilton Co Ltd.

The yearly bunkering returns were down again, a fall of twenty-three vessels on 1892, and the lumpers' (coal porters') standards were declining, some experienced severe hardship and hed to exist mainly on bread. In a typical month's figures of 23 vessels coaling CCC emerge as the major supplier: 16 were bunkered by CCC, three by Renwick & Wilton Co Ltd, two by G H Collins and two by J E Turner. The gas- and house-coal trade at Kingswear's quays was increasing, but not without problems. One

DARTMOUTH HARBOUR.

Regulations to be Observed in the Use of Steam Whistles and Syrens.

Under 57 and 58 Vic., "Dartmouth Harbour Order," paragraph 6, it is enacted as follows:

"No steam vessel within the jurisdiction of the Commissioners shall sound or use any steam whistle or syren except for purposes as are defined for the Regulations for preventing collisions at sea for the time being in force or so far if at all as the Commissioners from time to time may authorize the use thereof as a means of communication with local agents, pilots or crew. The master or managing owner of any such vessel shall be liable to a penalty not exceeding five pounds for the acts and defaults of any person on any such vessel so offending and the penalty may be recovered from and enforced against the managing owner in the same manner and by the same authority or authorities as provided for by section fifty-six of "The Improvement Act" Provided that this section of this Order is not to apply to steam vessels belonging to or worked by the Great Western Railway Company running backwards or forwards between Dartmouth and Kingswear."

EXEMPTION.

Under the powers conferred as above, the Dartmouth Harbour Commissioners approve of the following to regulate the use of steam whistles and syrens within their jurisdiction.

Definition of prolonged, long, and short blast:

Prolonged blast, duration 15 seconds, represented by

Long blast, duration 7 seconds, represented by

Short blast, duration 3 seconds, represented by ————

Duration of time between each blast:

The duration of time between each whistle shall be 3 seconds, represented by a blank space.

Time during which steam whistles and syrens may be used:

Steam whistles and syrens may be used between the hours of 6 a.m. and 10 p.m., as defined.

Use on Sundays prohibited.

The use of steam whistles and syrens is strictly prohibited between the hours of 10 p.m. on Saturday night and 6 a.m. on Monday morning, except those defined under paragraph 1 to 4 inclusive.

Syrens—Restrictions on the use of

Syrens are on no account to be used on board when steam whistles are available.

Steam vessels and steam yachts, on entering the harbour, consigned to local agents and others, are authorised to use once the following signals; and while at anchor or moorings the use of the signal, as defined in paragraphs 5 to 8 inclusive, once only:

1. Channel Coaling Company, Lim. ———— ———— ———— (2 long 1 short.)

2. Messrs. Collins and Co. ———— ———— ———— (3 long.)

3. Messrs. Renwick and Wilton. ———— (1 long 2 short.)

4. Mr. H. M. Turner, Lloyd's Agent. ———— ———— (1 short 2 long.)

5. Water Boat. In addition to any Flag or other signals in use, ———— ———— ———— (1 short, 1 long, 1 short).

6. Steam vessels waiting for passengers. 1 prolonged blast 15 seconds duration ———— as a notice to passengers previous to getting under way. Also to apply to steam tugs.

7. Steam vessels coaling and for Pilots. As a means of communication with agents or pilots half-hour previous to departure, ———— ———— ———— (2 short, 1 long).

8. Steam Launches and signal to owner. Not to use any steam signal, except such as may be necessary in the discretion of the master (or person in charge) for the purpose of avoiding collision; or as a means of communication to owner when on shore, ———— ———— (2 short.) Once only.

9. All other steam vessels are prohibited from using any steam whistles or syrens (except for the purpose defined by the Act), unless their signals (as a means of communication with agents, etc.) are previously approved by the Commissioners.

These Regulations are to come into force on and from December 1st, 1894.

By order of the Harbour Commissioners, Dartmouth.

WM. SMITH, *Clerk.*

Harbour Commissioners' Office.
DARTMOUTH, October, 1894.

---

problem was dredging; Renwick & Wilton Co Ltd's SS *Vanessa* drew only 17 feet but at low tide grounded 80 feet from the quay; berthing was another difficulty, with countless requests being made for extra quayage. Mr Wilton coerced the Dartmouth Chamber of Commerce to petition the GWR for two or three extra berths. He pointed out that in January and February eleven vessels had been detained a week or more, incurring heavy demurrage costs. The change from broad to narrow gauge had a reverse effect, for the new trucks (being narrower) carried less and took the same amount of quay siding; it took 180 new (narrow) trucks to equal 100 old (broad) trucks in capacity, and although they were supposed to take 10 tons, due to condition, most could only take three to five tons.

Meanwhile the expanding firm Renwick & Wilton Co Ltd purchased the Falmouth built 35-ton tug *Pendennis* (81ft x 14ft 7in x 7ft 6in) for towing, to compete with the River Dart Steamship Co's tugs *Hauley* (31 tons) and *Nimble* (17 tons). She was to supplement her returns by fishing in the Channel and despatching the daily catch from Kingswear station direct to Billingsgate Market, London. Unfortunately she caught fire twice and was sold away in 1897.

February heralded a danger signal for the bunkering trade: oil. The *Buka Standard*, (3,700 tons), arrived bound for Philadelphia; she was one of the first ships built to use coal or oil on long voyages and her bunkers could take either or both, as her furnaces were fitted with appliances to burn both fuels.

The *Chronicle* published details of the pilotage system stating that Dartmouth was part of the London District and as an outport part free, but part compulsory, with ten licensed pilots out of a 757 total. In an effort to appease local complainants the DHC obtained Board of Trade approval for a code of whistling for steamers, ie CCC (two long, one short), GHC (three long), R & W (one long, two

Above: Dartmouth Harbour Commissioners Code of Practice for the use of steam whistles and sirens in the harbour, which was to mitigate public complaints at uncontrolled signalling for tugs and pilots at all hours of the day and night.

DARTMOUTH HARBOUR & NAVIGATION AUTHORITY

Left: Albert Liwentaal, aerial inventor, in later years experimenting with powered flight.
BOB MARSH/SUE THOMAS.

Right: Model in Dartmouth Museum of the Mark II Aerostat made by Bob Marsh.
BILL RODGERS.

short) and so on. During all this activity, time appeared to stand still, for a while the harbour clock on Kingswear church had no hands! But there was movement of a different kind as the overcrowded village school at last received extra classrooms. At nearby Philips' yard the Dartmouth & Torbay Steam Packet Co's new paddle-steamer *Totnes Castle* was launched; it was 87ft x 13ft x 6ft 6in and replaced the old launch *Dart* (sold to Salcombe) on the Totnes winter service.

In late July the cottage hospital opened on the South Embankment, at a cost of £4,015, raised mainly by gifts and public subscriptions and generous help from Mr Wilkins, Brookhill. It had two main wards with six beds in each, an operating theatre and quarters for the matron, nurses and staff.

Regatta 1894 The highlight was the 169-ton American cutter *Vigilant*, winner of the 1893 America's Cup challenge over the Earl of Dunraven's *Valkyrie II*. She was owned by Mr Gould and had crossed the Atlantic to enter the RDYC over 40 tons race. There were only two starters, *Satanita* and *Vigilant*, and with *Vigilant* ahead, the committee abandoned the race as they could not complete in the eight hours allowed. The following day *Vigilant* entered the SBYC race for over 40 tonners and won the £50 first prize. Also present was an earlier America's Cup contender, Lieutenant and Mrs Henn's *Galatea*, on board which they lived in the harbour for many years.

LIWENTAAL – AERIAL PIONEER

Albert Liwentaal, a Swiss engineer working for Simpson, Strickland & Co, made an in-depth study of the soaring seagull and concluded that a lightweight man-made replica might resolve the mystery of flight, ie aerial progress on motionless pinions conquering the uncharted empires of the air. In a disused works shed at Sandquay, Albert Liwentaal constructed a model similar in outline to the seagull, the main body being a skeleton framework of light alloy on skids with a tail and 40-foot wide light timber-fabricated wings, with silken material stretched overall. Friends loaded the strange contraption onto Philips' launch *Star of the Night*; to the amazement of onlookers it proceeded with wings outstretched two miles upstream to land on a beach at Dittisham. Unfortunately wind and rain caused some damage, so the trial was aborted and the machine returned to base for repairs. Later in a strong wind from the same beach, Mr Liwentaal, astride a bicycle saddle behind the controls was pushed and took off, rising six or seven feet above the ground; he then swayed violently and crashed. The intrepid astronaut was badly shaken but unhurt and, undaunted, began to plan Mark II, based at Dittisham. This time, with a new tail and the skids replaced by a bicycle wheel, he tried again on a steep field and quickly rose a few inches, before crashing through a thick thorny hedge, wrecking the machine and wounding the pilot, who was tended in Dartmouth's newly opened cottage hospital. The attending reporter stated that photographs were taken of the machine, which today if located, would be a valuable record of early experimental flight. Liwentaal then moved to London and later abroad to continue with experiments and patents in powered flight for many years.

The second Aerostat *built at Dittisham. In flight, and moments before crashing into a hedge, injuring the inventor.*
PAINTED BY ANTHONY BRYANT

1895 The early months were dominated by the harbour, but static bunkering returns failed to deter Renwick & Wilton Co Ltd from purchasing its first large coaling hulk, the barque *Narwhal*, (1,356 tons), (capacity 2,100 tons), which had been wrecked on the Lizard. CCC acquired a grain elevator with a tower and an endless belt of bucket grabs as a coal store to take 700 tons and possibly to experiment with mechanical loading. Surprisingly in this business climate, a newcomer, Pomeroy Cross & Co, decided to open a house coal business and bypass the problems by importing their own coal. Many lumpers had recently experienced hard times and there were complaints that the soup kitchen's 1d (1p) per quart pea soup contained no potatoes or meat. Mr Havelock, manager GHC, was concerned for the 200 lumpers and their families in this bitter winter and urged the formation of a Welfare Society, with small weekly contributions to be put aside in good times for funding lean periods.

The Rt Hon Charles Seale Hayne, Post Master General, was entertaining the Prime Minister, the Earl of Rosebery, at his Kingswear Castle residence. This gave him the opportunity to fulfil several other engagements, one of which must have

1896, Floating Bridge No. 4 purchased by the Raleigh Estates from Philips, Dartmouth shown here with King Edward VII's coach and horses from Windsor here for the College foundation ceremony in 1902.
G WEATHERLY

The Reverend John Smart, vicar of Kingswear 1837 to 1880, with his daughter, school teachers and class outside Kingswear Church.

T CASEY

given him real pleasure as both founder and official receiver: the release from bankruptcy of the DHC. The 1894 Government provisional order supported by Harris, Buteel & Co, Plymouth, enabled them to borrow £35,000 in A & B Bonds at 4 per cent, issued at par, so allowed the DHC to compromise and clear old debts, and pay by instalments the loan to the Public Works Committee. Mr Seale Hayne's joy manifested itself in a speech given at the Lord Mayor's dinner, thus: 'My first love, the DHC, has now emancipated itself from the thraldon of the Court of Chancery.'

However, at the laying of the foundation stone for the Flavel church, he found little favour and caused conflict when he referred to the church as 'drifting towards Romanism'. At some stage differences appear to have surfaced between him and the established Church, for, on his death in 1903, he left most of his vast fortune to build the Seale Hayne Agricultural College, Newton Abbot, and the bequest included an anti-clerical clause.

Much interest was generated by the arrival of the Italian royal yacht *Saudia* with the Duke of Genoa aboard, accompanied by an Italian warship. The band played lively music on the New Ground, and on Sunday the Duke and is retinue attended divine service given by Father McCarthy at the Roman Catholic church.

Kingswear had recently been made a parish, and the newly formed parish council met to consider GWR correspondence about infilling part of Waterhead Creek. Two pearls of wisdom emerged that would apply equally to current events: firstly they decided the letters contained too many 'mays' and not enough 'shalls', secondly they were not going to be 'press taught'.

Ex-Mayor William Smith rectified an omission in Dartmouth's centuries-old regalia, the lack of a mayoral chain. Wealthy citizens and groups were to buy and present an inscribed link apiece. This was impossible for many people in this time of depressed trade, so a band of Lake Street residents appointed their own Mayor and ceremoniously presented him with a 'chain of office', taken from the smallest room in the house!

Regatta 1895 followed the normal pattern, but Mr Gould, owner of *Vigilant*, 1893 America's Cup participant, who had won last year's SBYC over 40 tons race, presented a 60 guinea cup to the club in thanks for hospitality. He had received equal hospitality from RDYC, but was aggrieved that, as with the Prince of Wales in 1880, the race was aborted on a time factor while he was in the lead.

The year ended with two major rebuildings; Glenorley, Kingswear, and Mr Bodley's Kings Arms restaurant on the Embankment corner (opposite the Raleigh Hotel), which was rebuilt in traditional style and raised two storeys in an extension to the existing Kings Arms Hotel.

1896 In January the boatbuilder Mr Hodges died. Previously he had worked for Redways, but after the great fire of 1878 he had started a small yard opposite the Floating Bridge Inn, earning a high reputation for fast small racing craft: a few frequent local winners were *Scaramouche, Editha, Picaroon, Jacko* and *Semibreve.*

February brought a flurry of Admiralty activity, when the RNC hospital on Ridge Hill closed and took accommodation at Fair View. A delegation was investigating building locally, whilst also considering property in Kingswear for convalescent cadets. Firstly Mount Ridley on Church Hill and then Bryndart were confirmed as leased by Admiral Sir F Bedford, but further developments were delayed due to the increasing likelihood of a permanent college at Dartmouth.

Mr Appleton's Le Suisse Chalet on Church Hill caught fire and became the victim of a local farce played out by the parish council members, who were also the fire brigade. They arrived in good time and were gaining control when they decided the village water supply could not spare any further water, so the fire brigade stood back and watched the house burn down. Luckily Mr Appleton was insured and insisted on rebuilding as before, but salt was rubbed into the wound when the local authority refused a water supply for building until after regatta. Another similar comic opera affected Mrs Barnes in Beacon Road. On demolishing Lincoln Cottage to build the present Glendene she offered, as the road alongside was only six feet wide, to sell the land for £10 to the council and set back the stone retaining wall to create a nine-foot road. Incredibly the council refused, and to this day ambulances and fire engines cannot reach several sizeable properties.

In the harbour GHC took delivery of a new 70ft tug *Verne*, shortly transferred to Portland, and Mr Turner arranged for Clyde Shipping Co to call weekly at Dartmouth *en route* from Glasgow to London; the fleet list was SS *Lizard* (1,175 tons), *Dungeness* (1,201 tons), *Copeland* (1,200 tons), *Pladda* (1,186 tons), *Fastnet* (1,170 tons), *Portland* (1,161 tons), *Aronmore* (1,169 tons) and *Sanda* (1,154 tons).

Coles Court, an Embankment area that belied its fine name, was offered for sale to the council. This area was home to numerous lumpers' families crowded together in little more than hovels, with not one closet on site,. The acquisition would enable a road to be cut from the ferry end of the Embankment to join Lower Street. Regrettably nothing was done for some years.

'Oracle' then reported delightedly in the *Chronicle*: 'Goodbye, old *Floating Bridge* with defective chains, crazy railings, worn out condensers and dilapidated

The fleet and membership list for the RDYC that year showed that 132 members owned 71 yachts, with a combined tonnage of 7,826 tons, an average of nearly 60 tons per member (110 tons per yacht). The adjacent Start Bay Yacht Club had 113 members owning 43 yachts totalling 4241 tons, an average of 37 tons per member.

THE R.D.Y.C. MEMBERSHIP BOOKLET

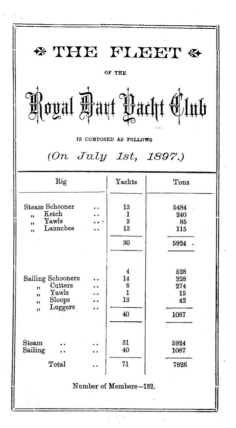

THE FLEET

OF THE

Royal Dart Yacht Club

IS COMPOSED AS FOLLOWS

(On July 1st, 1897.)

Rig		Yachts	Tons
Steam Schooner	..	13	5484
„ Ketch	..	1	240
„ Yawls	..	3	85
„ Launches	..	13	115
		30	5924
		4	528
Sailing Schooners	..	14	228
„ Cutters	..	8	274
„ Yawls	..	1	15
„ Sloops	..	13	42
„ Luggers			
		40	1087
Steam	.. ..	31	5924
Sailing	.. ..	40	1087
Total	..	71	7826

Number of Members—132.

OFFICERS.

Commodore:
H. STUDDY, Esq.

Vice Commodore:
Sir DONALD CURRIE, K.C.M.G., M.P.
S.S. *Iolanthe*, 634 Tons.

Rear Commodore:
Sir T. G. FREAKE, Bart.
S.S. *Energy*, 240 Tons.

Honorary Treasurer:
C. J. W. SEYMOUR, Esq.,
NATIONAL & PROVINCIAL BANK, DARTMOUTH.

Honorary Secretary:
H. W. POPHAM, Esq.

cog wheels': after twenty years and countless breakdowns the Raleigh Estates had obtained from Philips a new bridge, 47ft x 25ft. It was a vast improvement with chains running outside on steel helical-toothed cogs, the cattle penned away from passengers and the centre available for vehicles.

On the naval front *Britannia*'s tender HMS *Wave* was replaced by HMS *Racer* (971 tons).

Regatta 1896 The growing interest in sailing resulted in a total of twenty-two races: the RDYC ones were run on the 1895 RYA linear rules introduced to eliminate 'skimming dishes', the term for shallow, deep-keeled, cabinless racers. Sir T Freake, Vice Commodore, ran a private race and all boats carried distinct marked numbers on their sails, a big improvement on the former flag system.

A blow to Dartmouth's pride followed with the withdrawal of the lifeboat *Henry & Amanda Shaw*, which was offered for sale. She had never saved a life, only once rendered assistance, and received little local support. The year closed on an anxious note when the SS *Mashona* which was *en route* from Smyrna to London called for bunkers with a man aboard suffering from mild smallpox; Dr Soper refused quarantine so CCC ran a hulk alongside and the ship's crew coaled; then everything was fumigated and the ship and patient left for London.

1897 Queen Victoria's Diamond Jubilee year was when Dartmouth lost its grand old man Sir Henry Paul Seale, at ninety-one, the oldest baronet in the country, mentor of the *Floating Bridge*, founder member and ex-chairman of DHC and founder member of RDYC. The club also lost its secretary Lieutenant Colonel Gibbs, living adjacent in Priory Cottage (now Longford), who shot himself whilst depressed after major surgery; he was a superb yachtsman and much-loved locally.

On Bridge Road travellers stared and horses shied when Simpson, Strickland & Co's experimental motor car chugged up the hill. An engine and boiler had been mounted on a wooden platform with iron-clad wheels and was being driven by Mr Alexander, manager, with Mr Strickland, partner, as passenger. The GWR then opened the new railway footbridge to the foreshore, (cut off by the recent creek infilling) to create the new Waterhead sidings.

In Kingswear, as in Dartmouth, plans were afoot to celebrate the Jubilee, and so Mrs Walker, Bryndart, having just built Grasmere (The Keep) adjacent, offered sufficient land to extend the trust almshouses. The final choice to mark the occasion was a replacement clock in the church tower. It would be much appreciated as it served both communities, and the old clock had been inoperative for two years. It also provoked the following comment in the *Chronicle*: 'Kingswear has raised the £150 needed to celebrate the Jubilee and closed its subscription list, while Dartmouth has only raised £138 and Dartmouth should have provided three times that of Kingswear, even though Kingswear has some wealthy residents'.

Considerable interest was generated when HMS *Calliope*, with the gunboat HMS *Jason* and six torpedo boats, put into the harbour *en route* for the naval review at Portsmouth. *Calliope* (2,270 tons), was unusual for two reasons; she was one of the last of the masted sailing corvette cruisers with a steel hull encased in wood then coppered to the waterline. It was her great strength which enabled her, when caught in a hurricane in a Western Samoan harbour with seven American warships, to be the only ship able to raise steam and clear the harbour, amid cheers from the crews of the other doomed ships.

Regatta 1897 There was only one special Jubilee event, but seven town races, six for sail and one for steam launches, the RDYC departed from the usual events to hold one big class yacht race for over 30 tonners and some smaller classes. The big race had seven starters totalling 684 tons competing for a prize of £110, subscribed by members to commemorate the Queen's sixty-year reign. In harbour were 44 steam yachts, (28 over 100 tons, and 4 were 934, 715, 546, and 500 tons) plus 116 sailing yachts.

The year closed on a note of pathos, as a bottle was found by the *Floating Bridge* containing a message in a shaky hand from a seaman aboard a sinking ship recently bunkered at Dartmouth: 'Lost! Going down now, off Flamborough Head, SS *Princess* of Sutherland, November 13th. Should anyone pick this up please let my dear wife Susan Mustard, 26 Lawrence St, Sunderland know. Engines broken down, God help us. Going down further every minute. Goodbye to all, may God help my wife and little ones, may God forgive me all ....' (then followed a few indecipherable words). It was handed to Dartmouth Customs, who located Mrs Mustard to pass on the message. On a happier note, help was provided for the family and employment found for her. This happy ending belies the sailor's couplet: 'Where he goes and how he fares, No one knows and no one cares.'

1898 The bunkering trade showed a marginal improvement, though there was still considerable enforced idleness among the lumpers and the soup kitchen was kept busy. At the annual dinner of Renwick & Wilton Co Ltd at the Royal Dart Hotel Mr Abrahams the stationmaster stated that house-coal and gas-coal imports over Kingswear quays were increasing and quoted some figures to highlight the point: 1881 – 1,300 tons, 1886 – 35,000 tons, 1896 – 77,901 tons, 1897 – 84,166 tons. Several Danish ships and those of the Russian Reserve Fleet began to call for bunkers but the need for a powerful tug soon became apparent. Recently the Dartmouth & Torbay Steam Packet Co had sold the twenty-year old tug *Hauley* (32 tons), and the river launch *Nimble* (17 tons). The *Hauley* was bought by the Manchester Ship Canal Co, and the *Nimble* by Renwick & Wilton Co Ltd, but, because of her small size, was of limited use. A barque was forced to wait twenty-four hours in a strong wind and ebb tide, and eventually, to Dartmouth's shame she was towed in by a large yacht.

In May the schooner *Letitia*, (96 tons), was wrecked on the rocks at Mill Bay Cove, having missed stays on entering harbour. She quickly began to break up, but after heroic efforts the coastguards got aboard with ropes and all the crew were saved except the captain, who died aboard of a fit.

The *Chronicle* reported the old story of Kingswear's Nancy Tarrant who in 1824, only three weeks after giving birth, went out as steerswoman in Kingswear's six-oared pilot gig *Fly* in stormy weather in a race with the Dartmouth pilot gig *Dart*, to bring in the damaged Newcastle brig *Atlanta* from Brazil. Unfortunately

George Kingdon's patent compound engine and boiler, the basis of Simpson & Strickland's success as a major Dartmouth employer and premier builder of launches and steam yachts up to 200ft long.
CYRIL KING

Left: *A crowded scene in the boatbuilding sheds abreast Lower Noss Creek, showing clinker, carvel, and diagonally-sheathed craft in the course of construction.*
DARTMOUTH MUSEUM

Right: *1899. This unique photograph is probably Dartmouth's first motor car with a family of five aboard, and they would have no parking problems!*
ROY BARNES/DAVE GRIFFITHS

the *Dart* overturned, and Kingswear's chief pilot Hamilton in *Fly* failed to stop, though the crew were rescued. Henceforth the Kingswear sailors were called 'Turks', a race noted for their cruelty. The brig was found to have fever aboard and, to the pilot's anger, Nancy went aboard among the sick and the brig was brought alongside the quarantine hulk *Howe* at Noss. Nancy stayed aboard to nurse everyone, including the captain's wife and baby, back to health. For this breach of quarantine rules she was sentenced to death, but a twist in the tale brought a King's pardon. National rules had to be severe, for even in a small village such as Kingswear, 141 had died of the plague in 1671 out of a population of 200 to 300.

Regatta 1898 The Town Committee organized six sailing and fifteen rowing races, while the RDYC held four. The Duke of Abruzzi's *Bona* won the main race for yachts over 79ft in length. On day three the SBYC arranged three events, but the race for big yachts was marred when a crew member on *Ailsa* was lost overboard and the match abandoned.

Some excitement was engendered when the Russian SS *Tamboff* with 800 troops aboard called to take 1,000 tons of coal from Collins' hulk *Prince Henry*. A Russian soldier, liking what he saw, took off his uniform, jumped overboard and swam to Ravensbury to sit 'puris naturalibus' at the front door, to the horror of the female servant who opened it. He then fled naked to Little Dartmouth but was later arrested and returned to an unknown fate.

Meanwhile, twenty-three years since the first proposal to erect a shore-based naval training college with Dartmouth as the preferred site, the Admiralty (after four years of protracted negotiations with the trustees of the Raleigh Estates) announced that agreement had been reached and preliminary works were to commence. This news, was received with joy and jubilation in Dartmouth and shortly after came the announcement that the well-known architect Sir Aston Webb had been appointed.

Finally A H Bridson was appointed to the DHC where he was destined to play a major part for many years. William Smith's new ornamented Embankment House, adjacent to Mr Turner's shipping office, was opened as the Claredon Boarding Hotel.

1899 marked the close of a remarkable century, during which Dartmouth had developed from a small coastal port to a thriving bunkering station known to shipping on all world trade routes. The coaling trade was still improving, 409 vessels taking 46,073 tons against 376 vessels and 43,356 tons in 1897, an increase of 33 vessels and 2,717 tons. This year the main coaling agents began to acquire their own colliers to maintain supplies. Whiteway & Ball, Torquay, importers over Kingswear's quays, already owned the SS *Torquay* and ordered the building of the SS *Dartmeet*, while Mr Collins acquired the SS *Surbiton*, setting a pattern soon followed by Renwick & Wilton Co Ltd.

The SS *Wolviston* entered harbour for coals and reported every sailor's dream: the recovery of a rich salvage prize. They had found the Cunard passenger liner *Pavonia* adrift with her boilers blown and got her underway, losing her only to relocate her two days later to the joy of the passengers. They towed her safely to the Azores and for this received a huge reward of £5,000. The SS *Garton*, also in Dartmouth for coaling, had on board the second mate and six crew members of the barque *Galatea* which they had found sinking. The captain at pistol point had cast off in the only boat with the chief mate, steward, stewardess, and three men, leaving the others to perish with the sinking ship: there was some rough justice however as the captain's group was never seen again.

After being severely criticized for thirty-seven years for holding closed meetings, the DHC finally agreed to admit the public, and hired the Guildhall for meetings which they advertised. After six months only one person had attended, so they returned to meeting in their old offices in Fairfax Place. The *Floating Bridge,* managed from the outset by its owners, was offered for leasing and taken by Mr Percy of London, operator of the Penzance, Exeter and Menai Strait ferries.

In July Kingswear's self-taught but brilliant engineer George Kingdon died. His talent had served several masters well: W Pope's Waterhead Brass & Iron Foundry, William Froude's research into skin friction, oscillation and ship stability, Polyblank engineering, and Simpson, Strickland & Co, with whom as a partner he developed his patent Kingdon compound engine and boiler, laying the base of their fortunes. Coincidentally the then current issue of *Yachtsman* contained a report on Mr Simpson's ex-launch *Brownie* (now *Wyvern*) on the Yukon River. She was involved in the first hectic surge of the Klondyke Goldrush and, due to Kingdon's engine, was the only launch with the strength and speed to overcome the ice and difficulties on the Yukon River to reach Dawson City.

Regatta 1899 This, the last regatta of the exuberant nineteenth century, bore little resemblance to the official 1834 event, and a new class was introduced, the Western One Design. The town ran one race for this class won by *Mystery* owned by the Earl of Rothes, a relation of Colonel Studdy, who in *Jal-Manger* won the RDYC race for the same class on the following day.

The GWR implemented a long overdue scheme for the replacement of Kingswear's existing engine-shed 24-foot turntable with one measuring 55 feet. This entailed further infilling of Waterhead Creek and meant that larger engines could be accommodated, thus eliminating the need to change to smaller engines at Newton Abbot for the Kingswear line.

DARTMOUTH'S FIRST MOTOR CAR

The close of this exceptional century heralded great changes for the nation, mainly in the area of transport. Thomas Newcomen's genius had introduced the new age of prosperity with his invention of the atmospheric steam engine (patented 1705), which later led to the development of the steamship and locomotive. The next century was also to be dominated by transport, this time the motor car and the aeroplane, and Dartmouth was again at the forefront of developments. Work on the motor car took off in 1896 when the law demanding that a man precede the contraption waving a red flag was revoked, and all that was needed was a £2 carriage licence. Freed from restraint, the following year Simpson, Strickland & Co designed and built what was little more than a steam-driven cart for agricultural use. Basically the first motor cars were produced by local men with a touch of genius for mechanical engineering, and the cars were mainly developed in small workshops or garages behind their homes. Credit for the first Dartmouth motor car, completed in 1900, goes to H Inder, 110 Victoria Road, who in 1897 had been engaged by Simpson, Strickland & Co on their experimental vehicle. On completion he determined to build his own machine, a three-wheeler, with a top speed of 16mph, 5mph uphill, in which the passengers sat over the front wheels and the driver sat at the rear. The carburettor was bigger than the engine which had a three-inch stroke with a three-inch bore, and a belt

Within a decade or so the motor industry was established, resulting in a proliferation of makes of vehicles as shown in this rare photograph of a Dartmouth workshop.

ROY LOVETT/TOM CASEY

drive from the engine to a lay shaft, with the gear box on another lay shaft, and a chain belt to the back wheel. To make the wire wheels Mr Inder made the patterns and then had the hubs cast, while his father forged the axles and springs. The whole machine cost £100. The first trip took place one evening, with the policeman and many onlookers attending and professing, in the strongest possible terms, that 'these things will never catch on'.

He later built the first garage in Dartmouth in Ford Valley and retained the car for ten years, selling it to Mark Head, with whom he opened the garage business in Victoria Road, (later absorbed by Couch & Stoneman Ltd). The business then moved to the Embankment, to become Head & Co, later Head, Philip & Co, and was finally reabsorbed by Couch & Stonehouse Ltd. The second car owner in Dartmouth was Major Hockin, solicitor, followed by Dr H Harris, medical officer of health for the borough. Thus life progressed into the twentieth century during which this strange contraption gradually began to dominate everyday life.

CHAPTER 7

Trade, Transition and Turbulence

1900 to 1913

THOMAS NEWCOMEN

1900 The birth of the twentieth century evoked surprisingly little excitement or celebration locally, yet in Dartmouth there was clear evidence of unparalleled achievement, leading the community from one century to the next. In 1894 Albert Liwentaal had made an early aerial flight; in 1899 Mr Inder had built the town's first motor vehicle; and in 1900 work was started to illuminate Dartmouth with one of God's greatest gifts - electricity.

Britain had been a world leader in the nineteenth century, with great wealth and a mighty empire. By 1900 Dartmouth had been transformed from an isolated land-locked harbour into a thriving commercial port, with steamships calling for bunker coals and a rail terminus that was part of an extensive nationwide network. The evolution was due to utilisation of the power of steam, and thus our industrial base was mainly credited to the genius of Thomas Newcomen (1663-1729).

Surprisingly, for over 100 years no effort was made to acclaim or commemorate his creative talent. In their schooldays everybody had learned about Archimedes and his overflowing bath water and Newton's falling apple, but few people knew about Newcomen's singing kettle. His brilliance was mainly obscured and merit was given to his successors who further improved the original concept. However, in about 1840 (the era of Scott's romantic revival) Governor Arthur Howe Holdsworth, who knew of Newcomen's achievements and home, had created a magnificent memorial room at his mansion Brookhill, Kingswear. It embodied a moulded plaster ceiling studded with names and events associated with famous Westcountry families, and walls lined with oak panelling bordered by chain-link carving copied from panels purchased from Newcomen's home; each panel was signwritten with names and dates of other prominent local families, and individually hung purpose-made metal shields painted with their coats of arms. The *pièce de résistance* was the fireplace, reputedly Newcomen's, with marble lintel and carved timber surround, the recess lined with blue Delft tiles, all surmounted by an elaborate plaster cast overmantel from Sir John Gilbert's Greenway home. In the garden he erected 'Newcomen's bower', a gazebo lined with the original oak linenfold panelling purchased from Newcomen's house (removed in 1956 to Dartmouth Museum).

In 1851 Thomas Lidstone, a Dartmouth builder, had proposed the erection of a Newcomen memorial in St Saviours church, which failed to materialize through lack of funding. In 1863, 200 years after Newcomen's birth, Dartmouth council commissioned Bell's planned new road (now Newcomen Road), which involved the demolition of sixty-five properties between Lower and Higher Streets, including Newcomen's house and workshop. This enabled Mr Lidstone to obtain the jettied carved ornamental façade of Newcomen's house in Higher Street and some internal fittings and features from adjacent properties. In 1868 he used these to erect Newcomen Cottage on Ridge Hill. This almost private memorial also included two splendid plaster cast overmantels, one with a biblical scene similar to that in 10, the Butterwalk, and one dated 1635 with the initials of the Lidstone family. According to a Lidstone pamphlet, it contained Newcomen's fireplace and grate where he watched the singing kettle. Finally in 1873 Lidstone made another unsuccessful proposal to erect a public monument to the great man.

In 1887 to celebrate Queen Victoria's Golden Jubilee, the *Chronicle* reported on two further schemes: firstly a cottage hospital supported by public subscription at Bayards Cove, nominated by Francis Charles Simpson, Rear Commodore of the Royal Dart Yacht Club, Mayor of Dartmouth for six years and a major employer; and secondly, public pleasure gardens, to be named 'Newcomen Gardens', a park with a bandstand

Thomas Newcomen *1663 - 1729*
The Newcomen Enigma

Thomas Newcomen's invention in 1712 changed the pattern of life that had existed for centuries, but, as father of the industrial revolution, his genius received little acknowledgement. Belated attempts were made in the nineteenth and twentieth centuries to rectify this neglect, particularly by the Newcomen Society formed to commemorate his work, and recently, after meticulous research, by the late Ivor H Smart who published several pamphlets alleging that some previously held convictions were erroneous, as follows:

ALL R. TUCKER/ DARTMOUTH MUSEUM

Top left: The generally held opinion that the jettied ornamental facade of the house shown in R P Leitch's c1860 drawing of Lower Street was Newcomen's home is incorrect; it was Staplehill's house, Newcomen's being the plain facaded property in the foreground. (IHS)

Top right: At the sale of materials from the demolished properties, Thomas Lidstone purchased some parts and artefacts from Newcomen's house but more from adjacent buildings and built in 1868, Newcomen Cottage, Ridge Hill, which should be more aptly named Staplehill Cottage. (IHS)

Above left: *Governor A H Holdsworth's Brookhill memorial room circa 1830 and dedicated to Newcomen and local families. The fireplace is reputed to be Newcomen's (the contents today are dispersed.*

So, did the fireplace and fire-grate mentioned in Lidstone's pamphlet come from Newcomen's or Staplehill's house, or did Holdsworth acquire the genuine fireplace when he purchased Newcomen's panelling in the 1830s?

Opposite lower right: *Newcomen Cottage drawing room. overmantle, fireplace and fire-grate, also reported to be Newcomen's.* In 1925 the owner of Newcomen Cottage auctioned some artefacts and fixtures amongst which was claimed to be Newcomen's original fire-grate (where he was inspired by the kettle's escaping steam). Mr Brooksbank bought it for 27/6d (£1.38), then in 1927 sold it to Dartmouth Council for £2.

Opposite top left: Finally, there are reputed to be no pictures of Newcomen in existence, but Dartmouth Council acquired a small statuette entitled *Newcomen*, probably a model from a previous attempt to commission a memorial Newcomen statue.

Above: *Newcomen's Bower, built in the 1830s by Governor Holdsworth in Brookhill Gardens. It is a circular stone and thatched gazebo lined with Newcomen's oak linen-fold panelling now in Dartmouth museum.*
R. TUCKER/ DARTMOUTH MUSEUM

So Dartmouth Council should still own one of the most influential artefacts in the world, Newcomen's fire-grate which inspired the power of steam, and a statue that may bear some resemblance to the great man himself. It would be interesting to know where these nationally important items are today.

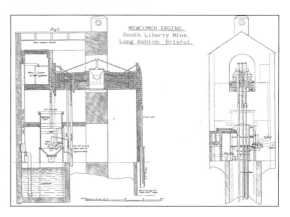

Above: *Elevations, drawn in 1895 by the eminent engineer Bryan Donkin, of the last functioning Newcomen engine, still working five hours a day, six days a week, 150 years after its installation in 1745. Few machines constructed today will be able to claim such longevity.*
THE ENGINEER, 1895
BY PERMISSION OF THE
BRITISH LIBRARY

Above: *Newcomen Gardens is what the gardens should be called as in 1887 funds were raised to celebrate Queen Victoria's jubilee, and honour the achievements of Thomas Newcomen. But mayor F C Simpson named them The Royal Avenue Gardens. This rare pre-1900 photograph shows a Sugg lantern, old cannons and Sir H P Seale's basic fountain at the Embankment end of the park.*
G WEATHERLY

and fountain on the one-and-a-half-acre New Ground, proposed by Jasper Bartlett, owner of Warfleet Brewery, several licensed premises and Borough grocery stores. Committees were formed, subscription lists opened and work started, but there was friction between the two men. The council, dominated by Simpson with his majority, owned the New Ground and imposed onerous restrictions, refusing to remove the ugly urinal that dominated the site, limiting the number of trees and insisting that ships continue to unload there. Meetings with the council failed to solve the impasse; it became obvious that the council controlled the future of the park and so the scheme was handed over to them. On 21 June 1887 the cottage hospital and the park, complete with Sir Henry Paul Seale's fountain, were officially opened. Ironically Simpson, (who was ambitious for a knighthood and was aware of Queen Victoria's happy visit in 1856 when she landed on the New Ground and granted Dartmouth the right to prefix her future regattas with 'Royal') exercised council prerogative and named the park not 'Newcomen Gardens' but 'Royal Avenue Gardens'.

Twenty-five years later, in 1912, ex-Mayor Charles Peek, E W Holdsworth and others revived the earlier call for a statue or, alternatively, an obelisk to be positioned outside the Castle Hotel. A later proposal was for a memorial museum and library, named the 'Newcomen Institute'; it found favour with the town council who offered to lease premises in the Butterwalk, but time passed and the Great War ensured its demise. In 1921 the memorial committee reconvened and, supported by the newly formed (1920) Newcomen Society and, using accumulated funds, a Haytor granite obelisk was commissioned. It has a superb copper plaque with details of Newcomen and pictures of his engine, and was erected in Royal Avenue Gardens, partly righting the wrong of 1887. Smaller plaques were positioned in Lower Street and the Baptist chapel. In 1995, thanks to the diligence of Newcomen researcher the late Ivor Smart, a plaque was placed in Newcomen Road marking precisely the position of his house. In 1964 to celebrate the tercentenary of his birth, the Newcomen Society, with help from Dartmouth's Percy Russell and others, located a disused Newcomen beam engine, formerly used on the Coventry canal. They arranged its transportation and re-erection in Dartmouth where it is now in working order and open to the general public at the Dartmouth District Visitor and Information Centre, The Engine House, Mayors Avenue.

The new century had dawned bright and clear with little obvious sign of the momentous events ahead. Coaling was still the staple trade of the port, but the pattern was changing, with diminishing numbers of steamships calling for bunker coals. The tonnage of the ships was increasing however, which allowed larger bunker capacity. This fact, coupled with the introduction of compound engines and the increasing use of oil as a fuel, later militated against Dartmouth as a coaling station, for steamers could travel further without re-coaling, and increased tonnage meant increased draft, which was important to a harbour of restricted depth. However, the 1899 Customs returns showed marginally improved total bunkering tonnage, although well below the record 1893 figures. Philips then announced that they intended to fulfil the harbour's greatest need and build a powerful tug, 55ft x 14ft x 7ft 6in, called *Venture*. This was particularly welcomed by the pilots whose number had been increased to ten, with two extra men on each of the two cutters. (*Rose* employed Messrs Dyer, Wright, Kelland, Croaker T, and Gatzais; *Gwendoline* had Messrs Weatherdon, Croaker S, Brian, Bird and Pillar.)

Concern arose early in the year over the collier, the *Vanessa*, on charter to Renwick & Wilton Co Ltd, which arrived several days overdue after encountering violent storms. The *Vanessa* was badly damaged, with her companionways and skylights boarded up, cabins gutted, lifeboats, ventilators, aft binnacle and steering-wheel washed away. Major repairs were necessitated at Simpson, Strickland & Co. The SS *Caprini* which was *en route* from the Black Sea to Bergen also limped into port with a heavy list, as her grain cargo had shifted. She was coaled on the opposite side to restore balance.

The royal yacht *Victoria and Albert II* with Princess Henry of Battenberg and her children arrived, coinciding with the news of the capture of Pretoria. Celebrations began with a firework display, during which some ratings firing rockets in a launch were hurt when one rocket backfired and set the launch alight. Several ratings jumped overboard and four men were burned and taken to the cottage hospital; the Princess visited them and presented the hospital with two photographs of the royal yacht. She also visited Brookhill and attended service at Kingswear church.

Left: W Martin, photographer extraordinaire, taking a self portrait in the garden of his home, Woodland Terrace, Kingswear.

W MARTIN/R HAWKE

Right: Tom Casey (doyen of the ferry men), daughter Kathleen and their dog in the garden of their home, Killarney, Wood Lane, Kingswear

P CASEY

Dartmouth received a major boost when the *Chronicle* announced that the national firm of Higgs & Hill Ltd of London had secured a contract to the value of £220,600 to build the Royal Naval College. In quick succession six steamships arrived with heavy plant and equipment, followed by numerous tradesmen and labourers, all seeking accommodation and bringing much-needed extra revenue to the town.

The Wilkins family at Brookhill gave Kingswear another new club in the square, the Cricket Institute, which within a few years suffered the same fate as previous clubs and closed through lack of support.

Regatta 1900 This year, for the first time, the initial day was called Town Day; it was marred by a lack of wind but racing continued with six sailing and six rowing races. The following day saw the handicap race over 30 miles for yachts, with a prize of £40, but the five starters were stopped after two of the three rounds, having taken two hours to sail only three-and-a-half miles. The magazine *The Field* stated that three large yachts refused to enter a race with such varying tonnage, from *Saionara* (a 12-ton yawl), to *Brynchild* (a 153-ton cutter). But it balanced out, for after a tedious day's drifting the handicap system worked well; *Saionara* won by

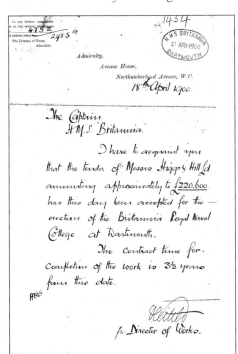

Left: After twenty-five years' deliberation and after considering thirty-two sites Dartmouth finally won the prize and the Admiralty awarded Higgs & Hill Ltd, London, the contract to build the Britannia Royal Naval College at Dartmouth. However it exceeded completion date by two years.

BAYARDS RESTAURANT

Right: Captain R H Cross RN of HMS Britannia *in his quarters. He believed he would command the new college but he was promoted to admiral and Captain Goodenough was appointed to implement an entirely new regime.*

G THOMAS

*William Casey on
float No.2 with
Derry's wagon and
driver. Aboard*
Blanche, *Casey's
first steam launch,
is launchman
Thomas Bingham
and his dog Spot
with boatman
William Tribble in
the stern.*

T CASEY/D GRAYHAM

only two-and-a-half minutes from *Caress* (78 tons), with *Brynchild* five minutes behind. In the harbour there were four sailing and six rowing races, which included a race for salmon fishermen with licensed River Dart boats. On the Saturday the Start Bay Yacht Club failed to enter a single event, blaming a depression in the yachting world. There was an amalgamation of events into seven races in which boats participated, including a randan race for coal lumpers and a shovel race. Outside the regatta, the newly formed Minima Club ran six races out on the Range.

In the autumn two well-known Dartmouth characters died. Thomas Binham, forty-four, a ferryman who had in 1867 become a launchman on Tom Avis's *Pioneer*, the first lower ferry steam launch. He joined the next ferry owners W & A Casey as launchman on their first steam launch *Blanche*, where with his dog Spot, he became a general favourite with all. It was a hard life, exposed to all weathers, and in one twelve-hour day the takings were just 3d (1½p). The other character was Sydney Hodges, a gifted portrait painter of celebrities and the nobility; he committed suicide in poverty in London and, like so many others, received recognition only after his death.

As the year closed the *Chronicle* commented on a debate in the council chamber about the demolition of the Manor House and lumpers' homes in Coles Court, and urged the building of some low-cost homes to rehouse them and local men, who would soon be returning from South Africa after the relief of Mafeking and capture of Pretoria. Two interesting remarks were reported: the first was by Dr Searle in the debate that 'men with long tongues, short memories and unbounding ambitions monopolized two-thirds of the council's time'. The second was by Lord Baden-Powell, hero of Mafeking, who, on returning home, was asked if he had any political ambitions and said that he had not but that he had joined the local Conservative club as they had an excellent first-class championship billiard table.

1901

saw the death in January of that exceptional lady Queen Victoria, and the nation and empire mourned the loss of their longest-reigning monarch. Nearer home Robert Cranford died: in 1854 he had been founding editor of *The Dartmouth Chronicle*, in effect almost Dartmouth's conscience, for he had loved the town, reporting affairs fully, fairly and without bias, and he had been a strong supporter of the Embankment scheme.

Fortunately the founder's high standards continued, for after the loss of the Belgian seagoing tug *Soudan* in Start Bay the newspaper berated Dartmouth for disposing of all its powerful tugs. She had signalled with flares and burning blue lights for assistance all night, but Dartmouth had only underpowered launches, the *Nimble, Water Lily,* and *Kingswear*. Captain Weatherdon in the pilot cutter *Gwendoline* finally rescued the men before *Soudan* sank, returning to Dartmouth towing the tug's two lifeboats crowded with survivors. Fortunately there was no loss of life in this case, though Dartmouth and Kingswear's close proximity to the river and the sea meant fatality was no stranger.

The great reaper with his scythe in the enclosed environment of the Dart gleaned a rich harvest of characters with tales to tell of experiences gathered across the seven seas. Captain William Henry Harrison Curtis, The Pines, Kingswear, who died in July, was such a man:

> He was born in Maine, 1841, and became a lieutenant in the US Navy in the American Civil War 1864-1865, and received an award for bravery in the Potomac River action. He then joined the English merchant service in command of the shipping firm Watts, Ward Steamship Co. He was later present at the bombardment of Alexandria embarking under fire British nationals for return to Britain where he married the eldest daughter of Tom Avis, Kingswear. Soon he was back in America in command of millionaire Trevor C Parkes SY Sultana then Col J J Astor's SY Nourmahal and was appointed chairman of the committee formed to entertain the British challengers for the America's Cup, Sir T Lipton and crews of Shamrock and Columbia.

The *Chronicle* also reported a near disaster which illustrated the need for vigilance at all times, even on a simple river crossing:

> The paddle steamer Totnes Castle standing in for Dolphin on crossing from Kingswear loaded with passengers caught the hawser holding the collier SS Celeste on No. 3 buoy. There was great consternation among all on board when the mast, funnel, ventilators and steering wheel were swept overboard and Captain Fleet on the bridge escaped death by a miracle, eventually bringing the vessel and passengers safely up on the Embankment.

Meanwhile the changing times were clearly reflected by the composition of the Harbour Commission. Since its formation in 1862 it had been the preserve of the landed gentry, mainly RDYC members, and usually chaired by the Seale family. The chairman was Andrew Hugh Bridson, one time RDYC member, whose father Henry had been an early Vice Commodore. But within two years the three main local captains of industry, employers in the coaling trade, became commission members. They were Thomas Wilton, Mayor and partner in Renwick & Wilton Co Ltd; Jasper Bartlett, owner and managing director of the Channel Coaling Co; and George Henry Collins, managing director of his own company.

Mr Collins, the last elected, promptly tried to rescind previously passed resolutions relating to the areas of the harbour allotted to hulks and the coaling trade, intent on securing increased working space and dredging. This infuriated the yachting fraternity, and Major Dean, RDYC member and Kingswear's representative, protested strongly and a period of verbal and written aggression commenced. During the next two months Mr Collins bombarded the *Chronicle* and had published in seventeen full-page columns, all in small print, copies of twenty-four letters to him, even those marked private and confidential. This bitter exchange resulted in a modest triumph for the commercial companies with some extension of the coaling line and area, but the yachting interests, whilst losing a little, had contained expansion to a small area. Little love remained between the contestants.

Regatta 1901 Edward VII, now King, agreed to continue as patron. The Dart Boat Sailing Club, formed in 1873, with Samuel Lake as captain, and the Minima Sailing Club, combined to form the Dart Sailing Club (DSC). The Dartmouth Rowing Club brought honour to the town by winning the handsome Orr Ewing Cup, worth 50 guineas for the third time: large crowds congregated at Kingswear station and carried the cup in triumph to Dartmouth. Regrettably, the Start Bay Yacht Club failed once again to arrange any races and the RDYC organized Friday and Saturday races, the new Dart Sailing Club also organized five races on the Saturday. The steam launch race of previous years was abandoned because a new by-law restricted speed to five knots. However, the turn-out of 164 craft was high, composed of 56 steam yachts, 10 schooners, 41 yawls and 57 cutters.

In Dartmouth the coastguard premises near Bayards Cove were replaced by nine new cottages and offices above Compass Cove. In December the DHNA board met to consider a scheme commissioned from their engineer Cuthbert A Brereton, son of their previous engineer R. P. Brereton, to dredge between the railway ferry and *Floating Bridge* a channel 600 feet wide to a depth of 25 feet at low-water spring tides. This would mean hulks could be moored and attendant vessels could swing the full width of the dredged channel. The project would cost £18,000, and it was passed to the Admiralty for approval and some financial support (the latter requirement always ensured oblivion).

1902 dawned with feverish preparations afoot for the visit of King Edward VII and Queen Alexandra. The story of the foundation stone laying ceremony of the college has been well documented, but many gems remain untold; the asides are often more interesting than the event.

Thomas Abrahams, stationmaster, and Harry Thorne, captain of the *Dolphin*, were suddenly thrust into the limelight. Harry Thorne promoted locally to 'Admiral Thorne', and the ageing *Dolphin*, thirty-two years old, was withdrawn from service for beauty treatment. The hull was repainted and a gold stripe added, while the funnel was painted bright red with a black top; decks were stripped and treated and the saloon transformed into a regal drawing-room with specialist furniture, later sold at Torquay for £100. The staff received new uniforms not to be worn until the special day. Kingswear station was decorated with numerous flags and bunting, and a red carpet laid down marking where everyone should stand, according to status. The royal train, the *Baden-Powell* (renamed *Britannia* for the occasion), arrived at 2.55pm, when Miss Popham, daughter of the RDYC secretary, handed the King a floral bouquet. Kingswear schoolchildren waited for the royal party in the station yard as five minutes were allowed for this part of the visit. Then the *Dolphin* was boarded and mate Harry Gurney unfurled the royal standard, a supreme accolade for the old boat. The royal party adjourned to the deck saloon, nicknamed locally the 'cucumber frame'. Captain Thorne was on the bridge and to use the *Chronicle*'s uncomplimentary phrase, 'the royal hulk cast off'. Contrary to oft-quoted statements the cockaded officer seen in official photographs on the bridge was Admiral Sir Frederick Collinson (no relation of mine) and not the King, who remained with the Queen in the saloon. They were received on Dartmouth pontoon by the Mayor, Corporation and Dart Harbour Commissioners and after a brief official welcome they mounted their own landaus and moved off for the Royal Naval College, arriving ten minutes later. Here the ceremony of laying the foundation stone and the casket promptly commenced. The casket was of solid silver, richly gilded and enamelled and medallioned on each side, one showing Kingswear Castle, the other Dartmouth Castle, and contained a handsome illuminated loyal address. The royal party then took the coach back to the pontoon, crossed over on the *Dolphin* and caught the train for London at 4.10pm.

The whole event lasted only one hour fifteen minutes, but was much enjoyed. However, it was the King's landaus that delighted the local population over the next two weeks. They had come by train from London to Churston station, then down Bridge Road to cross the *Floating Bridge* and on to Lady Freake's stables at Warfleet. From there the landaus were driven daily with seven horses, four coachmen and two mounted postillions.

Soon more mundane events prevailed. An auction of wines belonging to H C Collier, late landlord of the Royal Castle and Royal Dart Hotels, was held; it consisted of 137 bottles of vintage port dating from 1830 to 1896, the value of which would be incalculable today. Far from the realms of Bacchus the news came that a former curate of St Petrox (1830) had died as the eminent Dean of Sydney, Australia, at the age of ninety-two.

After ten years on Bayards Quay the Channel Coaling Co followed the earlier example of G H Collins & Co and moved to the South Embankment into brand-new offices constructed on part of the old Coles Court complex (now the Dartmouth Yacht Club). They were designed by S Parkes of Plymouth and the contractors were Anderson & Wills. The building was three storeys high with the

No. 3374, the royal train Baden Powell, *renamed* Britannia *for the occasion, decorated with the royal coat of arms and crown in Kingswear station and being admired by local residents.*

P RUDLING

The old Dolphin's *moment of glory, Dartmouth bound, flying the royal standard with the King and Queen as passengers in the embellished saloon, with Admiral Sir Frederick Collinson and Captain Thorne on the bridge in charge of pilotage.*

R TUCKER/DARTMOUTH MUSEUM

The old Dolphin's *deck saloon, nick-named the 'cucumber frame', was transformed for fifteen minutes' royal occupation with fine furniture which was sold two days later for over £100 in Torquay.*

R JONES

The stage is set in the specially erected pavilion for laying by crane of the Royal Naval College foundation stone and a silver casket by King Edward VII.
R TUCKER/DARTMOUTH MUSEUM

ground floor set above high-water level and a wide side passage alongside in Coles Court to facilitate the transport of gigs to a boat store behind. The ground floor consisted of a hallway, a 22-foot square directors' office, with a private 14-foot square office and toilets behind. The first floor had the secretary's office and boardroom overlooking the river and two smaller offices at the rear, while the second floor was used for storage. The façade was moulded limestone with ham stone dressings above with rubbed bricks, similar to the college. There were two big bay windows and a balcony.

THE MOROCCO LINE

Sir Dudley Forward, chairman of Forward Brothers Co trading as the Mersey Steamship Company, had been recently negotiating with the Harbour Commission and the GWR to make Dartmouth the station for a regular service by their liners, the SS *Morocco, Zweena, Telde* and *Oranago*, to Morocco and North Africa. Agreement was reached with the GWR for the provision at Hoodown Point, at Forwards' cost, of sidings, loading platform and coal shute to load barges with rail-freighted steam coal to bunker their ships; the costs were to be recovered by an agreed rebate on coals transported. In July the first liner SS *Zweena* arrived and anchored on the old Castle buoys in The Bight to bunker and collect mail and passengers. Later a 'recherché luncheon' was held aboard and Ernest Forward paid tribute to the Dartmouth workers; being unrestricted by rules and regulations like workers in London he was saving money, a voice was heard saying 'a little monarchy is Dartmouth'.

Regatta 1902 Hayne Smith resigned as secretary of the Start Bay Yacht Club which failed for the third year to organize any races, and this time RDYC did not take over. There were two full days' racing which included three interesting events, one for Blue Boats, another for twelve-oared cutters (naval ships in port) and one for college gigs. Entries came from HMS *Britannia* and *Racer*, the naval yard, the coastguard and the Artillery Volunteers. The Dart Sailing Club ran their races on the third day, but again there was no regatta ball. The illuminations provided by the gas company were exceptional, possibly because of future competition from the new Urban Electricity Company. Large crowds attended, with steamships from Bournemouth and Plymouth. However only 127 vessels attended this year, 37 fewer than the previous year.

A few weeks later, after sixty-six years of gaslight and two years' work by the new electricity company, Dartmouth was bathed in electric light, to the wonder and delight of the inhabitants. The newly opened naval hospital was the first to benefit, quickly followed by streets, shops and other properties.

In November the collier SS *Torquay* (Whiteway & Ball, Torquay) ran aground outside the RDYC while rounding Kittery Point and required three tugs, *Warrior*, *Northumberland* and the recently launched Philips' tug *Venture*, to free her on the next tide.

Finally Princess Beatrice and her entourage arrived by train to visit her two sons at the college. The Royal Dart Hotel was refurbished and commandeered by the royal party for a week, to the delight of Kingswear.

1903

Sport now played a prominent part in the area, particularly in Kingswear, where P A Wilkins, gold-bullion dealer and owner of Brookhill, generously provided the main ingredient, cash. The newly formed Kingswear Football Club held its first AGM, declaring a profit of one halfpenny. The Kingswear Cricket Club also received from its patron and president Mr Wilkins a brand-new spacious pavilion which served the club for many years, until its closure and removal to where it stands today, derelict, opposite The Quillet. The Cricket Institute, also provided and funded by Mr Wilkins in 1901, closed for lack of popular support. In October the philanthropic Mr Wilkins purchased the bulk of Gallants Bower from the Hugh Muir Estate (presumably this is the reason why it has remained undeveloped to this day and a place of beauty, for it did include ten building sites). Dartmouth owes much to Kingswear benefactors, for, some years later, the Rev P C Bayliss secured for Dartmouth the adjacent Dyer's Hill, and Sir Thomas Lennard bequeathed Rock Park Estate to the Dartmouth Corporation which included Sugary and Compass Coves, Dartmouth.

Mr Earnsby, manager of the new Forward line to Morocco, set up Kingswear's own co-operative society, with shares limited to two per family. Churston Golf Club clubhouse (designed by Sewell Appleton, son of the well-known Kingswear architect Edward Appleton) was opened, a long-awaited local facility.

Gas had been available in Dartmouth for sixty-six years, but although near its warmth and illumination had never crossed the river, as it was considered uneconomic to lay a gas main across the harbour and build a holder in Kingswear. But this year an electricity supply was laid from Sandquay, on cables wound around three large drums and mounted on special stands onto a lighter which was made fast to the side of the *Floating Bridge*; at low water it slowly traversed the river, unwinding and dropping the cable onto the river bed. The feeder cables were connected at each side and the supply laid along the railway line to Kingswear. At 5.30pm on 22 October after centuries of darkness, except for half-a-dozen oil streetlamps, came the brilliance of electricity. The supply was switched on and the inhabitants moved off to enjoy the sights, going first to the Beacon, then up the hill to the Redoubt, then back to Firmount at the head of Waterhead Creek, and finally back to the church, passing *en route* the mansions of the gentry, all gaily lit. A total of twelve street lamps were placed around the village, which no longer needed to cast covetous eyes on gaslit Dartmouth. Kingswear could not match her big sister when it came to liquid refreshment, however, for Dartmouth boasted twenty-six public houses for 6,062 population against Kingswear's three for 764 population, excluding the Rock Inn at Noss.

This year young Tom Casey, later doyen of the ferrymen, married Susie, daughter of Captain Oliver, Dublin. The river he served so well needed constant vigilance. In April when Casey was crossing in charge of the horse-boat, the ketch *Lord Napier* became difficult to handle on entering the harbour and collided with the horse-boat, her bowsprit cutting through the coverings of one of two 'Derry' wagons on board. Luckily the draymen were experienced and held hard onto the horses' heads, preventing them from taking fright and bolting overboard. With difficulty the ketch was disengaged, only to nearly collide with the *Floating Bridge*. She then ran aground near Noss, remaining stuck for several days.

After over twenty years' service as Dartmouth's town clerk, Osmonius Smart Bartlett was arrested for misappropriating funds. Mr Bartlett had been appointed in November 1883 after the cutting dismissal of Percy Hockin, an Embankment supporter, by the new Mayor Francis Charles Simpson and his vicious anti-Embankment committee. Mr Bartlett was sentenced to three years' hard labour, and, unlike today, it would have been hard. He was the first of several future official Dartmouth appointees to commit misdemeanours and fall foul of the law.

Then came the annual beating of the bounds of Dartmouth by the Corporation and townspeople. This involved parading to the four two-foot high bondstones. One was at Lady Freake's stables, Warfleet, one at the top of Vicarage Hill, one at Mount Boone, and one elsewhere. The procedure was that they would stand on top of the stones and quote: 'God bless the Mayor, and all the town, Give me a favour, and I'll jump down.' Then green rosettes were pinned on their chests.

The coaling trade continued unabated. Its three powerful leaders, G H Collins, J Bartlett and T Wilton were the main employers and the power base in the harbour, though Mr Wilton was concentrating on importing gas- and house-coals over the Kingswear quays and making urgent requests to the GWR for extra berths. Renwick & Wilton Co Ltd, (re-registered as Renwick, Wilton & Co Ltd), had been using chartered vessels to bring coals from the north-east ports for some years, the principal boats were the *Mezappa, Vanessa* and *Sabrina*, built by Fowlers & Co, Newcastle, for J Fenwick & Co, London. Sadly the *Sabrina*, built in 1865 (831GT, 211ft x 28ft x 17ft), after many years' service was to become a coal hulk in the harbour, replacing Channel Coaling Company's hulk *International*. The company made a policy change and in October purchased outright the *Vanessa*, having already bought the *Mezappa* in January, both built in 1872 (1164GT, 257ft x 30ft x 17ft).

The Morocco liners were now plying a regular service and, with the passengers and coaling, were to bring much-needed extra revenue into the town. However, Dartmouth became the final port of destination for two passengers from the SS *Zweena*. With thirty-two other passengers allowed shore leave for the coaling period, two chose to finish their game of billiards in the Royal Castle Hotel in spite of the steamer whistling, a seaman ashore trying to locate them and the landlord warning them 'your ship is calling'. On finishing their game they found their luggage neatly stacked on the Embankment.

In March an anchored French trawler broke adrift in the harbour during a savage storm, colliding with and damaging first the schooner *Ella*, then Sir George Jackson's salvage steamer *Zeppa* and hopper, and finally with Mrs Henn's America's Cup challenge boat *Galatea*, on which she had resided for many years. Some details of this remarkable lady were outlined in a later edition of the *Chronicle*:

> *Mrs Henn married in 1877 Lieut Henn RN of County Clare, and bought the 80 ton yawl* Gertrude, *in which she made her home, cruising in the Mediterranean. On the death of her brother she became the owner of the* Celia, *and in 1884 decided to build the* Galatea, *especially to challenge for the America's Cup. The* Galatea, *a steel cutter of 90 tons, was intended to go over to America with the* Genesta *in 1885 so as to be ready if that boat failed to race. Unfortunately, owing to defective ballasting of the* Galatea, *she was not able to leave, so did not meet the boat she was intended to race, and which easily defeated the* Genesta. *Instead she sailed against the* Mayflower, *which was one of a set of racing machines chosen to defend the following year, and which beat the* Galatea. *While the* Galatea, *having to cross the Atlantic under her own sail, was a stout, heavily built boat, the* Mayflower, *owned by General C J Paine, was a light-draft boat, with extreme beam and centreboard. As the* Galatea *in every case beat the conqueror of the* Genesta *in club racing, Mrs Henn*

Left: *The 1885 America's Cup challenger* Galatea *preparing to set bowspirit spinnaker before rounding the Sandy Hook lightship, USA.*
YACHTING WORLD

Right: *Lt W Henn, RN, owner of Paradise Hill, Shannon. In 1860 he was a cadet aboard the training ship* Trafalgar. *Then he served aboard the frigate* Galatea, *in 1872 he was appointed second in command of the search for Dr Livingstone. He retired from the navy in 1874 and acquired many yachts and in 1884 he commissioned Mr Beaver Webb to design the 90 ton cutter* Galatea *in which he crossed the Atlantic with his wife, a keen yachtswoman, who became the first lady to cross to America in a racing yacht.*
YACHTING WORLD

always thought that but for the delay they would have brought the cup to England ...Mrs Henn was a stamp collector for a lifetime, her collection being priceless. She was also the possessor of a fine collection of silver, which included four large replicas of the Warwick Vase. On board the yacht also she had two miniatures of the America's Cup, both exact reproductions of the famous trophy, and standing only two inches high.

After this accident Mrs Henn moved *Galatea* from Dartmouth to moor up in Plymouth. Coincidentally in the same year, Sir Thomas Lipton's yacht *Shamrock III* was attempting to regain the America's Cup, pitted this time against the American yacht *Reliance*. There was great interest in this event in Dartmouth and the *Chronicle* reported a system of signalling devised to inform the general public of the results. Coloured lights were hoisted onto the borough flagstaff as follows: 'green: *Shamrock*, red: *Reliance*; green over red: *Shamrock* leads, or vice versa: *Reliance* leads. Winner hoisted to the top of the flagstaff. White light: race off or unable to finish.' Sadly the *Shamrock* green failed to predominate even once.

Regatta 1903 occurred at the same time and was poorly supported due to bad weather and the fact that some owners were in America supporting the British entry. Again the Start Bay Yacht Club failed to participate. In its place the Town Committee arranged four sailing races for very modest prize money while the RDYC ran four races, yachts exceeding 48 tons TM having a £50 prize, yachts not exceeding 52ft LR a £20 prize, South Coast One Designs a £10 prize. The Western One Design race for the Commodore's Cup over 10 miles was won by Thomas Wilton in *Naiua*. The Dart Sailing Club covered the Saturday with six assorted races.

In December the Dartmouth & Torbay Steam Packet Company was renamed the River Dart Steamboat Company; the GWR in 1901 had refused to renew the 1877 lease to manage the *Dolphin*.

Finally the *Chronicle* reported the death of a man who could fairly claim to have done more for Dartmouth than any other, the Right Honourable Charles Seale Hayne, MP, initiator of the river steamboats, the railway company, the Harbour Commission, the Embankment and much more. He died a bachelor, leaving a large estate and great wealth, £150,000 of which he bequeathed to build the Seale Hayne Agricultural College at Newton Abbot. For a lifelong churchman his will contained a most unusual anticlerical clause: 'The testator specially desired that no part of his legacy should be used for the building or endowment of any consecrated church or chapel or for the payment of any chaplain or minister, and that no clergyman, priest or minister of any denomination whatever should hold any post or office in the said college.' It seems that there must have been a fracture in his relationship with the church at some stage.

1904 The first issue of the *Chronicle* reported two matters relating to the busy harbour. The first was the Customs return for the previous year, which showed 594 steamers had bunkered, taking 66,917 tons against 585 steamers taking 70,155 tons in 1902, an increase of nine vessels coaling but a shortfall of 3,238 tons, 269 tons a month. The editorial stated that the Harbour Commission should take heed if it was to retain its position as the best bunkering port in the English Channel, by deepening the water in the standing hulk line to allow ships of larger draft to come alongside at all states of the tide. This was never achieved as there were insufficient funds due to legal costs incurred in the totally unnecessary anti-Embankment opposition.

The second event was a Christmas tale that illustrates the dangers posed by even a simple river crossing:

> *The ageing* Dolphin *on Christmas Eve loaded with passengers for the Paddington train had just left Dartmouth pontoon and taking a wide sweep on a strong tide noticed the collier* Vanessa *bearing down on a similar course. As the distance closed, alarm began among the passengers who prepared to jump overboard while the master of the collier, realizing the* Dolphin *had little steerage screamed through his loud hailer to the* Dolphin *to make full speed ahead which with the kick of the tide straightened her up and the two vessels passed within inches of each other as women fainted and people on Bayards Cove hearing the pitiful cries made to launch boats, but a major disaster was just averted.*

A melancholy incident occurred in Kingswear when Mr Keely, the cemetery caretaker, depressed by his duties, was found by his wife hanging from the roof of the mortuary, where he normally attended to other unfortunates.

The anticipated confirmation arrived and announced the closure of the Start Bay Yacht Club, created in 1889. Headquarters had been established in Edward Marsh Turner's new offices (now Somerfields), then moved in 1894 to palatial quarters in York House (now Forbuoys); in 1897 they had 113 members and 43 yachts totalling 4,241 tons and organized races for large yachts on the third regatta day. For the last three years they had failed to do so; after thirteen years they gave away the regalia, hauled down their flag and auctioned off their effects.

In March the lifelong friend and business associate of Charles Seale Hayne, William Smith, solicitor, died. He was a man of high calibre, a large and wealthy property owner. A founder member of the Dart Yacht Club, he took on the onerous duty of secretary, a post he had also held in the Harbour Commission. His skills had been invaluable in achieving the construction of the Embankment. He was also responsible for eventually healing the acrimonious dispute between the town council and the Harbour Commission, and he was later appointed Mayor, instigating the Dartmouth regalia and much-admired mayoral chain. He was chairman of and major shareholder in the River Dart Steamboat Company, and had three sons, one called Hayne Smith (named after his friend) who continued as secretary to the Harbour Commission.

In spring the whole estate of the late Charles Seale Hayne MP was offered for sale at the Castle Hotel, Dartmouth. It comprised 853 acres which included Kingswear Castle, Glenorley (Kingswear Court), Kingscliffe (White House), Coombeside (Pinewoods), Warren Cottage and rabbit warren, Brownstone Farm, Higher Fugue, all his London properties and some property and coalyards on the Embankment. Adjacent to the Channel Coaling Company's brand-new offices more dilapidated corporation properties in Coles Court were being demolished at last.

Three months later the RDYC mourned the death of the Lancastrian Thomas Ridgeway Bridson, for many years Vice Commodore. He was an extremely wealthy man who lived on the headland adjacent to the Imperial Hotel at Rock End, Torquay, (later the setting for a story by Agatha Christie, *Peril at End House*). His brother, the late Henry Bridson, had been Vice Commodore in 1875, living at Derwent Lodge and Warfleet House, and was also the first Vice President of the Royal Yachting Association. Henry Bridson died in Madeira in 1879 and his brother Major Bridson who in 1880 gave two beautiful brass cannons to the RDYC to commemorate his death.

Mrs Betts, The Grange, Kingswear, and two daughters mounting a wickerwork two-seater conversation pannier for a two mile donkey-trip to the village for provisions.

W Martin/R Hawke

Thrussell the village store in The Square, Kingswear, which from this picture seems to sell only Fry's, Cadbury's, and, regular regatta contender, Sir Thomas Lipton's tea, coffee, cocoa, and chocolate.

W Martin/J Diss

Regatta 1904 The Town Committee arranged five sailing and seven rowing races, the RDYC only two, a handicap race for 50 tons and over with five starters, the £50 was won by *Rosamund* (63 tons). *White Heather* (143 tons) was first home but could not beat the handicap having to allow thirty minutes. The second race was for yachts not exceeding 52ft, and there were four starters, the £20 being won by *Maymon*. Again there was no regatta ball, and the illuminations were powered by electricity. Yachts attending numbered 121: 39 steam yachts, 7 schooners, 37 yawls and 36 cutters. Attendance was below average everywhere. This regatta was missed by Mrs Henn, the owner of *Galatea*, for the first time in twelve years.

USS Cleveland *built in 1901, on a courtesy visit 22 October 1904. She carried ten 5in guns, eight six-pounders, 350 officers and men. The foremast is embellished with the crew's washing, and Mr Uran, Kingswear lighthouse-keeper attends to the lantern (once housed in Dartmouth Castle turret) on the* Eclair *pier.*

W MARTIN/R HAWKE,

On the river the new *Kingswear Castle* arrived to join the Totnes' boats, while Renwick, Wilton & Co Ltd took delivery from Philips of a new tug *Victor* (45ft x 10ft x 5ft 6in). The star attraction was the arrival from America of the cruiser USS *Cleveland* at the invitation of the Harbour Commissioners. Moored opposite the Boat Float, she was much admired by the locals.

At the adjacent Bayards Cove Seamen's Mission, established in 1883, an auction was held for funds for the Dartmouth & Kingswear Cottage Hospital. On offer was an unusual work of art, an autographed quilt with the signatures of Princess Beatrice, titled people, gentry and townspeople in 464 silk squares surrounding a centrepiece of the Dartmouth coat of arms. It was sold for 11¹/₂ guineas to Mrs A Betts, The Grange, Kingswear, wife of W S Betts, ex-chief manager of the South Indian Railways.

1905 At last, after seven years' construction, the magnificent Royal Naval College was completed, but there were mixed feelings in Dartmouth. There was justifiable pride in the fine building and in the fact that Dartmouth had been chosen as its site, but during those seven years hundreds of labourers, tradesmen and others associated in its construction had lodged in the town and spent their money, whereas the cadets would be housed and victualled in the college itself, thus terminating the welcome extra source of revenue.

One bonus was an illuminated clock located 120 feet up in the centre tower, which would be visible over the harbour and would be the only public clock in the world to strike with ship's bells. The clock could be heard a mile away and soon became the object of strident complaint, necessitating toning it down to an acceptable level.

Meanwhile cadets completed their last term aboard the *Britannia*. A special parade was held to mark the occasion, and with bands playing, the cadets marched away to entrain at Kingswear. They fitted a special paying-off pennant on to the engine which stretched the full length of the train.

The 1904 Topaz class cruiser HMS *Sapphire* (360ft x 40ft) arrived with a torpedo flotilla and moored in the harbour. The old two-rater *Hindustan* with gunports sealed was towed away after forty-two years in the service of the college. Her mooring was taken by the newly built but already obsolete HMS *Espiegle*, a 1,070 ton Cadmin class small-masted light cruiser (185ft x 33ft), for cadet training.

The college opened in September with 100 cadets, yet there was no opening ceremony. There was some surprise on hearing that cadets were to be taught dancing for twenty minutes each day and forty minutes on Sunday, and the town jokers soon began to speculate that future officers might also have to pass a board of dancing masters. At the same time the radical Keir Hardy raised a question in Parliament objecting to the use of public funds on the Britannia beagle pack.

Meanwhile the coaling returns for 1904 showed a further decline in bunker coals: 530 vessels bunkered taking 58,411 tons, against 585 vessels taking 66,917 tons in 1903. The Forward liners alone accounted for 20,000 tons per annum and a policy change was instituted, abandoning bunkering with rail freighted coals, shute loading into barges from their sidings at Hoodown Point, and substituting loading the liners in The Bight direct from colliers. The lumpers and their families were experiencing lean times and an article published in the *Chronicle* highlighted their precarious livelihood:

> *A stranger was standing on Bayards Cove when suddenly a number of lumpers idling about close by sprang into movement. The men rushed towards a ladder at the lower end of the quay. The first to reach it swung one leg quickly over the uprights and cried 'one', the man at his heels did the same and shouted 'two', and the third and the fourth and the fifth and the sixth and still the game went on, and then the men returned to their places. It is this way: the look-out on Compass Hill (two miles from the town) had spied a steamer heading for the harbour, presumably to take bunker coal, and his arrival at speed at Bayards Cove was a signal. Gangs of lumpers are required to bunker steamers in proportion to the quantity of coal required. One, two or three gangs may be needed, and precedence is taken in strict order, and that order is determined by the rush for the ladder which is regarded as equivalent to getting into a boat. It is ever so much safer than a general scramble down the ladder in order to get first afloat would be. 'Ladder legging' is quite a normal occurrence at Bayards Cove now. Other lumpers on the North Embankment would rush for their boats when they saw the butcher's boat leave the quay. He had been alerted by the ladder legging and wanted to the first to reach the steamer.*

The executive staff of the Urban Electric Supply Co. Ltd, fronted by the general manager, Mr G F Smith. They are holding in the Guildhall, an exhibiton of electric lighting, (the wonder of the time). The proceeds to go to the hospital. Mr Smith was married to Mary Knowling Lake, daughter of Dartmouth entrepreneur Samuel Lake.

MRS B GOATHAM, HAROLD HUTCHINGS

SS Morocco *in harbour 8 April 1905, being coaled from barges chute-loaded at the depot at Hoodown Point, Kingswear, prior to her departure for North African ports.*

W MARTIN/R HAWKE

The declining number of steamers calling also reduced the income of the pilots; the cutter *Gwendoline* was sold to Falmouth pilots and the pilotage system was restructured to reduce costs: 'In future only one pilot boat the *Rose* would remain on sea station, relief would be at sea and a new all weather relief boat provided, and there would be only two extra men instead of the present four to work the cutter which must never return to harbour except for stress of weather.'

Friction arose in the summer when the pilots tried to stipulate that visiting yachtsmen could only enter port with the services of a pilot. The situation became so tense that town tradesmen, fearing loss of revenue, petitioned Trinity House, who advised that the practice was 'not recommended'.

However, further business was secured when Renwick, Wilton & Co Ltd negotiated for Dartmouth to become a fortnightly port of call for Langland & Sons (Liverpool) Princess line of eight steamers on a 1,700-mile round Britain tour.

The Dartmouth & Kingswear Steam Laundry, who had recently announced that they would only accept the BRNC laundry, grandly stated that during August they would accept washing from visiting yachtsmen. As these facilities were not available in Dartmouth, a new company, the Dartmouth Sanitary Steam Laundry opened with premises in Victoria Street (the name board is now displayed in the forecourt of the Alf Resco café in Lower Street).

This year the RDYC's founder Henry Studdy JP, retired. He had been Commodore for thirty-nine years since the formation of the club in 1866 and was replaced by the Duke of Somerset, who retained the post until 1920.

24 June 1905. A fine photo showing Ophir *No. 3408, at Kingswear station, the spare horse-float and three of J J Tolman's paddle-steamers and RW&Co Ltd's tug* Nimble *moored adjacent to their Hoodown workshop.*
W MARTIN/T CASEY

Rare photograph of GWR senior staff (one using the newly arrived telephone system) standing in front of a grounded South Devon Railway coach (ex-broad gauge).
P RUDLING

Regatta 1905 This year had a new regatta steward, RDYC member Sir Dudley Forward, chairman of the Forward Line, who presented several handsome prizes, including those for the randan lumpers' races. A full programme was organized and raced in brilliant sunshine. There were thirty-five sailing and rowing events, water polo and swimming in the Boat Float, three alfresco dances and two nights of fireworks. The number of participating vessels dropped to eighty-four and F C Simpson, chairman of the Noss Engineering Co, won two of the three races for Western One Design boats in his yacht *Fifine*.

The council appointed a new town crier and made it contractual that he should wear a uniform, as the previous one had refused.

In Kingswear a near disaster was averted when a train driver noticed flames coming from under the timber structure of the Higher Noss viaduct. He stopped the train and the whole of Simpson, Strickland & Co's workforce formed a chain with buckets of water from the river and from the engine tender, with which they doused the flames. The GWR later sent a sum of money to be distributed among the men for their share in saving the viaduct from destruction.

Finally there was some succour for the lumpers and coaling trade when the Channel Coaling Co secured a contract to bunker the Eastern Asiatic Co steamers working St Petersburg/Vladivostok. The first, SS *Arconia,* was coincidentally the ex-

1905, SS Princess Beatrice *982GT built in 1893 by Langland & Sons, Glasgow, one of eight ships:* Princess Maud *1466GT,* Victoria *1249GT,* Louise *952GT,* Olga *950GT,* Irene *765GT,* Ena *636GT, and* Alberta *being built. The photo shows Coles Court (partly demolished for Renwick Wilton & Co's new offices and a new road), the old Newman Building, G H Collins & Co coaling agent (now DHNA), Channel Coaling Co (now DYC), and Pomeroy Cross's coaling offices the old Ludwell House and yard.*

CYRIL KING

Donolly Castle, the former Donald Currie line ship which traded Dartmouth/Cape Colonies from 1872 to 1891. She bunkered 1,200 tons and took on board 1,000 iron bedsteads from Birmingham for Russia, and repatriated Japanese prisoners of war from Nogi to Odessa. Then before Christmas the SS *Malaya* (1,500 tons), with more bedsteads, and the SS *Kita* (1,400 tons), were bunkered.

1906 The annual Customs returns made unpalatable reading for the coaling trade: the figures showed an alarming decrease in steamers calling to bunker, only 371 against 530 the previous year, and a shortfall in coals of 12,547 tons. This resulted in considerable hardship for the lumpers and their families and concern in the coaling offices.

In Dartmouth St Saviours' 1707 chime-only turret clock was replaced by J Derby with a new chiming four-dial tower clock officially started by Miss Tracy. This fulfilled a long-felt need, for since 1860 the only visible clock in the area had been that of Kingswear church, until the addition in 1905 of the college clock.

For some years the condition of the port's floating contagious disease hospital ship *Mayfly* had been deteriorating, and the Port Sanitary Authority decided to try and buy *Britannia's* surplus tender - formerly Lord Delaware's yacht *Wave* - as a replacement. This proved expensive and the tender was sold to Anglesey for £925 with a contract clause that she should eventually be broken up in this country and the machinery mutilated beyond repair. So the Plymouth Maritime Inspector agreed that *Mayfly* should be beached and the interior lined with concrete, which was carried out for £39 by Simpson, Strickland & Co.

In early January the Torbay & Dart Paint Co Ltd on the Embankment at Coombe caught fire. It was erected in 1874 by George Parker Bidder, Sir George Elliot, and Samuel Lake. Paint had not been manufactured there for some years, and it was used as a levigating works for crushed powder for the main works at Brixham. The fire was eventually extinguished using Dartmouth's 1734 second-hand fire-engine (purchased in 1872) and assisted by Avis & Owen's water boat *Water Lily*. The severity of the fire and inadequacy of the equipment so alarmed the town council that they placed the old hand-pump fire engine up for sale. There were no buyers, so it was (as today) housed in an ante-room in St Saviours church, and a new horse-drawn steam fire engine was purchased from London for £330, capable of pumping 200 to 300 gallons a minute to a height of 156 feet.

In the same month another Dartmouth personality died, Percy Hockin, who, among many achievements and at the cost of losing his position as town clerk, played a major part in ensuring the construction of the jewel in Dartmouth's

These two pre-Embankment water-colours show Coles Court before its demolition to construct the new Coles Court road. **Left:** *The end property of Dartmouth's Lower Ferry Slip, and Hutchings the sailmakers.*
DARTMOUTH MUSEUM
Right: *The arched entrance to Coles Court from Lower Street.*
DARTMOUTH MUSEUM

crown, the South Embankment. Three months after his death an event occurred which would have given him great satisfaction: the town council appointed a committee of three to consider extending the Embankment as far as Sandquay, but it was another twenty-four years before this happened.

The *Chronicle* reported that a vacancy had occurred for the DHC Kingswear representative and the usual curious election procedure was held in the Royal Dart Hotel. Voters could only take part if the rateable value on their property was above £20: those up to £50 got one vote, between £50 and £100 two votes, £100 to £150 three votes, £150 to £200 four votes, £200 to £250 five votes, those exceeding £250 six votes. During the last two elections only two people had attended, making the whole procedure an expensive farce.

Another unusual event occurred at Philips' yard at Sandquay, where Philips completed the first of three tugs for Brazil, the *Viking*. She was modelled on their own tug *Venture* and built in teak (48ft x 12ft x 6ft 3in), and although possessing powerful engines the propeller was lashed on the deck, her boilers were filled with drinking water and she was rigged as a small schooner. Thus she safely sailed over 6,000 miles to Brazil with a Salcombe captain and five local men who returned in a Royal Mail steamer.

On 30 May the former Dartmouth & Torbay Steam Packet Co became officially incorporated as the River Dart Steamboat Co, with John Jago Tolman, William Ball and George Cliff as directors; and transferred all their assets, property and vessels, *Berry Castle* (1880), *Dartmouth Castle* (1885), *Totnes Castle* (1894) and *Kingswear Castle* (1905).

Dartmouth reacted with shock when another corporation official Mr Smith, the borough surveyor, accused of account irregularities, took his life with a shotgun in his office in Duke Street.

The yachting scene was marred by an incident in May involving the steam yacht *Evona* belonging to Henry J Mason, Rear Commodore, RDYC. A collier had been moored on an adjacent berth, as all other buoys were occupied, and it began

Left: *Dartmouth's first fire-engine, dated 1734, built by the inventor Richard Newsham, London, and purchased second-hand in 1872 for £55, gave the town good service for 34 years.*
R TUCKER/DARTMOUTH MUSEUM

Right: *Dartmouth's second fire-engine purchased for £330 from Shand, Mason & Co, London, after the 1906 Torbay & Dart Paint Co Ltd disastrous fire.*
R TUCKER/DARTMOUTH MUSEUM

unloading coal into barges 30 feet below deck. The fine coal-dust enveloped the freshly painted *Evona* and other yachts, resulting in the Dart Harbour Commission allocating specific dates and buoys for the discharge of colliers.

Regatta 1906 This year was sparsely attended with only seventy-four craft: the large yachts' race had only two participants and was abandoned due to a flat calm, while there were no entries for yachts exceeding 52ft LR or the 25 to 50 ton class.

In the weeks after regatta, there was considerable local interest in experiments carried out by C J Heinke & Co, manufacturers of submarine outfits. Philips took a party composed of the manager, assistant and two divers in their tug Venture to a spot two miles out, where divers G Baldwin and W May (the latter holder of the world's deepest dive record in recovering £9,000 frm the wreck SS *Catterthum*) went down 16 fathoms and carried out successful twenty-minute telephone conversations with those on the deck of the tug.

Finally, the 260-year-old Castle Point Battery received two 6-inch breech-loading quick-firing guns, replacing the two remaining obsolete forty-six-year-old muzzle-loading guns.

DARTMOUTH CASTLE BATTERY

Dartmouth Castle (1481), Kingswear Castle (1491) with its secondary defences, Godmerock Castle and the Redoubt, and Bayards Cove Castle, Paradise Tower and Gallants Bower Redoubt in Dartmouth were all built as harbour fortifications, with ordnance as their main feature. In the sixteenth century a seaward earthwork 'Lambert's bulwark' was formed at Dartmouth Castle and in the following century rebuilt in stone; it was then extended in 1747 to accommodate a second storey, making it a twelve-gun battery. There was a small regular garrison and from 1837 Sgt Major Furness also maintained the harbour light, a large oil lantern placed in the small castle turret. The local MP made a £20 annual payment for this service. When payments ceased the port was left, incredibly, without a harbour light until late 1856 when the adjacent lighthouse was erected. In 1856 Charles Seale Hayne, restored the ruined Kingswear Castle as a summer residence, while Paradise Tower was demolished during the building of Ravensbury mansion. Bayards Cove Castle was used as a store and Godmerock Castle (subject of a romantic story *The Grave of the Unknown* by Governor Holdsworth) and the two Redoubts were abandoned and reverted to nature.

After the Crimean campaign (1853-1856),warfare underwent dramatic changes mainly due to the evolution of the metal fighting ship and improved armaments. In

This rare photo of Castle Point Battery shows the officer, NCOs, men of the garrison and a rifled muzzle-loading gun on its traversing-carriage with shot, powder and ramrods.

R TUCKER/DARTMOUTH MUSEUM

Dartmouth Castle when used as garrison quarters. The exterior was slate-hung, the fireplaces, chimneys (using bricks from Sandquay brickworks, 1870-1871, stamped 'Armeson') and sanitary services were added. Also shown is the lighthouse turret and window, since sealed; for centuries this was the Port's leading light until 1856 when the adjacent lighthouse was built.

A C CARPENTER

1859 an altercation with France, and the fact that the French were building a powerful armoured battleship the *Gloire*, caused Lord Palmerston's government to counter with HMS *Warrior*, the world's most powerful warship, and ordered a revamp of coastal defences and the formation of local volunteer units (in Dartmouth this was the 6th Devon Artillery Volunteers). In 1860-61 the *Chronicle* reported that Dartmouth Castle's old bulwark at St Georges Green was to be demolished and Harvey, a contractor from Plymouth, was to build a new battery, a two-storeyed structure of granite, the lower casemented and bombproof with three 68-pounders and a 10-inch howitzer at the angle facing the sea. The upper battery was to be open with two 10-inch guns on traversing platforms with a guardroom communicating with the magazine and battery below by a spiral stone staircase.

In 1871 the castle was upgraded to improve the garrison quarters and the exterior slate hung for weatherproofing; more fireplaces and chimneys were added and sanitary facilities improved. At some period the 2nd Devon Volunteers, Royal Garrison Artillery was formed and in 1903 the regular unit was withdrawn along with three of the five remaining obsolete guns. The auxiliaries took over the two remaining guns for drill practice only and not for firing; then, as mentioned, they were replaced by the two modern 6-inch breech-loading guns.

1907 As the new year opened, the old Marine Tavern (now Hope Cottage) on the Lower Ferry Slip closed. For centuries business had been transacted behind its walls, on which still remains the figure of Fortuna, Roman goddess of good luck and fortune. Sometimes Fortuna stood on a ball or a globe, while a wheel represented the shifting of favours, or a rudder symbolised the guidance of world affairs. Fortuna carried a cornucopia from which she distributed good luck and sometimes she was blindfolded or veiled. 'Fortuna Virginensis' protected newly married women; while 'Fortuna Virile' preserved their beauty. Fortunately the Marine Tavern reopened higher up the Lower Ferry Slip on the corner of Lower Street.

The Customs returns gave welcome news of an increase in steamers calling to bunker, 527 vessels taking 61,313 tons of coal as against 371 vessels and 45,864 tons the previous year.

Adverts were placed for tenders for the Royal Navy's most bizarre vessel, a floating bathing tray, as follows:

Prestigious premises were a prerequisite for the principal participants in the coaling trade, and these new shipping offices designed for Renwick Wilton & Co, South Embankment, met this requirement. (now 'Room with a View' *restaurant.)*
DAVID BURNHAM

Tenders are invited for BATHING-TRAY, built of fir, and housed in. Dimensions: 44ft 6in by 8ft 3in; depth 7ft. A deck 2in thick and 4ft wide is fitted round the bath. A deck-house of fir is carried round the whole on an angle frame, and contains swinging glazed sashes. The whole structure supported on 6 rectangular air-boxes. Also an open BATHING-TRAY, 50ft 6in by 14ft. Depth 6ft 3in. Fir platform 3in thick and 3ft wide around the bath. Fittings included: 4 ladders, 6 air-boxes, 12 iron stanchions and wire jackstay.

Tenders were also invited for a new and commodious post office to be built on the South Embankment adjacent to Embankment House (now Fulfords, estate agents) to the design of E H Back. It was to replace the old post office established in 1889 in the (then newly built) Raleigh Hotel.

Renwick, Wilton & Co Ltd then vacated its rented upper-floor offices in the late William Smith's Embankment House and, like the other two coaling companies, moved into prestigious new premises built on the Embankment. Their new offices were on a corner site, part of the demolished old Coles Court, and almost next to the Channel Coaling Company's 1902 offices. The move received general acclaim, for after twenty years a new short road could be cut behind the Lower Ferry Slip and Sunderland Terrace, linking the Embankment with Lower Street.

DEVIOUS DEALINGS IN DARTMOUTH

This time, surprisingly, problems arose not between the coaling and yachting concerns, but between the coaling companies themselves.

There was friction when Forwards again decided to change the method of coaling their liners. Firstly they coaled with barges from a special railhead GWR jetty at Hoodown, then they changed to coaling direct from colliers, now they requested permission from the DHC to moor a 1,500 to 2,000-ton coaling hulk on the river, accompanied by a thinly veiled threat that without permission they would withdraw their liners from the port. This caused consternation, for a hulk of this proposed size could service their liners *and* have sufficient spare capacity to compete in bunkering other calling steamships. Their request was strongly resisted by the existing companies, particularly by Mr Bartlett, managing director of the Channel Coaling Co, who formerly had not been particularly partial to the yachting circle. Now he became surprisingly supportive of the yachting community, strongly protesting about how it would find the proposal unacceptable. However, the result was a foregone conclusion and reluctant permission was given for a hulk to occupy the station previously occupied by Renwick, Wilton & Co Ltd's hulk *Narwhal*, which had been withdrawn as the company's business was concentrated over the Kingswear quays.

By November the obvious had happened: a notice appeared that a new coaling company had been formed by Forwards, the Dartmouth Coaling Co Ltd with a share capital of £50,000. The barque *Stratford* arrived, her gear was stripped out and offered for auction on the New Ground, she was placed on station and business commenced.

Regatta 1907 Infighting on the harbour front by some of the top people did not deflate preparations, and a full programme was arranged. There were three special races for launches, while the Dart Sailing Club ran a handicap race to Torcross and back; in total twenty-five different launches participated. The racing on the Saturday by the regatta committee was over the old Start Bay Yacht Club course, Range/Torcross/Skerries/Range two rounds, 20 miles in total. In the Dart Sailing Club handicap races for cruisers 4 to 10 tons F L Carslake's *Ranee* won as usual. The result was so regular that it was surprising the *Ranee* had any contestants.

Just prior to regatta the old 1885 *Dartmouth Castle* river steamboat was sold away to Myrtle Grove, Ireland, but, there was a Dartmouth connection even in Ireland, for the quay by the church was given to Sir Walter Raleigh in 1579 for suppressing a local rebellion. Reputedly it was where he planted the first Virginia potatoes, and there are claims that he smoked the first pipe of tobacco there - although this is also claimed

by Greenway, Iron Acton and others. The new *Dartmouth Castle*, 71 tons, was built by Cox in Falmouth, and she was well patronized for the rest of the season. She was 100ft x 14ft x 6ft, 120hp, with cockpits fore and aft with spiral teak stairways, brass handrails to the upper deck and bars in the fore cabin.

The year closed with the death of Nathaniel Baker of Butts Hill, Kingswear, barrister to the GWR and local benefactor. The town council and George Philip made moves to acquire the Coombe Mud from the Raleigh Estates. Wild schemes were mooted to fill in the Boat Float and create another Boat Float there, or to build three docks and quays. These were forerunners of many schemes, but it was twenty-three years before any real progress was made.

1908
The appalling weather of the previous few weeks continued with many vessels sheltering in Dartmouth harbour and over 240 fishing trawlers in Brixham harbour. Renwick, Wilton & Co Ltd's collier SS *Vanessa* arrived from Shields damaged by hurricane-force winds, a carpenter was washed overboard (then fortunately back again), while another crew member was injured against the bulwarks, and one thrown over the wheel by a jerk of the rudder; Captain Smith said the vessel was in imminent danger of sinking.

Their collier *Mezappa*, returning to Dartmouth ran ashore at Flamborough Head and became a total wreck, but there was no loss of life. A few months later R D Renwick, the principal partner, retired and sold the controlling interest to Mr Wilton, who promptly ordered a replacement boat from Wood Skinner & Co Tyneside, their first purpose-built collier, the SS *Kingswear* (1457GT, 245ft x 36ft x 17ft). Mr Renwick, founder, had concentrated on the larger and more profitable Torquay branch, but his departure ensured the advancement of the capable local manager, Frank Dobson, first to a directorship and later in 1932 to a partnership.

The Customs returns for 1907 brought relief in the coaling offices, showing 657 visiting vessels and a further increase in bunkering figures: 1905: 45,837 tons, 1906: 61,313 tons, 1907: 71,873 tons, an increase of more than 10,000 tons over the previous year and a massive 26,136 over the year before that.

A *Chronicle* obituary announced the death of another stalwart of Dartmouth, Captain Henry Thorne, for forty years he had been captain of the railway ferry *Dolphin*. He was

20 May 1908. This photo was taken two hours after the arrival from Cox & Sons, Falmouth, of the brand new railway ferry The Mew, *90ft x 23ft x 9ft, twin-screw, 10 knots, costing £5,100 and capable of carrying 547 passengers.*

W MARTIN/JUDY DISS

121

*8 April 1908.
Special train No.
2173 chartered by
the Swedish
government arriving
from London, with
the exhumed body
of the Swedish
philosopher
Emanuel
Swedenborg (died
1772) being received
by a guard of
honour prior to
transportation to
Sweden for reburial
and belated honours
(136 years overdue).*

W Martin/Judy Diss

known to thousands of passengers and nicknamed 'the Admiral' after conveying King Edward VII and Queen Alexandra across the Dart in 1902. He had come to Dartmouth in 1864 as a steersman on the first railway ferry *Perseverance*. Captain Thorne missed, by four months, the arrival of the new GWR ferry, *The Mew*, which gave even longer service (forty-six years) to the river crossing. A consolation was that he also missed the departure of the forty-year old *Dolphin* for Appledore, whither she was towed by the tug *Challenger* for scrapping.

Arrivals and departures are commonplace at a railway terminal but in the spring there were two unusual arrivals. The first was John Lee (see 1885) 'the man they couldn't hang'. After his recent release he arrived to visit relatives in Dartmouth, one of whom was a licensee; John Lee became engaged, and, in the following year, married and set up business in London as a tobacconist, finally emigrating to America. The second arrival was a special train from London carrying the remains

*Swedish cruiser
Fylgia 4,810GT,
built in 1906, 23
knots, with eight
6in guns, which
included six in
barbettes, the
smallest armoured
cruiser in the
world, in keeping
with Sweden's
neutral policy, and
in Dartmouth to
convey home
Emanuel
Swedenborg.*

W Martin/Judy Diss

of the famous Swedish scientist, philosopher and theologian Emanuel Swedenborg, from the Swedish church in east London, where they had lain since his death in 1772. They were received on Kingswear station by a large guard of honour of officers and crew of the Swedish cruiser *Fylgia* anchored in the harbour. The remains were transported back to Sweden - 136 years after his death - and were to reburied there, after belated due ceremony and honours were paid to him.

Meanwhile the new Dartmouth Coaling Co set up offices sharing the registered headquarters of the parent company Forward Bros Co Ltd in Morocco House, Bayards Cove Quay. They had barely commenced business when an announcement appeared in the *Chronicle* of a meeting of creditors of Leach, Harrison & Forward, Liverpool, Forward Bros & Co, London, and Forward Killack, New York, which set alarm bells ringing. This was promptly followed by a request to the Harbour Commission to transfer all agreements with Forward Bros & Co to the Dartmouth Coaling Company. Then came a further announcement that Forward Bros & Co (The Mersey Shipping Co Ltd) and all its assets had been acquired by the Southampton-based Royal Mail Line of steamers, who promptly placed three of Forward's liners for sale on the open market.

There was understandable dismay and anger in the Harbour Commission and amongst the established coaling companies (whose principals were members of the Commission), for, in 1907 under the threat of Forwards' withdrawal of the service from the harbour, the Harbour Commission had approved a further coaling hulk assumedly to coal the now-departing liners, as suspected, the hulk promptly became part of a competing coaling company to share a diminishing amount of business in the harbour. All the time, the owners had been aware they were in financial difficulties, and today it would be called a 'confidence trick'. The port had hoped that the Royal Mail Line would continue to use Dartmouth harbour but the service was recommenced from Southampton.

Another prominent man with civic positions, Henry Square, solicitor, was arrested for misuse of funds. He had in 1904 taken over the solicitor's business of Osmonius Smart Bartlett, the former Dartmouth town clerk, who had received three years' hard labour in 1904 for a similar offence. In this instance Mr Square was sentenced to six years' hard labour, which was physically severe in those days, particularly for a professional man moving in the higher echelons of society.

Regatta 1908 attracted the smallest number of visiting yachts and participants for many years, only 55 craft, 13 steam yachts, 1 schooner, 13 yawls and 28 cutters. Sir Thomas Lipton's 1,243-ton steam yacht *Erin* was prominent and was much admired. His America's Cup yacht *Shamrock* was also present to participate in the RDYC race for 23-metre yachts. Bad weather caused the big yacht owners to obtain agreement from the club sailing committee to race on the Saturday instead

Left: A photograph of three Kings, Edward VII with his son and grandson the future George V and Edward VIII, taken on board the royal yacht about 1908. As Princes, George and Edward attended the Royal Naval College.
DEBRETTS

Right: Mercedes II *on trials off Scabbacombe Head showing this unique vessel flying Simpson and Stricklands house flag.*
CYRIL KING

Left: *Captain James Boxell on the bridge of the* Mew, *behind the carved wheel set adjacent to the funnel and the all important steam whistle cord.*
H HUTCHINGS

Right: *The* Lower Ferry Float *(Built Philips 1907), with an early tourer and saloon car aboard, flying their rally flag on the lifting stanchion. The remains of the float remains lying in Waterhead Creek, Kingswear.*
DAVE GRIFFITHS

of the usual Friday. Races for Friday were contained in the harbour, with just two races for launches and seven rowing events. The big race on Saturday had only three entrants, and because the weather was so poor it was run over the old Start Bay Yacht Club course: the Range/Torcross/Skerries/Range, which offered some shelter from the severe south-west winds, which, combined with the ebb tide, resulted in very lively seas. *Shamrock* was judged first and *White Heather* second.

Simpson, Strickland & Co launched, their biggest yacht ever the SY *Mercedes II* (136ft x 15ft) for E J Mercedes of motor car fame. She aroused international interest, claiming to be the fastest steam yacht afloat with the speed, 21.5 knots, the appearance of a torpedo boat and the grace, comfort and lines of a yacht. She had two funnels and pole masts with rigging and sails, electric lighting and heating, a magnificent mahogany saloon, four state-rooms and the usual bathrooms. Her engines were those of a destroyer, two triple expansion 490hp each, built at Noss works, and among the boat's superb equipment were compasses, telegraphs and speaking tubes supplied by H Adams of Dartmouth. Captain Carey of Kingswear and a crew of fourteen delivered her to Nice flying the Austrian flag.

1909 Several prominent characters died. Robert Moore, seventy-six, shipbuilder, chief clerk to his uncle Mr Kelly, an early Dartmouth shipbuilder who unfortunately went bankrupt in 1861. Robert Moore then became a shipbuilder in his own right at Higher Sandquay, where the engineering shops of the Royal Naval College were later built. He was also owner of Kingswear's Alma Steps properties and part owner of Kingswear's Steam Laundry. The second was William Owens, 55, former engineer to the Dartmouth & Torbay Steamboat Co, the son of the late William Francis Owens, Owensville (Kingswear House), formerly chief engineer to the Kingswear rail terminus. The next was Mrs Olive Bartlett, 67, Little Dartmouth, wife of the powerful Jasper Bartlett JP, Bartletts Stores, chairman of the Channel Coaling Co Ltd, and Dart Harbour Commissioner. She was followed by Roope Brooking, prominent member of the old Dartmouth Brooking family and wealthy Kingswear property owner. Then R F Wilkins, gold-bullion dealer, Brookhill, and a local benefactor also died. Finally, last but not least, 'Jim' died.

"JIM".Kingswear.

Jim was a handsome collie dog found dejected and abandoned in a railway carriage at Kingswear station in January 1901. Attempts to trace his owner proved unsuccessful, so the stationmaster T Abrahams took him on the 'staff'. His duties were to collect contributions for the GWR's Widows and Orphans Fund in a small brass box fastened to his collar. He did this with great success, being a general favourite with everyone, while living the high life. Jim soon learned to distinguish the dining car from an ordinary passenger coach, and the close proximity of the Royal Dart Hotel kitchens, the galleys of the steamers and the jetties all provided rich hunting grounds. In 1906 there was consternation at the terminus when, in spite of a wide search of the station and Kingswear, Jim was not found. However a telegram from Captain Smith, of Renwick, Wilton & Co Ltd's collier *Vanessa* reported that they had a stowaway; Jim had boarded the collier at Kingswear and after a good meal from the galley had curled up asleep. He was wakened by the rough waters outside the castle, was very seasick, and after a voyage to Newcastle was greatly relieved to return to a joyous welcome from all the railway staff. His adventure did not stop Jim, a gallant Lothario, from occasionally crossing to Dartmouth on either the lower or railway ferry to do a little courting, after which he plied his trade for contributions before returning to Kingswear. Sadly during 1909 he was struck by one of the new-fangled motor cars and died shortly afterwards. There was great sorrow among both staff and villagers and he was buried on the railway embankment below Fore Street. His simple grave, with headstone, is still there to this day. His greatest moment had been in 1908 when the Prince of Wales visited the college and placed a guinea in his collecting box.

The port towing services were undergoing some change. Philips disposed of the tug *Venture II* to South America but laid down a new tug *Venture III*, (67ft 6in x 14ft 6in x 8ft). Only two small tugs, *Vulcan* and *Vixen*, were left to provide towage. Then Casey & Heal ordered a new ferry tug, *Hauley* (34ft x 8ft x 5ft), while Simpson, Strickland & Co also received an order from Renwick, Wilton & Co Ltd for a general-purpose tug to be called *Totnes* (60ft x 12ft x 7ft).

The town and harbour slowly began to recover from the loss of the Forward liners, and the coaling companies, now increased to four, had to share very modest returns. The 1908 bunkering figures of 61,930 showed a shortfall of nearly 10,000

Left: '*Jim*' *the collie dog, a Kingswear favourite and official station collector for the GWR Widows and Orphans Fund.*
GREAT WESTERN
MAGAZINE

Right: *Frederick Heal, Adam and young Tom Casey pose for a photo by a gate that once spanned Kingswear's lower ferry slipway.*
TOM CASEY

tons below 1907, but later in the year rumours began to circulate that another coaling company was expressing interest in establishing a base in the harbour. One bright spot was the unusual sight of a school of porpoises in the harbour, catching salmon, tossing them into the air and leaping up to catch them (would they could today).

THE SECRET INVASION

Casey's new tug Hauley *built at Philips in 1909 to supplement launches* Blanche *and* Forester *on the lower ferry service.*

T CASEY

The *Chronicle* reported an unusual and alarming event that could have had a serious effect on national security:

> On the instruction of the German War Department two large steamships were commandeered at Hamburg and a large number of soldiers were ordered to converge on the port and marched aboard. Then as dusk fell they set sail across the North Sea unobserved and proceeded to England and into the river Humber, and after staying for a short while quietly slipped anchor and returned to Hamburg. The event when it became known caused considerable alarm and Sir George Doughty raised a question in Parliament as to why the German manoeuvre had been able to be carried out without being observed by any British warship, guard ship or authority.

The foregoing is probably a pure coincidence, yet it mirrored the main theme of the plot centred around yachting and secret German manoeuvres in Robert Erskine Childers' gripping novel *The Riddle of the Sands*, written six years earlier in 1903. Childers was an enigma and from a distinguished family. During the late 1860s Admiral Sir Hugh Childers, First Lord of the Admiralty, was involved in the tragic loss of HMS *Captain* with 500 lives including that of his own midshipman son (see 1870). A twist in the tale is that Robert Erskine Childers later grew disillusioned with the establishment, became involved in the Irish troubles and was eventually executed for treason.

Regatta 1909 attracted sixty-eight entries this year, including again Sir Thomas Lipton's huge steam yacht *Erin*, with some eminent personalities aboard, including Lloyd George, the Duke of Leeds and the Bishop Boyd Carpenter. The latter became so attached to Dartmouth that he purchased a home in Kingswear (Riversea) to which he retired and lived until his death in 1918.

SS Smolensk *7270GT built in 1901, 486ft x 58ft x 26ft for the Russian Volunteer Fleet, plying from St Petersburg to Vladivostok, seen in 1908 from Kingswear lighthouse being coaled by the collier SS Swiftsure. She was on charter to Channel Coaling Co.*
W Martin/J Diss

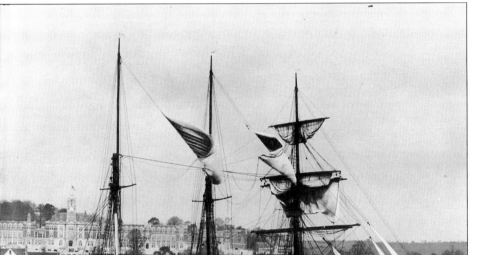

SY Sunbeam, Earl *Brassey's fine steam yacht in 1908 drying sails in the harbour after one of her round-the-world cruises.*
W Martin/J Diss

The principal event was the RDYC's 23-metre race, sailed over the usual course four times (40 miles). The result was the reverse of the previous year, M B Kennedy's boat *White Heather* beating *Shamrock*. Both boats had sailed forty matches during the season, each winning twenty races, though *White Heather* also won the King's Cup at Cowes.

The regatta committee ran four races on the Saturday in the Range, the handicap race for under 26ft with ten starters being won by *Oliviase* owned by Miss Emily Windsor of Pinewoods, Kingswear. She was wealthy, a superb yachtswoman and a very extrovert character.

As the year closed the college training ship HMS *Espiegle* was replaced by the 1899 Pelorus class cruiser HMS *Pomone* (2,135 tons, 300ft x 31ft), twice the tonnage and length of *Espiegle*.

The GWR announced that they were abolishing second class on all their services, so only first and third classes remained.

Finally Francis Charles Simpson retired, a former Mayor and bitter opponent of the South Embankment scheme and its commissioners, also chairman of Simpson, Strickland & Co, a firm he founded in 1879 to manufacture his protégé, George Kingdon's patent compound engine and boiler. Originally started with two or three men in an outbuilding behind his house Combecote, Ridge Hill, Dartmouth, the business had grown into a major engineering and shipbuilding company with a 25-acre works complex at Noss Point employing over 300 local men.

THE RANKS CLOSE

1910 For Dartmouth the word 'turbulent' best describes the second decade of the twentieth century, for as 1910 dawned, local battle lines were being drawn. Old wounds caused by the Mersey Steamship Co/Forward Bros/Dartmouth Coaling Co dispute were forgiven. An uneasy alliance was formed between the three established coaling companies and the newcomer, to enable them to act as a consortium within their power base the Harbour Commission, and repel any further intrusion into what they regarded as 'their' territory. Their leader Thomas Wilton was, for the first half of the decade, divisive, and for the second (the war period), patriotic.

This year saw the introduction of that indispensable item, the telephone. It was promptly installed and heavily utilized by the coaling factors. In the late days of 1909 the Dart Harbour Commission received a request from a powerful group, Denaby & Cadeby Main Colliery Co Ltd, for permission to station a shifting coaling hulk anywhere on the River Dart. This promptly alarmed the top management of the old-established coaling companies, who had eighteen months before been pressurized into accepting the new Dartmouth Coaling Company, and had no intention of accepting another. Trade was slack in the harbour, so to thwart the intruder the coaling companies applied for extra berths. Poverty was rife and the request was welcomed by the lumpers, traders, town council, and certain commissioners, namely A H Bridson (chairman), R Row (Dartmouth Town Council) and Basil Joy (Kingswear). However, the application was fiercely resisted by the vested interests who, aided by the GWR and college representatives, forced through the following resolution, which rang hollow: they gave yachting as the main reason for its rejection, whereas, although they were wealthy self-made men, they were not considered socially acceptable for membership of the yacht club. The resolution ran as follows: *'That none of the applications be granted owing to the fact that if coal hulks are permitted above HMS* Britannia, *the amenities of his majesty's naval establishment and also of the yachting interests would be injuriously interfered with.'*

This provoked more anger in the town council and proved to be a serious miscalculation, for Denaby & Cadeby, anticipating opposition, had also applied to the Brixham Harbour Committee for a similar berth for a coaling hulk in the outer harbour. In this instance they were welcomed with open arms and permission immediately given. The news was greeted in Dartmouth with dismay and resentment against Thomas Wilton, for although he was town representative on the Harbour Commission, he had acted in his own business interests and voted contrary to the town council's wishes. Moves were made to deselect him and a candidate was raised to oppose him in the forthcoming county council elections. A cartoon, produced by local artist J L Wimbush, portrayed him with two faces, standing straddled over the harbour, one foot by both castles, uttering comments unsupportive of Denaby & Cadeby's application. A threat of legal action brought its withdrawal and Mr Wilton retained his seat.

Meanwhile the new Brixham company expended £15,000 on facilities. Two vessels, the SS *Persia* and SS *London City*, arrived for use as hulks in Brixham harbour with attendant shifting hulks and two tugs, the *Dencade* and the *Torbay Scout*, and bunkering commenced. This caused further gloom in Dartmouth, for a rival bunkering port was established a few miles distant . By September 50 to 60 lumpers were employed at Brixham, to the concern of the Dartmouth lumpers, 180

Rear Commodore RDYC, Mr Mason's fine steam yacht Evona *in the Dart prior to regatta; regrettably the following day she was veneered with coal-dust from a discharging collier.*
W Martin/J Diss

of whom petitioned the town council to press the Harbour Commission to reverse their decision. The offending 1909 resolution was again debated and once again rejected by the coaling consortium. Further efforts were made to discipline Mr Wilton but, despite acting unilaterally, he survived.

Recent events had overshadowed the annual Customs returns for 1910, which, in spite of the new depot at Brixham, showed an increase of 4,950 tons over the previous year with 575 vessels bunkering, a total of 49,109 tons.

These events had so dominated affairs that the wreck of the Brixham trawler *Morning Star* passed almost unnoticed. Seeking shelter from a gale, she had anchored abreast Kingswear Castle and Renwick's tug *Totnes* was hailed for a tow, which was agreed, but surprisingly the full crew of the *Morning Star* hoisted anchor and all boarded the ship's boat with a warp which was not long enough to reach the tug in her fixed position. Consequently with no one aboard, *Morning Star* quickly drifted onto the rocks below Kingswear Castle and became a wreck; and was probably later beached at Warfleet Creek.

During the quarrelling between the coaling factors and the town the yachting circle had remained on the periphery, probably quietly against further hulks, but friction arose again when Mr Mason, Rear Commodore of the RDYC, was once again smothered in coal-dust in his fine steam yacht *Evona*. Previously the Harbour Commission had stipulated that no colliers could discharge on buoys three, four, five and six between May and October, but Mr Binloss, the new manager of the Dartmouth Coaling Company was unaware of the order and allowed the SS *Suran* to discharge adjacent to the yacht, reopening old wounds.

Regatta 1910 The two 23-metre yachts *White Heather* and *Shamrock* both had accidents in Torbay and missed the event, but this was partly compensated for by the novelty of a hydroplane built in the Royal Naval College and on trials in the harbour. This year, participating craft dropped to 31 steam yachts, 1 schooner, 16 yawls and 31 cutters. The most unusual race was in the Boat Float, a 50-yard dog race won by *Spot* against nine competitors, several taking a very erratic course.

On Friday in the RDYC 12-metre race, tragedy struck the *Cintra* two miles out in a half gale, when a squall caused her mast to snap off 15 feet above the deck, dragging three of the crew of seven overboard with the big sail. Dressed in oilskins, only two crew members could swim. Two drowned and one was saved by the competing yacht *Javotte*, the race being abandoned. All bunting and flags were taken down except for one at half-mast on the principal flag poles.

Left: *Warfleet Creek showing Sir Thomas Freake's thatched two-storey wet-boathouse and the hulk of a wrecked Brixham trawler probably* Morning Star *awaiting final demolition.*

AUTHOR'S COLLECTION

Some years previously the Dartmouth saddler C H Kenucky had received an order from the owner of a visiting circus, Sir Robert Fossett, for a headcollar for the world's largest horse, standing 22 hands and weighing 1.5 tons; he now received a further order for a headcollar for the world's smallest horse, only 27inches high.

J L Wimbush, who, a few years previously had painted a portrait of Edward VII, was now commissioned by the Toronto Constitutional Club to paint a portrait of King George V in admiral's uniform.

The *Floating Bridge* continued to be a source of concern, for since 1908 it had lain derelict and abandoned by its owners, the Raleigh Estates, on the foreshore at Sandquay. There was so much concern that senior council officials from Torquay, Paignton, Brixham and Dartmouth convened to consider the possibility of purchasing it, but they failed to reach agreement, each being wary of the other. So the estate threatened to withdraw the current substitute, an inadequate small rowing boat carrying a few passengers, and abandon the *Floating Bridge* altogether.

Simpson, Strickland & Co, who during the year had built boats for seven countries (Britain, India, Italy, Brazil, Belgium, Russia and Argentina) completed the year by launching a yacht for the Prince of Monaco and one for the Grand Archduke Stephen of Austria.

1911

Hopes for an uneventful start to the new year were dashed when a group of Mormon missionaries arrived and began campaigning house to house, mainly when the men were out working, for girls to go to Salt Lake City and adopt the doctrines of Brigham Young. There was also indignation at a leaflet, which read: 'Wanted, several hundred good looking girls and women, married or single, for Salt Lake City. Apply Mormon Agency, Dartmouth. Free pass to Salt Lake City, but no returns', making things difficult for the missionaries who denied they were polygamists and hurriedly left empty-handed. It was later discovered that some local wag had issued and distributed the leaflets.

There was equal surprise at the announcement of a stag hunt in Kingswear from Lupton Court. A full field turned out and set off, but there was a distinct shortage of stags in the Kingswear area!

Philip & Son, shipbuilders since 1864, became shipping owners for the first time, forming the Dartmouth & South Coast Steamship Co Ltd to trade Brixham/Dartmouth/Plymouth. A purpose-built vessel, the iron single-screw *Start Bay* (90ft x 18ft 6in x 9ft) was launched, but the enterprise was not successful and the *Start Bay* was sold away in 1915 to the British Red Cross Society. At the same time Renwick, Wilton & Co Ltd launched at S P Austin's Sunderland Yard a second new collier SS *Paignton* (2,009GT 280ft x 40ft x 18ft).

Above left: *The* Duke of Devonshire *berthed alongside the South Embankment to embark passenger.* T CASEY

Above right: *The sea-going paddle steamer the* Duchess of Devonshire *belonging to the Devon Dock, Pier and Steamship Co Ltd. landing passengers at Torcross beach from a precarious bow mounted hinged landing stage* T CASEY

Below left: *1912, and poverty among the lumpers caused local dignitaries to open a soup kitchen issuing twice-weekly pea-soup at ¹/₂d a quart. Here at the Market Square kitchen lumpers are queuing to receive their quota while children with brew-cans, bowls and other containers line up to take rations home to feed the families.*
R JONES/R TUCKER/DARTMOUTH MUSEUM

Right: *Lumpers Maddo and Maggot Stone enjoying their rations.*
R JONES/R TUCKER/ DARTMOUTH MUSEUM

Mr Wilton, who in 1908 had gained control of Renwick, Wilton & Co Ltd, owning the colliers SS *Vanessa*, *Kingswear* and *Paignton*, embarked in October on a new venture 'time charter shipping'. He formed a new company, Wilton Steam Shipping Co, and as chairman and managing director purchased from his other company (Renwick, Wilton & Co Ltd) its latest acquisition, the SS *Paignton*, and placed it on charter.

The *Chronicle* reported events relating to the arrival in Dartmouth and meteoric progress of Thomas Wilton. They were the deaths of two prominent north countrymen, coaling factors who probably knew Mr Wilton in Shields in the 1880s and could have influenced his move over 400 miles south to the small port of Dartmouth. The first was Mr Heppel owner of the Cwmaman Colliery group, of which Mr Wilton became local manager in Dartmouth on his arrival in 1885; the other was R D Renwick, who, with Mr Wilton as partner, formed Renwick & Wilton Co Ltd in 1893.

Left: *A postcard advertising the Roseville Roller Rink which opened in Victoria Street in 1909.*
H HUTCHINGS/DARTMOUTH MUSEUM

Right: *A delightful photograph of Donald Hitt, son of the proprietor, dressed in his skating outfit onto which his mother has darned protective knee-pads.*
H HUTCHINGS/DARTMOUTH MUSEUM

Meanwhile the Brixham bunkering station was affecting Dartmouth and there was anger and poverty among the lumpers. A soup kitchen dispensed pea soup two days a week and a blanket society was formed to supply one blanket per household to the deserving poor.

To make matters worse, Denaby & Cadeby took offices in William Smith's Embankment House (next to the new post office) and advertised in the *Chronicle* that they would supply household coals at well below the prices of local merchants, and inhabitants should stock up as a coal strike was imminent. They loaded a large barge at Brixham and then with their tug *Dencade* towed it round and moored it at the Embankment adjacent to the office, so supplying the general public direct. When empty it was replaced by another barge. Local merchants were soon aggrieved and applied to the DHC to station barges on the Embankment themselves, but this was refused as their barges would be permanent and not mobile. The Denaby & Cadeby barges also paid harbour dues. The argument with

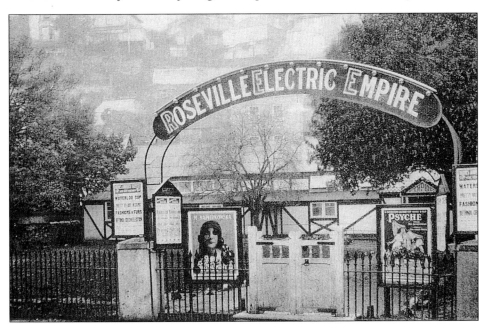

By 1913 the Rink had succumbed to the latest craze, the cinema, and become the Roseville Electric Empire.
H HUTCHINGS/DARTMOUTH MUSEUM

Floating Bridge No. 5, commissioned by the new owners (after 40 years' control by the Raleigh Estates) differs from all previous bridges in that it is propelled by wire ropes instead of chains.

G THOMAS

the town council became more vitriolic after coaling factors on the DHC, particularly Mr Wilton, again refused to rescind their 1909 resolution, so in return the town council demanded increased representation on the Harbour Board.

CARDIFF TAKES CONTROL

Jasper Bartlett, recently retired from the Channel Coaling Co Ltd, remained a commissioner. Rumours circulated that the new Dartmouth Coaling Company had taken over the other companies, but this was denied. Robert Row, the town council, and other representatives began to complain bitterly that it was now a cartel of coaling companies under the auspices of the Cardiff owned Dartmouth Coaling Company. The company was owned by Evans, Thomas & Ratcliff (later Evans & Reed of Cardiff) and, although the other companies retained their separate identities, they were in fact amalgamated and able to control prices.

Regatta 1911 met with change when the Royal Yachting Association set the RDYC's race day as the Saturday. However, strong reaction by the Dartmouth Committee and a good programme brought revision and it reverted back to the Friday, to follow the Torquay Regatta. Entrants increased to 78 vessels, including 24 steam yachts, 1 schooner, 19 yawls, 2 ketches and 22 cutters. The RDYC 19-metre class race (40 miles) had four starters and all four raced on both days for the first time. The 6-metre class was won by *Ouananithe* sailed by that yachting legend Morgan Giles.

Although a busy commercial port, Dartmouth had for some time been growing in stature as a holiday resort, with more visitors arriving by rail to enjoy the town and to take trips on the river steamboats to Totnes. An increasing number had been arriving by seagoing paddle-steamers such as the *Duke* and *Duchess of Devonshire,* owned by the Devon Dock & Pier Co (directors Wilton, Aitken et al) and by vessels owned by Cosens & Co of Weymouth and by the Southampton & Brighton Steamship Co. Problems arose because of their size and draft, as at certain states of the tide, passengers could only land from small boats. The proposal was revived to erect a landing pier (119ft x 25ft), made from greenheart piles and level with the Embankment. It would have rounded ends and lower decking with a stairway to the upper deck to enable landing at all states of the tide. The proposal had been mooted before in the past ten years, the last time was in 1904 with a price of £450, but the Board of Trade had insisted that a Provisional Order must be obtained which would cost £350, thus destroying the scheme's viability. The Commission and town council decided to reconsider the proposal.

HMS Dartmouth, *a light cruiser named after and adopted by the town, visiting to receive an official welcome and the presentation of silver plate.*

R BARNES/D GRIFFITHS

1912 The Roseville Roller Rink, Dartmouth reopened as the Roseville Electric Empire theatre.

Trouble came when the threatened coal strike became a reality and over one million miners downed tools. Very quickly the lifeblood of Dartmouth harbour began to dry up and great hardship ensued; some families existed on a loaf of bread per day, and due to the high prices, coal was bought in pennyworths. A fund was started to subsidize house coal from the local merchants. The bunkering trade had almost ceased due to the lack of supplies and men were laid off at Philips' and Simpson, Strickland & Co's shipyards. Fortunately the confrontation was resolved, and the miners returned to work.

Meanwhile Renwick, Wilton & Co Ltd sold the SS *Vanessa* to Greece so she ended her days in the sunshine, unlike her sisters: the SS *Mezappa* was wrecked at Flamborough Head and the SS *Sabrina* was a coal hulk in the harbour.

There was some jubilation, however, for after four years of closure and great inconvenience to passengers, in Dartmouth in particular, the Raleigh Estates sold the *Floating Bridge* No. 4 for £265 to John Williams, Davenport, along with the tolls, the roads and the foreshore rights. He promptly ordered from Rogers & Son of Plymouth a new *Floating Bridge* No. 5, (77ft x 24ft x 5ft 6in). This was worked by wire ropes around drums, not chain driven as before. She arrived towed by *Venture* and went into service in November.

In June the light cruiser HMS *Dartmouth* (5,250 tons), arrived to receive a gift from the inhabitants of Dartmouth, a solid silver shield and a card tray, both decorated with the Dartmouth coat of arms and other embellishments and inscribed 'Presented by the Mayor, Aldermen and burgesses of the borough of Clifton, Dartmouth, 1912. Charles Peek, Mayor'. Unfortunately the Admiralty ordered she should not enter the harbour but anchor in the Range, which was surprising as a few weeks previously a ship of 10,500GT and two Swedish warships of similar tonnage had safely moored in the harbour. However, the locals made the best of a rather unsatisfactory situation.

Around this time Archibald Hine-Haycock purchased Kittery Court. He became a leading light in Dartmouth and Kingswear, becoming a Harbour Commissioner and participating in all local activities, a tradition carried on by his family to this day.

The smouldering anger, regarding the refusal of the coaling consortium on the Commission to allow Denaby & Cadeby, (now firmly established at Brixham), a hulk in the harbour, was rekindled when the Grand Canary, Tenerife & Atlantic Coaling Company applied for the same. The application met with similar opposition and was rejected, incurring further wrath against Mr Wilton from the town council and the citizens of Dartmouth.

Regatta 1912 Entries were at an all-time low, with only 50 vessels including 11 steam yachts, 2 schooners, 13 yawls and 24 cutters. The crack boats did not attend. One interesting contender was the Rev E C Bayliss, Kingswear, who, in his yacht *Elsie*, won the handicap race for yachts not exceeding 32ft. His munificence was later to play a major part in securing Dyer's Hill for the enjoyment of Dartmouth's citizens. Another interesting personality was the Earl of Mount Edgecumbe, who on the Friday in *Eilum* won the RDYC handicap race of 20 miles for 26 to 44 footers, while *Cintra*, Major A Croak's yacht beat *Ieana* in the 12-metre class.

In December Mrs Marianne Simpson, wife of Francis Charles Simpson, died at Maypool. Her body was ceremonially carried on a barge draped in black and accompanied by two similarly covered barges for mourners and was towed by Casey & Heal's launch *Blanche* to Dartmouth for interment in St Clements. Simpson, Strickland & Co's workforce of over 300 lined the foreshore, hatless, to pay their last respects to the wife of the firm's founder.

The ongoing saga of the Newcomen memorial continued with a sensible proposal to turn part of the Butterwalk into a museum, a commendable idea, but one which did not take shape for forty-two years.

1913
In the new year, the *Chronicle* announced the death of Mrs Susan Setter, eighty-eight, of the Trust Houses, Kingswear. As sexton's wife she cared for Kingswear's church, but this humble position concealed the fact that her son by her first marriage was the Hon Henry Turley, later President of the Australian Senate.

A tragedy occurred when William Douglass, son of the late Sir James Douglass, designer and contractor of the Eddystone lighthouse, drowned while sailing just outside the harbour. He was at Dartmouth for the regatta with his wife and son Edward, and visiting his mother Lady Douglass, Gramercy Tower, Dartmouth. William and Edward took a partially-rigged sailing boat out in a stiff breeze, and when one-and-a-half miles out, they capsized. The accident was witnessed by two men in a dinghy by the castle who could do little, so they rowed over to an 35-foot motor launch *Kangaroo* whose occupants declined to assist as it was 'too rough'. The event was also witnessed by Alfred Neil Hill, Warren Cottage, Kingswear, and from nearby Glenorley, he telephoned the college who dispatched a *Britannia* launch. Mr Hill bravely, pulled hard for the scene in a very small dinghy. Meanwhile Langland's round-Britain cruise ship *Princess Victoria*, after leaving the harbour, arrived on the scene and launched a boat, to find only Edward alive. After searching the area for William for some time without success, she proceeded on her journey. The inquest heard that Mr Douglass had narrowly escaped from death thirty-three years previously while supervising the construction of the new Eddystone light. During the demolition of Smeaton's old Eddystone light, (now erected on Plymouth Hoe), he fell 70 feet towards the rocks below, but was caught by a huge wave that carried him aloft and into the vicinity and safety of the supply boat. The jury recorded accidental death, and commended Mr Hill for his bravery, while deploring the lack of courage shown by the occupants of the launch *Kangaroo*. Mr Douglass's body, when found, was interred alongside his father Sir James in St Petrox churchyard.

There was anger and public outrage in Dartmouth when Councillor Scammel, scourge of the Harbour Commission, as lessee of a Butterwalk property (now the museum), proposed to sell the magnificent King Charles II fireplace and panelling in the room to a non-resident. The *Chronicle* entered the lists, stating that some years before an even more magnificent chimneypiece, illustrating the judgement of Solomon with life-sized figures of the twelve apostles in carved oak, was removed from another house in the Butterwalk and sold for £30 to an unknown country house in the Midlands.

This alerted the town council to the ongoing threat to Dartmouth's old buildings, many thoughtlessly destroyed, and their diminishing collection of treasures, and this forced them to take counsel's opinion. In the meantime Councillor Scammel, aware of the voters' anger, with brass-necked cheek offered

to sell back to the council for £700 the unexpired portion of the lease he had bought from them four-and-a-half years previously for £650, with the promise not to remove the fireplace and the panelling. However, counsel's opinion was that he did not have the legal right to dispose of the same, and thankfully they remain to this day in the museum for all to admire.

Consternation arose in the Commission when the chairman Mr A H Bridson resigned after a disagreement with Mr Thomas Wilton. He felt so aggrieved that he had the reasons for his resignation printed in full and distributed. His departure was a sad loss to the board; he was an intelligent and independent wealthy country gentleman who, for fourteen years, had chaired many contentious meetings and handled fractious members, including Mr Wilton, with great skill. Then Captain Clift of the River Dart Steamboat Company and Mr G H Collins also resigned, for reasons of ill health. The latter had controlled his own company for the last thirty-seven years, though lately Mr W J Medway had been director of operations. His departure, along with the recent retirement of Mr Jasper Bartlett, confirmed that the Dartmouth Coaling Company was in full control of the three bunkering companies, as Renwick, Wilton & Co Ltd had ceased bunkering some years previously.

Mr Jasper Bartlett, still a commissioner, was appointed chairman in place of Mr Bridson. Mr Wilton saw this as a golden opportunity to stabilize his often turbulent position of trying to be an independent harbour commissioner, whilst also a representative of the town council. So he shrewdly resigned both posts, then, with a little help from his friends, had himself re-elected by special order as a commissioner only, with no affiliation to the town council. The town council could increase its representation on the Harbour Commission and re-affirm its avowed intention that its representative would be duty bound to implement its chosen wishes, while Mr Wilton was now a member in his own right. Then to replace Mr Bartlett the town council elected councillor Mr G N Philip, though there was some concern that, as a shipbuilder, he had vested interests. Alderman W J Medway was appointed to the vacancy caused by Captain Clift. Mr Medway had for many years been a severe critic of the Harbour Board, but since those contentious days, he had become the senior member of the bunkering firm G H Collins & Company Ltd. So the commission had turned full circle from being the domain of wealthy country gentlemen, mainly members of the RDYC, to being a consortium of wealthy self-made businessmen.

A picture of happy children paddling in Warfleet Creek; of special interest is the adjacent quay and Warfleet Kiln with attached thatched cottage, a timber unloading-crane and stocks of limestone.

AUTHOR'S COLLECTION

By this time Renwick, Wilton & Co Ltd was experiencing difficulty in maintaining contract coal supplies over Kingswear quays, as they owned only the SS *Kingswear*, so in November Mr Wilton placed orders with John Crown & Son Ltd, Sunderland for two new colliers, one for each of his companies.

However, the dogs of war were stirring and the forthcoming regatta was the last one for several years. There was no sign of the upheaval ahead, indeed the King's yacht *Britannia* and the Kaiser's yacht *Meteor* lay alongside at anchor and in harmony on the placid waters of the Dart.

Regatta 1913 appeared to be regaining its previous popularity, though there was surprise when the Dart Sailing Club, formed in 1873 as the Dart Boat Sailing Club and merged in 1903 with the Minima Sailing Club, announced it was to dissolve, and give its cups and trophies to yacht clubs within three miles distance of the Dartmouth pontoon.

A magnificent prelude to the festivities was a Venetian fête held in aid of funds for the Dartmouth & Kingswear Cottage Hospital:

> *Prizes were offered for the best illuminated and decorated launches and rowing boats and thousands of residents and visitors watched the proceedings. The competing launches and rowing boats were prettily decorated and there were some remarkably fine illuminations. A procession was formed and wended its way slowly down the harbour headed by a miniature of the old cadet training ship* Britannia, *the clever work of the men of HMS* Pomone. *As the Embankment was passed a salute of twenty-one guns was fired from the* Baby Britt. *The hospital also provided a very nicely decorated gondola. The launches and boats with hundreds of lights presented a brilliant spectacle. Mr Philip A Wilkins later gave a fine display of fireworks on his Dartmouth property Gallants Bower. Whilst the fete was in progress collectors for the hospital were busy ashore.*

A full three-day programme of events was organized by the regatta committee and the RDYC. The Marquis of Ailsa's yacht *Bloodhound* again took part and F L Carslake's *Maharanee* won her race as she did every year. Ninety-two vessels attended. *The Times* reported that this was a good regatta, and stated 'there was little wind which was fickle and rather shifty'. In view of the events of the following year that description might well apply to the German attendance.

The year was also memorable for some of the Kingswear hierarchy who made the headlines for all the wrong reasons. The erratic and very wealthy Miss Emily Windsor, Coombeside (Pinewoods) was forcibly removed by two policemen from the Esplanade Hotel, Paignton, drunk and using foul language. She was then arrested for refusing to depart in the chauffeur-driven Rolls Royce, spent the night in jail and was fined 40s(£2). The chauffeur stated she always gave him her purse to pay all transactions.

Captain Evan Llewellyn of Nethway House, Kingswear, aide-de-camp to General Sir W H Manning, Governor of Jamaica, decamped with Lady Clara Maud Manning, the Governor's wife. The manageress of the Royal Dart Hotel, Miss Alice Calderbank, committed suicide on Friday the thirteenth by drowning herself at Lighthouse Beach, in spite of several brave attempts to save her.

Finally, Dartmouth achieved a free weekly library. A small private library had previously existed, owned by the Dartmouth Literary and Debating Society, but Mrs Frean started a free library (two evenings a week) in 1911 with 368 books. Readers paid 1d ($^1/_2$p)per annum, with a free reading room. In 1913 premises were taken in Cromwell House, but costs ran to £60 or £70 a year and a request was made to the town council for funds. It offered a paltry £10 which was refused.

CHAPTER 8

War and Peace

1914 to 1925

THE OLD ORDER CHANGES

1914
As this fateful year dawned relations within the House of Hanover still appeared normal, but the King and the Kaiser were about to engage in the bloodiest conflict of all time, which was to alter forever a social structure that had existed for centuries.

Locally the year began on a tranquil note, for in 1912 the Rev de Courcey Ireland had been appointed the new vicar of Kingswear and made an immediate impact, drawing large congregations from both sides of the river. He was well liked and promptly set in motion a grandiose scheme to improve and enlarge Kingswear church. He was supported by the Rev Boyd Carpenter, Dean of Westminster, the local gentry and four other wealthy highly placed clerical gentlemen residing in Kingswear, plus J A Reeve, of Yarrow Bank, an ecclesiastical architect. Mr Reeve produced some excellent plans which transformed the church into what appeared to be a mini-cathedral. These were approved by the Ecclesiastical Commission, to proceed in two stages, and the vicar promptly set about raising the necessary funds. He was particularly successful and by early spring the first phase of the improvements began, namely a new choir vestry and organ chamber, removal of the choir stalls from the rear to the chancel, installation of a central heating system, and redecoration.

Dartmouth was visited by two eminent people, firstly Mr Winston Churchill, who visited the college in the Admiralty yacht *Enchantress.* His visit was fortunate for, two years later when First Lord of the Admiralty, he decreed that before *Britannia* left for demolition at Blyth her figurehead should be removed and remain at Dartmouth Royal Naval College. The other visitor was the great philosopher and poet Rudyard Kipling whose family came for a brief holiday.

Proposed improvements to Kingswear church to be undertaken in two stages; the first was completed but phase two, the nave extension, new quadrantal vestibule, and castellated boundary walls, was abandoned when World War I commenced.

DARTMOUTH CHRONICLE

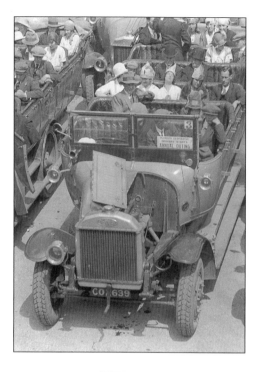

THE ARRIVAL OF THE TRADE UNIONS

The bunkering trade was at a very low ebb and there was much poverty, which provided fertile ground for Dan Hillman, Plymouth secretary of the Dock, Wharf, Riverside & General Workers' Union, who was keen to form a branch in Dartmouth. He shrewdly invited Ernest Bevin, national organizer, from Bristol to address the lumpers, and, being a born orator, Bevin persuaded them to form a new branch. The new order soon obliterated the good relations that had existed between employers and men since 1852, for two months later whilst bunkering the SS *Romany* with 1,800 tons of coal from Collins' hulk *Juno*, a 50 per cent pay rise was demanded, and work ceased. The captain then arranged to coal from a shifting hulk pulled alongside, but the lumpers boarded and threatened the crew, so the police were called. A rise of 25 per cent was settled and the vessel proceeded, but the aggrieved combined coaling companies stationed a tug at the harbour mouth and diverted coaling vessels to their other depot in Portland. Mr Bevin met the employers in London where the Union was recognized, and a considerably reduced pay rise was agreed and accepted by the men. Unfortunately the Portland workers, unaware that the dispute was settled, went on strike in sympathy, but paid a heavy price for they were locked out: although the Dartmouth men expressed their support they did not strike and as a result coaling at Dartmouth increased. Over the next few years the Union certainly helped the workforce, who were sometimes less than patriotic when it came to a conflict between the war effort and personal interest.

Dartmouth's first mechanical refuse vehicle, quickly nicknamed the 'Dreadnought'. It was bought in 1909 for £444 but was a mechanical disaster, breaking down fifteen times in the first year, and was finally sold in 1914 for £40 to Mr Soper, Slapton. The Council then reverted to genuine horse power for the war and for many long years after.
R TUCKER/DARTMOUTH MUSEUM

THE GREAT WAR

When Britain declared war on 4 August a great crusade ensued, but patriotism soon gave way to reality. To cheering crowds, and with bands playing, a whole team of cadets marched away to war, entraining at Kingswear for service in the reserve fleet. The majority died a few months later when the *Aboukir, Hogue* and *Cressy* of the Seventh Cruiser Squadron were torpedoed off the Dutch coast. In Dartmouth people rushed to join the Old Pals Brigade in Kitchener's army, and some lumpers joined the Pick and Shovel Brigade. Mr Wilton agreed to be Mayor and performed the duty diligently throughout the war years.

On 3 August it was agreed that because of the crisis in Europe there would be no regatta, a situation not remedied until 1919.

In the autumn, the Naval Bank at Dartmouth collapsed, bringing great distress to many local businesses and citizens, including the Dart Harbour Commission which lost £2,500. Eventually Lloyds Bank took over limited liability, paying only 25 per cent in the pound.

The Customs returns for 1913 confirmed that trade was still being affected by the Brixham depot. A total of 516 vessels bunkered in Dartmouth in 1911, 465 in 1912, and only 436 in 1913. Two or three years before, Brixham harbour had been £800 to £900 in debt, but now it had a trading surplus of over £1,000, and rates had been reduced.

In the harbour Mr Wilton was dominant, for he had sold Renwick, Wilton & Co Ltd's tug *Totnes* to Constantinople. Its new purpose-built collier the SS *Torquay* (870GT 200ft x 30ft x 8ft) arrived, but ran aground at Torquay, laden with coals, three months later. A large quantity had to be thrown overboard to the delight of local fishermen; thirty boats abandoned fishing and trawled up the coal, a much more profitable catch. In September, the Wilton Steam Shipping Co's second new collier, the SS *Churston* (2,470GT) arrived, but shortly after she was commandeered by the Admiralty along with the other colliers SS *Kingswear, Paignton* and *Torquay* to coal the fleet at sea. Tolman's River Dart Steamboat Co bought from Cox in Falmouth a new paddle-steamer *Compton Castle* (108ft x 18ft), to carry 450 passengers. The steering wheel was set six feet above deck for all-round vision, and the aft saloon was in bird's-eye maple and mahogany with gold cushions and damask curtains. The fore cabin was in varnished pine with a commodious bar, managed by Mr Dawes of the Criterion on the quay (Taylor's Restaurant). The existing ageing cutter *Rose* was replaced by a fast new 1910 Plymouth-built pilot cutter *Millie*, (50ft x 14ft x 8ft).

1915 There was consternation early in the New Year when a large section of Kingswear's main road collapsed and fell, demolishing the major part of the engine shed. On a brighter note the energetic Mrs Fitzherbert, Glendene, received a letter from Buckingham Palace thanking her for organizing the knitting of seaboot stockings for the Fleet. A total of 2,296 pairs had been distributed, the work being carried out by local people and needy trawlerwomen whose men had lost their lives at sea, and whose traditional work of net making had practically ceased.

The Admiralty released two colliers the SS *Torquay* and *Paignton,* and Mr Wilton sold the latter, (which his company Wilton Steam Shipping Co had bought in 1911 for a nominal sum from Renwick, Wilton & Co Ltd), for a handsome profit. The SS *Torquay* returned to transporting coals from Blyth to Dartmouth, but two months later she struck a mine which ripped open the port side and destroyed the engines and boilers. One man was killed and two badly injured, and the captain and crew took to the boats, whilst the vessel was towed back to the Tyne for repair and return to service. In June the other collier SS *Churston* was mined and sank with the loss of four men. This was a blow as both the ships were modern colliers, fitted with double bottoms and ballast divided fore and aft for trimming purposes, double derricks and winches to each hold, and electricity throughout, all fitted to the highest standards.

The demand for manpower from the forces was acute and it became difficult to maintain the ferry and other services. Casey and Heal obtained a small steam

Philips' tug Venture *built in 1903, a prototype of several later vessels built by the firm and given the same name.*
CYRIL KING

launch, the *Edna,* for passengers and abandoned the centuries-old rowing ferry, while a new much larger launch was ordered from Plymouth. In March an unusual sale of surplus craft was held on Kingswear Beach: '*1) Open rowing ferry boat 18ft 6in x 6ft 6in, 2) another 18ft x 6ft, 3)open two bowed ships longboat 30ft 6in x 8ft 6in, 5 tons, suitable for herring fishing, 4) open boat 38ft 6in x 8ft 6in, 8-10 tons, working or 80 passengers, 5) steam launch* Edna.' In May Casey's new launch *Relief* arrived, giving quicker and more efficient service, though the old rowing ferrymen were missed for their friendly banter.

Philips also had manpower problems, and after a protracted period Renwick, Wilton & Co Ltd's new tug was launched and named appropriately *Dartmothian* (50GT 63ft x 15ft x 8ft). She promptly salvaged the full-rigged Italian *Macodiarne* (2,350tons), which had lost all sails in the Channel, and towed her into Dartmouth. *Dartmothian*'s arrival was fortunate, for a few months later Philips sold the only other harbour tug *Venture,* and this was quickly followed by the disposal of the *Start Bay* to the British Red Cross Society.

Meanwhile shipping losses were becoming severe, and the Commission chairman stated that receipts were well down, as coals arriving by sea were only 40 per cent of the pre-war period, much now coming to Kingswear by rail. The jetty trade was also very depressed. There was a near disaster when Channel Coaling's hulk broke into flames in the forecastle while the Dutch ship SS *Zeus* was coming alongside. The ship pulled clear, sounding her sirens, bringing the locals out to see the night sky lit up by the fire. The harbour tugs and Mr Avis's *Waterlily* arrived to spray the hulk, and then Casey's horse ferry appeared with the Dartmouth fire engine and brigade aboard. Between them they prevented the flames reaching the main hold containing hundreds of tons of valuable bunkering coals.

Philips' only venture into commercial trading between Plymouth Dartmouth and Brixham, the Start Bay *built in 1911 for the Dartmouth & South Coast Steamship Co. Seen here with Red Cross insignia after her sale to the British Red Cross Society in 1915.*
CYRIL KING

Above: **A Dartmouth Trawler** *1867. One of the Lake, Armeson, Twyman, Dartmouth fleet of twenty sailing trawlers moored up against the New Ground. A basic vessel with rudder steering and low bulwarks. The top hatted gentleman is probably one of the owners.*

G WEATHERLY

Opposite page
Top left: **Sir Henry Paul Seale,** *1806–1897, owner of the Mount Boone estate, which he sold in 1878 to the Raleigh estate, who in 1898 sold it to the Admiralty to build the present Britannia Royal Naval College. Eleven times mayor of Dartmouth.*

DARTMOUTH TOWN COUNCIL

Top right: **Arthur Howe Holdsworth,** *1780–1860, the last governor of Dartmouth Castle, (the title ceased in 1857). In-filled the pool for the market, and connected Dartmouth to the Toll Road system. Twice mayor of Dartmouth.*

DARTMOUTH TOWN COUNCIL

Bottom left: **Francis Charles Simpson,** *1846–1923, an ebullient north countryman who arrived in Dartmouth in 1873. His credit rating was to establish Messrs Simpson & Strickland Engineering Co Ltd, employing over 300 men, his debit was to conduct a bitter feud against the South Embankment. Ten years mayor of Dartmouth.*

DARTMOUTH TOWN COUNCIL

Bottom right: **Charles Seale Hayne,** *1833–1903. Dartmouth's greatest benefactor, the railway, harbour commission, and the South Embankment, the last only achieved after vitriolic opposition which motivated him to leave Dartmouth to become Ashburton's Liberal Member of Parliament, and Mr Gladstone's Paymaster General.*

PROFESSOR F. HARPER, PRINCIPAL, SEALE HAYNE AGRICULTURAL COLLEGE.

The College Afloat *This placid painting shows H.M.S.* Britannia *and H.M.S.* Hindustan *floating serenely on the waters of the Dart in 1890. Painted by C W Fothergill – Chief Instructor of Drawing and Surveying, Sandhurst.*

These former warships were converted into training ships for naval cadets in use until BRNC was established ashore in 1905.

BRITANNIA ROYAL

Architect Sir Aston Webb   Builders

ROYAL PRINCES AT BRNC, DARTMOUTH

Prince Albert	*1877/79*	*later Duke of Clarence*
Prince George	*1877/79*	*later King George V*
Prince Edward	*1909/11*	*later King Edward VIII*
Prince George	*1911/12*	*later King George VI*
Prince Philip	*1939*	*later Duke of Edinburgh*
Prince Charles	*1971*	*later Prince of Wales*
Prince Andrew	*1980*	*serving RN officer*

NAVAL COLLEGE

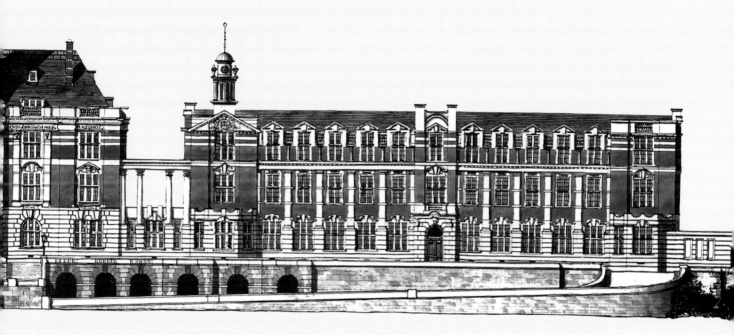

gs & Hill Ltd, London   Completed 1905

This section of a measured architectural drawing by Dale Goffe shows the fine detail of Sir Aston Webb's classic design for the Britannia Royal Naval College, Dartmouth. Contracted by the Admiralty in 1898, Higgs & Hill Ltd. began construction in 1900, the foundation stone was laid by King Edward VII in 1902 and the College opened in September 1905.

Top right: **The *Terrier*** *built 1873 by Philip's (with a dogs head figurehead) as a brigantine for Newman and Hunt's Dartmouth fleet of vessels engaged in the annual Salt Cod trade with Newfoundland. Later owned by Kingswear's Captain Angel who converted her into a three masted schooner (with Raffee Topsails). Painted by the celebrated Pier Head painter Reuben Chappell, of Fowey, Par, and Charlestown.*
AUTHORS COLLECTION

Top left: **The *Gabrielle*,** *Circa 1880, an R.D.Y.C. member's yacht off Naples. The painting was given to the club by the Royal Torbay Yacht Club and was painted by the well known Neapolitan Pier Head painter, De-Simone*
ROYAL DARTMOUTH YACHT CLUB

Left: **The 1868 Regatta** *showing the Dart Yacht Club, (later R.D.Y.C.) race about to commence from anchored positions, (the last time a fixed start was used) and includes the tug* Pilot *(1852). The picture was presented to the R.D.Y.C. by Mr E Kensington, who lived in Higher Wilderness, now, Derwent Lodge, and who took part in the race with his 15 Ton cutter* Una. *The painter was H. Forrest.*
ROYAL DARTMOUTH YACHT CLUB

The Jersey Lily *The lovely Lillie Langtry, an occasional clandestine visitor to Kingswear and Dartmouth with her consort, the Prince of Wales. Painted by E. Poynter*

Bertie *Edward VII, Prince of Wales, debonair in a role he did so well, 'Bertie' the rakish 'Man about Town'. Photograph by Bassano 1875.*

War and Peace—*1916*

1916 Early illusions that the war would be short and exciting soon evaporated. One casualty was the closure of the Rock Inn, Noss, one of Kingswear's four pubs. It was small, just a taproom, with a few domestic rooms, stable and coach house, while the only other properties nearby were another cottage, the Britannia Halt, and the level crossing keeper's house. Being some distance from Kingswear, The Rock Inn's trade had disappeared, as the principal customers were men from Simpson, Strickland & Co's works, many of whom had joined the forces. This caused a severe shortage of skilled tradesmen and eventually caused the closure of Simpson, Strickland & Co. Nethway school, Kingswear (now Dragon House), reduced to only sixteen pupils, closed indefinitely.

A new naval barracks had been built in Dartmouth to replace the old 3-rater *Britannia*, and a national scheme to save her was launched belatedly by the Duke of Manchester. The target was £16,000 and the plan was for her to remain in Dartmouth and become a training ship for 300 boys whose fathers had been killed in the war. The Mayor, Mr Wilton, started a local fund, but times were grim and money was not forthcoming. On 4 July 1916 after forty-three years on the Dart, *Britannia* was towed away by the tugs *Jollic*, *Homer* and *Asna*, under pilot J Pillar. With great dignity she sailed slowly past Dartmouth Castle to be saluted by Major Lawson dipping the flag. She was a grand old ship; broken up in Blyth, her timbers, advertised by catalogue, were sold as war memorials and souvenirs.

Colonel Studdy of Waddeton Court sold his property of 1,053 acres to Sir Alfred Goodson, who was later to play a major part in local and RDYC affairs.

In the Harbour Commission Captain Angel aired a strong grievance about the composition of the Dartmouth sub-committee of pilotage. As he started to speak, Mr Medway suddenly remembered some urgent business appointment and hurriedly left, but Captain Angel continued, making the most of the fact that the Harbour Commission affairs were fully reported in the press, whereas the pilotage meetings were private. His complaint was that two men appointed to the sub-committee had little nautical experience: Mr Medway, commercial and general manager of the coaling companies, and G N Philip, shipbuilder. He also felt that the Brixham pilots should have a representative; the result was that after twenty years' service both he and Captain Buckpitt, real seadogs, resigned, depriving the Commission sub-committee of its most experienced men.

Military tribunals were formed which met quarterly to review the positions of men who remained in reserved occupations. One such young man was R L Dennis, who, through the vicissitudes of war, was thrust into a senior controlling position in the coaling companies, which he retained for many years. Newspapers published long columns of names of the dead and missing, and details of rewards for bravery. The area had its share of both; for example, Trooper W A Simpson, son of Francis Charles Simpson, was killed digging out a comrade during a bombardment; Lieutenant Boyd Carpenter was killed in action; Corporal Veale, Dartmouth, was awarded the VC; Lieutenant de Courcey Ireland, son of Kingswear's vicar, gained the Victoria Order, 4th Class.

Trade unions sometimes used their indisputable muscle for profit rather than patriotism and anger arose when workers at Philips refused to work on Bank Holidays unless they got double pay, a choice not available to Kipling's poor Tommy Atkins.

In Kingswear the Rev Ernest Bayliss had converted Ridley House into a preparatory school for twenty-five sons of serving officers, and fifteen went on to Osborne College. Colonel Edward Appleton FRIBA died this year. He had been architect to the Cary Estates, Torquay, the Luttrell and Llewellyn Estates, and responsible for many fine Torquay properties, the rebuilding of Kingswear church (1845-47), the waterworks, the Vicarage, most of the local gentry's houses, and Dartmouth's Fairfax Place.

The year closed with a great gale which caused havoc in the harbour. The schooner *Princess of Thule*, anchored abreast the coastguard station, started to drag towards the Western Blackstone rock. She slipped anchors and turned into the wind to make for harbour but, as she tried to hoist sail, a huge sea turned her on her beam end and the wind ripped her jib to ribbons. The captain tried to

Bronco Bill's Circus in wartime Dartmouth with clowns, bands and native Red Indians parading elephants, camels and yaks. The show's grand finale was a re-enactment of an Indian attack on the Deadwood Stage.
Tom Casey

A driver from Hawkes, coal merchants, who took his orders for door-to-door service too seriously on Crowthers Hill.
R Tucker/Dartmouth Museum

bring her up with the mainsail but a heavy sea drove her broadside onto the rocks off Kingswear Castle where she quickly broke up, with the loss of five lives. In the crowded harbour the SS *Yankalilla* broke her warps, so she dropped anchors and steamed all night to maintain position, while the hulk moored alongside broke adrift to strike the brigantine SV *Huntley*, carrying away her fore top gallant masts. Having cleared, the hulk then drove into the SS *Columbo* which broke adrift to collide with the collier SS *Emma Minloss*, which came loose and sank the standing hulk *Sabrina*. Three other hulks and the *Floating Bridge* broke away and were run up on the Kingswear shore, and numerous small craft were sunk on that violent night.

1917
Death was now so commonplace that the demise of Arthur Henry Enoch, sometime resident of Kingswear, in January 1917, passed almost unnoticed. Known as the 'artist of the Dart' he was a talented man who left behind a rich tapestry of local scenes, one of which, 'Beautiful Dartmouth', once hung in Buckingham Palace.

The war had little to offer that could be considered good, but the resulting comradeship was a small bonus, and the men of the London Regiment stationed in Dartmouth enjoyed an abundance of camaraderie with the local people. When the regiment was ordered to France, and embarked on the railway ferry *The Mew* to entrain at Kingswear, the steamers whistled in the harbour and people cheered. A little light relief for the citizens came when the original Bronco Bill's circus came to town, complete with native Red Indians and elephants.

In Kingswear, Glenorley, adjacent to Kingswear Castle, acquired a new owner, Thomas Lennard, later knighted ((in 1920). A rich man, he was owner of a chain of over 200 nationwide shoe shops. He became a major benefactor to the area, and Kingswear in particular. His first action was to rename Glenorley with the more up-market title Kingswear Court.

A few months later the owner of another highly desirable residence, the foremost in the land, decided to change his name proclaiming: *'I declare that the name of Windsor is to be borne by this royal household and family, and relinquish the use of all German titles and dignities... George R I.'* Dartmouth responded by renaming Hanover Street, Anzac Street, after the Australian and New Zealanders who had taken part in the Gallipoli campaign (World War I).

The harbour remained very depressed and in May the *Chronicle* published a report that a smaller number of ships had been sunk, only 26 that week as against 62, 59, and 64 respectively in the previous three weeks. Such losses were reflected in the harbour, with coal at a premium, as ships had to take priority and domestic supplies were decimated. The difficulties of heating and cooking were the main concerns. A champion of the poor was Father Daniel, priest of Dartmouth's Roman Catholic church. Aided by the trade unions he crusaded against the council and the coal factors for better supplies at affordable prices. He was chided that 'for a minister to descend from the sub-limits of the pulpit into the unconsecrated atmosphere of practical business was a dangerous step.' But he had some success for the unions placed at the Embankment a barge selling limited extra coal shipped over from Kingswear station at slightly cheaper rates. The Mayor, Mr Wilton, concerned for the very poorest, offered to place a barge free of charge adjacent to the Embankment at the disposal of the Food Committee, and to provide ten tons of coal per week at cost price direct from the barge to those in need. The towage of the barge would be paid for by others wishing to help.

The *Chronicle* reported that the cruiser HMS *Dartmouth* had been torpedoed but not sunk in the Adriatic, with the loss of seven lives and eight wounded men.

After many years the Harbour Commission moved its offices from Cromwell House, Fairfax Place, to Lloyds Bank Chambers, Spithead, and the free library, now owning 1,600 books, moved from Fairfax Buildings to 10 Victoria Road.

The final blow of the year was the offer for sale of Simpson, Strickland & Co's business and works, formerly employing over 300 men. Swan Hunter, national shipbuilders, was rumoured to be interested.

Manpower shortage was so acute that to maintain essential bunkering services against union opposition, mechanization was introduced – wooden pontoons surmounted by mechanical grabs.
CYRIL KING

Ella Trout MBE, (right) who, as a young girl, was honoured for her bravery in rescuing seamen from a torpedoed ship in Start Bay, with Mrs Adams, (left) wife of a long-line fisherman who in post-war regattas frequently won races in Sailor
S WIDDECOMBE

1918

The war was in its fourth year and its appetite for the flower of British manhood was unsated, making the task of the military tribunals almost impossible. Most of the coaling companies' lumpers had joined the services; where formerly they had ten clerks they now had three. Mr Taylor, chief clerk to all three companies, had recently died and this continued the exemption from service and elevation of young R L Dennis to manager. From then on, he played a major part in harbour affairs. The manpower situation became so acute that mechanization was introduced with its attendant problems. This solved one of the 'm' problems, manpower, but created another 'm' problem, money. This was strongly taken up by the unions, who had considerable muscle, for the original twenty-one members had risen to 438; they refused to work the grabs installed on the coal hulk *Sabrina* unless the employers engaged the same number of men as previously, or paid the reduced numbers the same amount as they had paid the whole gang. Undaunted, the coaling companies obtained permission from the Harbour Commission to station two floating grabs on the mooring previously held by the departed hulk *Stratford,* to be moved alongside the hulks or steamer to be coaled.

The 'Sailors' Rest' (formerly the Newman Building, Hudson's Bay warehouse, G H Collins & Co Ltd's offices) founded by eminent local people to offer accommodation to calling seamen. Now the DHNA offices.
R TUCKER/DARTMOUTH MUSEUM

Patriotism was overlooked again, and eventually the unions agreed to accept the same terms as existed in Bristol Channel ports. But discontent continued, for whereas previously forty to fifty men were needed to coal a vessel, now only ten men and a grab were required. However, the tribunal solved the problem by stating that those who objected would be found another job (in the Army).

At the other end of the scale, the Duchess of Marlborough started a Jewel Fund to receive jewels, gems and gold to support the war effort.

Many homes still received that dreaded telegram. A typical case was that regarding Bombardier William Jolliffe, twenty-one, the only son of Mr and Mrs Jolliffe of Warren House, Kingswear. He had joined the services in the first week of the war and had been gassed twice and wounded twice which seemed so unfair. Acts of gallantry were commonplace. One young girl, Ella Trout, and a small ten-year-old boy fishing off Hallsands, saw a nearby steamer torpedoed. They rowed through the wreckage to a single survivor and, with great difficulty, this frail pair hauled him aboard, saving his life, and for this Ella was awarded the MBE. Other behaviour brought no credit to the area. The torpedoed SS *Clan Sutherland* (3,820 tons), was towed into Dartmouth harbour and beached. The officers and surviving crew were taken to Plymouth and not allowed to return for three days, during which time all their personal belongings, food, spirits and navigational instruments were looted from the ship.

In July, after long negotiation the principal residents on both sides of the river established a sailors' rest in the old Newman Building, formerly Collins' offices, now the DHNA offices. This was to provide comfort and accommodation to visiting sailors until 1923.

For Philips the year proved a catalyst. For years the town council had dallied over purchasing the Coombe Inlet from the Raleigh Estates, and in June 1914 Philips had resolved the issue by purchasing outright the area known as Coombe Mud. The outbreak of hostilities two months later suspended their original intention to develop the area with new buildings, quays and slipways. However, in 1918 the final closure of Simpson, Strickland & Co created a flurry of activity in the harbour and caused the alarm bells to ring in Dartmouth and particularly at Sandquay, when Swan Hunter, major national shipbuilders, announced proposals to purchase the firm. It prepared plans for major improvements to create a major shipbuilding yard. This motivated Philips to engage Dr J A Purvis of Exeter to prepare a grandiose scheme on their Coombe

Mud site, which included a dry dock, fitting-out quays, new workshops and slipways. They formed a new and enlarged company with T Wilton, the Mayor, a director, and began negotiations with the Admiralty to obtain approval, offering it a strip of land free of charge to erect a new improved 50-foot wide approach road to the college. However, after months of negotiation the Admiralty decided an enlarged shipyard at Sandquay would interfere with the college amenities, and refused approval. During that interim period Swan Hunter decided a major shipyard so far from the main steel supply centres would be uneconomic and withdrew its interest. Quickly and shrewdly Philips, alarmed by the Admiralty's backtracking and anticipating refusal, proceeded with financial support from Swan Hunter to purchase Simpson, Strickland & Co's yards at Noss. New plans were quickly produced for extensive improvements there, local authority and Harbour Commission approval was obtained, and the refurbishment commenced.

During this period Mrs Mary Knowling Lake died at her daughter's home in Shrewsbury. She was the widow of that exceptional man the late Samuel Lake, who, in 1870, was the architect and builder, amongst other projects, of Coombe Terrace, which was put for auction up by the trustees. The close proximity to Coombe Mud made Coombe Terrace of considerable interest to Philips who, with others, attended the auction, but failed to meet the reserve. Shortly afterwards Philips purchased it by private treaty to accommodate some of their staff. Coombe Villa, the most imposing of the terrace, and Mr Lake's old home, was occupied by a senior member of the Philip family for many years. The houses were unique in being the first permanent prefabricated poured-concrete houses constructed in the country. They are as sound today as when they were built over 120 years ago, yet concrete houses at Townstal built after the Second World War were demolished barely forty years later due to concrete cancer (so much for progress).

In July Renwick, Wilton & Co Ltd's tug *Dartmothian* was released from Admiralty service and purchased by the Wilton Steam Shipping Co, its first commercial transaction since the SS *Churston* had been lost in 1915 and the SS *Paignton* had been sold away.

The Great War ended on 11 November 1918, though there had been nothing 'great' about it. Although we had won, we had paid a great price, America being the only real beneficiary. We were impoverished and denuded of skilled manpower; however, there was great rejoicing, for at long last the killing had stopped.

A NEW BEGINNING

1919 With the onset of peace, normality returned to the area. Thomas Wilton was Mayor for the fifth successive year and still fulfilled his duties conscientiously, and for this he was awarded a knighthood. He had previously offered the town a generous gift of four houses for returning disabled ex-servicemen and women. This was later revised to two houses and premises to form an ex-servicemen's club 'Comrades of the Great War', (forerunner of the Royal British Legion) which was duly opened at Cromwell House, Fairfax Place, Dartmouth.

The men, some of them, returned very different from those bright-eyed young men who had blithely marched away to war in 1914. The monumental mason, woodcarver, gilder and other craftsmen were kept busy on memorials to the fallen and prominent, departed personalities. In Kingswear the death was recorded at Riversea of Bishop Boyd-Carpenter, Dean of Westminster. Since retirement he had been devoted to working for the war effort and grateful parishioners presented Kingswear church with a superb, richly carved pulpit to honour his memory. The crew of HMS *Tiger* donated a fine stained-glass window to the late Commander Valentine F Gibbs, RN, The Cottage, (Longford), Kingswear. This was to commemorate the gallant part he played in the storming of Zeebrugge in 1917 where, though mortally wounded, he had remained on the bridge of HMS *Iris* whilst directing operations, maintaining the highest traditions of the service.

Meanwhile ships began to return to the harbour, including three captured German submarines. Dartmouth was also presented with a war souvenir, a six-inch German field gun, while all British guns captured by the Germans and used to line Berlin's main thoroughfare, Unter den Linden, and other German cities, were returned to Great Britain.

Sadly peace was dominated by a malaise that persisted for several years: strike action. The year started with tradespeople, then bakers, railway workers, miners and others walking out, to the despair of industry, which in turn was accused of profiteering. The harbour was full of American shipping, prompting the following letter in the *Chronicle:*

> *During the period since July 8th about 41 large cargo vessels put in for bunkers. Of the 28 quoted, 24 are Americans, all of which put in for bunker coal only. I wish the strikers could spend a week in Dartmouth and see how the advantage won by our Navy and Army is being thrown away by the home non working industrial hosts. The Americans, with the signing of peace, are all out to take the trade that we turn down, Germany, the countries of Scandinavia: it's all alike to the US trader: he's out to sell and buy goods as quickly as possible.*

Tragedy occurred aboard one of these American steamships, the SS *Western Maid,* due to the Americans' habit of carrying firearms. Friction, already existing between the second engineer and two Irish firemen, erupted when the latter returned from ashore rather the worse for drink. A fight developed, the two men against the engineer; a fellow officer, fearing injury to his colleague, fired at the firemen, but hit and killed the second engineer.

Jasper Bartlett accepted, for the last time, the position of Commission chairman and ordered that Kingswear foreshore from Ballast Cove to Waterhead be cleared of the wrecked hulks that had accumulated there during the war years. The dormant Wilton Steam Shipping Co ordered a collier from Murdock & Murray & Co Ltd, Port Glasgow, the SS *Paignton II,* (2,400 tons deadweight, 240ft x 36ft x 21ft), with triple-expansion engines and in July sold at a handsome profit the tug *Dartmothian,* the third vessel to go to Constantinople, which it had purchased only ten months before from Renwick, Wilton & Co Ltd. There was also some excitement in the town when two seaplanes touched down on the waters of the Dart, bearing the King of Belgium, who had come to visit his second son at the Royal Naval College.

German field-gun along with a floating mine presented to Dartmouth after World War I as war souvenirs. The former was melted down in World War II and returned to Germany as bombs.
R Jones/R Tucker/Dartmouth Museum

*Two seaplanes on
the Dart give rise
to local hopes that
Dartmouth would
be chosen as a
seaplane base; the
Admiralty chose
otherwise
however, although
several later
landings did
occur.*

R Tucker/Dartmouth
Museum

The town council resurrected the idea of a suspension bridge across the Dart. It was ninety years since Rendel & Foulton had prepared plans and specifications for a crossing at Greenway, and later proposals had been made by the South Devon Light Railway, but all to no avail.

In July the Mayor received a reply to a letter written the previous September from the townspeople of Dartmouth, Massachusetts, population 5,500. They were delighted to make contact and said they had 130 townspeople in the forces overseas. In reply Mr Wilton invited any of those members to spend a few days' free holiday in Dartmouth.

Miss J P Henley, sister of that remarkable Dartmothian William Henley, offered to give his lifetime work and collection to the council, provided they found suitable premises to house and always display them. Miss Henley also confirmed that Henley's clock on the shop at the corner of Duke Street and Foss Street, belonged to the town as it had been funded by public subscription. On a lighter note the town found pleasure in the acquisition of its first fish and chip shop.

Regatta 1919 After five long years of absence regatta returned. It formed the basis for all future regattas, being three-day-events organized by the Town Committee, with the Royal Dart Yacht Club running only some handicap races fortnightly from June. A race was held in the Boat Float for what must have been the forerunner of water-skiing, a '*motor boat toboggan*' (competitors can be dressed in bathing costumes standing on planks pulled by a motor boat).

The year closed with the death of two interesting men, firstly G H Michelmore, seventy-two, owner of the Dartmouth & Kingswear Steam Laundry. He was formerly an engineer for the South Devon Railway and later Great Western Railway, responsible for carrying out the building of wooden viaducts on the South Devon line to Plymouth. The other was yacht club member Sir James Brooke, Sheepstor, Dartmoor, the white rajah of Sarawak who virtually ruled that ancient nation in New Guinea for many years. He was a frequent visitor to Lupton House as guest of Lord Churston.

1920 A new decade, the roaring twenties, started with a whisper; the 'roar' was to come later. We had won the war but found peace difficult to handle: war weariness, food shortages, manpower deficiencies, unfulfilled expectations, social upheaval, union power and trade slipping away to peripheral allies, presaged another decade of conflict. The *Chronicle* started the year by reporting that there was a surfeit of women in the country due to the appalling losses suffered in the recent conflict. In total 790,000 men, mainly aged between twenty and forty, had been lost; this was particularly evident in the mining industry as coal,

KINGSWEAR DOCKS COMPLEX

The railway was rerouted around Philips' shipyard replacing the line crossing the two creeks over wooden viaducts, as this had bisected the works.

G PHILIP

This, the third unsuccessful Kingswear scheme to promote a docks complex for the Port of Dartmouth, probably failed for reasons of transportation, for road communications were minimal and the adjacent rail terminus was only a single line. Had it been successful it would have materially altered the village of Kingswear because Waterhead Creek would have been cut off and in-filled for marshalling yards, storage, sidings and warehousing.

DHNA

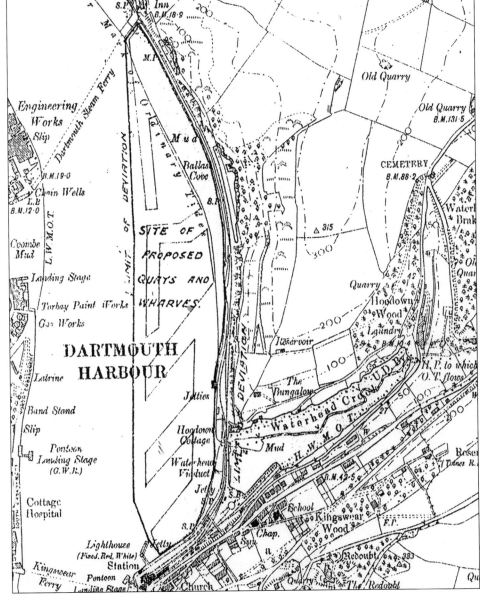

the country's lifeblood, was in short supply. However, the Harbour Commission reported that coaling was increasing, if slowly. Commissioner Medway, aged 61, had died. He was general manager of the three combined coaling companies, and the situation was further complicated when, three weeks later, A Dennis, senior manager of the same group, also died. This furthered the meteoric rise of young R L Dennis, who took over both posts, and also Mr Medway's position as Harbour Commissioner.

In 1919 the Admiralty released from war service Renwick, Wilton & Co Ltd's two colliers SS *Torquay*, built in 1914, mined in 1915 but saved, and SS *Kingswear*, built in 1909. They were both promptly sold.

Mr Williams, Devonport owner since 1912 of the Noss Higher Ferry, offered the business for sale by auction, the tolls, *Floating Bridge*, slipways and Bridge Road. The *Chronicle* reported that a payment of £40 a year to the Duchy of Cornwall had remained unclaimed for the last forty years, and that a right existed for the bridge owner to erect a toll house at Hillhead and levy a fee from all travellers other than relevant house and land owners. However, a bid of £500 from Philips failed to make the reserve, and the sale was withdrawn.

KINGSWEAR'S DOCKS COMPLEX

Commissioner Captain Angel promoted a scheme for a docks complex to be constructed at Ballast Cove, Kingswear. This was a development of an earlier 1901 scheme by G H Collins, former Commissioner and owner of one of the coaling companies. It received broad approval and was forwarded to the GWR, the landowner. As the GWR would have to fund the project, the scheme made no further progress.

Mr Peeke, the energetic Mayor of Dartmouth and a Commissioner, obtained the council's approval to purchase old properties at Burrough's Slip to build a new road from the Embankment to Newcomen Road (Raleigh Street). At the same time he was canvassing hard for the absorption of Kingswear into a greater Dartmouth, which, if successful, would have included the new docks complex. With the approval of the Commission, the GWR and the town council, he toted the scheme around several major national engineering construction companies in London. It found favour with Matthew Wrighton & Co Ltd, who produced plans which, although still in Ballast Cove, differed marginally from Captain Angel's plan in that the quays were set at right angles, whereas Captain Angel's were parallel to the shore. It was negotiated with the GWR and a Parliamentary order was applied for. However, as a result of second thoughts, the Parliamentary bill was withdrawn. Had Mayor Peeke's commendable efforts succeeded it would have reduced the port's dependence on

Philips' engineering facility matched the high quality of the vessels built. This splendid photo shows engines in the course of construction for (left to right) SS Sunflower, *SS* Bou Regreg *and SS* Oued Mellah.

G PHILIP

steamers calling only for bunkers, and created additional trade and employment, possibly making Dartmouth today a small commercial port, like Teignmouth, with a happy mix of commercial and pleasure boating.

Meanwhile strike action still prevailed, and, to the relief of the employers, the unions began fighting amongst themselves with accusations of poaching each other's members.

In Kingswear the GWR began rerouteing and straightening the rail line at Noss, which ran on a wooden viaduct, designed by R P Brereton in 1863, over the two creeks and then through the centre of Philips' works. It involved removing the viaducts and re-laying the line from the tunnel mouth to run behind the works. It was not without cost, for Mr G C White, a Dittisham labourer working on the tunnel cutting for the contractor Relf & Sons, was buried in a landslip.

In a lighter vein, Thomas Lennard, Kingswear Court, shoe shop magnate, received a knighthood.

Regatta 1920 attracted a record 20,000 visitors, proving that the committee was right to re-activate the event so soon after the war. The port committee ran two sailing races on the first day and four outside on the Saturday, while the RDYC also arranged four races outside. Yacht racing received a boost when King George V had *Britannia* recommissioned, and several other big boats attended: *White Heather, Westward, Paula III, Terpsichor* (later *Lulworth*), *Nyra Moonbeam, Susanne, Zinita, Joyetti, Brynhild* (1899), *Valdora*. All these took part in the regatta races on Friday and Saturday.

During 1920 Sir Alfred Goodson became Commodore of the RDYC when the Duke of Somerset, Commodore for the previous fifteen years, died. The Duke was without issue and his first cousin once removed, General Sir Hamilton Seymour, was next in line. Before acceding to the title he had to prove the validity of the marriage of his great-grandfather Colonel Francis Seymour, which was reported in the *Chronicle* as follows:

Reparation German warship Stuttgart, *lying off Philips' newly-acquired shipyard at Noss, awaiting the removal of her heavy guns and equipment prior to being taken to her owners' Wards Yard at Teignmouth for final demolition.*
G PHILIP

Reparation German destroyer T189 *wrecked on Roundham Point, Torbay, was later abandoned, sold and demolished in situ; her sister ship was wrecked on Preston slipway, towed to Brixham, demolished and her hull allegedly hulked in Coombe Mud, Dartmouth.*
R TULLY

Kingswear's Jim Thorpe, transport and salvage expert, with his trusty Austin in his Paignton depot; he salvaged destroyer T189's *valuable turbine engines in 1946 after their 21 years' immersion under Torbay's waters.*
J THORPE

The discarded hull of a British submarine and the bow of a former German destroyer, both demolished at Brixham and then hulked in Coombe Mud, Dartmouth, to assist in land reclamation.
R JONES/R TUCKER/
DARTMOUTH MUSEUM

The story of this marriage and of the difficulties it has caused might have been borrowed from the pages of a sensational novel which had been thrown aside by the impatient reader on the ground that that sort of thing did not happen in real life. After hearing the arguments of learned counsel, referring to musty rate books and land-tax returns, inspecting a ship's log, Indian burial records, the faded archives of the long-dead East India Company, and examining parish registers, the Committee of Privileges has decided that it happened as follows: Mr Perkins, a Woolwich publican, permitted his daughter, Leonora, to marry John Hudson in 1768. Two years later Perkins died, and Hudson, who seems to have been in partnership with his father-in-law, took over the licence, and held it until 1775. Affairs seem not to have prospered with him, for in 1785 he shipped before the mast on board the Manship, *belonging to the Honourable East India Company, and sailed for Calcutta. Here he died on 27 September 1786 and was buried on shore. News of his death reached England, and his widow proved his will, and on 3 September 1787, married Colonel Francis Seymour, son of the Dean of Wells and grandson of the 8th Duke of Somerset. Thus ten years after her first marriage the widow of the publican turned merchant seaman married into a family which had twice married potential claimants of the Throne.*

The regatta had hardly finished when the harbour was visited by Sir T Lipton's fine yacht *Shamrock* with a crew of twenty-two.

As the year closed a great storm arose and two reparation German destroyers anchored in Torbay broke adrift. Despite gallant efforts by the Brixham lifeboat, which nearly overturned, Denaby & Cadeby's main colliery tug *Dencade,* and two smaller Dartmouth tugs, the destroyers went ashore, but with no loss of life. One came up on Roundham Point and the other at Preston Slipway, and both were written off and sold. They were built in 1910, costing over £40,000 each, and were over 220 feet long. The *T189* (646 tons) lying on the rocks at Roundham Head in the more difficult position made only £100. The other, the *S24* (555 tons) in the more accessible position on Preston Beach, made £545. H W Shaw, who had purchased both vessels, demolished *in situ* the *T189*, taking only the more easily removable parts and leaving the sea to reclaim the rest, including the valuable bronze propellers and turbines. These were recovered in 1946 by Kingswear's enterprising Jim Thorpe,

Floating Bridge *No. 6, built at Philips in 1920 immediately after their purchase of the ferry, slipways and Bridge Road.*
R Tucker/C King/Dartmouth Museum

who owned a mechanical and salvage company at Paignton harbour. The more accessible wreck the *S24* was patched and towed to Brixham to be broken up there. Mr Shaw then purchased a British submarine for £1,000 from Davenport, which was also towed to Brixham and opened to the public for inspection at a fee, before being demolished. The enterprise proved so profitable that Mr Shaw, his foreman Fred Rennels and another employee amassed sufficient capital to resettle in Australia. Interestingly it was stated by Mr Rennels in a local newspaper that the stripped hulls of both the destroyer and the submarine were towed to Dartmouth and run up on the Coombe Mud to act as breakwater to further landfill, and it is believed that they were the two hulls that were buried under what is now Coronation Park, formed after Dartmouth's North Embankment was built in 1931.

Ten Prince liners that safely made harbour to lay up – the Burmese, Korean, Trojan, Galician, Serbian, Grecian, Siamese, Spartan, Manchurian, *and* Arabian Princesses.

R TUCKER/DARTMOUTH MUSEUM

1921

Philips had purchased by private treaty the Higher Ferry, the tolls, *Floating Bridge*, slipways and Bridge Road. They promptly laid down a replacement ferry, the sixth (yard number 548), which was launched in May. It was larger and built entirely of steel, measuring 55ft x 32ft x 24ft, with 24-foot prows at each end, and a 7-foot house each side to accommodate passengers and machinery. Between these was an 18-foot roadway to accommodate four large charabancs or lorries. A new innovation was propulsion by paddle-wheels, with guide wires to ensure a straight and quick passage across the river. Though incomplete, it was immediately placed in service and propelled by a small steam launch until work on the machinery aboard was completed.

It was an exceptional year, starting with the arrival from Barry, South Wales, of a once-proud ship, the 1,633-ton *Sorkness*, a Norwegian four-masted steel barque, 252ft long and built in Glasgow in 1894 for Captain Clink, (who had named her *Zinita*, after a 26-rater of Fife design). He was a keen yachtsman, naming his fleet after famous racing yachts: *Samoan, Thistle, Valkyrie,* and *Zinita*. She was renamed *Sorkness* on being sold to Norway and sadly was to end her days in Dartmouth harbour as a standing hulk for the Dartmouth Coaling Company. The wooden gun sloop, ex-HMS *Falcon*, well known in Plymouth, also came to serve as a shifting hulk.

Around this time the three-funnelled German cruiser *Stuttgart* arrived from Cherbourg and anchored abreast Philips' works at Noss. She was purchased by the Channel Shipbreaking Co Ltd of Teignmouth, as the two German destroyers wrecked in Torbay had been originally, but as she drew 14 feet of water and the Teignmouth yard could only accommodate 10 feet, Philips removed her heavy guns and gear to lighten her, prior to towing her to the Teignmouth yard.

The SS *Broadmayne* (3,120 tons), on passage from London to America, called for bunkers. She arrived one evening in heavy weather and signalled for a pilot, but continued to make harbour giving the engine an occasional kick; but she failed to allow leeway and caught the Castle Ledge buoy, snapping the cable, which wrapped around and jammed the propeller. She then drifted onto the rocks at Inner Froward Point, Kingswear, and a night of bravery followed both at sea and ashore. The Brixham life-saving apparatus team - supported by that great, and by no means young, farmer Tom Bulley (Brownstone Farms) and his son - made Herculean efforts to reach the wreck. Finally the Brixham lifeboat *Betsy Newton* saved most of the men, while some, who had reached the cliff face, were hauled to safety by the shore party. The wreck later broke in half and was sold to Johns & Co Ltd, Port Talbot, and demolition commenced. The major portion, the bow and midships, was floated clear and towed to Millbay Cove, beached and demolished there; the stern, which included the engines, was stripped and later slid off the rocks and disappeared under the deep water. The pilots were cleared of dereliction of duty, but criticized for failing to have more powerful motor launches to cope with the heavy seas.

SILENT SENTINELS ON THE DART

After four years of bitter conflict, change was inevitable, although not always palatable, and this was particularly noticeable in the harbour. There were well over 10 million tons of shipping surplus to requirements, so owners began to lay up their vessels as rates were insufficient to cover operating costs and outlay on capital. This had a beneficial effect on the cash-starved Harbour Commissioners through lay-up fees. The SS *Glenbridge* was the first to lay up by Kiln Gate, quickly followed by six more, then a positive galaxy of vessels from all the principal shipping companies, foremost being the Prince liners. The latter laid up vessels in tiers in the main harbour, others abreast upriver, way past Noss, a process that was to continue for many years.

This brought little revenue to the area and severe hardship prevailed particularly among the lumpers. In some weeks no ships at all coaled, and the port reduced the number of lumpers to 180, of which 163 were unemployed. The fishing industry was also badly hit and it was proposed that a third of the fleet should lay up. To compound the misery, the miners demanded more money, declaring a national strike and depriving the port of the coal necessary to support the diminished bunkering trade. The situation was so serious that the Government declared a state of emergency; the strike and attendant hardship lasted six months and cost millions of pounds.

Meanwhile Renwick, Wilton & Co Ltd was again using chartered vessels and, having disposed of their only colliers, the SS *Torquay* and SS *Kingswear*, ordered a new replacement collier from the Clyde Shipbuilding Co. In Brixham the rival Denaby & Cadeby Main Colliery Co scrapped their old standing hulk *London City* and purchased from the Denaby Shipping & Commercial Co, Southampton, the larger SS *Susquehanna* (3700GT ex-Union Castle Line), renaming it also *London City*. Denaby Shipping & Commercial Co established an oil depot in a harbourside quarry at Brixham to service the growing numbers of oil-burning ships, and these improved facilities further depressed the Dartmouth trade. The Commission again came under intense criticism from the town council, lumpers and expanding Labour Party. The wealthy A H Bridson, who had previously been Commission chairman for thirteen years and had changed his political colours, strongly advocated removal of what he called 'anachronistic anomalies'. All parties were still incensed that Mr Wilton and the coaling companies had refused to grant moorings to Denaby & Cadeby in 1910, forcing them to Brixham. The town council had improved their representation on the Commission, but were still outvoted as Mr Aitken, pleasure

Top left: *SS* Broadmayne *was wrecked at Froward Point, Kingswear; all were saved due to the heroic actions of Brixham coastguard, rocket crews, lifeboat, and a local farmer and his family.*
DARTMOUTH MUSEUM

Middle left: *Mr Tom Bulley, Brownstone Farm, whose participation and local knowledge on that wild and stormy night in 1921 was a major factor in the rescue; he also provided warmth and shelter for the survivors at his farmhouse.*
M FARDON

Middle right: *A cheerful land-girl, who assisted in the rescue and when the war ended, continued working at Brownstone Farm.*
M FARDON

Bottom left: *The salvaged bow-section of the* SS Broadmayne *beached in Millbay Cove prior to demolition. The 'castle' was previously a lime kiln converted by Neil Hill with a water wheel to generate electricity for Mr Jolliffe's adjacent Warren House. Unfortunately the stream's riparian owner, Mr Bulley, diverted the watercourse.*
R TUCKER/DARTMOUTH MUSEUM

craft representative and director, as was Wilton, of the Devon Dock & Pier Co (part of the Renwick, Wilton & Co Ltd group), voted with the consortium. A provisional bill was sent to Parliament which resulted in a new board of thirteen members and doubled the town's representation from two to four. The chairman, Channel Coaling Co's ex-managing director Jasper Bartlett, and the clerk, Mr Palfrey did not relish the change and so resigned. Sir Thomas Wilton temporarily took the chair.

Regatta 1921 This was again highly successful and well attended; the swimming in the Boat Float was watched by 3,000 people. The highlight was the Embankment Gardens, described as 'a feast by day and night'. The gas and electric companies together with Mr Johns, horticultural chief, transformed them into a dreamland. The display included an illuminated model of the yacht *Shamrock I* with 'GB' in lights over the entrance to the gardens. There were thirteen sailing races arranged by the two committees, Lord Birkenhead winning the six-metre class, while the motor launch race, 'Bang and Go Back', had five starters.

The two old rivals, Dartmouth and Brixham, began again to cast covetous eyes at Kingswear, for if there was any chance of a dockside complex it would be at Ballast Cove, Kingswear, which already possessed the essential rail network. Dartmouth, the major contender, courted Kingswear assiduously and there were rumours that there was to be a tunnel under the river linking the two communities. However, Kingswear spurned both overtures although Brixham was to pursue her claim with vigour, petitioning Devon County Council to absorb both Kingswear and Churston Ferrers within its boundaries. They quoted the following figures:

Place	Acres	Population	Per Acre
Brixham	5,626	7,954	1.4
Churston	2,518	572	0.23
Kingswear	101	841	8.3

So tiny Kingswear had six times as many people per acre as Brixham, and thirty-three times more people per acre compared with Churston parish. The final result, to Kingswear's delight, was a rejection by the Devon County Council to any change.

This hectic year ended with a major blow. The Dartmouth & Kingswear Cottage Hospital, sustained by voluntary subscription, closed through lack of funds for the first time since its opening forty-four years previously. Fortunately the untiring efforts of H J Boyd Carpenter, Riversea, Kingswear, raised sufficient moneys for the hospital to reopen the following June. Kingswear church received superbly carved replacement oak seating around the whole building from an anonymous donor, found after her death to be Lady Lennard of Kingswear Court. Kingswear's Captain Angel published *The Good Ship Sheila*, based on his long years at sea in square-rigged ships; then sadly he died, thus depriving Dartmouth of a rich character.

The Moravian Mission ship Harmony *in Dartmouth harbour prior to making her yearly trip to Labrador and the South Arctic to trade with the Eskimos.*

J HORSLEY

1922 The old wooden two-decker *Hindustan*, built in 1824, and on the Dart with the college for thirty-six years before being towed away in 1905, was finally broken up at Woolwich. In January the new collier for Renwick, Wilton & Co Ltd was launched in Port Glasgow, (2,470GT, 292ft x 42ft x 19ft) and named *Haytor*. Amalgamated Industrials Ltd (Sir Thomas Wilton was a director and Renwick, Wilton & Co Ltd was part of their holding) experienced severe cash problems, so before the SS *Haytor* could commence service she was sold on to Spain and renamed *Dilluns*. HMS *Pomone* was paid off and launch No. 63 HMS *Osborne* was renamed *Britannia* and became the replacement depot ship at Dartmouth. The depression was widespread and many more ships were being laid up along the coast, many in the Dart estuary. The economic situation continued to deteriorate; the *Chronicle* announced that 1,700,000 tons of British shipping was laid up, and in the shipyards building work was being suspended as owners were unable to pay. The bunkering trade declined and trouble arose when attempts were made to reduce the pay of the lumpers, who because of the recent war and prior union strength had much improved their wages and conditions and had imposed restrictive practices, such as the payment of all trimmers whether needed or not. There were standoffs on both sides for some eight months, which ended with mutual compromise.

Since 1919 Sir Thomas Wilton's health had been declining, so he sold his Dartmouth home for almost thirty years, Hawarden, South Town (Woodlands), and moved to Haytor, near Bovey Tracey; he also purchased a property in London. His business of Renwick, Wilton & Co Ltd was ably run by his sons Thomas based locally and Clifford, based in Newcastle-upon-Tyne, and by his partner Frank Dobson in Torquay. In January 1922 he created with his two sons a private company, Vale Investments Ltd, to manage family investments, and in June he implemented an earlier decision to place the Wilton Steam Shipping Company in voluntary liquidation. For some time he had been extending his interests beyond the limits of the business that had served him so well, and moving into the more precarious and complex fields of banking and brokerage, which were to cost him dear. In 1916 he had become vice chairman of a large London company, Amalgamated Industrials Ltd, who had absorbed Renwick, Wilton & Co Ltd; in 1921 he resigned to become an ordinary director. The company became bankrupt in June 1922, although Renwick, Wilton & Co Ltd was able to continue trading. More disastrously,, he had in 1920 accepted a directorship in the newly formed London-based Anglo Baltic & Mediterranean Bank, which had made some unsecured loans, and had become involved in law suits which bankrupted it. To his credit, Sir Thomas personally repaid many friends and associates whom he had persuaded to invest in Anglo Baltic & Mediterranean Bank. He resigned his brief chairmanship of the Harbour Commission, as he felt unable to accept the changed circumstances, since the coaling factors had lost their monopoly. He presented the town with a fine gold medallion to add to the mayoral chain. Lady Wilton, not to be outdone, also presented a splendid medallion for future mayoresses to wear, which redressed the imbalance that existed on civic occasions between the Mayor and the Mayoress.

St George, *a beautiful three-masted barquentine waiting for repairs at Philips.*
CYRIL KING

*Regatta tug of war
in the Boat Float
between twelve
oared cutters*
G WEATHERLY

Regatta 1922, though highly successful, was smaller, for no big yachts competed, only *Terpsichore* having been commissioned this year. However, the season saw the start of the 12-metre international class, built to the new 'second international rule'. There were only two races outside on the set course, West Blackstone/Sands Hotel/ Skerries/Finish, while on the Saturday a new race was held for service cutters of the Britannia Royal Naval College.

As the year closed the harbour was graced by the arrival of a small but beautiful barque-rigged auxiliary sailing vessel, the *Harmony*, under Captain Jackson. She was owned by the Moravian Missionary Societies, and every year loaded stores and provisions, which ranged from flour to tombstones, and left for the Labrador Missionary Post, taking out and relieving the missionaries, some of whom had thirty years' service abroad. In the Arctic she also traded clothing, tinned food and other stores with the Eskimos for furs, whale oil and seal skins, partly to assist the people and partly to finance the mission. The Moravians had a romantic history after the German Reformation, sending missionaries worldwide. The first missionaries went to Greenland and the West Indies, and they reached Labrador in 1761. However, the crew were murdered and ten years later the London Moravians sent a second expedition which succeeded, and they supervised the work with a ship per year ever after. The vessel, 223 tons, was built in 1864 of oak and teak and copper sheathed to the waterline. She was built for the East Indian tea trade and named the *Lorna Doone*, with a figurehead of the comely heroine of Blackwell's famous novel. She passed to a Dundee firm and spent some years whaling before becoming the property of the missionaries, who renamed her *Harmony*. She called at Dartmouth once a year, and in 1925 she rescued the crew of the Hudson Bay Company ship *Eskimo* which had been caught in the ice and had sunk. In 1927 the Hudson Bay Company took over the trade. Shortly afterwards this lovely old ship, known affectionately to sailors and to Dartmouth as 'Gin and Bible,' was sold to the breakers' yard.

1923

was dominated by the river; the Royal Dart Steamship Company had acquired the Dittisham ferry and its rights, and decided that offices and a new pier extending further into the river were necessary to service the increasing excursions to that lovely waterside village. Meanwhile Philips had for the Royal Dart Steamship Company launched another new paddle-steamer for the Totnes run, the second to be named the *Totnes Castle*.

Several local men died in quick succession. Francis Charles Simpson JP, and County Councillor died at his Maypool home. He was Mayor of Dartmouth for ten times and Rear Commodore of the RDYC for eleven years; he founded the defunct Start Bay Yacht Club, the large shipbuilding complex at Noss and the cottage hospital. He was also the scourge of the Dart Harbour Commission and the South Embankment scheme. Next followed H J Boyd Carpenter, Riversea, Kingswear, who since the death of his father the Bishop Boyd Carpenter in 1918, had tirelessly carried on his father's local charity works. He was mainly responsible for the reopening of the cottage hospital. Finally, there was the sad accidental death of the disabled Mr Pearn, a Strete fisherman who, when returning down Bridge Road in his van from Brixham, ran straight onto the *Floating Bridge* at Noss and off the other end, drowning in the deep water.

The normal tranquillity of Kingswear was disturbed by the appointment of the new vicar, the Reverend Michael Dowling Ryan, MC. He was a man of strong character with leanings towards the Catholic church, and keen to introduce incense and mass into his services, which brought him into conflict with his parishioners and caused trouble for several years.

Trade continued at a low ebb and the *Chronicle* reported that the world tonnage of oil-fuelled ships now exceeded that of coal-burning vessels; this threatened the future of the bunkering trade. Shipbuilding was so depressed that Philips began building twenty-five barges, for the Thames, just to keep the works open, (which they had never done before), and at £9 per ton they could not even cover costs. They also tried to sell to the town council for £5,000 the Coombe Mud, which they had bought for £1,000 in 1914, with the condition that the town council should build and lease them a dry dock. On investigation the town clerk established that the dry dock would cost about £70,000 to £80,000, thus making it an offer the town council found no difficulty in refusing.

Regatta 1923 was surprisingly held one week earlier than usual, 23-25 August, and only a modest number of craft, three steam and seventeen sail, were listed in the harbour. A new dinghy class was introduced, the Dart One Design, which raced in every regatta until 1963. An interesting winner of the yachts not exceeding 20ft was *Firefly*, sailed by Prince John-de-Mahé.

The *Chronicle* also reported the arrival of another graceful sailing vessel, the three-masted brigantine the *St George*, to undergo repairs and alterations at Philips prior to a ten-month 21,000-mile scientific expedition, sailing to the West Indies through the Panama Canal and to the lesser-known islands of the South Seas. The ship, 275 tons net, was built in 1860 by Ramage & Fergusson Ltd, sheathed with teak and coppered below the waterline. She was owned by the Scientific Exploration Research Company, formed by a band of adventurers and academics to promote expeditions to more remote areas of the world. Never in Devon's history had so many intellectuals gathered in such a small area; the party included nine fellows of the Royal Society, professors and doctors of the Archaeological Institute and other august bodies. Some were paid, while others were paying fees to undertake serious scientific study, mainly on the Easter and Cook Islands, Tahiti, Rappa and the Marquesas. The town was intrigued by this concentration of academics, and rumours began to circulate that the trip included treasure-hunting in the Cocos Islands. Commander D Blair OBE was in charge, and the party included eminent photographers and a later famous marine artist, Montague Dawson. However, all was not well from the very beginning; she was only scheduled to be in Dartmouth for six weeks. She finally left nine months later, after a ceremonial dinner given by the Corporation, and sailed away to cheers from the townspeople. The borough band played, flags flew and many of her seventy crew manned the rigging. The expedition during the following eighteen months collected many rare specimens, but was dogged by misfortune; financial problems were such that at one stage they were unable to meet the crew's wages and the London offices were besieged by wives demanding payment. The ship suffered some damage and several members left and made their separate ways home. However, the *St George* made a triumphant return to Dartmouth in September 1925. Later, when in Plymouth for repairs, writs for £4,900 were nailed to her mast and she was declared bankrupt. She was offered for auction, but sold privately for £16,000 for use as a training ship in Plymouth, being broken up in 1929.

At the end of the year the town was rocked by the announcement that S T Pope, Dartmouth's town clerk for the last twenty years, had been asked to resign. This was embarrassing as now four town clerks, with long service, had been dismissed. The first one was Percy Hocking in 1882, suspected of influencing council elections but mainly because of his strong support for the South Embankment scheme; the second town clerk was Osmonius Bartlett in 1902 for misappropriation of funds with yet a third in 1907. In this case irregularities had been found relating to some small accounts and Government grants totalling several hundreds of pounds which had been lost due to the clerk's failure to make the necessary applications and to reply to correspondence. In Mr Pope's case an open council meeting was held with the public in attendance; Alderman P B Atkins carried out a spirited defence of the town clerk requesting that he be given another chance. He succeeded in splitting the council vote 7/7 and it was only on the casting vote of the Mayor that he was requested to resign, which he duly did and a new town clerk, J J Day, was appointed.

Mr Pope set up business locally and in the following year stood for the town council. Surprisingly he was elected at the top of the poll and was carried in triumph to the Guildhall shoulder high by his supporters. However, after only attending one meeting, further anomalies were discovered in the affairs and accounts of the Port Sanitary Authority, where he, as town clerk, had also served as secretary. Proceedings were started and his champion Alderman P B Atkins resigned all his public appointments and sold his drapery business in Duke Street (now HSBC Bank). Matters dragged on: although the money involved was small, his main misdemeanour was again non-compliance with his duties and the consequent loss of grants. One glaring item was that for years the Port Sanitary Authority had been trying to replace the decaying 1893 isolation hospital boat *Mayfly;* eventually they purchased the River Dart Steamboat Company's *Kingswear Castle* for £500 and converted her for over £1,000, only to find that the Government had in 1918 stopped demanding a separate floating isolation hospital. The committee members, had not been informed by Mr Pope. The *Kingswear Castle* was eventually stripped, towed away and hulked further upriver near Totnes. Meanwhile Mr Pope had moved away, and secured steady employment elsewhere, and the council decided to take no further action.

1924 started quietly and trade continued to improve. Upriver a cloak-and-dagger event was unfolding aboard one laid-up Russian ship SS *Jupiter.* She had arrived in September 1922 flying the old imperial flag, her owners, Compagnie Russe, had moved to Paris before the Revolution. In March agents of the Soviet Union boarded her and persuaded the captain to haul down the old flag, run up the red flag and hand over the ship's papers. The Admiralty ruled that the vessel belonged to the Soviet Republic, who took full possession and sold her to Italian owners.

Meanwhile Philips, despairing of Dartmouth ever having a dry dock, negotiated with their north country co-owners Swan Hunter to purchase from them a large fairly new floating dock (260ft x 60ft) with a holding capacity of 2,000 tons and a docking draft of 14 feet. She arrived at Noss in April, towed by the Dutch tug *Humbert*. In May a Brixham trawler skipper saw a full-rigged German ship

Dartmouth Floating Dock

Every
Class of Vessels
up to
1,500 Tons
displacement,
260/270 ft. Length,
58 ft. Beam.
MEAN
Maximum depth
over blocks,
14 ft. at
Middle Spring Tides.

Telegrams:
" Philip, Dartmouth."

All Latest Appliances
including
Pneumatic and Electric Tools
for Riveting, Caulking,
Drilling, Scaling,
Paint Spraying, etc.
Bottoms Cleaned and Coated.
Electric and Acetylene Welding, and
Pneumatic Floating Plants.
Every description of work
to Hulls above water line,
and to Machinery on all
classes of Vessels,
including Oil Tankers, up to
20,000 Tons executed
with the utmost despatch.
Dock close to Machine and
Ironworkers' Shops.

Telephone :
No. 12 Dartmouth.

Proprietors:

PHILIP & SON, LIMITED,

Shipbuilders and Engineers,

DARTMOUTH.

Landkircham, (1,796GT) ashore at Downend Point. He alerted Philips who promptly despatched their tug to claim the prize, towed her to Dartmouth and berthed her in their dry dock. There was justifiable pride at this event in Dartmouth, but no hint of the misfortune to follow. Work commenced immediately and 700 tons of ballast were removed from her. Later in the evening, when the forty-one crew were settling in their bunks, a sudden list to starboard created panic and the captain ordered the men ashore. At two in the morning the dock sank, but fortunately the ship, freed of her mooring ties, was able to float free, mainly unharmed. Philips engaged a salvage vessel *Ringdove Aid* from Falmouth and after several unsuccessful attempts to raise the dock applied to the Dart Harbour Commission in August for permission to abandon the sunken dock after cutting off the sides. This would have given 30 feet of clear water at spring tides, but the request was refused. So the salvage vessel returned, the dry dock tanks were sealed and pumped clear of water, filled by compressed air and brought to the surface. Thus the dock, so nearly abandoned, returned to give a further thirty-seven years of service.

Philips fulfil a major Dartmouth need, by providing a floating dock that continued to give good service for thirty-seven years.
DARTMOUTH MUSEUM

The first Kingswear Castle after launching in 1904 at Falmouth. In 1924 she was sold to Dartmouth Corporation and converted into hospital ship at a cost of £1500, only to find later it was not required. She was then offered for sale as a houseboat, but there no takers so she was hulked upriver near Totnes.
CYRIL KING

175

Regatta 1924 mirrored the nationwide improvement in trade, for forty-five yachts were listed. Harold Clayton, later Sir Harold, entered the winners' lists, (a practice he was to repeat for many years ahead), whilst in the big yachts exceeding 50-tons King George V's *Britannia* beat *White Heather.*

The religious turmoil that had started in Kingswear the previous year when the new incumbent introduced Catholic practices continued unabated. Several senior residents resigned their positions in the church and Sir Thomas Lennard, wealthy shoe magnate of Kingswear Court and the vicar, the Rev Dowling Ryan, exchanged blows in the church vestibule over the matter. Civil action resulted in the Brixham court but, possibly because of their social standing, both were persuaded to withdraw their summonses. The unrest continued, however, with Sir Thomas Lennard withdrawing all his moral and financial support from the church.

1925 was the mid-point of what was to be a traumatic half century, the first period of which was blighted by a horrific war, and which experienced great social change. Sadly, the following generation appeared to have learned no lessons from this, for the second twenty-five years were to be a repetition of the first.

The year started with a macabre advertisement in the *Chronicle* by the 'Dart Board of Conservateurs', anxious to preserve salmon stocks: 'the board in future is increasing its payments for Herons' Heads from 2/6 to 5/-'.

News came that the three-masted schooner *Terrier* had sunk off Milford Haven. She was built in 1873 by Philips for Newman Hunt & Co Ltd for the Newfoundland trade (143GT, 104ft x 21ft x 13ft,) with a dog's head as a figurehead, but she had been purchased by Kingswear's Captain Angel and converted in 1896 for the coasting trade.

The cottage hospital had recovered since its closure and reopening in 1921, and had sufficient funds for R Pillar & Sons to build a sizeable extension. At the same time the town council purchased all the adjacent dilapidated old properties and demolished them to construct a new road (now Hauley Road). Sadly the nearby sailors' rest at Oxford House (DHNA) was forced to close because the lease had expired and there was insufficient money to purchase it.

Trade, however, continued to improve. The coal strike was virtually over; shipbuilders were working longer hours for lower wages to receive orders; Elders & Fyffe 'banana boat' passenger liners were calling more frequently. To profit from the improving mercantile position Sir Thomas Wilton, in spite of declining health, formed a new company in March, the T & C Wilton Shipping Co Ltd, with himself as chairman and two sons, Thomas and Clifford, as directors. For the Kingswear jetty trade and time chartering, they ordered from Crown & Sons of Sunderland a new collier, the *Haytor* (1,189GT, 220ft x 356ft x 15ft), the second of their boats to bear this name. After three-and-a-half years Elder Dempster Line's SS *Indora* sailed to resume trading, thus leaving the main harbour clear of laid-up shipping for the first time in nearly five years. Since the arrival of the SS *Glenbridge* in March 1921, 101 vessels had laid up and there were still seven ships on the river above Noss. They were beneficial locally, in terms of harbour dues, ship repairs and provisioning, and as objects of interest to passengers on the paddle-steamers and day-trippers' boats.

Many visitors wishing to see Dartmouth Castle were deterred by its remote situation and the lack of a suitable landing place, so Councillor Richards persuaded the council to build one, Stumpy Steps, adjacent to the castle, and invited boatmen to tender for a summer castle ferry service (today well served by ex-pilot Dave Griffiths and his colleagues).

Regatta 1925 attracted even more yachts, the star being Sir Thomas Lipton's *Shamrock*, which won the handicap race for over 70-tonners, against four competitors, for a prize of £80. The handicap race for yachts under three tons drew fifteen entrants, the largest number of starters to date, and was won by Mrs Morgan Giles, while in the launch races there was one for motor-boat tobogganing. There was also much acclaim for the Embankment Gardens, again lit up like fairyland.

The excitement engendered by regatta had barely subsided when the GWR, owners of the Lower Ferry, refused to renew Casey & Heal's lease, informing the public by a notice in the Chronicle; shortly afterwards came the following notice by the town council:

IMPORTANT NOTICE: CLOSING OF HORSE FERRY Passengers and
Drivers of Motor and Vehicular Traffic are requested to IMMEDIATELY
NOTIFY THE TOWN CLERK of any Delay or inconvenience caused in
the use of the GWR New Ferry Service on 'The Mew'.
J J R Day, Town Clerk, Guildhall, Dartmouth, 2 October 1925.

There was consternation in the town, for this action ended almost fifty years' sterling service by the Casey family. However it was not unexpected as the GWR also owned the adjacent railway ferry *The Mew*, and had been modifying it during 1924 to carry vehicles as well as passengers. To the GWR it was common sense because road transport had increased considerably, including their own fleet of vehicles, and so they were having to make considerable cash payments to Casey & Heal to transport their own vehicles on their own ferry.

There were several drawbacks to the new scheme, as the railway ferry had to transport the cows and flocks of sheep, previously carried by the Lower Ferry along with the passengers. The town council took up the matter and by October the head of the GWR, Sir Felix Pole, made a present of the Lower Ferry service and float to the town council for a nominal sum of £100 and the payment of £5 per annum for the use of the slips.

Mr Heal retired, and the locals were delighted when his partner Tom Casey placed a small twelve-seater passenger launch, *I'll Try*, in the service, which lasted ten months, running from the privately owned Gibbs Steps (Longford) adjacent to Kingswear Slip. Shortly afterwards the town council offered the service for tender and received only two replies, one from Tom Casey (only blank forms as a mark of protest), the other from Mr Peters, (recently a partner in the firm Peters & Raymond, coal merchants, Bayards Cove, Dartmouth) and Mrs Blanche Heseltine of Kingswear, who was a sleeping partner in his firm. The latter's offer of £250 per annum for a term of fourteen years was accepted. After purchasing some of Mr Casey's fleet, the service recommenced following ten months' closure, much to the local inhabitants relief.

SS Haytor, a collier built in Glasgow in 1924 for T & C Wilton Co's (Newcastle to Hollacombe, Torquay) gas- and house-coal trade over Kingswear quays.
NEIL WILTON

The end of the year was marked by the opening of the superb new Kingswear Village Hall, which had been given by the wealthy Sir Thomas Lennard. It was palatial for a village, built in restrained Tudor style on two floors, with a men's club below with two full-sized billiard tables, one given by Mr Hine-Haycock, Kittery Court, the other by Sir Thomas. Above was an assembly hall with a stage and balcony and seating for 200 people. The hall was dedicated to the First Kingswear Girl Guide Troop, of which Lady Lennard was captain. The large reception was attended by all the top people of the district, with one notable exception: the Rev Dowling Ryan.

After severe pounding by storms in the Bay of Biscay, Sir Ernest Shackleton and Captain Scott's famous ship *Discovery* put back into Dartmouth for repairs at Philips prior to another voyage. This time the voyage was not for purposes of exploration but for scientific research, and was planned to last for two-and-a-half years. Her first port of call was to be Tristan da Cunha, and followed by South Georgia to gather information on the migration of whales. A small bow-mounted harpoon would fire a silver-plated pellet, numbered and dated, which pinned onto the skin of the whale and which asked whalers and the station to return these details and claim a small reward. She was the only British ship built solely for exploration, and was packed with scientific instruments. Her frame was solid oak, 11 inches thick to resist the terrific pressure of the ice. Before sailing the officers and crew of thirty-one were entertained by the town council at a civic banquet at the Royal Castle Hotel. It was a further two years before she returned from the Falkland Islands, her base in the Southern Ocean, her laboratory packed with thousands of crustaceans preserved in spirit for further investigation and with numerous water-colours of brilliant fish recovered from the deepest oceans.

The *Chronicle* records show that by pure coincidence on the day preceding the departure of the RSS *Discovery* for the Antarctic the beautiful three-masted barquentine SV *St George* returned to Dartmouth, her port of departure for the Antarctic two years previously. She was greeted outside the harbour by the Mayor and councillors in the PS *Berry Castle* to cheering, whistles and rockets. For a few brief hours these two graceful vessels lay abreast on the lovely placid waters of the Dart, bringing to a peaceful close the first quarter of the twentieth century.

Sir Ernest Shackleton's and later Captain R F Scott's RSS Discovery *here for repairs at Philips whilst en route for a two-and-a-half-year tour in the Antarctic.*
R BARNES/D GRIFFITHS

CHAPTER 9

The Lean Years

1926 to 1939

LABOUR AND THE UNIONS UNITE

1926 will be remembered as the year of the General Strike and the eight-month-long miners' strike that nearly crippled the country. The recession persisted, ships returned to lay up in the harbour and depression loomed.

The year began sadly when tragedy overtook the London barge *Lord Kitchener,* (69 tons) on passage from Poole to Par for china clay. An intense gale had reduced visibility to 20 yards when she struck the rocky cliffs between Redlap and Rockvale Coves just outside the harbour mouth. The vessel rapidly broke up and three crew clambered up the mast which collapsed shorewise, throwing them into the water. Only the captain reached the shore, and after searching for the mate and boy for three hours, he managed to scramble up the almost sheer 80-foot cliff face to reach Redlap Farm, where he alerted the coastguard. This was the second tragedy to occur here, for ten years previously a small sailing vessel, *Kingswear Castle,* had come ashore with the loss of all hands.

In February the *Chronicle* received from S Ferris, Gothic Cottage, Weeke Hill, a copy of an unpublished letter dated 23 January 1905 from the great explorer Henry M Stanley who found Dr Livingstone in Africa. It praised the late R Ferris for the great contribution he had made to the success of Stanley's second African expedition, as follows:

> *Dear Sir,*
> *It is now twenty-nine years since your father, delayed at Zanzibar, undertook to make for me some alterations in the* Lady Alice *boat. That his work was exceedingly effective may justly be conceded, since by the alterations we were enabled to transport the boat something like three thousand miles, and endured the rough handling of the porters, the frequent putting to and dismounting of the sections, and safely survived the stormy lakes Victoria and Tanganyika. It was also through the* Lady Alice *that we were able to navigate 1,800 miles of the Congo, and make known its course to the Atlantic. Certainly Ferris's name will always be associated in my memory with what the* Lady Alice *was able to achieve. Mr Ferris was, besides, a good honest fellow, and it was one of my happy lucks to have met him at the right time and to have secured his able assistance when he was most needed. I am sorry he has passed away without my being able to see him and give him a hearty greeting and acknowledging the good turn he did the expedition at Zanzibar in 1871.*

HEADS NORTH AND THE LUALABA; TAHS KATANGA."

DARTMOUTH'S CONTRIBUTION TO H M STANLEY'S 1871 EXPEDITION

Above: *Henry Stanley and Frank Pocock tossing a coin to decide their route, whether north, or south through cannibal territory.*

Left: *The* Lady Alice, *their only means of progress (apart than by foot), prior to her modification by Dartmouth's R Ferris. She was delivered in five sections, which was too big for jungle transportation.*
BOTH EXETER WESTCOUNTRY STUDIES LIBRARY

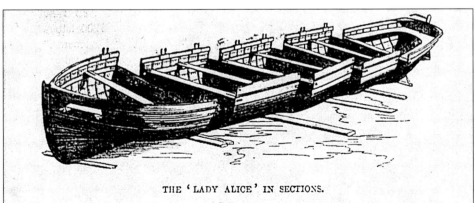

THE 'LADY ALICE' IN SECTIONS.

I thank you for your memorial card and beg you to accept my sincere sympathy in your great loss.

Yours faithfully, Henry M Stanley.

The episode was also related in Stanley's 1894 book *Through the Dark Continent*:

In April 1874 the news came that Livingstone was dead, and the Editor asked him to complete Livingstone's work in Africa. Prominent among the equipment was a barge invented by Stanley consisting of five sections, and named the Lady Alice. *'After my return from the Fufiju Delta, the steamer* Euphrates *had brought the* Lady Alice *to Zanzibar and I discovered that four of the sections weighed 280lb each, and that one weighed 310lb, but in her present condition her carriage through the jungles would necessitate a pioneer force a hundred strong. Then I was informed that a very clever English carpenter named Ferris was about to leave by the* Euphrates *for England, and for a 'consideration' promised to do his utmost to make the sections portable without lessening her efficiency. I explained that the path was often only 18 inches wide in Africa, and hemmed in on each side with dense jungle, and that any package six feet broad could not be conveyed along it. Therefore each of the four sections should be sub-divided to obtain eight portable sections, each three feet wide, and that an after-piece be made upon arriving at the lakes. Mr Ferris furnished me within two weeks with the newly-modelled* Lady Alice. *Mr R E Ferris was in Zanzibar after lighthouse construction work at Batavia.*

Meanwhile industrial strife surfaced again, as the coal industry was making substantial losses and the miners' leaders, representing 1,127,000 men, thought the shortfall should be made up by the Government. This view was not shared by Prime Minister Mr Baldwin and his cabinet, and matters degenerated to the extent that the miners' leaders, with the tacit support of the expanding Labour Party and the Trades Union Council (TUC), received plenary powers and a General Strike was called.

The Lady Alice *successfully withstands attack by hundreds of cannibal Bangalas in a fleet of canoes.*
EXETER WESTCOUNTRY STUDIES LIBRARY

This was considered a challenge to the Government and the constitution and immediate moves were made to counter the situation. Volunteers from all walks of life were mustered to run essential services, a local example being the manning of Churston station. Captain Ferrier, Mr Evans and the sons of two local baronets, Arthur Clayton and Hugh Goodson, became porters, and were surprised to receive tips for their freely-given services. Fortunately the General Strike ended quickly, but the coal dispute dragged on for several months.

The effect was nationwide and Dartmouth was one of the first casualties, because of its dependence on coal for the bunkering trade and the Government ban on the export of coal. By June household coal was almost exhausted and the collier *Camberway* thankfully arrived with 1,000 tons of German coal, which was quickly unloaded at Kingswear jetty. The coal situation was acute and fortunes were made when laid-up shipping, even that due for the breakers' yard, was pressed into service, scouring the world for coal for British industries.

Out of the 1,127,000 miners who went on strike, nearly bringing the country to its knees, 850,000 had drifted back to work by November and the strike was virtually over. (Now there are only a few thousand miners.)

For centuries Dartmouth's only water supply was from hillside streams by aquaduct and conduit. This changed in 1908 when this happy picture of the town council was taken at the opening of the Old Mill Creek Water Works. It was further extended in 1926.
DARTMOUTH MUSEUM

Miss Helena Mary Wotton, aged 16, Church Park Cottages, Kingswear, the G W R Queen in her finery at Belle Vue, Manchester. With 50,000 people she attended a pageant where actors, with elephants, camels and other animals portrayed transport through the ages, followed by a display of contrasting railway engines from Robert Stephenson's (who attended Dartmouth's 1857 regatta) Rocket *to modern engines.*
ALISTER GILL

A return to normal heralded more mundane events, such as Kingswear forming a Women's Institute, and Philips launching for the River Dart Steamboat Co a new 70ft long 300-passenger motor-vessel, the *Clifton Castle.* The *Chronicle* also reported the death of self-taught artist Tom Rowden, whose water-colours encapsulated the essence of Dartmoor.

On the Dart the hulk *Sabrina* departed to be broken up (the final ignominy) after fifty years' service, first as a collier then as a coal hulk.

The town council eliminated the boatman's perk of one boat towing another to avoid paying two tolls. The Seamen's Mission announced a scheme for the adoption of lighthouses and lightships by private groups to improve the lot of the keepers.

Regatta 1926 This event boasted several steam yachts and forty-five sailing yachts, and was dominated by the over 70-tons outside race of 40 miles, which was won by RDYC member Sir Maurice Singer in *Lulworth,* beating *White Heather II, Corona* and *Westward.* However, more fun was generated by one of the rowing races, the shovel race. There were, as every year, alfresco dances and fireworks.

After the regatta a marriage, which figured high on the London social calendar, occurred between Miss d'Oyly Carte and Lord Cranbrook. They were to have strong connections with Kingswear, for three months previously her father Rupert d'Oyly Carte, son of Richard d'Oyly Carte (the impresario of Gilbert and Sullivan fame), had taken possession of his newly built home Coleton Fishacre, one of loveliest of the many mansions surrounding Kingswear. It was designed by Oswald Milne, a disciple of Sir Edwin Lutyens (architect of Castle Drogo), and he created at Coleton Fishacre a magnificent 20-acre show garden. In 1982 the Estate became the property of the National Trust.

Finally, Lord Churston's nearby fine mansion Lupton House caught fire and was totally destroyed, although the contents were saved and stored in the stables.

1927 started with red faces in the Kingswear station when the *Chronicle* reported that some wag had defaced notices in first-class carriages from 'To lower the window pull the strap towards you', to 'To love the widow pull towards you'.

The GWR had already given the Kingswear Lower Ferry to the Dartmouth Town Council virtually free. It then offered to give away the 100-mile long east/west broad waterway of the Kennet & Avon Canal, connecting the rivers Thames and Avon. There were no takers and deterioration continued until 1955, when enthusiasts formed an association, later a trust which raised over £2 million to restore the waterway. It was reopened by the Queen in 1990 and the canal has since been allocated a lottery grant of £27 million.

The year also concluded the reign of Miss Helena Mary Wotton, queen for two years of the GWR's centenary celebrations. She was daughter of Kingswear's railway porter and was chosen as the railway queen from numerous contestants. Thirty special trains converged on Manchester with all grades of officials and staff for the biggest ever railway gathering. She stayed at the five-star railway-owned Midland Hotel, was waited on hand and foot, and met the highest ranking people in the land. She attended various meetings and took part in two railway films; one aboard *The Mew* was shown locally and she won much acclaim for the gracious way in which she carried out her duties. Her final act was to open Kingswear's first public library, established in the small committee room of the village hall. Meanwhile station communication was greatly improved when the Geddes' small private bus service from Brixham was replaced by a major operator, the Devon General Bus Service, which covered a wider area including Paignton and Torquay.

On the river the T & C Wilton Steamship Co Ltd took delivery of a further new vessel from Crown & Sons of Sunderland. She was 305ft x 42ft x 24ft, with a carrying capacity of 4,500 tons, and named the *Newton Abbot* by Mrs Haroldeen Wilton. The three coaling companies continued their policy of replacing the existing standing coal hulks. Channel Coaling Company Ltd's *Sabrina* had gone to be broken up the previous year and had been replaced by the Norwegian barque *Dagny* (1,115tons, 222ft), built in

Liverpool in 1889 as the SV *Tulca*, a handsome vessel with a fine cut of bow, painted ports and a graceful figurehead. G H Collins' *Juno (*220ft), once an elegant paddle-steamer belonging to the Bristol Steam Navigation Co Ltd on the Bristol/Cork service, was towed away for breaking at Preston, Lancashire. Also during this period the Harbour Commission renamed Robin Hood Cove at Kingswear, Newfoundland Cove.

Regatta 1927 was complemented by the gift to the Royal Naval College of the famous 28-ton yawl *Amaryllis* given by the sister of the late Lieutenant G D H Muhlhauser. In 1920 he had sailed 31,159 miles around the world, crossing the Atlantic from Dartmouth to the West Indies, Panama Canal, the Marquesas Islands, Australia, New Zealand, the Torres Strait, Java, Ceylon, the Red Sea and the Mediterranean, arriving back in Dartmouth in 1923.

The regatta was again graced by King George V's *Britannia*, competing against four others in the RDYC's over 70-ton handicap race of 40 miles, which she won handsomely. In a much smaller class, yachts exceeding 20ft, H L Goodson, RDYC won against *Joy* in his *Uno*.

Coleton Fishacre, the lovely home of the D'Oyly Carte family standing in twenty acres of magnificent grounds.
COURTESY OF THE NATIONAL TRUST

Lady D'Oyly Carte launching a skiff for the Dartmouth Amateur Rowing Club at Messrs Philips' Sandquay Yard.
R TUCKER, DARTMOUTH MUSEUM

A new feature of the regatta was that prizes were given for the best decorated premises, business and private, the former was won by J H Smith, Duke Street, and G W Pillar, Lower Street, and the latter was shared by three winners. The regatta was attracting an increasing number of spectators from a wider area. This was illustrated by the *Chronicle* reporting that, since the issue of the first car registration number, A1, twenty-four years previously, the alphabet was now completed and a new system was needed. The newspaper also stated that the historian Hugh Watkins had presented a copy of Thomas Newcomen's transcript in the Berlin museum to the town council, and the council had purchased for £2 what was probably the most famous grate in the world:

> *There will be satisfaction in the town over the purchase by the Town Council of the fire grate ... When Lower Street was demolished in the sixties, the grate was incorporated in Newcomen Cottage, Ridge Hill, and was acquired by Mr Brooksbank at the sale of effects which took place there about three years ago. Mr Brooksbank is thanked for allowing it to pass into the possession of the Dartmouth Corporation.*

[But where is it today?]

THE NORTH EMBANKMENT SCHEME

As the year closed the town council finalized the Coombe Improvement Scheme, which had been under consideration since 1924. The proposal was to continue Samuel Lake's existing South Embankment a further 312 yards north (a seawall and road) across the Coombe Mud, owned by Philips, to the *Floating Bridge*, infilling the Coombe Mud area to create pleasure gardens. The town council applied for a Parliamentary bill with powers to borrow £40,000 to purchase the necessary area and property. It also applied for a compulsory purchase order to acquire the Coombe Mud. These orders were obtained and work commenced in November of the following year but the project was long in execution and fraught with problems, it partly opened in 1932 and was fully completed when the pleasure gardens were opened in 1937.

1928 The main topic of conversation was the town council's £40,000 North Embankment scheme with its implications and benefits, for at last Dartmouth would have a recreation area. Therefore there was surprise when the Dartmouth Gas Company successfully applied for permission to erect a coal conveyor on the existing Embankment, sited virtually at the starting point of the proposed new Embankment. There was resistance in the council when it realized that the structure would be 60ft high at the waterside and span the road 80ft into the gas works; its concern was that their expensive new scheme would be dominated by the high appliance, accompanied by the possible attendant coal-dust problems, and compounded by the fact that the council finances would not benefit by a penny.

The council was also committed to further expenditure on a contract to purchase Lancaster House, Higher Street (now the Hooked restaurant), for £1,200. This fifteenth-century half-timbered house, partly restored fifty years before by Captain Ridgeway, was in poor repair but still worthy of preservation. A Dartmouth museum was mooted and an appeal for restoration funds started by Mr A H Bridson, who had 7,500 leaflets printed and distributed mainly to professional bodies and organizations.

In Kingswear, to the joy of local inhabitants, spring brought the end to twelve months of construction work replacing the old 55ft turntable with one 65ft in diameter, and replacing R P Brereton's 1865 wooden three-span single-line viaduct over Waterhead Creek, with a new double line concrete and steel viaduct. This enabled the heaviest locomotives, such as the *Torbay Express*, a clear run to Kingswear, for previously they were too heavy to cross the old wooden viaduct and were exchanged at Paignton for a lighter engine. Sadly this work involved the demolition of the former Old Passage House Inn, from where a pulling ferry had once operated to the New Ground.

The North Embankment Scheme *1928-1937*

Left: Coombe Inlet, (note hull of ex-German destroyer).

Right: Works start at Torbay Paint Works.

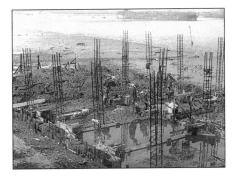

Left: A dredger arrives.

Right: Strip foundations and column reinforcement cageing.

Left: Shuttering columns and main road beams.

Right: Main deck work at Floating Bridge end.

Left: Wheelbarrow race.

Right: Piling almost complete.

Left: The dredger Cam back pumping behind roadworks.

Right: Completion, a through road.

ALL R TUCKER
DARTMOUTH MUSEUM

Dartmouth sadly did not always care for her heritage as the following pictures show:
Above: *Two views of Mount Boone Mansion in ruin (now housing).*
Left: *Lancaster House (now* Hooked *restaurant).*
Right: *Speedwell House, Lower Street (now Masonic Hall.)*

R BARNES, R TUCKER,
DARTMOUTH MUSEUM

On Kingswear's border Lord Churston, owner of the adjacent Lupton Estate, suffered another serious loss. Two years previously the main house had been completely destroyed by fire and the mansion was being completely rebuilt. The contents had been saved and the pictures, library books and antiques had been stored temporarily in the nearby stables. In February another fire occurred in the stables and all the family heirlooms were lost.

Change was also taking place in Kingswear where the controversial vicar, the Rev Dowling Ryan, to the sorrow of some and the joy of many parishioners, exchanged the benefice of Kingswear for that of the Rev Burt in Whitley Bay. A more traditional service returned to Kingswear, but in Whitley Bay the Rev Dowling Ryan continued his pursuit of Catholicism with renewed vigour, which resulted in near riots among the more ebullient northern parishioners, who defected from his services in droves. An ecclesiastical enquiry took place and he was instructed to temper his leanings.

Trade continued to improve. During the previous year 838 steam and sailing vessels entered, the former mainly to receive bunker coal. The deadweight was 472,184 tons, an increase on 1926 of 108 vessels or 117,918 tons. One tanker alone the SS *Valetta* took 1,250 tons from the Channel Coaling Co Ltd.

Regatta 1928 This drew a fair number of entrants, particularly among the big yachts. The race for over 21-metres, the first such, had six starters and was won by Lord Waring's *White Heather II*, while the Port Committee arranged four races outside the harbour for day three. This time there were six starters in the over-21-

Left: A late twenties picture of Hauley I *(the latest 1999 being* Hauley VII*) with the first purpose-built float to accommodate eight vehicles, (nicknamed 'Big Jumbo').*
ALAN KITTRIDGE

Middle left: Robert Cranford's printing works and offices in Fairfax Place, designed by Edward Appleton, Kingswear architect, in Tudor style.
G WEATHERLY

Middle right: 1863 Maypool five arch stone viaduct, designed by I K Brunels former chief assistant, R P Brereton.
G WEATHERLY

metre race, and Sir Thomas Lipton's *Shamrock* won, and in the international 12-metre Mr T O M Sopwith's *Mouette* won.

The regatta days were so busy that the Lower Ferry employed both floats, while the GWR's chunky rail ferry, (oddly named after the soaring seagull, *The Mew*) carried 20,137 passengers, and on the last day 207 vehicles were transported by the three ferries.

Three days after the regatta ended a Manchester-bound lorry loaded with crates and running down the covered Dartmouth gantry to *The Mew* jammed solid. It was a subject of annoyance and gave rise to absurd advice from standard passengers as to its removal. The year closed with the spectacular sight of three flying boats landing and taxi-ing downriver; a submarine entered the harbour with a seaplane mounted on its bows, which later made a demonstration flight over the town.

1929
The last year of the roaring twenties started badly, for the Lower Ferry drifted seaward due to mechanical failure and was only recovered (much to the passengers' relief) when well past Warfleet Creek. Since the service had recommenced in August 1926 under Peters & Heseltine, it had relied on second hand craft (some of Tom Casey's old fleet), and two old horse floats. However, with motor traffic increasing it became obvious that the existing council-owned old floats built for horse traffic were completely inadequate, and a programme of replacement was instigated.

In February the town council invited tenders and ordered a much larger float capable of carrying eight vehicles, which was delivered in July. Then the ferry tug (Casey's *Hauley* of 1909) proved inadequate, finding the bigger float, which acquired the nickname *Big Jumbo*, too difficult to handle. The owners applied to the Commissioners for permission to run the ferry on guide-wires similar to the Higher Ferry. Not surprisingly permission was refused in such a busy part of the harbour. So Peters & Heseltine ordered from Peter Mitchell, *Portmellon*, a new and more powerful tug *Hauley I* (first of the present-day line of tugs to *Hauley VII*), which took up station in the following year.

There was also a replacement programme for the passenger ferry service and Ferris & Blank, Coombe Mud, delivered *Perseverance* for the service, possibly one of the last vessels from that yard, for shortly afterwards they moved premises to Old Mill Creek. The adjacent yard of Couch & Lavers moved to South Town as both were displaced by the Coombe improvement scheme.

Meanwhile as work was steadily proceeding on the North Embankment scheme the town council decided to make further improvements to the South Embankment road approach to the Lower Ferry Slip. They demolished the end house of Sunderland Terrace (formerly the Marine Tavern) and two adjacent properties in Lower Street (later rebuilt as the Good Intent), giving better visibility and an improved turning circle.

This year was a particular milestone for the Labour Party, or the 'People's Party' as it liked to be known, and it was briefly elected to power. Since 1900 its supporters and representation had grown from 62,689 to 8, 317,035 and from 2 MPs to 288 MPs.

Labour Growth in Parliament

Date	Votes	Members
1900	62,698	2
1906	323,195	20
1910	370,802	42
1918	2,244,945	57
1922	4,236,733	142
1923	4,348,379	191
1924	5,487,620	151
1929	8,317,035	288

The upsurge had begun immediately after the end of the last war during a period of great social change, but the party's triumph was short lived for it was another seventeen years before it secured a further period in power.

At the other end of the social scale, Sir Thomas Lennard, squire of Kingswear Court, made a fine gesture in presenting Dartmouth Town Council with Rock End Park Estate, which included Sugary Cove, part of the Little Dartmouth Estate, which he had purchased earlier.

Regatta 1929 Not since pre-war days had the harbour presented such a spectacular scene. It included Sir Walter Preston's fine steam yacht *Lorna* and T O M Sopwith's *Vita*. The big yachts were there in force and the Port of Dartmouth Regatta Committee organized (among other races) a race outside the harbour for £80 for yachts exceeding 21 metres, and another for £20 for 12 metres. Those competing (with their season's placings) were as follows:
Winning Flags for the season (from the Western Morning News*)*

Yacht	Owner	1st	2nd	3rd
23 Metre				
Shamrock	Sir Thomas Lipton	29	10	1
White Heather II	Lord Waring	8	10	5
Candida	H A Andreae	3	7	8
Cambria	Lord Camrose	6	3	6

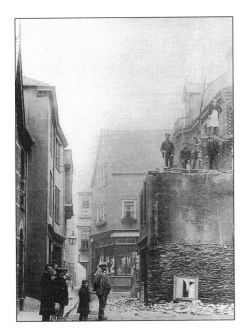

The ferry end of Lower Street widened at various dates since 1900,

Left: *the* Alf Resco Café, **Right:** *Private house facing the Lower Ferry Slip.* **Middle:** *The* Good Intent. **Below:** *Now top of the Lower Ferry Slip, (formerly The second* Marine Tavern).

R Tucker, Dartmouth Museum, G Thomas.

12 Metre

Mouette	T O M Sopwith	24	7	4
Flica	C R Fairey	6	8	2
Iryuna	Sir Wm Burton	5	9	10
Iris	Ben S Guinness	5	6	5
Moyana	W Leuchars	5	3	4
Rhona	J Lauriston Lewis	4	7	8
Zinita	R C Connell	2	5	3

The Great War, that great leveller, had ended over a decade previously, yet inequality still existed, and the following quote from a London newspaper, reported in the *Western Morning News*, says it all:

> *VC but no job. Ex-corporal seeks job. What offers? Owns VC (Victoria Cross). TT. Non-smoker.*

It transpired that this poignant little advertisement had been placed by Dartmothian Corporal Theodore William Henry Veale (born in Clarence Street on 11 November 1893) who had served with the Devonshire Regiment.

When the war was over a popular refrain was that 'Britain would be a land fit for heroes to live in', but somehow this was forgotten. Corporal Veale returned and was presented with his VC by King George V. He received a hero's welcome in his home town of Dartmouth and then found employment in the building trade, but work was intermittent and he moved to London. When interviewed he said:

> *There I obtained employment in the film industry and had parts in the films The* Somme *and* Q Ship, *but the film firm had a run of bad luck, the introduction of 'the talkies' affected its activities and I with others was discharged.*
>
> *I receive no pension from the army as I was not wounded. My staple resources are the 4s [20p] a week award which accompanies the Victoria Cross. I believe I could do good service as a doorman, porter, attendant, or helping builders or decorators. All I ask is a job in London to keep my wife and two bairns from feeling the pinch of want.*

Two weeks later he had several offers of employment and had accepted a situation. Corporal Veale, although living in London, often returned to his beloved Dartmouth to partake in the 'Monkey Town' and the main Regattas, and on the outbreak of the World War II he rejoined the services as a dispatch rider. However, his financial problems must have persisted, for some time afterwards his VC and war medals were found in a dealer's window for sale and thankfully were purchased and returned to the Devonshire and Dorset Regimental Museum where they are proudly displayed. It is incredible that, eighty years after the cessation of hostilities, no official local memorial exists to commemorate the bravery of Dartmouth and Kingswear VCs: Corporal T W H Veale VC or more recently, Colonel H Jones VC of the Falklands campaign (1982).

The growth of the motor car had created the need for fuel service stations and these spread across the countryside. Kingswear built its first at Hillhead, at Brixham Cross. In the village the GWR commenced long overdue improvements to the railway terminus by lengthening the platform, roofing over the booking office, and extending the trackwork.

In November two prominent members of the coaling industry died. The first was Sir Thomas Wilton, chairman of Renwick Wilton & Co Ltd, and the other was Jasper Bartlett, Channel Coaling Co Ltd. Together with George Henry Collins, (ex-chairman of G H Collins & Co Ltd, who died in 1932) they virtually controlled Dartmouth's bunkering trade from the 1880s until 1911, when the Cardiff-based group Evans & Reed Investment Co Ltd founded the Dartmouth Coaling Co Ltd and took over the other two companies to form a tripartite group with coaling businesses in many major ports.

Corporal T. W. H. Veale, VC
1893-1980

Corporal 'Teddy' Veale of the Devonshire Regiment awarded the Victoria Cross for 'most conspicuous bravery'.

The gallant rescue of Lieutenant Eric Savill, (later Sir Eric Savill) on July 20th 1916.

THE MILITARY MUSEUM OF DEVON & DORSET (BOTH)

This Dartmothian's bravery at the battle of the Somme in 1916 is recorded in the following citation in *The London Gazette*:

> *For most conspicuous bravery. Hearing that a wounded officer was lying out in front, Private Veale went out in search, and found him lying amidst corn within 50 yards of the enemy. He dragged the officer to a shell hole, returned for water, and took it out. Finding he could not single-handed cary in the officer, he returned for assistance, and took out two volunteers. One of the party was killed when carrying the officer, and heavy fire necessitated leaving the officer again in a shell hole. At dusk Private Veale went out again with volunteers, to bring in the officer. Whilst doing this an enemy patrol was observed approaching. Private Veale at once went back and procured a Lewis gun, and with the fire of the gun he covered the party, and the officer was finally carried to safety. The courage and determination displayed was of the highest order.*

1921. The Prince of Wales in Dartmouth signing Corporal Veale's autograph book.   DARTMOUTH MUSEUM

Above: **The Rock Inn** *This rare photo of the Rock Inn, Noss Point, shows Mrs Palk, the landlady and customers, from all walks of life shortly before final closure in 1916. (Note – The caged bell rope, used to summon the Floating Bridge Ferry).*

ANON

192

Above: **Coleton Fishacre** *This unique weather vane map was commissioned by Spencer Hoffman, for Oswald Milne designer of Coleton Fishacre, built in 1926 for Rupert D'Oyly Carte.*
TORQUAY LIBRARY THE MAP COURTESY OF THE NATIONAL TRUST.

Below: **The Mew** *The much loved old railway ferry 'Mew' 1908–1954, with her distinctive tall Woodbine funnel, prior to her conversion in 1924, to carry road vehicles. Painted by G. S. Cooper.*
POSTCARD

Dartmouth's School of Artists, *Sydney Hodges, G. Whitaker, J. L. Wimbush, H. B. Wimbush, A. E. Enoch and William Hopkins Way, who painted the pictures on both these pages.*

Above: Lifting crab pots off Warfleet Creek. Circa 1840. DAPHNE HINE HAYCOCK

Below: Relaying the Checkstone Buoy outside the harbour mouth. Circa 1840 DAPHNE HINE HAYCOCK

Above: *The Rock Inn, Noss and* Floating Bridge *No 2.* J Collins & Sons, Bideford

Below: *Bayards Cove, with the castle and Mission to Seamen.* Dartmouth Museum

DARTMOUTH
Foss Street

DARTMOUTH
The Butter Walk

DARTMOUTH
From the Boat Float

DARTMOUTH
The Butter Walk from the Quay

H. B. Wimbush: Commissioned in the early years of the last century by Messrs Raphael Tuck & Sons, to paint watercolours of local Dartmouth scenes for reproduction as postcards called 'Aquarettes', as follows:

Top left: *Lower Ferry Slip and Island House*

Middle left: *Bayards Cove and Castle (then complete with battlements).*

Bottom left: *St Petrox Church and Dartmouth Castle.*

Opposite page top left: *Tudor House, Foss Street.*

Top right: *The Butterwalk*

Bottom left: *Southern corner of the Boat Float*

Bottom right: *Northern corner of the Boat Float*
ALL G WEATHERLY

Above top: *The first tangible signs of the new college, the foundations, dominated the harbour. Two German cruisers, the* Irene *and* Gefion *were here on a courtesy visit in 1901.* POSTCARD

Above: *During World War One, this Motor Torpedo Boat Squadron was stationed in Dartmouth, and engaged in raids across channel and escorting convoys, the personnel were billeted in Dartmouth and Kingswear. Painted by Frank Mason.* ROYAL DART YACHT CLUB

Opposite top: *July 15th 1940. The Hurricane from 215-213 Squadron flown by Sub Lieutenant Bramah was shot down when engaging an enemy Dornier 17 but the pilot was then rescued off the Mewstone by the destroyer HMS* Scimitar *commanded by Captain R D Franks, R.N.* DARTMOUTH MUSEUM

Opposite: *An armada of landing craft slipping out of Dartmouth Harbour, in the early hours of April 24th 1944, rehearsing for the forthcoming invasion of Europe. Painted by Commander Dwight Shepler, U.S.N.* DARTMOUTH MUSEUM

Above : *A galaxy of sailing ships assembled in the River Dart for the 1956 International Tall Ships race from Torbay to Lisbon. In the middle line foreground is the Portuguese barque* Sagres, *while bordering the picture is the Norwegian barque* Christian Radich *with BRNC Captain's barge passing. Painted by Harold Ing.* DARTMOUTH MUSEUM

Below: *A time capsule of when Dartmouth had a thriving ship building industry, showing Philip & Son Ltd floating dock (1924–1961) off Sandquay with a Trinity House lightship* The Bar *docked for repairs with HMS* Venus *of the Dartmouth Training Squadron in the background. Painted by Harold Ing.* DARTMOUTH MUSEUM

The Sailor Queen. *A delightful 1946 picture of our present Queen in Torbay behind the wheel of* Windstar, *owned by Sir Percy Mitchell, Commodore of the Royal Yacht Squadron. (The yacht was constructed by Percy Mitchell, Portmellon, who also built Dartmouth's first three* Hauley *lower ferry tugs). In that year, Princess Elizabeth and Princess Margaret, with the Windsor Sea Rangers, spent several happy days in Dartmouth aboard the* Golden Hind *the Sea Rangers Training-ship.*

SYLVIA CLARK – COURTESY OF THE GIRL GUIDES ASSOCIATION

THE HUNGRY THIRTIES

1930 The new decade brought little cheer and the death of further prominent local people: in Dartmouth, William Lamb Hocking (solicitor), and Captain Fleet of the River Dart Steamboat Co Ltd; in Kingswear the active Mr Gibbs of The Cottage (Longford) and Captain Jack Goldsmith, Ridley House, a member of the Holdsworth family.

The harbour presented a mixed picture. Ships were still arriving to lay up: twenty-two vessels were already moored upriver bringing added revenue. The Commissioners also received an unusual request to lay up two more ships; unusual in that they were 113- and 130-year-old ex-Navy training ships, the 1817 38-gun frigate HMS *Foudroyant* and the 1800 HMS *Implacable*, a 74-gun two-decker which had been a French battleship captured at Trafalgar. They had previously been moored at Falmouth but were seeking new berths. Regrettably they did not come to Dartmouth.

Philips assisted the harbour trade by dispatching a recently completed vessel on the Norwegian ship SS *Beldis*. The latter arrived with her decks already crowded with six locomotives, tenders and numerous carriages. A large crowd of interested spectators watched the loading with alarm, as the vessel listed shorewise over 30 degrees; however, she righted herself and sailed safely.

There was also much interest when the small, but unusual, river suction dredger *Cam* arrived under tow from Kings' Lynn for dredging on the new Coombe improvement scheme.

Hardship continued among the coal lumpers as the shipping industry was still at a low ebb, and consequently bunkering a shadow of its former self. It was ominous for the future that more motorships were being built than steamships. There was, however, sufficient trade to cause concern that colliers were unloading into smaller vessels adjacent to the cottage hospital on the Embankment. Archibald Hine-Haycock, Kingswear's representative on the Commission, secured an instruction that buckets on the mechanical grabs should only be released at the deck level of the receiving craft, to minimize the coal-dust nuisance.

Sir Thomas Wilton and family outside their home Harwarden, South Town. Left to right, Thomas, Editha, Harold, Clifford, Eric, Sir Thomas, and his second wife, Alice Lucy.
From Harwarden Sir Thomas could oversee his business activities, the coaling hulks in Ballast Cove, and the Kingswear jetty trade.
NEIL WILTON

Regatta 1930 The highlight was the winning outright of the magnificent Kingswear Challenge Cup by the Dartmouth Amateur Rowing Club. This superb large specimen of silversmith's work was given in 1920 by Sir Thomas Lennard of Kingswear Court, and if won five consecutive times, could be retained by the club concerned. Seventy-six yachts attended and an unusual race, held on the third day, was for International 12-metres where the owners of these fine yachts changed boats. It was won by T O M Sopwith's boat *Mouette* sailed by A C Wilson. Another novelty for Dartmouth was the arrival during regatta week of talking pictures; the house was full for the whole week. Again noticeable was the number of visitors arriving by car, the *Chronicle* reported that between 1920 and 1930 road tax licences issued in Devon (excluding Exeter and Plymouth) had risen from 13,000 to 78,000, while horse and carriage licences had dropped from 12,000 to 3,000.

A parade to collect funds to purchase souvenirs for members of the Dartmouth Amateur Rowing Club, who in 1920, won the last of the five races necessary to win outright Sir T Lennard's magnificent Silver Challenge Cup.
R TUCKER, DARTMOUTH MUSEUM

Meanwhile the discussion over whether there should be a suspension bridge across the Dart continued.

Despite the depression and their closing of the East Dock, Cardiff, the GWR still displayed confidence in Kingswear, and implemented a big improvement scheme, reported in the *Chronicle*:

> *Details of extensive alterations are being carried out at Kingswear by Industrial Constructions Ltd, of London. The work was begun with the removal of the old 1865 jetty. The piles, numbering 70, have all been drawn. A new wharf is to be constructed of reinforced concrete, 360ft long, extending from the old fish wharf to the crane men's hut. The existing wharf is to be entirely reconstructed; the present wooden piles are being cut off to just below the waterline. This will enable two colliers of the average length to be berthed simultaneously for discharging.*
>
> *Electric cranes will replace the familiar steam appliances, and the depth of water will be considerably increased.*

The late Sir Thomas Wilton of Renwick Wilton & Co Ltd had advocated similar improvements without success since 1886, and had, for decades, imported coals over Kingswear wharf, often with steamers awaiting berths and occurring demurrage.

During this period the Paddington Railway Museum held an exhibition of all the coats of arms of their amalgamated companies, including the Dartmouth & Torbay Railway Co Ltd. The main GWR coat of arms was an amalgamation of the coats of arms of London and Bristol.

Children and ladies of the Dartmouth Rowing club in their finery outside the gas works in Mayors Avenue for the launching of a new skiff gaily decorated for the occasion.

R TUCKER, DARTMOUTH MUSEUM

1931

The first *Chronicle* of the year reported that the cruiser HMS *Dartmouth* (5250 tons), was to be scrapped. Launched in 1911 she had visited the town the following year, but the Admiralty decreed that she should remain outside the harbour, even though larger ships used the port. At a civic reception a large handsome engraved solid silver shield and card plate, subscribed by the inhabitants of the town, were presented to HMS *Dartmouth*. Not knowing what happens to artefacts of value at a ship's demise, the town council wrote to the Admiralty asking if they could buy back the plate. This request was misunderstood, and the Admiralty replied that ships' nameplates were not sold, but that the council could buy the gun tampions; the matter was dropped, but it would be interesting to know where the plate is today. The ship's bell was later acquired and hangs alongside that of *The Mew* in Dartmouth Museum, while Geoff Smales (RDYC member) acquired one of the brass gun tampions and presented it to the RDYC.

Meanwhile the suspension bridge controversy continued, reinforced by some costings, with a figure of £300,000 being quoted. However, another lesser but equally vociferous party, pressed for a tunnel under the river from Waterhead Creek, Kingswear, to Coombe Mud, Dartmouth, and pointed out the savings and advantages to be gained by using the soil to fill in Waterhead Creek for the GWR sidings, recreation grounds and parking. More soil could be used to fill in the truncated Coombe Mud site at Dartmouth and creating a new recreation ground behind the newly formed North Embankment Road. However, because of cost the project engendered more steam than action for many years.

The Mayor of Dartmouth, Dr H J Campbell, like several previous incumbents, favoured a bridge and an amalgamation of Kingswear with Dartmouth, thus securing both ends of any crossing, high, low, or under.

The newly completed Kingswear Quay with the fixed quayside track and cranes, with Messrs T & C Wiltons Steam Ship Co Ltd's collier, the Haytor *alongside.*

A general view showing both cranes, with one unloading from the Haytor *into wagons belonging to five differing railway companies.*
BOTH DHNA

Regrettably there were now 274 unemployed in the town, seventy-four being dockers (the new up-market title for lumpers), while in April twenty-four ships were laid up, totalling 84,084 tons. By June this had increased to thirty-four ships, including the Pacific Steam Navigation Co's line *Oropesa*, (14,075GT). Built in 1920 she was the largest vessel yet to lay up on the Dart, and this number was further increased by three Bibby Line troop ships, the *Dorsetshire*, the *Somersetshire* and the *Lancashire*, each around 16,855 tons. These three came every year (when we had an empire), to lay up until the start of the trooping season, and caused the same controversy regarding their moorings in the main harbour; sometimes the yachting fraternity, sometimes bunkering, sometimes individuals complained, but all grudgingly agreed that their presence did more good than harm to the commerce of the town.

In an effort to improve trade and returns, shipowners canvassed the Government for a reduction in fees for ships using the Suez Canal. The British Government owned 44 per cent of the canal shares, bought in 1875 for £4 million, and it received dividends of £36 million. The 1929 dividend was 267 per cent; and 57 per cent of the steamers using the canal were British; and vessels over 10,000 tons paid £2,000 for each passage. As 900,000 tons of British shipping was lying idle, and much of the trade was to the east, a reduction in tariffs would help trade.

Regatta 1931 The main feature was the appalling weather, and all six events organized by the RDYC for sailing outside the harbour on Friday were abandoned, disappointing many including the four J-class yachts and the four 12-metre class that were to have taken part. Races were held in the harbour for RDYC prize money. Foul weather on the Saturday again caused cancellation of outside events, though four races were held in the harbour. In the three DOD races W L Pritchard had won two and Miss MacAndrew one. There were sixty-four yachts attending.

The following weeks were an anticlimax apart from the arrival of the RSS *Discovery II* about to embark on her second voyage of scientific research to the Antarctic to survey the coastlines and oceans. She had only returned earlier in the year after eighteen months in the same regions. She had replaced Captain Scott's beautiful three masted steam and sail RSS *Discovery*, which had in 1925 also sailed from Dartmouth on her last voyage, returning in 1927 to London, but is now restored and berthed in Dundee. This voyage

Boat drill aboard, the Dorsetshire *and* Somersetshire *and a regular question asked by tourists was, why the lifeboat sails were hoisted in the harbour, to which a jocular reply was, if, when at sea, the engines failed, they would hoist the lifeboat sails and sail the liner back to port.*
R Green R Tucker, Dartmouth Museum

The Development of Dartmouth
Public Transport Services *1917-1934*

In 1917, the last stage coach left Dartmouth for Kingsbridge and was slowly replaced by intermittent road transport. In 1930, Mr C T Way with Mr W T Goodall, to fulfil a local need, formed the Dartmouth & District Bus Co in Mayors Avenue a service to Townstal, Dittisham, Cornworthy, and Totnes. A Morris 14-seater was acquired DV 4378, then later an 8-seater Rio and 14-seater Willys Overland, finally a Laffly 24-seater. In 1934 the Western National Bus Co to abort further competition, bought out the company, but the service continued.

R Tucker, G Thomas , Dartmouth Museum

A novel home made diving suit made by three enterprising Dartmouth boys for underwater exploration.
DARTMOUTH CHRONICLE

was to be highly successful, but was marred by an accident in 1933 when, almost home, she lost overboard (off Ushant) her popular captain, Commander W M Carey RN(Ret). *Discovery II* made another similar voyage eighteen months later, and she was then replaced by another beautiful, but regrettably never completed, RSS *Research*, built at Philips. In these events three Dartmouth men participated, R M Gourley, third engineer, H W Sandford, fireman, and M W Peachey, crewman.

Mundane affairs prevailed, but were enlivened by a fire in the Royal Dart Hotel. The flames were spotted by J Challacombe, employee on the railway ferry *The Mew*. The captain ordered the steamer's fire hose appliances to be fitted by the engineer, Mr Roper, (the first time they had been used since construction in 1908) and along with Dartmouth's firemen, who had crossed free of charge in the penny ferry, they soon gained control.

In Baker's Cove, opposite Kingwear lighthouse, Dartmouth's pilots R Gatzais and R H Roberts, aboard the newly built pilot boat *Good Intent* while returning from piloting the Swedish SS *Valencia* to the pilot limits, narrowly escaped with their lives when an explosion ripped through the boat, blowing pilot Mr Gatzais through the engine room hatch, and causing the boat to burst into flames. The two men took to the water and although Mr Roberts had a lifebelt he was no swimmer. He was helped by his companion but they made no progress, so Mr Gatzais swam to the shore for help. Ashore Mr Walsh pluckily jumped in the water and held Mr Roberts until both were rescued by a boat from Riversea, Kingswear. Meanwhile Dartmouth Coaling Co Ltd's launch *Meroe II* arrived, secured the pilot boat and towed it to Warfleet Creek, then chopped a hole in its side allowing it to sink in the shallows. Mr Walsh received an award for gallantry.

Finally Kingswear lost two prominent men. George Henry Collins died at Eastney where he had lived for over forty years. The other, Sir Thomas Lennard had, after fourteen years at Kingswear Court, left to reside at Cheriton Bishop, Exeter. He had been magnanimous in good works, including funding the seating in Kingswear church, the palatial village hall, the Boy Scouts' and Girl Guides' movements, and presenting superb silver tankards, chalices and skiffs to the Dartmouth Rowing Club.

1932 heralded a return to normal for Kingswear's harassed foreshore residents. In addition to the usual orchestra of steamers whistling on the river with trains and colliers discharging and loading at the quays, they had, for some eighteen months been assailed by a further chorus of construction noise from the International Construction Co Ltd, who at last had completed the redevelopment of Kingswear's new quays. The old *Eclair* pier and quay had been removed and replaced with new concrete wharfs with train tracks and two new electric cranes, though one of the four original steam cranes was retained. The new wharf could handle two or three steam-colliers at once. Peters & Heseltine's ordered a new second tug for the Lower Ferry service, from Percy Mitchell's yard at Portmellon named *Hauley II*. It was to service the transport of the increasing numbers of motor cars on floats, long known as 'horse boats' but now referred to as 'car ferries'.

With the completion of the North Embankment roadway and the isolation of the Coombe Mud, the full extent of the area reclaimed as recreational ground became apparent. In Kingswear it aroused thoughts of the benefit that might accrue if Waterhead Creek were infilled to provide a recreation ground and parking area. The parish council conducted a card vote between this and the cheaper alternative of using the old Boohay Road cricket ground, and fortunately the latter scheme won handsomely. Schemes to fill in the creek came and went, but some areas were being reclaimed for rail sidings and later for car parking. It was surprising in view of the popularity of the motor car that Kingswear's one and only garage proprietor, Mr Jewel, went into bankruptcy.

Sadness followed the news that a popular young man, Michael d'Oyly Carte, aged twenty-one, the only son of Mr Rupert and Lady d'Oyly Carte, Coleton Fishacre, had been killed in a road accident in Switzerland. He was travelling by motor cycle to Monte Carlo to train in hotel management, prior to taking a senior position in his father's business the Savoy Hotel Group, London.

Above: This inspiring picture of Barry Docks, with lines of merchant ships (including some bound for Dartmouth) tiered up awaiting coal chute loading. It highlights that in the Thirties we still had a sizeable merchant fleet and by controlling the Suez Canal, we exported goods (particularly coal) worldwide.

Right: Britain was also active in advancing knowledge in the field of oceanology and the research ship Discovery II arrived with three Dartmouth men aboard.

AUTHOR, R TUCKER, DARTMOUTH MUSEUM

Trade was still depressed with Dartmouth's soup kitchen dispensing 60 or 70 gallons of soup per week at a penny a pint, with 400 children amongst its recipients. Channel Coaling Co offered 6 tons of coal for distribution to the deserving poor, one hundredweight each. Laid-up shipping was slowly decreasing, but the vessels were being scrapped to avoid lay-up dues and maintenance. This was a worldwide problem and the British merchant fleets alone lost 631,230 tons. The *Chronicle* reported that Captain H N Railey of the New York Explorers' Club had arrived in Southampton and had selected Philips to supply the equipment and dry dock facilities for fitting out their vessel to search for the sunken wreck *Lusitania*, torpedoed in 1917 off Ireland. The main details are:

The steam yacht Marie *in the Philips' Sandquay yard on the slip for repair and a new propeller*
AUTHORS COLLECTION

An ex Navy 1919 Kil *Class Patrol Gunboat* Kilmartin *at Noss for conversion into a motor yacht (as money permitted), but she was towed away still uncompleted in the late twenties. Later Viscount Chapel completed her and in 1939 she was put under Admiralty control and was finally scrapped in 1952.*
AUTHORS COLLECTION

to take motion pictures at a depth never before attempted, to broadcast a description of the Lusitania *and carry out research in submarine lighting. The order for the great steel tube will cost £16,000 (at par), and placed with Philip & Son, of Dartmouth. It will have an overall length of 280ft. Within this will be a steel ladder, leading to the bottom observation chamber. The tube will be 5 feet in diameter and about 7/16ths of a inch in thickness. Dartmouth will be our constructional base and the vessel finally selected will be dry-docked, and the steel tube fitted.*

However, the enterprise (with shades of Jules Verne's *Twenty Thousand Leagues Under the Sea*) faded and nothing further was heard. At Philips the Norwegian ship SS *Belray* called with twelve barges already on her decks to collect a large twin-screw motor launch for an Indian prince, the *Muhara of Keutch*.

The launch in Sunderland of the T & C Wilton Co Ltd's first purpose-built collier, the Bovey Tracey was a happy occasion. One picture (left)shows the wife of a board member, holding the launching bottle, the other (right), the ship taking the water.
NEIL WILTON

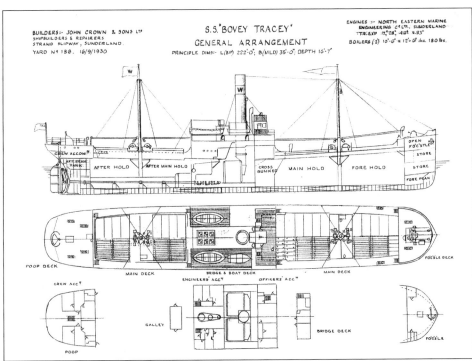

John Crown & Sons Ltd's, Ship Builders, plan of the Bovey Tracy, a vessel to serve the owners well until being sunk by enemy aircraft in 1941.
ERIC BOVEY
CYRIL KING

HANDS ACROSS THE SEA

Dartmouth now joined the Namesake Towns Association and presented the *Chronicle* with a report (not previously made public) containing items from a bound document received in September 1864 from Dartmouth Massachusetts, which was celebrating its 200th anniversary. It was from a W Crapo and is abridged as below:

> *Dartmouth has had an interesting past, but its namesake, which is part of the city of New Bedford, in Massachusetts, USA, appears to have an equally intriguing history. On September 14, 1864, the town celebrated its 200th anniversary, a bound report being published and a copy sent to Dartmouth, Devon.*
> *A Press representative has been privileged to see the report, which contains many interesting details of the town's history.*
> *In an address by William Crapo it is stated that at the June term of the*

Plymouth Colony Court in 1864 it was ordered that 'all the tract of land commonly called and known by the name of Acushena, Ponagansett, and Coaksett is allowed by the courts to be a township, and the inhabitants thereof have liberty to make such orders as may conduce to their common good in town concernments, and that the said town henceforth be called and known by the name of Dartmouth'.

FIRST NEW ENGLAND HOME

A message 'To the Mayor, Recorder, and Aldermen of the City of Dartmouth, County of Devon, England' read: 'We call to mind the fact that it was from Dartmouth, and in a Dartmouth ship bearing a name significant of that feeling of Concord which we trust will for ever characterise the intercourse between the nations to which we respectively belong, that Bartholomew Gesnold in 1602 put forth upon his voyage to America, landed upon our shores, and upon an island often called by his name, in sight from the spot upon which we are now assembled, erected the first white man's dwelling upon the soil of New England.
Deeper still have been our recollective associations as we have remembered that it was from your noble harbour and in the nobler hearts and homes of the then inhabitants of your city, that our Pilgrim Fathers found a shelter when the perils of the storm drove them from their course across the ocean to found an empire in the New World?'

Regatta 1932 The weather was much better than the previous year and there was a very full programme. RDYC members Sir Harold Clayton, Hugh Goodson and V W MacAndrew excelled. The events were numerous and well attended. The ideal weather on the first day allowed four sailing races and rowing events.

On Friday the RDYC held seven races with five J-class vessels racing the 40-mile course for prizes of £70, £20 and £10, and there was also the first recorded class race for the International-14s, E Morgan Giles winning twice. There were six rowing events, including a new event for mechanically propelled lifeboats from the troopships in the harbour, *Lancashire* being the winner. On Saturday there were six yacht races including a J-class and all old yachts exceeding 65ft rating; *White Heather II* won, beating *Britannia*, *Candida*, *Astra* and *Shamrock* in that order.

The regatta over, the River Dart Steamboat Company announced the erection of a new landing stage downriver from Totnes, which was in a deeper part of the river and which projected four feet further from the bank, enabling vessels to arrive earlier and depart later.

In December Lady Freake died at Warfleet House where she had lived since her marriage. Andrew Hugh Bridson JP also died at Rookville, Dartmouth at the age of seventy-two. He was born in Lancashire in 1860, later coming to Dartmouth to reside with his father Mr Henry Bridson at Derwent Lodge, and then at Warfleet House where he built a large model railway in the gardens. He was an old Etonian, a keen yachtsman and an RDYC member. During his long civic life he held numerous posts including the chairmanship of the DHC, and was a founder member of the defunct Dart Boat Sailing Club and Start Bay Yacht Club. In his early years he was a Conservative, but died as president of the Dartmouth Labour Party.

1933 saw the arrival of General Estates Co Ltd, Bond Street, London who had acquired the unexpired portion of the Lower Ferry lease from Peters & Heseltine. Mr Peters, the active member of the partnership, had diversified his interests during 1932 mainly into towage and pleasure boat services, and had ordered a second ferry tug, *Hauley II* from Percy Mitchell, Portmellon, and had also ordered a 72ft pleasure boat, the *Torbay Belle,* for trips from Torquay to Dartmouth and Dittisham. Prior to this, he had negotiated with General Estates Co Ltd the takeover of the lease, the tugs and launches, the floats being council-owned, and in July he alerted the town council of his future intentions, whilst offering them the option of purchasing back the unexpired

The Cam *suction dredger on completion of her hire from King's Lynn for work on the North Embankment was re-engaged by the Corporation for one month to dredge the Boat Float. Her funnel was lowered and manoeuvred into the Float and work commenced, but unfortunately a mishap caused her to sink and the contract time was exceeded, causing considerable extra expenditure.*

R TUCKER, DARTMOUTH MUSEUM

portion of the lease for the exorbitant sum of £12,000, later reduced to £8,000. Considering he purchased it in 1926 for £250 per annum it would have been an astronomical return on his investment. However, the council was as usual short of cash because of the North Embankment scheme so it agreed to transfer the lease to General Estates Co Ltd.

In March Lady Freake's Warfleet House and contents were auctioned and the house with seven-and-a-half acres and two boathouses was purchased for £3,000 by Finch Ingram of Stoke Fleming, who also purchased Woodlands, Warfleet Brewery and the nearby wharf and kiln at Warfleet which he later donated to the Council for public use.

In Kingswear the board school lost Richard Wedlake, headmaster for forty-two years who retired and would be greatly missed. Archibald Hine-Haycock, Kittery Court, paid him the following fulsome tribute at the presentation ceremony:

Richard Wedlake, centre, 42 years Headmaster of Kingswear School, poses for a final photo with his pupils, several of whom still live in the village today.

Four delightful young ladies from the school, a May Queen, and three handmaidens dressed in their finery.

BOTH ROY KELLAND

I feel sadness at the thought that we are losing one of the finest characters that has ever had the training of boys and girls. Mr Wedlake has been associated with the Kingswear School for 42 years, a lifetime of self-sacrifice, keen discipline, and thought for others.
Mr H Adams of Dartmouth said he remembered having many happy times at the school and 'some tender ones' (laughter).
He only wished that 'time would stand still', as then they would have Mr Wedlake always with them.

He was followed by Mr Fowles, County Chief Inspector of Schools, who also paid Richard Wedlake a handsome tribute.

Meanwhile trade was improving; 30,000 tons of laid-up shipping had left the port since the last survey, leaving only 53,000 tons. The annual pilotage for 1932 showed 722 ships had visited Dartmouth, 202 British and 520 foreign, but there were now only five pilots as against twelve in the port's heyday.

Mr Peters', Lower Ferry operator's new passenger launch Torbay Belle *built by Percy Mitchell (the builder of the first three* Hauley *tugs) precariously perched on the sea wall at Portmellon, prior to launching. He then started his new business of Torquay to the Dart pleasure cruises.*
Gary Mitchell

The Charles Jose, *having coaled in Dartmouth ran ashore on Slapton Sands, where the cargo of scrap iron was unloaded and the ship safely salvaged. To this day, pieces of scrap iron surface on the beach.*
R Tucker,
Dartmouth Museum

Regatta 1933 This year brought brilliant sunshine but light winds which curtailed some outside sailing. DOD boats continued to go from strength to strength, one race having seventeen starters. There were two races for J-class and old yachts, *Astra* and *Velsheda* winning one race each.

In the year's last quarter a disastrous fire at Galmpton Creek destroyed the major part of J Saunder's shipyard. Unfortunately the tide was out and the firemen were powerless as their hoses were clogged with river mud. The flames and smoke were seen in Torquay but no lives were lost. On Christmas Eve the Belgian steamer *Charles Jose* (509 tons), ran ashore on Slapton Sands close to the Sands Hotel. It was a wild night and eleven crew were rescued, two by breeches buoy and nine by the ship's lifeboat, the rescue being conducted in the light of car headlights turned seawards. Much of the cargo of scrap iron was recovered later, loaded into barges and brought ashore at Kingswear for onward transmission by rail. The ship was salvaged only to sink ten months later with the loss of nine lives.

1934

The early *Chronicle*s reflected the growing popularity of yachting with an advertisement saying that the large and commodious former gentleman's waterside residence, The Elms, South Town, set in two acres with a private beach had been converted into a comfortable and spacious 'yacht hotel' for visiting yachtsmen. Kingswear was still debating the urgent need for a public toilet to accommodate the ever-growing numbers of visitors and yachtsmen!

The world depression of the thirties ensured a steady flow of cargo and passenger vessels to lay up on the river, bringing much needed revenue for the cash starved Harbour Commission. These pictures give a general picture.
Top: *Tramp steamer with an unusual tall funnel and tobacco pipe ventilators.*
Middle: *The passenger liner* Pulaski.
Bottom: *PSNC liners laid up above Noss.*
RT TUCKER, DARTMOUTH MUSEUM
DAVE GRIFFITHS

Captain Brown, harbourmaster, retired and handed over responsibility to Captain Griffiths. Long lines of shipping stretched upriver, silent monuments to the depression, but there was some improvement. In the British Isles in 1934 there were 453 vessels, 1,079,021 tons laid up, as against 760 vessels, 1,863,814 tons in 1933, though many ships were not returning for trade but being scrapped. The Bibby Line troop ship SS *Hertfordshire* was sold for £9,500 for breaking up. A set-back was the decline in calling seagoing excursion boats. Bristol-based P & A Campbell's *Westward Ho* had ceased calling, as had two locally owned boats the *Duke* and *Duchess of Devonshire*.

The increase in tourism encouraged Mr Roberts, Hoodown Farm, to create a golf course on the hilltops between Noss and Kingswear. He enlisted the services of a professional golfer, E Povey, and laid out an eighteen-hole course, 6,136 yards long. There was one hole of 655 yards and another of 500 yards. On the heights overlooking the river he built a clubhouse, still known today as the Golf House, and formed a golf club.

It was officially opened by Archibald Hine-Haycock of Kittery Court, amid high expectations, but the scheme was ahead of its time and the club only survived for three years. The owner, Mr Roberts, after several unsuccessful attempts to develop Hoodown Farm and lands was forced to place the farm, golf course and building plots on the market. Lot No. 2 , the golf course, was advertised in the *Chronicle* as follows:

> *Lot 2:- The golf course clubhouse and building sites, with charming views of the estuary of the River Dart and surrounding county of Devon extending for many miles; in all about 100.463 acres of good agricultural land with full vacant possession on completion.*

Kingswear & Dartmouth Golf Course *1934-1937*

J. Sproule

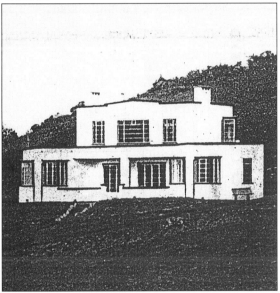

J. Sproule

AN IDEAL HOLIDAY CENTRE FOR THE
YACHTSMAN—GOLFER—FISHERMAN.

Professional: E. POCOCK.

GREEN FEES:
    Summer—3/- per day; 2/- per half-day.
    Winter—2/- per day; 1/6 per half-day.

Subscription until further notice—£3 3s. per annum.

No Entrance Fee for members joining before
May, 1936.

G. Thomas

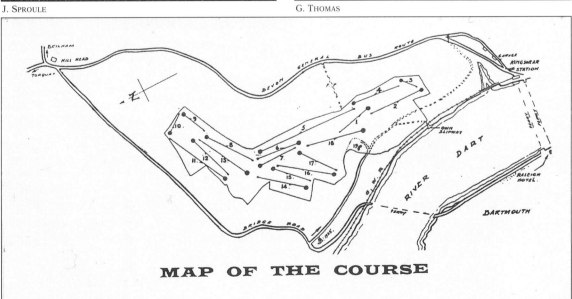

MAP OF THE COURSE

G. Thomas

*The damaged bow
of the W Class
destroyer shortly
before leaving
harbour, escorted
by HMS* Valorous.

The SS Luimneach
*in harbour after a
collision in Start
Bay in thick fog
with destroyer
HMS* Whirlwind.
BOTH R TUCKER,
DARTMOUTH MUSEUM

In May there was a near tragedy when, just outside the harbour in dense fog, the destroyer HMS *Whirlwind* ran head on into the bow of the SS *Luimneach*, bound for Limerick with coal. Two men asleep in the forecastle had a narrow escape, but fortunately extensive damage was restricted to above the waterline, and both vessels made the shelter of Dartmouth harbour. Philips carried out temporary repairs to the steamer, while the navy escorted the destroyer to Devonport for repairs.

Passengers on the railway ferry *The Mew* were surprised to be sharing the journey with three elephants belonging to a travelling circus, causing considerable debate as to the correct toll for elephants!

The Admiralty Yacht Enchantress *after unfortunately colliding with and sinking the Lower ferry float. On a happier note it was fortunate that* Winston Churchill *was aboard the* Enchantress *when she called in 1916, when old* Britannia *was leaving for break up in Blyth and he decreed her figurehead should remain in Dartmouth.*
DAVE GRIFFITH

If you are going to be wrecked, choose a good place as this ketch did near Compass Cove, Dartmouth.
DAVE GRIFFITHS

Five young naval officers from Hong Kong arrived at Dartmouth aboard the 54ft ketch *Tai-mo-shan*. They were welcomed by the captain and staff of the Royal Naval College after a twelve-month voyage which had taken them to Formosa, Japan, the Aleutian Islands, Vancouver, San Francisco, Mexico, Panama, Jamaica and Bermuda, the last port of call.

Regatta 1934 The event saw the return visit of the lovely American-owned four-masted schooner *Aldebaran*, formerly the late Kaiser's private yacht *Meteor*. She last visited Dartmouth for the 1913 regatta with the German royal family aboard, and had lain for the last time in friendship alongside the royal yacht *Britannia* before four bloody war years. The regatta was reported to be the most popular for many years, with thousands of spectators watching numerous events and a fine array of yachts in the harbour, including the J-class boats *Shamrock*, *Candida*, *Velsheda* and *Astra*, moored abreast of the RDYC.

After twenty-six years of devoted service to sailors and the people of Dartmouth, the Rev F R B Simpson retired. He was the son of the late Francis Charles Simpson, Maypool, and had recently officiated at the death of a previous partner in his father's firm, Major F Strickland, the son of Sir Charles Strickland. The latter was a brilliant engineer who had married into another famous shipbuilding family, that of Sir William Thorneycroft, a famous marine engineer.

The King Henry
VII, *more generally
known (hardly
surprising) by its
nickname* The
Bullet, *which
sometimes came to
Kingswear with
the* Torbay
Express. *It was a
King Class
locomotive no.
6014 fitted with
partial
streamlining and is
shown here at
Torquay on 24th
July 1936.*
COURTESY OF OAKWOOD
PRESS/C.R. POTTS *FROM
NEWTON ABBOT TO
KINGSWEAR RAILWAY*
PUBLISHED 1989

A tragedy occurred when the paddle steamer *Totnes Castle*, returning from Totnes, swamped a small rowing skiff with its backwash even though the captain had reduced speed. Sadly for the three occupants, two 20-stone men were sitting in the stern and a young girl was rowing; hence the bow was raised and the wash came over the stern, causing the death of one young man by drowning.

The year closed with yet another Dartmouth town clerk being requested to resign. After a series of irregularities Gilbert Jones was asked to leave without the customary period of notice.

1935 started with the Government making a determined effort to halt the decline of the British shipping fleet, by announcing the payment of a subsidy to shipping companies to replace ageing vessels on a scrap and rebuild basis; unfortunately this did not help Dartmouth for the ships being scrapped were coal-burning, and of the rebuilding programme only 37 per cent were cargo ships, and of this the tonnage of motorships was double that of steamships. Admiral of the Fleet Earl Jellicoe, formerly a Dartmouth cadet, had reported in 1914 that foreign countries had 14,300 ships, 25 million tons, but in 1935 they had 20,000 ships, totalling 43,500,000 tons, an increase of 5,700 vessels and 18,500,000 tons, while Britain had lost 1,500 ships and 1,500,000 tons. Consequently many British shipyards were closing. However, the number of vessels in the graveyard (as the lay-up moorings above Noss were called locally) was declining; two were sold recently to Italy, leaving only twelve, of which three were troopships laid up for the summer months and one was the 8,600 tons SS *Oropesa*.

Then Dartmouth Town Council broke with tradition and appointed an acting town clerk, Miss Mary Inder. She held this position with panache until Mr R Cuff was appointed. This was a difficult period as the council was endeavouring to find a tenant for the Torbay & Dart Paint Works, to develop the Coombe site and possibly use Lancaster House as a library and/or museum.

A near tragedy occurred on Whit Monday, when the Admiralty yacht *Enchantress* just cleared the troopships in the main channel and collided with the empty Lower Ferry, which sank in deep water, fortunately without loss of life. The chargehand jumped aboard the tug as the float sank, the ropes parting on impact. The float was the old wooden spare float and the two remaining new metal floats were utilized to maintain the service, while the Channel Coaling Co Ltd attached a small hulk flying red flags and lights over the wreck, and a few days later the float was raised and run up on the Kingswear shore by the RDYC.

Kingswear received a very special train, *King Henry VII*, whose rounded front gave rise to the nickname *The Bullet*. However, wonder turned to smiles when a copy of the famous Heath Robinson's cartoons *Railway Ribaldry* arrived at Kingswear station. It was commissioned to commemorate the GWR's centenary, and to illustrate that while running 'God's Wonderful Railway' they could also laugh at themselves. During this period Mr Bovey arrived as stationmaster to oversee a long period of quayside activity and his son Eric Bovey is, at the time of writing, a very knowledgeable doyen of Dartmouth.

Regatta 1935 started with seventeen entries in the DOD class race, won by W L Pritchard in *Olwen*, with Vernon MacAndrew again winning the West Sole restricted class in his *Artica*. The second day's outside racing by the RDYC was 'wisely' abandoned because there was 'a lot of sea running'. However, rowing in the harbour continued, including a two-oar cadets' race for the Kingwear Girl Guides. The final day for J-class and old yachts over 65ft was disastrous, for of the four starters, the American yacht *Yankee*, owned by Mr Lambert, was dismasted, as reported in the *Chronicle* and abridged below:

> *Yankee was leading with* Endeavour *astern and nearing the Skerries Bell Buoy* Shamrock *was next astern and* Velsheda *a little way off to leeward. Then* Yankee's *mast collapsed. Two men were washed overboard but were promptly rescued. The other vessels went to her assistance and the race was abandoned,* Yankee *being taken in tow by the trawler* Trojan *which chanced to be nearby.*
> *The steel mast had just crumpled about 4ft above the deck and also at the lower cross-trees. The boom also was badly smashed and splintered and the greater part of the mainsail went overboard. In the harbour she was put alongside a vessel where her wreckage was cleared by crane.*

Sir Harold Clayton in *Aslain* and *Watermouse* won two races. The *Chronicle* also published an article of interest, covering a matter that was considered abhorrent and unthinkable, but which is sadly relevant today:

> *As I sat on the Embankment and gazed upon the craft assembled in the harbour, there were the luxury boats of the great yacht owners. I thought of the men who owned these boats and I realized that for the most part they are active businessmen. Years ago old-fashioned snobbery would not have tolerated a businessman yachtsman.*
> *The* Vita, *Mr T O M Sopwith's handsome steam yacht, was built in Krupp's yard to American design. Mr Sopwith is now one of England's foremost manufacturers of aircraft.*
> *Mr Gerard R Lampert, with his schooner* Atlantic, *mistaken by many people for* Bluenose, *has spent many thousands on yacht racing.* Yankee *costs a small fortune to run.*
> *Mr C R Fairey's* Shamrock *was riding serenely on the waters. Mr Fairey, like Mr Sopwith, is a manufacturer of aircraft.*
> *Mr W L Stephenson, owner of* Velsheda, *is one of the chiefs in a big American business. Then there is Mr H A Andreae a merchant banker who owns* Candida: *Mr Hugh Paul, a big grain merchant, and another well-known owner, Sir William Burton KBE, who owns* Marina, *one of the big '12s', has a flourishing business in Ipswich. So the men who are*

keeping alive the greatest sport in the world have earned the joys that only sailing can bring.
I very nearly denoted these notes as a 'peep into the future' on utilizing mainsails of yachts for advertizing – a method one well-known whisky firm have already demonstrated with their slogan 'Don't be Vague'.
Yachtsmen have drawn lurid pictures of what might happen if this practice should grow, and in their lighter moments have envisaged a fleet of boats known by the names of the commodities they advertize in place of craft unmarked but for their numbers. In the meantime let me pray that such sights will never be seen.

[How wrong he was!]

The regatta was hardly over when disaster again struck in the harbour; an explosion almost wrecked the fine college yacht *Amaryllis*. Fortunately there was no loss of life, though a caretaker/skipper was injured when the decks were blown asunder and a raging fire caused much damage before being brought under control by the college staff and later repaired.

Normal events prevailed ashore though two of the oldest houses in Dartmouth were undergoing changes in Lower Street. Ludwell House was replaced by a new headquarters for the Ancient Order of Foresters, whilst the charming old Speedwell House underwent major alterations and was stripped of character becoming the Hauley Lodge of Freemasons. The *Chronicle* also reported the sad death of Sir John Valentine Carden in a crashed Belgian airliner. Sir John, named after his famous grandfather General Valentine Baker Pasha, was a former resident of Riversea, Kingswear, and of Ravensbury, Dartmouth, where he had lived with his mother Lady Carden. He was a brilliant engineer and well known for his work on tanks, and the half-shaft. He also invented the engine for the Flying Flea aircraft.

1936 The early part of the year was dominated by the death of King George V. The town council finally undertook to establish a town museum and library. It purchased the United Methodist chapel in Newcomen Road and after alterations it opened in September but as a library only. Meanwhile the Ministry of Works published a new list of ancient monuments which contained Dartside properties including Dartmouth Castle, Bayards Cove Castle, and Kingswear's Gommerock Tower. The latter is today isolated in private grounds and lost in undergrowth. Kingswear Castle was not listed, but is now under the ownership of the Landmark Trust, formed some years ago by Sir John Smith to save less well-known and less well-endowed architectural gems not accepted by the National Trust. Dartmouth also received a very generous gift from Kingswear's Rev E C Bayliss, Ridley House. He acquired Dyer's Hill, which had been long coveted by the council. When the site had come on the market, the town council was unable to afford the purchase price, so the Rev Bayliss purchased outright to save it from exploitation, then offered it back to the town council at a cost of less than one third the price he had paid for it. The delighted council promptly agreed and in appreciation were to construct on the heights a small park named Bayliss Park. at Dyers Hill which was opened after due ceremony in June. [Where is the park today?]

Progress continued with the demolition of old properties lining the 1892 Mayors Avenue from the George & Dragon onwards. A decision was later made to name the new Coombe recreation ground Coronation Park to celebrate the crowning of the monarch King George VI.

Activity in Dartmouth harbour was brisk. The 5,112 ton Swedish freighter *Sumatra en route* from Calcutta to Gothenburg developed a serious fire in No. 3 hold off Start Point and was towed into Dartmouth by the Dutch tug *Zwarte Zee*, listing heavily. Her 400 tons of cargo was unloaded into lighters, and the fire was extinguished. Two Italian salvage vessels, the *Arpione* and *Rampino* owned by Count Burragi, made the harbour their base, hoping to locate and salvage valuable copper and other metals from war wrecks in Start Bay. They successfully located SS *Chorley*, torpedoed in 1917, and recovered many copper ingots which were unloaded into Renwick Wilton & Dobson Co's barge *Goliath* for onward transportation from Kingswear station.

The Norwegian SS *Belmoira* called to collect from Philips the 56-ton tug *Kanvea* built for the state of Morvi. Already aboard were four locomotives and fourteen coaches on the deck and when loaded she developed an alarming list to starboard, which fortunately was righted and the ship sailed. Philips also received an order from Trinity House to build three lightships and a prestigious £100,000 order from the Government for a non-metallic all-wood teak vessel, the RSS *Research*, for scientific exploration. The two recently displaced Coombe firms launched their first vessels from new yards. Lavers & Co Ltd of South Town built a replacement 35ft passenger launch *Reliance* for General Estates Co Ltd's Lower Ferry service. Ferris & Blank Co Ltd of Old Mill Creek built a small ferry float for the River Dart Steamboat Co Ltd's river-crossing at Dittisham.

At this time the Earl of Dartmouth died, and so did the Rev Burt, vicar of Kingswear who was replaced by the Rev F H Keyworth. Miss Mary Bridson, daughter of A W Bridson who had done so much for Dartmouth, presented to St Clement's church a fine three-light stained-glass window in his memory. Then in a hands-across-the-sea ceremony there was an exchange of flags by the Dartmouth British Legion and Dartmouth Nova Scotia, and both flags are now proudly flown on civic occasions.

In Brixham a centuries-old way of life changed. The port had formerly been reliant on sail alone but a new venture, Brixham Trawlers Ltd, was launched with six newly acquired 110ft long steam trawlers from Hull. They were named the *Al*, *Auk*, *Ibis*, *Thrush*, *Kite* and *Ruff*, one trawler for each day of the working week, to ensure a regular fish supply and restore Brixham's position as one of the chief fishmarkets. Brixham was probably the last port in the kingdom to adopt, as standard, the steam trawler. In the 1870s, Samuel Lake and G P Bidder both from Dartmouth, had attempted to introduce steam trawlers, (the first in Great Britain) but were defeated by local prejudice.

A proposal was mooted that the council should purchase and demolish the property at the seaward end of the Lower Ferry Slip to recreate a new ferry slip at right angles to the existing one, thus forming an entrance directly off the end of the South

The Swedish SS Sumatra, *with fire raging in her forward hold, being towed into Dartmouth Harbour.*

The Norwegian SS Belmoira, *already heavily laden, being loaded with the Philips built 56-ton tug for India.*
BOTH DARTMOUTH
MUSEUM

Top Left: *Edward, Prince of Wales on a visit to the College making a spectacular landing by sea plane on the Dart.*
RICHARD WEBB

Top Right: *Copper ingots salvaged from SS* Chorley *torpedoed in Start Bay during the First World War, being unloaded at Dartmouth. The docker in front is Mr Knapman, Kingswear.*
DAVE GRIFFITHS.

Embankment. However, nothing was done and interest switched to the raising of the Lower Ferry float accidentally sunk by the Dartmouth slip. A mechanical coal-grab also sank in calm weather leaving just the mast clear of the water, and this was raised by the salvage vessel *Recovery of Leigh* and beached on the Kingswear shore, where it was dismantled. This was the second coal-grab to sink within months, the other sank in a storm. Confrontation arose between the town council and the coaling companies as to the need for so many hulks in the harbour. It was resolved by a committee decision.

The DHC announced with pride that its previous old debt of £40,000 incurred in the early 1880s by Francis Charles Simpson and his anti-Embankment Committee was now only £13,000. The reduction came from laying-up dues paid by ships in the Dart because of the continuing depression, so some good had come from the misfortune. Regrettably some of the boats now being sold up the river belonged to Elders & Fyffe, who had called at Dartmouth for some years previously. The Pacific Steam Navigation Co's *Oropesa* left for Liverpool.

Regatta 1936 The event started with the troopship *Dorsetshire* being opened to the public, a prelude to a very successful regatta. The big yachts predominated although there were twenty-two starters in the DOD class, and record crowds attending the rowing events.

There were thirteen events from the RDYC and the Port of Dartmouth Committee on Friday and Saturday, the premier races being for the J-class and old yachts with four starters, *Endeavour*, *Velsheda*, *Astra* and *Endeavour II*. There were also twenty-two swimming races in the Boat Float including a 50-yard race for dogs, with contestants bringing dogs from many parts of the country.

This regatta gained high praise from the *Suffolk Chronicle* making pleasant reading:

> *It is really impossible to believe the amazing contrast between two Royal regattas as take place at Harwich and Dartmouth.*
> *During a brief holiday in delightful Dartmouth during the royal regatta, I compared it with the Royal Harwich Regatta. Dartmothians make the royal regatta the three days of the whole year for which they live and save, days on which they are reborn and spend. It is no concern to a real Dartmothian to be completely 'stony' by the end of the regatta, they then live for the next year's carnival on the 'Rhine' of England.*
> *This vast organzisation is so perfectly carried out that I should have liked to transport the whole of Harwich and Dovercourt to Dartmouth, to see just how a royal regatta should be carried out.*
> *The more one reflects on the whole aquatic carnival, and dares to compare it with the Royal Harwich the more hastily does one exclaim 'Wake up, Harwich!'*

On 11 December King Edward VIII officially abdicated the throne.

The year closed with the death of Colonel R W Studdy, President of the RDYC, a local man who, like his father, had a long association with the river Dart, Dartmouth and its regattas.

The notorious runaway Grimsby trawler the Girl Pat *(famous for the exploits of the Osbourne Brothers in the South Seas) moored in Dartmouth Harbour alongside the troopship* Somersetshire *for a few hours, after her 8,000 mile return from Georgetown under the command of Commander R W Lawrence RN (Ret).*
DAVE GRIFFITHS

A half scale replica of the Golden Hind *is the centre of attraction on the South Embankment.*
CYRIL KING

THE WRECK OF THE ENGLISH TRADER

1937 In January fortune failed to smile on the Trader Navigation Co's 362ft SS *English Trader*, for when sailing too close to the castle she went aground on the Checkstone. The combined efforts of HMS *Witch* and four tugs failed to free her, and on the thirteenth day her forward tanks became holed and her bow broke away aft of the foremast. Ship surgery became her only hope, so with pumps working day and night, divers with heavy timbers erected temporary bulkheads and cut away the damaged fore section, thus freeing her bows. Then came the indignity of being towed stern first and beached at Ballast Cove, Kingswear, where steam pumps were employed to keep her hull free of water, while the temporary bulkheads were reinforced and braced with steel hawsers. She was again towed stern first to Southampton, then to Shields where the forward section was rebuilt, and she was returned to full service exactly 100 days after going aground. Meanwhile her abandoned bow section, still stranded on the rocks by the castle, was cut up, loaded into barges and deposited on Hoodown beach, Kingswear, for onward transmission by rail to South Wales for scrap.

Harbour events dominated, for in March snow fell and cold winds caused problems on the Lower Ferry. The tow ropes attaching the tug to the float broke, and the float with a car and several passengers aboard was swept seaward onto the rocks at Warfleet. Fortunately the float was undamaged and later recovered to the passengers' relief. Much interest was generated when the runaway Grimsby trawler *Girl Pat*, famous for the Osborne brothers' exploits in the South Seas, put into harbour under Commander R W Lawrence RN who had sailed her 8,000 miles from Georgetown bound for London. Because of her exploits she was under suspicion at every port of call. In French Guyana *Girl Pat* was suspected of involvement in the rescue of two French convicts, and in Philadelphia an armed guard of four was placed aboard for fear of smuggling, while, for every purchase, cash was demanded because of the boat's reputation. News of her arrival spread rapidly but she stayed only a few hours, disappointing visitors, many of whom had come from as far afield as Plymouth.

Meanwhile the annual grumble about the three troopships continued, the anti-troopship brigade being reinforced when it was learned that two large vessels refused to enter the port for coals because of the troopships' positions, thus depriving the lumpers of work and the town of trade.

A replica of Drake's *Golden Hind*, complete with bearded crew in traditional costume *en route* for Plymouth Navy Days moored alongside the South Embankment.

International Regatta, Coronation Year 1937 Preparations to celebrate the coronation of King George VI, formerly a cadet at Dartmouth, proceeded apace. Mayor W T Pillar, and his daughter Helen Pillar, Dartmouth's youngest Mayoress ever, engendered much enthusiasm. The town band received new uniforms and the reclaimed Coombe recreation area was formally opened and named Coronation Park. In Kingswear the first Kingswear Girl Guide Troop planted a small copper beech with a plaque at the head of Church Hill; at the time of writing it is over 100ft tall. Parties and street celebrations were held on both sides of the river, and in Dartmouth 2,530 electric lights and over 200 gas lights were erected, with four floodlights illuminating a large picture of their majesties.

The Norwegian cargo ship **SS** *Stargrad* arrived carrying the Crown Prince Olav's six-metre yacht *Norma*; after being unloaded her mast was stepped by the coaling company enabling her to participate in the racing events.

For the first time Dartmouth enjoyed two regattas in the same year to mark the occasion. Events were planned jointly with Torquay for an international regatta to be held from 19 June to 3 July with races for twenty-five classes of yacht; the Dartmouth dates were 28, 29 and 30 June. In addition the following 'feeder' races were arranged:

a) By the RORC, races from Southsea to Cherbourg to Eddystone to Torquay
b) By the Parkstone Sailing Club from Poole to Torquay

Below is a much abridged layout of the programme:

Torquay	*Sat 19 and Mon 21 June*
Paignton	*Tue 22 June*
Babbacombe	*Wed 23 June*
Torquay	*Thur 24 June*
Brixham	*Fri 25 and Sat 26 June*
Dartmouth	*Mon 28 and Tue 29 June*
Passage Race Dart to Torquay	*Wed 30 June*
Torquay	*Thur 1 July*
Torquay	*Fri 2 and Sat 3 July*

Races were offered for the following classes at most locations, although not all received sufficient entries to justify a race:

The Hundred Day Miracle of SS *English Trader*
1937

Left: *Aground on Castle Rocks.*

Right: *Combined towage fails to free her.*

Left: *The bow begins to break away.*

Right: *The bow cut away.*

Left: *Under tow with a timber bulkhead.*

Right: *Beached at Kingswear prior to leaving for South Shields.*

Left: *En route passing abandoned bow sections.*

Right: *Bow wreckage awaiting rail transit to South Wales.*

Left: *Damaged underside of hull.*

Right: *100 days later, back at sea.*

R TUCKER/
DARTMOUTH MUSEUM

In July, the Dutch liner Slamat *from Rotterdam entered harbour with 319 girl students aboard for a sightseeing and hiking holiday in South Devon. (The local boys, must have thought Christmas had come early!)*

R TUCKER, DARTMOUTH MUSEUM

An ocean-going sea trader being coaled in The Bight by a floating coal-grab direct from a South Wales collier.

DARTMOUTH MUSEUM

Six IYRU classes 12metres to 14feet, and four Handicap Cruiser classes for over-75tons to 25tons. There were also races for West Solent, Q class, Sunbeam, Olympic Monotype, Papillon, Solent X, National-12, Torbay H'cap ClassII, Jolly Boats, 31 sq mtrs, 22 sq mtrs, Canoes, Redwings, and Snipes.

First prizes for each day's racing ranged from £40 for the largest cruisers, £25 for 12-metres to £3 for Snipes. Many special cups and trophies were presented and silver medals were struck commemorating the regatta and presented to every competing yacht. The Royal Dart Yacht Club voted £200 towards prize money for one day.

The *Western Morning News* details in respect of the International Regatta were:

a) The Committee vessel was HMS Witch.
b) Crown Prince (now King) Olaf of Norway sailed in the 6 metre races.
c) All the courses were in Start Bay, the largest, of 14 miles per round, being triangular from the Range to the Skerries, to an eastern mark and return to the Range.
d) On the first day, Thendara, *a new Clyde-built ketch, carried away about 20ft of her mast shortly after rounding the Skerries when she held a commanding lead.*
e) On the second day there were fierce squalls and a number of the smaller craft capsized.

Regatta 1937 This year's event held from 26 to 28 August, was a much reduced affair, the big yachts having left for Glasgow immediately after participating in the earlier international event. On Thursday the regatta committee held only four sailing and eleven oared events, while the RDYC on Friday held only four races for smaller craft, supported by ten rowing races. The final day had a limited programme with only two sailing races, but the swimming matches attracted crowds of between 2,000 and 3,000 people, and large crowds attended the athletic sports on the newly opened Coronation Park. At least 10,000 visitors travelled to Dartmouth for the regatta.

According to the *Chronicle*:

> *Miss Helen Pillar, Mayoress, the eighteen-year-old daughter of the Mayor, in addition to carrying out her official duties which included selling flags for the Waifs and Strays and presenting swimming prizes in the Guildhall, had in addition a) pulled in the winning boat for the Girl Guides on the Friday, b) swum in the swimming event on the Saturday and won the Guides' event c) run in the 100 yards open race, finishing third only a few yards behind two trained members of the Paignton AAC.*

During 1937 the shadow of war cast by Adolf Hitler, that skilful but unstable leader of Nazi Germany receded, but reality returned when Miss Thurston, Dragon House, Boohay, Kingswear, gave a lecture to the Kingswear Women's Institute on the horrors she had experienced in the Spanish Civil War. Mundane events soon obscured talk of war for the Kingswear parish council was still debating the position of its long overdue public toilet, and the church organ underwent overdue repair and renovation. A man driving a heavy showman's vehicle on Bridge Road lost control and crashed through the railway gates and into the platform of Britannia Halt, completely blocking the line. The signalman, with great presence of mind, averted a major accident by running up the line with a red flag to halt the 1.30pm train 100 yards from the accident. Dartmothians were immersed in serious discussion as to the merits of the town's inns, once famous for white ale brewed at the Trafalgar, Sun, Seven Stars and the Globe. It was made as other ales, except corn was added as a grout with the barley malt and sugar and brewed in a boiler which resulted in a milk-like liquid. The white ale fermented strongly and would blow the cork out of any bottle used as a container.

This hectic year closed with Dartmouth, for the umpteenth time, dismissing its town clerk, Mr Cuff, again without payment and again for monetary irregularities. Dartmouth must have headed any league for picking problematic town clerks!

1938
The territorial ambitions of the Third Reich were casting long shadows over Europe, to the extent that rearmament was the order of the day. War preoccupations were commonplace and committees were formed to organise fire, ambulance and other services that air raids and war would necessitate. In the *Chronicle* correspondence raged over whether financial return or moral ethics should decide if German cruise ships from Himmler's 'strength through joy' youth movement should call in the harbour. The Harbour Commission returns were down again and the laid-up liner SS *Voltaire* was about to depart. Trade was in steady decline and the commissioners canvassed the MP for Torquay, C Williams, to petition the Government with the following:

> *deep concern that the bunkering trade in the country and Dartmouth in particular is being driven abroad by conditions and restrictions, and if conditions should be ameliorated in favour of the British coal industry without delay.*

A total of 12,000 leaflets were also printed for distribution to ships' owners eulogizing the benefits of Dartmouth harbour as a port of call. The folly of war was illustrated by the arrival of the Irish vessel SS *Lanahrone* for bunkers, with six

Left: The young boy holding the tail of a Thresher Shark caught locally has the making of a true fisherman who can always tell a tale of the one that got away.
R Tucker, Dartmouth Museum

Right: Commander Oliver at the controls of the glider built by the cadets under his supervision in the college grounds.
R Tucker, Dartmouth Museum

stowaway deserters aboard from General Franco's foreign legion; they were three Canadians and three Americans still dressed in their uniforms, who had hidden in the cargo of salt until thirst drove them on the deck. They were refused disembarkation rights in Dartmouth, remaining aboard until the ship reached her destination of Aberdeen.

There was resentment when the Admiralty decided not to pursue the possibility of Dartmouth becoming a naval seaplane base, disappointing many Dartmothians. It possibly inspired Commander P D Oliver and some college cadets to build a glider in their spare time, as M Liwentaal had done in 1894. It took eight months to complete and was 18ft long with a wing span of 33ft and cost £57. It could be assembled in three hours and was tested on Kingswear's old golf course with cadets pulling two ropes attached to elastic which dropped off when the machine gathered speed and took to the air. It flew over the course and landed and then was towed back up the hill by motor car for several other successful flights. The *Chronicle* recorded a little gem as to why some college cadets reach senior ranks in the services. It was as follows:

> *A cadet at his passing-out review by senior officers (which included an Admiral) was asked to name whom he considered his three most famous Admirals, to which he answered 'Drake and Nelson' then, turning to the Admiral presiding over the board said 'I did not quite catch your name, Sir'. Naturally, he passed.*

This happy group is the crew of one of the River Dart Steamboats on the Dartmouth to Totnes service and the lady is Mrs Mary Wood, neé Spear.
G Thomas

An artist's impression of a suspension bridge crossing the Dart from Sandquay to Noss. One of the many proposed since 1828.

DARTMOUTH CHRONICLE

The town regalia was enriched by Helen Pillar, the previous year's Mayoress, with a superb gold medallion displaying a cameo portraying the two princesses Elizabeth and Margaret. This was to partner the earlier gold emblem given in 1921 by Lady Wilton of Dartmouth for the Mayoress to wear on civic occasions. At the same time the council was debating yet again the construction of a bridge over the River Dart; this time a low-level bridge from Braithwaite was suggested. This was deferred for later discussion at a conference of local authorities who were meeting to discuss transport problems in the area.

A prelude to the forthcoming regatta was the award by Crown Prince Olaf of Norway of a decoration to R L Dennis, chairman of the DHC and principal of the Combined Coaling Companies, for help and courtesy received during the 1937 International Regatta. Mr Dennis said that he felt the award would be shared by the town.

Regatta 1938 The harbour had fewer visiting yachts than in previous years, and winds were fitful causing races to be shortened. The Dart One Design had twenty-two starters and took two-and-a-half hours to do one round, while in the RDYC big-boat races, kedge anchors were used. In the handicap yachts, 20 to 70 tons, of the eight starters only *Lady Anne*, Colonel Sir V Gabriel, finished the course of 27 miles. The West Solent and National 12 classes were also run.

On the Saturday the seven Port Regatta races were all competed for, with Vernon MacAndrew's *Trivia* winning the £40 International 12-metre race. In the harbour, rowing events were unaffected and attracted much public support. A new Friday event was for two-oared cadet boats from the newly established Warfleet Training School.

This excellent establishment was the brainchild of its benefactor, Vernon MacAndrew, millionaire shipowner of Ravensbury; he was also proud owner of the motor-yacht newly built by Philips, the 211 ton *Campeador V*, as well as *Trivia*. As Vice Commodore of the RDYC Vernon MacAndrew encouraged the sport of yachting, particularly the development of the Dart One Design class and he built up the club's fleet of these boats, organizing races in Dartmouth and at other nearby regattas. To these meetings, it was his practice to tow up to thirteen boats in line behind his luxury yacht, *Campeador V*, developing a system that required a helmsman only in the last boat of the line, while the remaining crews travelled in the comfort of the yacht.

His homes, Ravensbury and nearby Warfleet House, had been homes to many prominent flag officers of the RDYC. In earlier years big-yacht owners had manned their vessels with professional crews, but this was now proving difficult due to the diminishing number of sailing trawlers. These had previously supplied the superb seamen who had fished in the winter months and manned the big yachts in the summer. To rectify this Mr MacAndrew, supported by friends, decided to provide a reservoir of trained hands by using his surplus and vacant Warfleet House, and he allocated £20,000 for its conversion to a training school for deckhands and domestic servants. Warfleet House had been the Freake family home until Lady Freake's death in 1932. It was bought with seven-and-a-half acres in March 1933 by Finch Ingram, Stoke Fleming entrepreneur, for £3,000, mainly to develop the land, and Mr MacAndrew, anxious to preserve the ambience of nearby Ravensbury, promptly purchased just Warfleet House and Lodge from Mr Ingram. It had since been unoccupied although furnished with items purchased from Lady Freake's family sale; surprisingly it was left unlocked and only once was broken into by an intruder, when an unemployed sailor walked in and stole two oil paintings and two wall candelabra. He was apprehended in Avonmouth and sentenced to twelve months' jail.

The training scheme was announced in the *Chronicle* as follows:

> *The training centre is to be established on the banks of the Dart and boys between the ages of 15 and 18 will be eligible for the course, which will commence annually in June and terminate in April the following year. No fees will be charged, and £5 will be paid for each boy and will be returned at the rate of 2s per week in pocket money.*
>
> *It will accommodate thirty and instruction will be given in rowing and sailing, all deck duties, boatswain's work, stewarding, simple accounts, the use of charts and elementary navigation, also instruction in engineering, including the maintenance of petrol paraffin, and diesel engines and outboard motors.*
>
> *Boats will be supplied for the necessary routines, and the establishment will be run as ship, the students divided into 'watches'. One dormitory will be fitted as a forecastle complete with folding canvas bunks.*
>
> *A gymnasium will also be included, and an electric light plant installed similar to that used on yachts.*
>
> *The project will be under the direct supervision of the Boys Department of the National Council of YMCAs.*

The proposals were nationally acclaimed, while offers of equipment were received including the masts and yards of the former fully-rigged *Herzogin Cecilie* wrecked in Soar Mill Cove, which were accepted. Lady Freake was also remembered during Dartmouth's carnival when a display of the early postal services used her fine coach and four stately horses, lent by Finch Ingram of Stoke Fleming, who had acquired the coach with the house purchase.

The training scheme was short lived, however, due to the impending war in Europe, and the YMCA leased the house as a hostel to a doctor of music and former choirmaster of a church in St John's Wood, London. He brought some twenty choirboys to reside there and was in charge of their training and well-being; sadly he abused that trust and was brought to court on eighteen charges. His career was ruined, he received twelve months' hard labour, and the hostel closed.

Miss Ethel Tew of the Gunfield, a well-known RDYC member, in her 14ft centre board racing dinghy Tit Willow.
RDYC

Left: *Mr Vernon MacAndrew's novel scheme of towing to nearby regattas, behind his* MY Campeador V *thirteen DOD dinghies with only one man aboard the last dinghy.*
Right: *Mr MacAndrew, Rear Commodore, RDYC and Major Heskett-Smith RYS at a club At Home function.*
BOTH R TUCKER, DARTMOUTH MUSEUM

The schooner Jessica *belonging to club member Edward Tew, Dartmouth Harbour commissioner and owner of the Dartmouth mansion the Gunfield*
RDYC

Another happy launch. Dartmouth children aboard a new skiff in W H Ways coal yard.

R Tucker,

Dartmouth Museum

1939

War clouds were gathering over Europe, but there were still celebrations at the April launch at Philips of the all-wooden scientific vessel duly named RRS *Research*. Due to construction complexities, she was three years overdue with only the hull completed and had cost over twice her original estimate. She was 142ft 6in long and was to be rigged as a brigantine with 12,000ft of sail with an auxiliary engine. She was a superb and exceptional vessel as the *Chronicle's* abridged details show:

> *Its value will be appreciated even in time of war when it will carry letters of marque, signed by the Powers, to protect it from attack ...*
> *Brass, bronze, aluminium and other non-ferrous metals were used. It was not easy to bend and shape brass to a required design, nor to get brass of sufficient purity free from magnetic material.*
> *The timber was difficult, the Admiralty helping with teak of the finest quality*

Regrettably a few months later, international world events curtailed further progress and incredibly, on the cessation of hostilities, it was decided that RRS *Research* was no longer required and she was towed to Plymouth and broken up. What a waste of an expensive and unique vessel that would have made a superb sail training ship.

The impending crisis breathed some life into the harbour, however, and R L Dennis reported that John Hall & Co's line of steamers to West Africa would call fortnightly to land passengers. Laid-up shipping was also refurbished and pressed into service, so that by February only one ship remained laid up on the river. The 14,000-ton *Southern Express*, a whaling factory-ship with over a hundred British crew aboard, put into the harbour. They departed by train from Kingswear after seven months in the Antarctic where they had caught over 2,000 whales, which yielded 107,276 barrels of oil. Their wages of £9 per month seemed poor reward for such a hard life and most swore they would not be returning.

The Ill Fated RRS *Research - 1939*

The Hon Mrs Spencer Jones at the official ceremony at Messrs Philips' yard, driving home the first rivet on the keel of the new vessel. The second riveter was a relation of old Dartmothian Stan Widdicombe. In the picture is the respected club member the late George Philip, as a young boy who seems a little critical of events.

Also shown is the completed hull on stocks, and this lovely wasted ship taking the waters. She was to replace the American research ship Carnegie *destroyed by fire off Samoa in 1929. The* RRS Research *cost over £100,000 to build entirely with non-metallic materials to research earth magnetism, applied air and atmospheric electricity, meteorological observation, deep sea soundings and marine biology. She was aided by a marine collimator, sea deflector, and earth indicator, and to cruise mainly under sail, aided by an ancillary engine.*

R TUCKER, DARTMOUTH MUSEUM

Above: *The Royal Yacht,* Victoria and Albert III *moored in The Bight with many local boats around loaded with sightseers hoping for a glimpse of their majesties.*

Below: *Their gracious majesties on their visit to Dartmouth shortly before the outbreak of hostilities. A smiling Queen and the two princesses are seen by cheering crowds as they drive along the embankment.*
Both R Tucker, Dartmouth Museum

In July the royal yacht *Victoria & Albert III* arrived with their majesties and the princesses aboard. They were to spend two days at the Royal Naval College and in the town and were welcomed by the civic dignitaries and crowds of over 20,000 people. At the college the present Queen (HRH Queen Elizabeth II), then twelve years of age, met her future husband the young Prince Philip of Greece, who had been detailed by his uncle Lord Louis Mountbatten, aide de camp to the King, to entertain the princesses.

There was also celebration in Kingswear because the Rev Keyworth's appeal for £330 to repair the 1897 church clock, (which had been stopped for some time) and to repair and re-hang the church bells finally met its target. The tenor bell was recast and the two smaller bells, quarter tuned, and all were rehung on a steel frame in the 1170 tower. They were blessed by the vicar who wrote this pleasant hymn set to music for the occasion, the first verse of which is as follows:

Three bells in an ancient tower
weave their mystic rime
Two archangels great of power
Mary sweet of chime.

Further up the river Greenway House had a new owner, Agatha Christie. In 1939 the house was requisitioned by the Admiralty and occupied by US Marines and Agatha Christie's family has recently offered the house to the National Trust. Her short story, *The Regatta Mystery*, published in a short story collection of the same title in 1939, was set in The Royal Castle at Dartmouth.

Centenary Regatta 1939 The European crisis was not to prevent Dartmouth enjoying its centenary regatta. Much planning had extended it to a full week and it included races under the flag of the Royal Thames Yacht Club. It was a tremendous event starting with a public luncheon in the Guildhall, followed by a processional march to Coronation Park for athletic sports, followed by fancy-dress parades, illuminations, fairs, fireworks, two alfresco balls, the Centenary Regatta Ball, the Grand Alfresco Ball and united open air services, and so on. There were also sixty-two separate rowing and sailing events.

A sad event was the arrival of the 756-ton yacht *Xarafa* with the American flag flying at half mast and the body of its owner Franklyn M Singer aboard. Son of the late millionaire Isaac Singer of Oldway, Paignton, the founder of the Singer Manufacturing Co, he had died in Paris aged sixty-three and was returning for interment in the family vault in Torquay.

However, the dogs of war were evident. Two days after her arrival, the regatta guardship, the destroyer HMS *Brazen*, was recalled. Her sirens began sounding at 10.30pm to recall the men from ashore, while her searchlights swept the harbour and the town. At 11.30pm her sirens were sounded at full blast for five minutes before she sailed off at 12.45am. Gas masks were distributed, warden services started and war paraphernalia was put in place.

The Regatta guard ship HMS Brazen *which left the events and the harbour prematurely in spectacular fashion as the war clouds gathered.*
WORLD SHIP SOCIETY

Dartmouth's Literary Connections
1854-1954

Ever since Geoffrey Chaucer was sent to Dartmouth by King Edward III in 1373, and subsequently based The Shipman in *The Canterbury Tales* on John Hawley, Dartmouth has continued to feature in many books, films and television programmes and become the home of many talented writers and artists.

Authors from the Dartmouth area in the period covered by this book include these three, whose books have given pleasure to their readers throughout the world.

Flora Thompson *1876 - 1947*

In autumn 1928 Flora Thompson came to live at The Outlook in Above Town after her husband had been appointed Postmaster of Dartmouth in the previous year.

She later wrote her semi-autobiographic trilogy about life in the countryside which was combined as *Lark Rise to Candleford* and published in 1945.

Still Glides the Stream was published posthumously in 1948.

OXFORDSHIRE COUNTY COUNCIL PHOTOGRAPHIC ARCHIVE

Agatha Christie *1890 - 1976*

Dame Agatha Christie Mallowan, of Greenaway House, the world famous crime writer, born in Torquay wrote over 70 detective novels many featuring Hercule Poirot or Miss Marple.

In 1939 she published a short story set in The Royal Castle Hotel, Dartmouth entitled *The Regatta Mystery*.

Other titles with local connections include *Ordeal by Innocence* and *Dead Man's Folly* featuring Greenway. Also *And Then There were None* and *Evil under the Sun* which were set on Burgh Island, Bigbury.

A rare photograph of Agatha Christie with family and friends at Blackpool Sands near Dartmouth.

MRS ROSALIND HICKS

Christopher Milne *1920 - 1996*

Son of A A Milne, Christopher Milne received much acclaim for his sensitively written volumes of autobiography: *The Enchanted Places* (1974), *The Path through the Trees* (1979), *The Hollow on the Hill* (1982) and *The Open Garden* (1988).

He opened the Harbour Bookshop on 25th August 1951. He also co-founded the Dartmouth & Kingswear Society in 1959.

ANDREW HOLMES

CHAPTER 10

The Second Time Around

1939 to 1954

ANOTHER WAR TO END ALL WARS

That fateful day, 3rd September 1939, war was declared and the remaining months of the year were devoted to war preparations. The territorial army was called to the colours in August and the evacuation of children to safe towns started, rationing and the blackout were introduced, the latter necessitating the erection of railings around the Boat Float. The first war casualties occurred.

In the first month the aircraft carrier HMS *Courageous* was sunk with heavy loss of life, but the two Dartmouth men aboard, Chief Petty Officers D Westlake and R Wilcox, were saved. The former insisted the *Chronicle* saved his life, for after being on deck with CPO Wilcox discussing local affairs, he went below leaving the *Chronicle* behind. Ten minutes later he remembered his paper, and he was halfway up the companionway when the torpedoes struck, blowing him up onto the deck, while those below were killed. He and his fellow Dartmothian were later picked up from the sea by the escort destroyers.

1940 was an eventful year. In the early months, the Air Raid Precautions (ARP) and local defence volunteers, later the Home Guard, were formed, sirens were mounted and evacuees began arriving. Compulsory billeting was introduced and out of the 35,000 people already placed, Devon had accepted only 4,491, but by late spring Dartmouth had accommodated 576 children and Kingswear 107 children, one household in five became a home to an evacuee.

Troops poured into France and shipping losses by U-boats mounted, including the B-class destroyer HMS *Brazen*, guardship at the previous Dartmouth Regatta, which had left port in such dramatic fashion. The local MP for Torquay, Mr Williams of Greenway, surmised in an address that the Luftwaffe had not attacked because they were too frightened of the RAF; how wrong he was.

But everyday affairs continued: Kingswear's church clock was repaired and was given newly gilded hands. Then the neighbouring clock at St Saviours went on strike and stopped. Her four faces showed four different times, so the clock

Dartmouth quickly responded to the national emergency as pavements were painted, and principal buildings were sandbagged.
R TUCKER,
DARTMOUTH MUSEUM

*Smith's Pharmacy
(later Boots) in
Duke Street
adapted as an air-
raid shelter and
gas mask centre.*
R TUCKER,
DARTMOUTH MUSEUM

Left: *The gallant
little* Campeador V
*owned by Mr
Vernon W
MacAndrew, who
immediately war
was declared,
placed her under
Admiralty control.
They appointed
him, and two
fellow members of
the RDYC.
temporary
Lieutenants*
RDYC

Right: *A happy
band of brothers,
Commander C H
Davey OBE RN.
and temporary
Lieutenants J R
Muir, and C B
Turner aboard the*
Campeador V.
RDYC. CROWN COPYRIGHT

repairers moved over the water; shortly after its repair the vicar of St Saviours, the Rev A Shell, died. Manpower was a problem so ferry hours were cut and became erratic. A lean-to shelter was erected on the site of the demolished end house by the Lower Ferry Slip, and instructions issued that, in an air-raid alert, ferries should proceed to the Dartmouth side, while if at night crews were to marshal at the ferry slip and wait. The town council debated whether Warfleet Brewery (which they owned) could be used as a munition factory.

In France the Germans commenced their offensive and the British Expeditionary Force and her allies soon realized the folly of reliance on fortified fixed lines of defence, such as the French Maginot line, for the highly mobile German armies outflanked them and forced the British to beat a hasty retreat to the Channel ports, where the Dunkirk evacuation began. Many local men were rescued and several local boats took part in rescuing troops off the beaches. Even the 1908 Dartmouth rail ferry *The Mew* left to contribute, but after steaming at full speed to Dover, she was deemed unfit for the task and returned slowly to Dartmouth. Among the armada of small ships returning with survivors there were several Belgian and French trawlers determined to continue the conflict, and among them were the two French tugs *l'Isere* and *l'Aure* which sailed into Dartmouth harbour and remained there, giving good service throughout the war. Brian Bovey, a Kingswear schoolboy then, remembers the cargo consisting of purloined French racing cycles of which he and others became proud owners.

On 22 June a tragedy struck Vernon MacAndrew and his fellow officers and crew patrolling in his 111-ton luxury yacht *Campeador V*; after nine hard winter months of constant patrol in dangerous waters she struck a magnetic mine, was

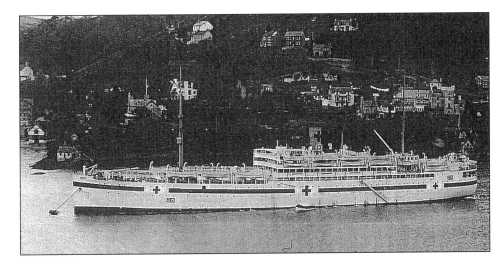

The troopship Dorsetshire *was promptly converted into a hospital ship and left the harbour to take up war station.*
DARTMOUTH MUSEUM

The Arandora Star *probably the largest liner to lay up on the Dart, leaving for service, and shortly to be torpedoed while transporting German and Italian prisoners of war.*
CYRIL KING

blown apart and sank in less than a minute, with only two members surviving. It was a bitter blow for Dartmouth, for temporary Lieutenants V W MacAndrew, J R Muir, and C B Turner RNVR were all local men and members of the RDYC. This happy band of brothers, in spite of mature years, had been promoted by the then First Lord of the Admiralty, Winston Churchill, with characteristic words: 'Promote them, age will be served'.

Another veteran, Dartmouth's ex-Corporal Veale VC, enlisted as a dispatch rider, while the old cannons on Bayards Castle and the 1918 six-inch German field gun were donated to assist the drive for scrap metal. News came that the *Andorra Star*, previously laid up on the river, had been torpedoed while crossing the Atlantic with 1,500 German and Italian prisoners of war. The killing field knew no bounds for the Air Ministry ordered the destruction of all peregrine falcons, which were decimating the carrier pigeons increasingly used to carry messages for the RAF.

As the year closed the harbour experienced its first air raid when, in November, a single enemy plane dropped four bombs over Kingswear, completely demolishing a farmworker's cottage at the junction of Slappers Hill and Hoodown Farm Lane. Mrs Violet Jane was buried but rescued from the debris seriously injured, while her husband was unharmed. Another bomb blew a huge crater in a nearby field (aptly named Wilful Murder) just a short distance from the centre of the village.

News came that the 144-ton schooner-yacht *Noroit*, belonging to Earl Beatty and previously laid up on the Dart, had been purchased by the American millionaire Harry B Clarke, managing director of Clarke Aircraft Products USA, to enable him to escape the London air raids and return to the States with a crew of six, which included M Middleton of Dartmouth. It was ill planned, and after fifty-eight days they arrived in Barbados. The engines had failed, the sails were ripped to shreds and they had been stopped by an Italian submarine and two German E-boats. Finally they landed starving and exhausted from after eating only pancakes made from flour and water and fried in engine oil.

*Right: The statue
of King George V
stood supreme
over the wreckage,
having withstood
greater threats
than the German
airforce (a plot by
cadets to decorate
him, causing a
near strike among
staff given extra
duty to protect
him).*

DARTMOUTH MUSEUM

*Below: The BRNC,
a prestigious
target, received
battle honours on
the 18th September
1942, when two
bombs fell. One
destroyed the bay
window section of
the front façade,
the other the
quarterdeck.*

DARTMOUTH MUSEUM

1941 brought little cheer, but Captain R T Paine, Dartmouth, was awarded the George Medal for bravery when his ship was torpedoed. The local people, as well as raising £2,000 towards a Spitfire, set out to raise £35,000 for a motor launch but ended up achieving the magnificent sum of £135,750.

A new town clerk T H Butt requisitioned ten houses, including the vacant Warfleet House, which already had a day nursery under Miss Pockett; it then later became a Wren base until 1946. Mrs MacAndrew, owner of Warfleet House and nearby Ravensbury, saddened by the death of her husband, left Ravensbury and loaned the house to the YMCA, who had previously received Warfleet House and £20,000 to establish the (now closed) training school for yacht crews. Ravensbury became a hostel for the growing number of service personnel arriving in the town.

Shipping was increasing, reinforced from Portland by Channel Coaling Co Ltd's powerful 1927 tug *Portwey* which remained until 1952, and is still in steam today. In Kingswear a sad accident occurred on the Hoodown railway-crossing when a lorry loaded with chippings was hit by the Churston train and carried down the line. Driver E C Blake was killed on impact and thrown into the river.

Meanwhile heavy air raids on London, Coventry, Manchester and other major cities including Exeter and Plymouth were taking a heavy toll of property and life, but fortunately Dartmouth remained unscathed. Heated argument continued as to whether cinemas should open on Sundays for lonely and bored service personnel. Spirit and patriotism were high, bolstered by the success in the Libyan desert of the 'desert rats' of the Eighth Army, while small bands of volunteers set targets of achievement; £21 bought three rifles, £160 a machine gun; supplementary targets for major schemes were regularly surpassed.

Finally Dartmouth, long the port of privateers, merchant seamen and the Navy, witnessed a change by the appearance of Wrens, in increasing numbers who were to play a valuable part in the war.

1942 The *Chronicle* reported yet another major fund-raising effort by Dartmouth and Kingswear, to raise £120,000, the cost of the hull of a destroyer, the HMS *Haldon*, and by March this total was exceeded. In Kingswear the Rev S H Keyworth delivering a fine sermon at the church of St Thomas à Becket stated that malaise and lethargy at home was as dangerous as any fifth column, and it was alright right to be 'a good hater' – strong patriotic medicine.

A letter in the *Chronicle* from A C Nicholl, The Chalet, Kingswear, returned to the campaign to kill peregrine falcons. They were such a serious menace to the Air Ministry's carrier pigeons that a core of fifty observers had been established, from which he received regular reports of sightings. He then dispatched a special team to the area to carry out their unpleasant task.

In mid-May the town was honoured by the visit of the King and Queen. They arrived by special train at Kingswear, arranged by stationmaster R H Bovey, and from there they boarded a naval launch to be received by Mayor and Mayoress W G Row to cheering crowds. They visited the college to see officer cadets and Wrens, then proceeded to Derwent Lodge to see off-duty Wrens, many of whom exchanged conversation with the Queen. The royal family finally departed in the evening by train from Kingswear station after a happy day in Dartmouth.

THE BOMBERS ARRIVE

At 11am on 18 September, after two years mainly free from air raids, Dartmouth was attacked by six Focke-Wolf bombers, without warning. They came in upriver low against the sun, then paired off to attack the college, coaling installations, and the shipyards. The college was machine gunned and struck by two bombs, one on B-block, the other on the quarterdeck. Considerable damage occurred resulting in the death of a Wren petty officer, and one other officer was injured. Casualties would have been considerable had the cadets been in residence. This episode resulted in the re-siting of the training college, first at Bristol then later at Eaton Hall, Cheshire, where there was a tenuous link with Dartmouth as it was the country home of the Earls of Devon.

The second two bombers concentrated on the coaling vessels in midstream, sinking the collier *Fernwood*, the hulk *Dagny* and a floating mechanical grab, causing the death of four lumpers. Several men were rescued from the water by a brave Wren in an 18ft ex-launch-tender, and she was later rewarded for her courage with an inscribed silver cigarette case from the directors of the Channel Coaling Co Ltd.

The main damage was caused to the shipbuilding yard of Philips at Noss, where twenty people were killed and forty injured, while the mould loft, machinery and plating shops were destroyed, leaving only the heavy cutting and punching machines intact. However, to the company's credit, the shipyards were reopened for limited production within forty-eight hours.

*The extensive
damage caused to
Philips Noss
Works killing and
injuring many
employees and
destroying
buildings and
machinery.*
R TUCKER/
DARTMOUTH MUSEUM

1943 After nearly three-and-a-half years of war a watershed was reached in the late summer of 1942 with the victories of the gallant Eighth Army in North Africa. Strident voices called for a second front, and Dartmouth was no exception. The town council included a few new councillors who were Labour supporters with strong non-socialist leanings, and who had taken to wearing red stars in the council chamber and addressing other members, to the annoyance of some, as 'brother' or 'comrade'.

In January evidence of a change from defence to attack became apparent in the harbour, when the Royal Navy took over the top floors of Kingswear's Royal Dart Hotel, which was commissioned as HMS *Dartmouth II*, later changed to HMS *Cicala*, and established as the coastal forces' base. It included a cipher and confidential books section. At the same time the vacant BRNC was recommissioned as HMS *Dartmouth III*, later HMS *Effingham*, and became the headquarters of the Combined Operational Services. From then on, the first flotilla of an ever-growing fleet of landing craft arrived in the harbour to carry out practice landings on Slapton beach.

The growing influx of service personnel to Dartmouth and its vicinity soon placed an intolerable strain on the facilities of the small civilian Dartmouth & Kingswear Cottage Hospital, and a small auxiliary hospital was established in the rectory at Stoke Fleming. It was fully equipped and had eighteen beds for civilian sick, thus freeing Dartmouth for service personnel. Also on January the 23rd a Motor Torpedo Boat (MTB) flotilla, manned entirely by members of the Free French Naval Forces, arrived to take up station in the harbour. They had been trained and equipped with new vessels at Portland and, after inspection by their commander General de Gaulle, were in combat readiness. They were accompanied by a British depot ship HMS *Belfort*, built in 1919, and their base was in Kingswear at the 1902 Forward's wharf at Hoodown (today the workshop of the DHNA). This also served as a torpedo store, and four fuel tanks were located in Waterhead Creek. Several local gentlemen's residences in Kingswear were requisitioned for accommodation: Longford, (adjacent to the slip) for the officers, Brookhill, Kingswear Court, Inverdart, The Mount, and Ridley House for the men. From Kingswear they participated in several engagements inflicting considerable damage on enemy convoys and sinking several ships. Serving among the crews was General de Gaulle's son Philippe. They remained at Kingswear until September 1944 and established a firm bond of friendship with the village, which exists to the present day.

Free French Motor Torpedo Boats (MTBs) and their depot ship HMS Belfort *moored alongside their Hoodown headquarters.*

DAVE GRIFFITHS

Crew members aboard a MTB enjoying a well-earned break after loading torpedoes from the adjacent jetty, prior to a foray across channel.

DAVE GRIFFITHS

This upsurge of naval activity had probably not passed unnoticed by the German intelligence services. In 1993 when alterations were made to a house in Fore Street, Kingswear, which possessed panoramic views of the harbour, an extensive network of powerful aerials was found fixed to the underside of the rafters.

On 13 February Dartmouth suffered its heaviest air raid when, according to the *Chronicle*, four enemy planes flew in low from the sea without warning, machine-gunning and dropping high explosive bombs, while the anti-aircraft guns opened up a heavy but mainly ineffective barrage. One of the bombs landed in woodland while another fell alongside the Yacht Club Hotel, damaging its high embankment walls and rendering the building unusable, but fortunately there was no loss of life. The other two bombs fell in the town centre causing considerable damage, heavy loss of life and many injuries. One bomb landed in Higher Street destroying the public house The Town Arms and its adjoining grocery shop, and damaging a nearby girls' council school. Customers drinking in the bar had a miraculous escape, one of them, C G Lorette, told the *Chronicle* reporter, with true British phlegm, 'When I got up I looked at my beer to see if it was still worth drinking'; sadly it was not. In a more serious vein, next door, the grocer's wife Mrs T Ball and her daughter were killed.

The fourth bomb did the most damage, killing thirteen and injuring another forty people. It completely destroyed the Midland Bank (now HSBC Bank) in Duke Street and a row of three shops with flats above as far as Henleys Corner, Foss Street. It also severely damaged the Tudor House, a Dartmouth gem, so much that it had to be pulled down. The Butterwalk, two churches and several adjacent properties were severely damaged. In the following days frenzied activity by all the rescue services saved further loss of life.

The Free French Navy was further reinforced by the transfer of the newly built destroyer HMS *Haldon* for which £12,000 plus had been raised by Dartmouth and Kingswear. However, the town council had anticipated the money would be for a British-manned vessel, so the Admiralty offered a further new vessel, building HMS *Caesar* for adoption, which was accepted by the town council. Mundane events went on as usual and there were bitter complaints that the penny ferry launch, was now run only between 7am and 8am in the morning and the car ferry between 8am to 8pm. Staff shortages were blamed, and the town council agreed to loan one of their staff to help General Estates Ltd to run longer hours. Once again the town clerk left, but this time of his own accord. Another 'Wings for Victory' effort was started on both sides of the river to raise £50,000 to build sixteen fighter planes and £93,227 was raised in only four months.

Left: Mayhem and destruction in Duke Street as one bomb tore the heart out of the main shopping area, killing and injuring many. The rescue services strive to make the damaged buildings safe to recover those trapped in the wreckage.

This year, 1943, was also the turning point in the war. The German and Russian armies were still engaged in mortal conflict on the eastern front. Nearer home the liberation of Europe really began; the Eighth Army had secured North Africa and then carried out the first invasion of Europe by landing at Syracuse in Sicily. The Devonshire Regiment, part of 50th Division, played an important part. Their commander General Bernard Montgomery had, as a brigadier with the 9th Infantry Brigade in 1938, presented a statuette of a fully equipped British soldier to the Royal Naval College as a mark of appreciation for the hospitality the brigade had received whilst stationed there when practising the first combined landings on Slapton Beach, with our only three landing craft. These invasion exercises were soon to be repeated on a bigger scale.

Above: Clearing up alongside the Butterwalk which was badly shaken but still standing.
ALL R TUCKER, DARTMOUTH MUSEUM

Above (both): In October 1943, American troops training at Slapton, where General Montgomery in 1938 practised invasion exercises. During this period to become battle worthy their amphibious forces suffered a reverse losing two LSTs, damage to others and many lives to German E-Boats.

Below (both): The damaged LST US 289 making Dartmouth Harbour.

ALL DARTMOUTH MUSEUM

BETTER LATE THAN NEVER

In early October Lord Fortescue, Lord Lieutenant of Devon, with General Sir Hugh Ellis and an American general from the European theatre of combined operations and other officials, chaired a meeting in the crowded Slapton parish church to acquaint the families and representatives of 3,000 people, 840 homes and 200 farms from six parishes with the fact that the whole area was to be commandeered for battle training. They had six weeks (until 20 December) to evacuate their homes to allow the area to be used for battle training and invasion practice by the US Army.

Naturally there was distress amongst the people who had lived in the area all their lives and where homes had been in families for generations. Twenty threshing machines were dispatched to the area with 300 to 400 service men and women as Land Army personnel to help lift the crops, and move the 6,000 cattle and 12,000 sheep. The authorities were to pay for removals and storage but only for the first two weeks of accommodation which had to be found in neighbouring towns and villages. The later return and restitution of damaged property would be recompensed in full.

This was the prelude to a massive influx of American forces in November. The first contingents from the US Navy Advanced Amphibious Division took quarters at Sandridge and Waddeton Court, and as the size of the force expanded, Hunterswood and Maypool were also occupied. In late December the first units arrived to take possession of the vacant BRNC, which was to become the headquarters of the US Navy.

1944 Service personnel were arriving in increasing numbers and accommodation was at a premium, so the town's few level areas were quickly commandeered and large camps were set up for use as workshops, stores, launching slips and so on. The river began to fill with naval vessels and landing craft of all types, mainly purpose-built for offensive action. Exercise landings on nearby Slapton Beach were commonplace. Sadly one operation, Operation Tiger, on 20 April, resulted in disaster when seven enemy E-boats infiltrated the convoy and torpedoed two large fully-loaded tank-landing-craft, resulting in the loss of hundreds of American lives. This tragedy was kept a

The Build-up to D-Day *1944*

D-Day nears, the training over and the harbour hums with activity and is crammed with 468 invasion craft filled with anxious men awaiting countdown.

A US tank trundles along the North Embankment with the Ship-in-Dock *pub in the background.*
ALL DARTMOUTH MUSEUM

secret for many years after the war had ended. In the same month the 3rd Canadian division (with General Eisenhower supreme commander of the allied forces, and Mongomery in attendance) also carried out invasion exercises on Slapton beach.

On 6 June hundreds of large and small landing-craft sailed from many ports in Britain, including 485 from Dartmouth, fully loaded with anxious soldiers and their equipment, to begin the invasion of France after almost five years of bloody conflict.

Those men in the invasion craft would have experienced the same tensions and fears as the troops of William the Conqueror, who had carried out a similar but reverse invasion almost nine hundred earlier in 1066.

The victories and achievements of this exercise, Operation Overlord, and the eventual liberation of Europe have been well documented elsewhere. At this point in Dartmouth and Kingswear people began to concentrate on what the future would hold for the area after the war.

With the departure of the American and British forces the population was greatly reduced and the presence of so many servicemen and women was sadly missed, particularly by the shopkeepers whose income diminished considerably. The imbalance was not so obvious in the public houses, as due to the war there were more women visiting licensed premises, often alone.

1945 Confident of early victory, the Dartmouth & Kingswear Cottage Hospital annexe at the Stoke Fleming rectory was closed down and the staff returned to Dartmouth. After the departure of the forces, shipping in the harbour became negligible.

It was almost two years since the American forces had arrived in Dartmouth and there was a strong possibility that the US Navy base at the college would close. To commemorate the bond of friendship established with the town the US Navy authorities added a further link to the mayoral chain, a gold and enamel replica of the US Navy badge. It was presented to Mayor W G Row at a ceremonial parade at the college by Commander P D Crocket of the US Navy Advanced Amphibious Base.

Two weeks later the town suffered a set-back to civic pride when Alderman W D Pillar JP, ex-Lord Mayor, and a freeman of Dartmouth with twenty-two years' public service, was found guilty on twenty-two charges of obtaining money on Government contracts by false pretences and issuing fraudulent invoices to the value of £2,557. He was sentenced to three years' penal servitude.

This folly, according to many prominent local people from all shades of the political spectrum and those who held high office on both sides of the water, was completely out of character with the man they knew, who had done so much for Dartmouth. It was summed up by Captain T Wilton of Kingswear: 'He has been a very fine example of a true Britisher, who has brought up a family which many Britons could be proud of.'

Happily the nation did not suffer any loss as all the money was paid back out of a trust fund by his devoted family.

ALL QUIET ON THE WESTERN FRONT

VE (Victory in Europe) day on the 8 May dawned bright and clear. It was a day of great celebration and rejoicing after Prime Minister Winston Churchill's historic broadcast announcing victory and the end of the war in Europe. All local church bells rang, steamers hooted and sounded their sirens, trains in Kingswear whistled, car horns were sounded and flags appeared in every window. There were parties with dancing and singing and speeches well into the night. In spite of the blackout, lights were switched on and searchlights from anchored warships made victory Vs in the sky, while public houses exhausted their supplies in one glorious evening. The war may have been over in Europe, but in the churches, people prayed for the safe return of loved ones and those who had sacrificed their lives for the freedom of others.

The shaping of peace began but it still retained a strong offensive nature, as fifty-eight sea cadets arrived to claim Ravensbury from the War Department. They formed the 15th Cadet Training Corps under the command of Lieutenant E A W Grey, with

HMS Ceasar *the ship adopted by both Dartmouth and Kingswear during the war after their magnificent achievement in fund raising towards the cost of its construction.*
<small>WORLD SHIP SOCIETY</small>

The Mayor and happy families celebrating at VE Day street party, at Brown's Steps, Dartmouth.
<small>BOTH A L CLAMP</small>

Free French Forces assembled for the colourful ceremony of taking the salute on the lawn of Kittery Court, Kingswear prior to leaving to return to France and homes.

Victory at last, school children celebrating in Kingswear Square. Note the archway under Armesons 1870 building blocked up as an air-raid shelter and the shops adopted as ARP centres.

Kingswear Parish Council Chairman William Todd with high ranking French Government member receiving an illuminated address thanking Kingswear for the hospitality given to the Free French Forces stationed here during the war.

ALL WILLIAM TODD

the Royal Naval College providing facilities for swimming, boatwork, sports, trips on motor torpedo boats and gunboats and training with machine guns and pompoms. The Admiralty allocated the cadets a 115ft long B-class MTB which moored in Warfleet Creek and remained there until 1947 when it moved further up the harbour.

The Americans erected a monument on Slapton Sands as a memorial to their training there and to their fallen men.

Celebrations continued and the town received a visit from three high-ranking officers of the three armed forces who each presented a flag to commemorate the raising of £450,000 for the war effort. The Admiralty sent Dartmouth's adopted destroyer HMS *Caesar* to the Dart on an official visit under the command of Captain D H Brewer, a former college cadet. The ship was dressed overall and open to the public and over 2,000 people visited and met the officers and crew. After hospitality visits the happy ship left concluding her three-day visit by flying 'Good Luck Dartmouth' signals; at Ravensbury the Sea Cadet Corps 'manned ship' as she passed.

In August the *Chronicle* reported a tragedy on the river. A collision occurred at Sharpham between the paddle-steamer *Kingswear Castle* and a launch with eighteen passengers aboard. Surprisingly both vessels were running abreast. The launch sank, and the only two passengers who could swim helped others ashore. Sixteen-year-old Arthur Morley dived fully clothed from the steamer, the only one to do so, to rescue and help four women and a five-year-old child to cling on to the half-sunken launch; he then swam to a rowing boat moored nearby and returned to save six others who clung to it until the rescue boats arrived. Sadly one man was drowned but Arthur Morley saved eleven people, and it is hoped his bravery was well rewarded.

Finally this momentous year ended, proving war changes everything and yet nothing, particularly in politics. In Dartmouth the Labour Party held sway in the council chamber, as in the country, and everything was once again set for social change. One progressive member wished to nationalize everything that moved, wanting the Lower Ferry service returned to council control, but it was left as a private concern. Although they had several council representatives on the harbour board, the council regarded the Dart Harbour Commission with deep suspicion. At one council meeting, the councillors refused to go and meet the DHC, even though it was to the council's benefit, and demanded that the Commission should attend the council.

1946
The nation's mood was still ebullient and the war machine began winding down. Demobilization was implemented, with some long-serving personnel and prisoners of war returning as men, not as the boys they had been at the outset of hostilities. They had sacrificed their youth for little immediate return and were to queue not 'at the cookhouse door' but for the modest number of jobs available.

With the capitulation of Germany the allies concentrated on defeating the Japanese forces, who surrendered after the horrors of Hiroshima and Nagasaki. The country then embarked on a further round of celebration.

RESUMPTION OF REGATTAS

Regatta 1946 After six years of absence a limited event was planned, and sadly this time the weather was the enemy; torrential rain marked the opening and on Friday half the races were cancelled, the remaining five being transferred to the harbour course. There was great disappointment when a special race planned for five reparation German yachts of the 50-square metre class, and owned by the Royal Navy, was cancelled. Although the weather improved on the final day, sailing outside was again cancelled and races scheduled in the harbour were controlled by a committee boat at Warfleet. Rationing and shortages still prevailed with tobacco and beer in short supply. This regatta resulted in the formation two months later of a new class of dinghy built by Morgan Giles of Teignmouth, known as the Royal Dart One Design (RDOD).

Left: *The lovely* Royal Sands Hotel, *once the retreat of many and frequented by royalty.*

Right: *Sadly, the same hotel when handed back in 1946, after (perhaps) over-excessive American war practice. Regrettably, it was never rebuilt.*

Both Harold Hutchings

In November the town council, high on the Government promise that permanent prefabricated housing would solve all housing problems and promote a better new world, took the surprising decision to take legal action to demolish the ancient Butterwalk even though it was a listed building. After the damage suffered in the 1943 air raids the building had been shored and boarded up and the council appeared more concerned about the loss of rates and the new social order than preserving their heritage. Fortunately the Minister of Town and Country Planning scheduled it an 'ancient monument', provoking howls of rage in the council chamber and such remarks as: 'It was to bring matters to a head that we decided to pull it down and now a bunch of cranks have done a bit of wire pulling'. Hooray for the Minister of Town and Country Planning!

1947 brought the coldest spell of weather to Dartmouth since 1891, with 18 degrees of frost and the heaviest snowfall for twenty years. Dartmouth lay under three feet of snow and sledges were used on the streets to assist with shopping. Electricity supplies were interrupted, transport was almost non-existent, pipes froze and an unusual and eerie silence settled over the town. In Kingswear Waterhead Creek iced over and drifts of snow at Hillhead were 20 feet high, and the village was completely cut off for several days.

In Dartmouth the appalling weather did not stop the talking, for two years after the cessation of hostilities, the housing committee had met forty times, talked for 200 hours, used 5lb weight of paper in 500 pages of foolscap, but had not built one new house! After fierce discussion and on the casting vote of the Mayor H G Middleton an order was placed for fifty permanent 'Cornish' prefabricated units to be sited somewhere on top of the hill. The first sixteen prefabricated houses arrived and were rapidly erected and occupied. The later units were supposed to be a short-term solution to the housing problem, with a life expectancy of ten years, whereas the permanent prefabricated units were to have an indefinite life, but times proved that the reverse was the case. Accommodation in Dartmouth was further reduced when fire swept through the Queens Hotel (formerly Kings Hotel, now Riversea). The fire service was quickly on the scene and was reinforced by the arrival of Channel Coaling Co Ltd's tug *Portwey* which sprayed the fire with powerful hoses. Although the building was completely gutted the fire was prevented from spreading to the garage with its petrol pumps next door.

The Totnes Rural District Council approved the erection in Kingswear of a flat-roofed block of seven flats, which are now thankfully hip-roofed, in the Redoubt Quarry, and the local builder J Tribble converted the village smithy at the end of Wood Lane into a modern dwelling and threw it open to the public to show what could be done with old property.

Philips launched a new steel ferry float for General Estates Co Ltd, and the Lower Ferry manager, Captain N Bray, attended the launching. A new passenger launch *Reliance* was placed on the Lower Ferry run. (The previous penny ferry was also called *Reliance* and had been built by Lavers and introduced to the service in 1935, so presumably this was a replacement launch.)

Dartmouth decided that the newly reintroduced Bayards Cove regatta should be held on 28 June, and some old customs were revived. It would be known as the

'Monkey Town' regatta and would consist of a water carnival, open-air dancing and a full programme of nine swimming and thirteen rowing events. The area would be flagged and independently roped off from Dartmouth for the day and have its own Mayor wearing a top hat crowned with a toy monkey; it would also have a Mayoress, town clerk, and a town sergeant in robes of office, and the president would be Finch Ingram. It was fully supported by the Royal Naval College whose captain was officially received along with the Mayor of Dartmouth and other dignitaries. It was a huge success and well attended. Also present was the World War I Dartmouth VC, Corporal T W H Veale, who came from London and took part in the marathon not expecting to win but just to finish the course. The *Chronicle* gave a brief history, supplied by Miss Henley, of the origin of 'Monkey Town', as follows:

> *During the first world war men of the British fleet were issued with a rum ration which was known as a 'monkey', and when in Dartmouth harbour it was usually issued when they were lying off Bayards Cove, which in turn acquired the nickname 'Monkey Town' for its association with the rum ration.*

Kingswear was often envious of Dartmouth's Mayors and events, but was appeased when the parish council leader received a letter addressed to the 'Lord Mayor of Kingswear'.

The ever increasing number of cars coming into the village posed a problem for there was no suitable turning place other than in the square, and this caused chaos with the ferry traffic. Proposals for change were made but the problem was not resolved, although debate mentioned several place names which have disappeared today: 'Hawkes Corner', 'Dead Men's Lane', 'Wilton's Corner', 'Brew House' and 'Nelson's Steps'.

A landslip caused by heavy rains occurred adjacent to Inverdart Cottage on Castle Road isolating the Castle, Brookhill, Kingswear Court, The Grange, and other country houses for five months. Only a 4ft width of roadway remained, as the rest had slid into the River Dart 200ft below. The only alternative road was a long detour via Boohay which was boycotted by many because of the roughness of the route. Supplies were taken by vehicles to the edge of the landslip, transferred across by wheelbarrow, and put into another van on the opposite side. This was inconvenient and expensive for the properties, particularly Kingswear Court and Brookhill. Both had now been de-requisitioned as service quarters.

Kingswear Court had been acquired in 1930 by the Holiday Friendship Association which was back in business and receiving up to 600 visitors in the summer. Brookhill had been acquired by D Sanderson and was established as Fountain Violet Country Club. A Dartmouth boatman, C Alexander, established a partial solution to the problem by running a water taxi service from the station and ferrying hundreds of passengers to Brookhill and Kingswear Court slips. Devon County Council was unable to help as the road was privately owned, and after several months of isolation, D Sanderson, Sir Frederick Fowke, Major E J West, Herbert Jones, and the Holiday Friendship Association supported by two local MPs, obtained a wartime Bailey bridge, slung it across the ravine and set it on 10 tons of concrete foundations, thus reconnecting the area to the rest of Kingswear.

A most unusual event occurred in August at Kingswear when an earth tremor brought phenomenal tides. The river level dropped suddenly leaving the car-float with cars aboard and its attendant tug high and dry on the Kingswear slip. It was freed later by the passenger launch, only to be stranded again in Dartmouth when the tide rushed in while cars were being loaded, carrying the float and tug too far up the slip.

Further drama occurred with the death of A Cash of Kingswear in his privately owned aircraft, an Auster Autocrat three-seater. Watched by his wife and two children he tried to take off from a sloping field at Penhill Lane, Hillhead, failed to clear the hedge and trees and crashed nearby, causing his death and seriously wounding his passenger.

The famous gaff-rigged schooner, Westward *135ft long, with 15,498 sq ft of sail, after some years laid up on the Dart, she is leaving harbour lashed to the tug* Portwey *for sinking off Guernsey as the late Mr Davis decreed. She had raced against all the famous J-Class yachts,* Astra, Britannia, Candida, Endeavour, Shamrock V, Velsheda, *and* Yankee.

DAVE GRIFFITHS

There was a sad prelude to the forthcoming regatta on Monday 14 July when the superb J-class yacht *Westward* went to her ocean grave, as abridged below:

The *Westward* lashed to the *Portwey* slipped out of Dartmouth harbour about midday on Tuesday as instructed in her owner's will. She had been lying in the Dart since 1929 and the date of the sailing was kept a close secret even from those on board, two old members of the millionaire's crew, skipper Bill Aldis, and James Foster, a sailmaker. A complete ban on all press and newsreel men was imposed, and Captain Griffiths, harbourmaster, believed up to the time of the arrival of the explosives expert with specially prepared scuttling charges that the *Westward* was to go to Falmouth for final stripping as her lead keel of 80 tons was valued at more than £4,000. The hooting of the tug's siren brought people from their homes to watch the departure of the famous yacht in the dusk The *Westward* frequently raced against *Britannia*, King George V's yacht, which after his death in 1936 was sunk on his instructions. The *Westward* was built for an American owner in 1910, at Bristol, Rhode Island, USA, and in the following year at Kiel Regatta swept all before her. In 1912 she was purchased by a German company, Norddeutschen Regatta Verein and renamed *Hamburg II*. After World War I she was acquired by an American financier Clarence Hatry who renamed her *Westward* but in 1924 he was jailed for 13 years for fraud. She was then offered for sale and purchased by Mr Davis. The *Westward*, devoid of splendour and mastless, sank within five seconds of a double explosion which ripped her apart in Hu Deep, near Guernsey, Channel Islands. The *Portwey* reached Dartmouth after a round journey of nearly one hundred miles, which with the scuttling had taken 22 hours, and the crew headed by Captain Griffiths went ashore immediately after 24 hours without rest and in the last stages of exhaustion.

In Dartmouth, Fairview College closed; it was established in 1918, when it transferred to Dartmouth from its previous buildings at Southend, which were wrecked in a Zeppelin raid.

At Dittisham disagreement surfaced between the Totnes Rural District Council (TRDC) and the River Dart Steamboat Company over the sum the steamboat company demanded for its premises at Dittisham which contained vital toilet conveniences which the TRDC required for public use. The matter was resolved after the council threatened compulsory purchase. The toilets were for the use of Dittisham car-ferry passengers, as the service had recommenced after a gap of many years. The paper also reported another river crossing, by a Lakeland terrier called 'Bundle', owned by the manager of the Royal Castle Hotel. The dog had a charmed life, having previously been buried for thirty-six hours in the London Blitz, it was enjoying the quiet life of Dartmouth. It was seen entering the river at its widest point, calmly swimming over to Kingswear and then travelling down the railway line to the Lower Ferry to return without paying the penny fare. It arrived safely back at the hotel.

The *Chronicle* also contained instructions, two years after the war, as to how to obtain one's ration book and identity card.

Regatta 1947 started in brilliant sunshine and was much larger than the trial postwar 1946 regatta which fortunately had been successful. Sixty boats raced, controlled from the old coastguard station at Compass Point where Percy Russell, Dartmouth historian, gave a commentary of events. The Thursday races were between twenty DODs, the three from the Royal Naval College being disqualified for arriving late, while in the new RDOD class the pioneering yachtsmen were Captain T Wilton, Major H D Teague and Major Eric Wilton, with Clive Barr and Major H D Teague winning. The Redwings' race was held over while the race for Nationals had six combatants and was won by *Laughter*, B P Moore and J Holt.

The remaining two days were outside and controlled from the flagpole again at Compass Point and there were eleven races.

Hostilities over, the implements of war were surplus to requirements and began to stockpile in shore bases, airports and harbours, and Dartmouth Harbour soon started to fill with redundant ships awaiting disposal.
H G CASSERLEY, DAVE GRIFFITHS

The fairground proprietors this year gave a sum of money towards asphalting the area of the New Ground which had been a sea of mud the previous year.

As this busy year began to ebb, the King and Queen visited Dartmouth, arriving at 10.15am at Kingswear station. They crossed by Navy launch to Dartmouth to meet dignitaries, then visited the college, crossing Coombe Park on the new concrete road laid by the Americans. There were more meetings, then they returned to Kingswear to catch the 4.30pm train to London.

A fine stained-glass window was presented to the college by the officers and men of the Combined Operations base stationed there four years previously. This was called the 'St Boniface Window' after a saint born at Crediton and martyred in Germany in 755. The window contained the Combined Operations flash and the badge of HMS *Effingham*, the name of the college during the war, chosen by Admiral Mountbatten as it was thought better to name it after HMS *Effingham* sunk off Normandy in 1940 rather than becoming HMS *Dartmouth III*.

The year closed in a blaze of colour in Kingswear when the street lights were once again turned on and a meeting was held in the village hall to celebrate the fifty years of the Royal Ancient Order of Buffaloes. The Mayor of Dartmouth, F Scardifield, and the four local chairmen from Salcombe, Stoke Gabriel, Kingswear and Totnes attended. The Grand Chamberlain told the meeting that the Order had been formed by stage people who adopted the name of a popular song of the 1880s '*We'll hunt the buffalo*', and they invented a weird and wonderful series of ceremonies which were kept up when people from other walks of life joined the Order.

The last day of the year saw the drowning of Arthur Ball, seaman from the collier *Moses Gay*, who after a night ashore carousing decided to swim back to the ship instead of waiting for the shore boat.

1948
Rationing still prevailed which encouraged a flourishing black market for many items, including the humble egg. So Mr C J Shuttleworth, former Minister of Agriculture, lecturer and poultry farmer, and Gunfield Hotel owner, advocated a scheme to eliminate eggs from the local black market. He purchased for £1,500, the near derelict council owned Warfleet Brewery with one-and-a-half acres to create an intensive poultry farm run on American lines, with all-electric hatching and rearing apparatus for 20,000 hens to lay 150 eggs per bird per year, a target of three million per annum. However, the Ministry of Agriculture at Exeter refused the large amount of animal feed needed, as did Whitehall, as 200 tons per year could not be guaranteed. Subsequently a London firm, Glysons Products, purchased the brewery to manufacture cosmetics and perfume but these products were short-lived, so they applied to build a kiln to make domestic and decorative pottery. The council agreed and Mr Harry Caute arrived as design director. He had served 22 years with Torquay's Watcombe Pottery, owned his own business, Lemon & Caute and later Daison Art Pottery. Today his pieces are eagerly sought after, making any of his signed Dartmouth pottery a collector's item. Production then commenced with a thrower and handler from Staffordshire, and a local girl, and quickly prospered soon employing over forty staff. The Dartmouth Pottery has recently been totally renovated and refurbished to a high standard and is once again making quality pottery.

Meanwhile, ratepayers were unhappy as rates were amongst the highest in the country, and the council met in closed session. The *Chronicle* was vigorous in pursuit of more openness, highlighting an excess of officials, over expenditure on training courses, and costly direct labour schemes. Arbitrary power was given to the borough engineer to 'hire and fire staff without question' to counter slacking and pilfering on the Townstal Estate projects. This brought furious accusations from the Labour group on the council, led by Alderman Scardifield, of creating 'little dictators'. Matters came to a head later, when estimates were received for ten traditional houses at Townstal, three from private contractors and one from the council's Direct Labour Department. The council's bid was the highest at £18,471, whereas the lowest was that of a private contractor at £15,319, a difference of £3,152. The contractor also had to make a profit, whereas the council labour force did not.

Left: *This ex-M T B 620 was renamed the* Golden Hind *and allocated to the Sea Rangers as headquarters, and moored at Old Mill Creek, Dartmouth. In 1946, the Princesses Elizabeth and Margaret spent several happy days aboard.*
COURTESY OF THE GUIDE ASSOCIATION

Right *Dartmouth's old jail, St Saviours Square, built in 1825 and demolished in 1948.*
DARTMOUTH MUSEUM

Miss Henley then highlighted the old regatta joys. Everyone ate gingerbread ,men made in Mr S Widdecombes Smith Street confectioners shop, (the moulds are in the Henley Museum). There was the greasy pole, bowl of treacle, Punch and Judy and mutton pies. The commercial stalls included, saw sharpening, chair making, scissor grinding, shoe blacking, basket making and clock mending. There were many carved and gaily decorated gypsy vans and gleaming steam and traction engines.

Concern surfaced at Bayards Quay, when it was discovered that the centuries-old cobble paving was disintegrating, and the cobbles were being thrown into the river. To his credit Finch Ingram, who owned the Old Customs House, offered to locate suitable cobble replacements and make a £25 grant towards the cost of repairs.

Problems were also becoming acute at the old Butterwalk, which was becoming more and more dilapidated and a danger to the public. No Government department was willing to authorize payment even for temporary repairs, let alone restoration.

At this time, a meeting of ex-members of the Prince of Wales' 5th TA battalion of the Devonshire Regiment was convened, and it was decided to re-form the unit. Before World War II it had been the 7th battalion, then later in 1941, the 87th Anti-Tank Regiment serving in the North African campaigns.

A gruesome discovery was made when demolishing the old jail of 1825. Five skeletons were found, one buried face down. They were assumed by Percy Russell, antiquarian and founder of Dartmouth museum, to be monks of the pre-monstratensian Order belonging to the fourteenth-century Chapel of Holy Trinity, on the site of the present church of St Saviours. Father F W Hodge, of St John the Baptist Roman Catholic church, kindly arranged for the reburial of the remains of the monks.

In lighter vein, a Dartmouth butcher was taken to court for using unsaleable scraps of meat to make his sausages, which on analysis were found to contain only 21 per cent of meat against the 50 per cent required by law. For this he was fined £2, and £1 analyst's fee.

Regatta 1948 Attendance was up. One name dominated and was to do so for many years ahead: Anne Hine-Haycock, who in her *DoDo*, a Dart One Design, won all the races in her class, on all days, both inside and outside the harbour.

In the big yacht races for over 25 tons *Flica* won, and in the 9 to 25 ton race *Meme* won. The other classes were West Solent, Dragon, 50 Sq Metre, 3 to 9 tons, 3 tons and under, RDOD, Redwing, National-12 and Firefly, and non-classed open boats not over 16ft. These events were watched by 2,500 people, and the athletics were held at Norton Park.

Finally three representatives of the RDYC and Dartmouth Regatta Committee joined the Torbay Yachting Association.

Continuing on a nautical theme, *The Mew*, which had been to Devonport for her annual overhaul, returned to service with alterations to her bridge and her old tall Woodbine funnel replaced by a new short funnel painted black and yellow, the colours of her new owners, British Railways. At Old Mill Creek aboard the ex-motor torpedo boat and training ship *Golden Hind*, Miss Ann Hopkins, senior member of the movement, with the aid of local Sea Rangers completely redecorated the ship before the arrival of the year's intake for training. In 1947 Princess Elizabeth and her sister Princess Margaret had lived aboard for a few days with members of the Windsor Sea Rangers Company

Another worldwide depression and shipping, like these Elder Dempsters' vessels and other major companies again began to return to lay up in the Dart above Noss.
However, locally, they brought a modest amount of trade and revenue for the Dartmouth Harbour Commission.
E K GREEN,

Finally, Brigadier-General Evan Henry Llewellyn DSO died at Coleton Fishacre, the home of his friend Rupert d'Oyly Carte, as his own house Nethway had been commandeered by the Ministry of Health during the war to accommodate evacuated children. He had served in the Boer War and World War I, and between wars had returned to South Africa to raise and train 30,000 native soldiers to serve under the country's leader, General Smuts.

1949 started with rumour and counter-rumour that Dartmouth Town Council was keeping secret the fact that the lessee of the Lower Ferry, General Estates Co of Southampton, was not going to renew the lease when it expired on 25 March and the service might close down. On 16 March the town council confirmed the rumour that the Lower Ferry was to revert back to the corporation, but that it would not close down. At a meeting a ten point resolution was passed, abbreviated as follows:

> - *To rescind all resolution that the Council will not operate the Ferry after March 25, 1949.*
> - *To accept the County Council offer to bear 50 per cent of any loss incurred during the forthcoming year.*
> - *That the Dartmouth Corporation shall carry on the Ferry Service of the Kingswear Lower Ferry passenger and vehicular as a Corporation, as from March 25, 1949, when the present lessees relinquish their lease.*
> - *That the Ministry of Transport and Devon County Council be informed of this decision but if the Ferry Service is likely to prove a burden to the taxpayers of Dartmouth, the Ferry Service shall be curtailed.*
> - *That the General Estates Co be advised of the Corporation's decision to take over the existing Ferry plant at an agreed valuation cost.*
> - *That the Ferry Sub-Committee proceed with the continuation of the service, the acceptance of the two floats and the engagement or otherwise of the existing staff.*
> - *That the Town Clerk apply to the Ministry of Health and Transport for consent to the necessary loans.*
> - *That the Borough Treasurer negotiate the necessary mortgage.*
> - *That the order to pay shall be sealed by the Council*
> - *To make application to the Ministry of Transport for authority to increase the Ferry tolls for passengers.*

The last clause caused considerable concern as the passenger toll was to be increased by 100 per cent, from 1d to 2d ($\frac{1}{2}$p to 1p) to cross the river on the float or on the launches *Reliance* and *Perseverance*. Friction also arose over the allocation of free tickets to selected people, but on 25 March it was business as usual.

COMMUNIST COLLUSION AT DARTMOUTH

For many years Dartmouth's political scene had been mainly dominated by a Tory or a Whig, often depending on the amount of hospitality dispensed by the candidate. The meetings were generally good humoured, sometimes boisterous but never violent, although 1949 was the exception. After World War I, a new movement, the Labour Party, found favour and prospered and, after the close of World War II, the party had progressed enough to form the government of the day. During the late conflict the Red Army's struggle against Nazi Germany had earned it many admirers, particularly among Labour members with strong left-wing leanings. On the cessation of hostilities, Stalin's refusal to withdraw from occupied territories, the Berlin blockade and wall, and warlike intentions caused many to temper left-wing leanings. However, a small but vociferous group formed the Dartmouth and Brixham Communist Party, and one member, E A Holtham, succeeded in becoming the treasurer of the Dartmouth Carnival Committee, to the concern of many. The Dartmouth Chamber of Trade and others threatened to withdraw their support unless he resigned and the carnival was put in danger of closure. He refused to resign, and supported by Alderman F Scardifield and Councillor A E Bragg (his brother-in-law), called a meeting to protest at the Chamber of Trade's action. This was attended by some people from outside the area with similar leanings and after a short and noisy meeting, a hand vote on their resolution condemning the Chamber of Trade was taken, which declared 45 to 45, but in favour of the motion when the two counters Mrs Holtham (wife) and Councillor Bragg (father-in-law) cast their votes. There was uproar in the hall because many present were from Brixham and elsewhere and the result was unrepresentative. A demand was made for a ballot, which was refused by Alderman F Scardifield, leader of the council Labour group. Anger and resentment against the Communist Party increased nationwide when twenty-four members of the Royal Navy were killed on HMS *Consort* going to the aid of HMS *Amethyst* trapped on the Yangtse river in communist China; one Dartmouth man was injured and one Petty Officer J C Akhurst, son of Councillor C F Akhurst, was killed which increased anger locally. Matters came to a head when Mr Holtham invited Britain's only communist MP Harry Pollitt to address a meeting in Dartmouth. Feelings ran so high that no hall could be hired and the meeting was held in the open air and at night for safety, outside the police station at Mayors Avenue. A very large angry crowd assembled to shouts of 'throw them into the Boat Float' and worse, and after Mr Pollitt started speaking, Councillor Akhurst approached with a noose and a letter suggesting how it could be used. The small number of police present could not restrain the crowd which lost patience and surged forward striking and knocking both Mr Pollitt and Mr Holtham to the ground. With police aid they retreated to Councillor Bragg's house at South Town, followed by a noisy and aggressive crowd. Britain's only communist MP beat a hasty retreat via a back window and across fields to a car for Totnes where he caught a train to London. Thereafter little more was heard of the Dartmouth and Brixham Communist Party.

During this turbulent period the BRNC reinstated the post-war beagle-pack breakfast, where sixty-five powerful landowners and farmers pledged their continued support for the hunt, and expressed their pleasure at the defeat in Parliament of a Labour-sponsored anti-hunt bill. In Kingswear church a handsome carved memorial tablet was dedicated to the dead of two world wars, and at Philips there was occasion for celebration when the SS *Wimborne* (420 tons), was launched, the biggest ship ever built at Noss. However, rejoicing was tempered by the fact that far fewer ships were now calling in the harbour as oil-burning vessels far outnumbered coal-burners, and bunkering had almost ceased. Strident calls were made for alternative harbour trade and the Harbour Commission reviewed yachting charges, hoping to make the harbour a yachting centre. Another proposal was to make the Dart a home for houseboats; fortunately, only a few arrived, including *Water Gypsy* and *Marguerite*, which moored locally and became a continual problem.

Regatta Fair.
'All the fun of the
fair' held on the
New Ground, for a
few glorious days
of Dartmouth's
annual regatta,
held since its
official start in
1834.
R TUCKER

DARTMOUTH MUSEUM

Regatta 1949 Attendance was high and all races were run, as in 1948, and with more entries. But although the committee had made economies, there was a deficit of £130. On the bright side, the Government had lifted the ban on lighting, and the illuminations began to return to their pre-war standard. Queen Victoria had visited the 1856 regatta, and had granted Dartmouth the right to prefix future regattas 'Royal'. Now the Home Office was checking all authorities regarding the use of the word 'Royal', and that doyen of Dartmouth, Rodney Tucker, provided the secretary of state with sufficient information for him to write saying he did not wish to interfere with the existing arrangements. Another age-old custom was also revived, the holding by the RDYC of their annual regatta cocktail party on the lawns of Kittery Court.

Finally, a stirring event occurred when the home-made 20ft sloop *Nova Espero*, sailed by two brothers Stanley and Colin Smith arrived from Dartmouth, Nova Scotia, after a West/East Atlantic forty-four-day crossing. The RDYC cannon was fired, steamers whistled, crowds cheered and the Mayor and Corporation gave the pair a civic welcome, after which they retired to a civic luncheon at the Commercial Hotel, Victoria Road.

1950 The new decade, the halfway point of the twentieth century, gave Dartmouth and the country little to celebrate as most commodities were in short supply. Rationing still existed and a black market ensured that traders were poorly supplied. To improve the situation Major Benson, Dartmouth Chamber of Trade and a Harbour Commissioner, proposed the erection of a deep water jetty to enable the numerous visiting pleasure-craft to land passengers at all states of the tide and so bring extra revenue into the town. Finance was the problem, however, as similar projects had been mooted before and failed to materialize for lack of money. It was agreed that the harbourmaster Captain Griffiths would liaise with a Kingswear contractor to obtain preliminary costings for further discussion.

In the town concern was mounting regarding the deterioration and perilous state of the old Butterwalk, and the bad impression it gave to visitors. The council was able to report that the Ministry of Works had stated that rebuilding, including extensive work to the west wall would cost £49,000, as preliminary borings had been taken to 40ft without finding solid ground. One councillor was stated as saying that he was 'sorry the German bomb had not done a better job'.

The *Chronicle* reported that the Admiralty, aided by an appeal, had purchased a superb ivory and bone model of *Britannia* and Admiral of the Fleet the Earl of Cork and Orrery, presented it to the Captain of BRNC, Dartmouth. Miss Pamela Henley of the newspaper's '*Museum Corner*' stated that many of the timbers from the old *Britannia*, broken up in 1916, adorn the facade of Liberty's in London.

The family of the late Sir Thomas Wilton presented St Barnabas church with a handsome carved oak memorial reredos suitably inscribed. (In 1965 the surviving family members added a further two-wing extension to the reredos, but sadly St Barnabas church closed a few years later, and the reredos was transferred to St Saviours church; it was subsequently lost, but rediscovered in 1998).

W H Gooding, owner of the decaying Warfleet Boathouse (previously Dartmouth Sea Cadets' headquarters, YMCA hostel, MacAndrew's Deckhand School, and Lady Freakes' boathouse), at this point proposed its conversion to the Dartmouth Sailing Club (similar to the Dart Boat and Dart Sailing Clubs, first started in 1873 by Samuel Lake, Bridson and Simpson). He was refused a drinks licence but nevertheless called meetings and appointed a Commodore and committee; with local support he registered a burgee which was later proudly flown on *Nova Espero* on her return Atlantic crossing to New York.

Kingswear expressed dissatisfaction at the way the Dartmouth ferry committee ran the Lower Ferry: the parish council complained that the work-boat failed to comply with council's own rules, obligatory for others, having no life-saving or fire-fighting gear aboard. When the ageing twopenny passenger ferry *Perseverance* was out of commission, a good launch should be chartered. It was felt

Regatta Night. At night a fairyland of light, excitement and activity frequently illuminated by spasmodic bursts of pyrotechnical brilliance.
R Tucker,
Dartmouth Museum

For centuries a rowing ferry operated from Kingswear to Dartmouth, until 1915 when the first motorised passenger launch, the Relief *was introduced, followed by the* Perseverance *then later these two launches* Reliance *and* Newcomen.

<small>TOM CASEY, DESMOND GRAHAM</small>

Perseverance was unseaworthy as she had to be beached every week for patching, and the other launch *Reliance* was anything but reliable as she was still beached for repairs started last October. It also wrote to British Rail suggesting *The Mew* should run more often, say, every twenty minutes. Feelings were so strong that the old question of a Dart bridge or tunnel was resurrected.

This possibly had an impact as the Dartmouth council promptly ordered a new passenger launch from Blackmore's, Bideford, which was named *Newcomen* and started service in the following year.

In 1916 Finch Ingram had invented the modern Boddy-Finch life jacket that was in use until after World War II. He made a generous gift to Dartmouth of a valuable finely carved marble statue 'Piscatorie' which he had acquired in Florence. The council debated whether it should be displayed in the Royal Avenue Gardens or in the borough museum, for there was concern that if it was placed in the gardens it could be subjected to vandalism. This latter fear proved correct for while it was in the gardens it did suffer damage, and had to be restored more than once. As Sir Henry Paul Seale's 1887 gift of a garden fountain has been restored to celebrate the Millennium, and both the fountain and 'Piscatorie', a delicate and much-admired work of art are now protected by fine wrought iron decorative railings

Mr Finch Ingram presenting the Mayor of Dartmouth, Mr B Lavers with a fine Florentine marble statue for display in the Royal Avenue Gardens.
RICHARD WEBB

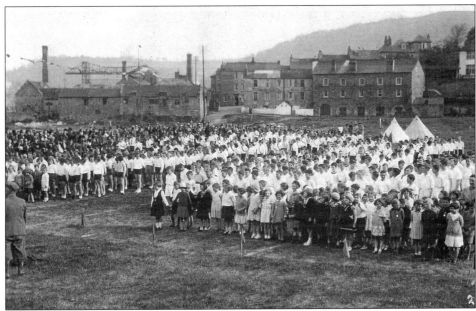

Children of all the Dartmouth schools assembled in 1936 on the infilled Coombe Mud inlet which today forms Dartmouth's second open space, Coronation Park.
G. WEATHERLY

BRNC Beagle pack with huntsmen. For some years Admiral Sir Frank Hopkins, previously Captain of the Ark Royal *and President of the RDYC was Master of the Beagles.*
G WEATHERLY

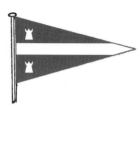

Dartmouth Yacht Club
In 1948, W H Gooding, a newcomer and owner of Warfleet Boat House, found that Dartmouth had no sailing club. Determined to rectify this, and after collecting 214 signatures, he called a meeting in the Guildhall in 1949. Here he elected a committee and formed the Dartmouth Sailing Club, but W H Gooding's later application to convert the boathouse and obtain a drinks licence was refused. In 1950, Major G R Benson convened another meeting and was elected club commodore with its headquarters based at the Dartmouth Arms. A burgee was created and the club then participated in the annual Royal Regattas. In 1952, the 100 year old coaling trade ceased and in 1954 the Channel Coaling Co's South Embankment premises were purchased by P Perrin Thoms, who became the club's second commodore and he leased the premises to the club. In 1965, through membership loans, the club purchased the freehold and in 1974, changed its name to the Dartmouth Yacht Club.

R L Dennis, Harbour Commissioner and chairman of the Combined Coaling Co's, had refused to explain the bunkering position, but signs that the 100-year-old coaling trade in Dartmouth was drawing to a close came when the standing hulk and once proud barque *Juno* slipped her moorings and was pulled by the tug *Saevar* past the castle *en route* to Iceland; she shed her tow-line and had the dignity of sinking at sea.

Regatta 1950 This year the two big races for yachts over 25 tons and yachts 9 to 25 tons were replaced by races for 30ft rating and over, and for under 30ft rating. A record number of entries was received, many from Torquay, but foul weather prevented their attendance so entries for smaller classes were few. Outside on the Friday most races were cancelled and on the Saturday there was no racing at all. As a result of the repositioning of the Castle Ledge buoy a new start line had to be introduced. This was the first regatta in which the newly founded Dartmouth Sailing Club officially participated.

The *Chronicle* reported that the county council had since 1948 provided and funded a traffic warden in Kingswear during the summer months to control the incoming ferry traffic, relatively modest by today's standards. Funding a traffic warden in Kingswear seems strangely difficult fifty years later.

Finally, Captain R Clifford Primrose had started building a new type of racing yacht in 1949 at the Dolphin yacht yard, Dittisham. The class name and first vessel was *Scimitar*, a canoe-stern dayboat, 15ft LOD with a sail area of 113sq ft and a fixed keel. She was reported to be unsinkable and cost only £120. He hoped that, with her two sister boats *Kukri* and *Sabre* she would soon be racing at Dartmouth starting a class of their own, but this did not materialize.

1951 saw the death of Miss Pamela Henley, founder and curator of the first Dartmouth museum, the Henley collection in Anzac Street. As sister of the late William Henley she had given his collection to the borough on condition that it was to be kept on display in perpetuity. No two people loved Dartmouth more or were more knowledgeable about the area and she wrote a regular feature, 'Museum Corner', in the *Chronicle*, comprised of snippets from bygone days but still as relevant today.

Meanwhile, the Dartmouth Harbour Bill was making slow progress through Parliament. Brixham had always wanted a seat on the Harbour Commission. The DHC feared that opposition from Brixham would make passage of the bill time-consuming and expensive so it was decided to offer Brixham a seat on the board. In June royal assent was received for a new board of sixteen members, composed as follows:

Government nominees 5, Harbour and Embankment members (Commercial) 3, Kingswear Council nominee 1, Brixham Council nominee 1, Dartmouth Council (elected) 6.

The town council got what it wanted, increased membership from four to six, to counter what it thought was an over-powerful commercial section. Their original 1863 representation was two, later increased to four, but there was concern because Kingswear did not appoint a free agent, but nominated Captain T Wilton, who in a private capacity was Chairman of Messrs Philip & Son Co Ltd, whose Managing Director already had a seat on the board.

Two nautical events followed. First, the 20ft sailing sloop *Nova Espero*, after two years, set sail for New York. This time Stanley Smith had a new companion Charles Violet, and they took letters of goodwill, presents, and copies of the *Chronicle* for the Mayor of New York. They were given a civic send off, and departed as previously stated flying the burgee of the recently formed Dartmouth Sailing Club. The second event was the sinking off Start Point of the much-loved 37-ton college yawl, *Amaryllis*. She had belonged to the late Lieutenant G H P Muhlhauser who had circled the world in her; on his death in 1924 his sister had presented her to the Admiralty for use as a training boat, on condition that when they had no further use for her she was to be sunk. A convoy of college boats accompanied her on her last voyage to Start Point where she was blown apart by explosives.

On a happier note the *Chronicle* reported an aside taken from the *British Railways Magazine*, of a signalman on the line who was completely mystified to receive the following box-to-box message:

'*SMOKING VIRGIN fourth coach from engine, 7.10 Cheltenham. Train need not be stopped*'.

The handsome wooden motor yacht Anne of Anstie *which was owned by Mr W. E. Vacher and was, for some years, moored in the Dart. In 1951, a serious fire aboard was brought under control by two nearby vessels and Dartmouth's Fire Service.*

MRS MARY NICOLLE

Dartmouth's third fire engine, the first to be motorised, which was driven aboard the Lower Ferry float and transported alongside Anne of Anstie, *from where her powerful pumps soon brought the fire under control.*

R TUCKER,
DARTMOUTH MUSEUM

The accuracy of the wording was questioned and the signalman in the next box declared it was as he received it, but eventually it was discovered the message should have read:

'Smoke EMERGING fourth coach from engine, 7.10 Cheltenham. Train need not be stopped'.

Regatta 1951 As last year, bad weather interrupted events: the Friday and Saturday races and most of the outside events were forced to use harbour courses. On Saturday the athletics events were held at Norton Park and the swimming ballet (synchronised swimming) took place in heavy rain. Again, in spite of economies, a loss was recorded.

On 25th August 1951 Christopher Robin Milne opened the Harbour Bookshop. Son of A A Milne and the original Christopher Robin of the *Winnie-the-Pooh* books, he received much acclaim for his sensitively written volumes of autobiography: *The Enchanted Places* (1974), *Path through the Trees* (1979), *The Hollow on the Hill* (1982) and *The Open Garden* (1988). Previously he had been a Cambridge scholar; served as an Army officer throughout World War II and then became a bookseller when he moved to Dartmouth. He also co-founded the Dartmouth & Kingswear Society in 1959.

In the harbour in late October flames broke out on the wooden 121TM 100ft twin-screw motor yacht *Anne of Anstie*. Fortunately the owner W E Vacher, his wife and three daughters were aboard, and the girls in the launch motored to the nearby survey ship HMS *Scott*, which then drew alongside, as did *The Mew*, turning their hoses on the fire. The Dartmouth fire engine boarded the Lower Ferry and with the two ships gained control and doused the flames, saving the vessel. The yacht had been built in 1925 at Camper & Nicholson's Gosport yard for the millionaire Baron De Rothschild.

'Companions in Adversity', the last two standing hulks to leave the harbour they had served so well for almost thirty years. The Dagny *(with the ex-gun sloop* Falcon *in attendance) and the* Sorkness *sail for break up at Grays, thus ending the 100-year-old Dartmouth bunkering trade.*

JOHN HORSLEY, DAVE GRIFFITHS

THE END OF THE COALING TRADE

In June came an anticipated yet unwelcome announcement from R L Dennis, chairman of the Harbour Commission, that bunkering in Dartmouth harbour would cease by Christmas. There were only 4,000 tons of coal in stock, and when that was exhausted it would not be replaced. In a small but excellent editorial the *Chronicle* complained bitterly about the secrecy that surrounded the announcement. It had many times requested and been refused information on the possible closure of the 100-year-old bunkering trade, which once employed 300 to 400 men, but now was reduced to to only ten. The *Chronicle* felt that positive steps should have been taken earlier to replace the lost revenue, whereas the board was about to discuss what could be done.

Finally it was announced that the harbour's only tug, *Portwey*, owned by the Channel Coaling Co, was to be restationed at Falmouth in the new year. The British Iron & Steel Federation had purchased the two remaining standing hulks on the river for scrap. The United Towing Co's tug *Tradesman* towed away the *Sorkness* (on which some coal had been left for ballast), to Grays on the Thames for breaking up. Then the tug returned for *Dagny*, her ballast being taken from a smaller hulk broken up at Kingswear. Thus ended Dartmouth's 100-year-old bunkering trade.

Above: Collier unloading gas coal into rail wagons, with Mr Hawke and one of his cart horses in attendance to replace loaded trucks with empties.
ERIC BOVEY

Below: FT Everard & Sons Ltd, MV Similarity leaving Kingswear quay after discharging her cargo for Torquay gas works.
DARTMOUTH MUSEUM

*The gas works
between Mayors
Avenue and
Clarence Street,
showing the yard,
two gasholders,
offices and the
superintendent's
house.*
G. WEATHERLY

*The telpher coal
conveyor erected in
the 1930's to
receive coal
supplies from
Kingswear, and
mechanical
unloading direct
into the works.*
CYRIL KING

THE REVIVAL OF THE GAS COAL TRADE

1952 During the war the maritime trade over the Kingswear quays (because of the submarine menace) mainly reverted to rail. From 1945 it slowly revived from eight vessels a year, to in 1955 a maximum of 79 vessels a year, then declined and in 1963 reverted back to rail. House and gas coals from Goole, Tyne and other north-eastern ports which were unloaded at Kingswear jetty into rail trucks for local distribution and onward transmission to Torquay and Hollacombe gas works. According to Eric Bovey this trade was virtually monopolized by E T Everard & Sons Ltd, Greenhithe, Kent, with their vessels *Similarity, Stability, Serenity, Fred Everard, Security, Superiority* and others. Their normal weekly cycle consisted of one day loading, two days sailing, two days discharging and one day returning, in ballast. Renwick, Wilton & Dobson Co Ltd, Torquay, were the main agents who notified the colliers' departure, progress, and anticipated arrival times to R H Bovey, stationmaster, for him to organize wagons and unloading. Another company engaged in the trade was E Foster & Co Ltd, Blackfriars, Manchester, with shipments from Hartlepool and Sunderland.

Top Left: RDYC new gantry, with DOD's racing with (as usual) Miss Anne Hine-Haycock in the lead.
RDYC

Top Right: Two J-class yachts, Britannia *and* Shamrock *and a DOD helmed by Helen Pritchard, cross the finishing line in Start Bay, with club members watching aboard the committee boat.*
RDYC

Middle: The Duchess of Devonshire, *her happy working days numbered, laying beached and neglected in Galmpton Creek.*
JOHN HORSLEY

Bottom: 'Home Is Where Your Heart Is'- when your wandering days are over, just come ashore (with your boat) as these two (now beachcombers) have in Galmpton Creek.
JOHN HORSLEY

The cargoes were unloaded by Kingswear's two Clyde Crane Co electric cranes fitted with hydraulic grabs of 30cwt and a three-ton lift. They had a 35ft sweep, and traversed the quayside on a 7ft-wide in-built track. They were operated by two men who normally worked as porters but who had received special training to work as crane drivers when required, and their station duties were covered by other staff on an overtime basis. Renwick Wilton & Dobson Co Ltd's men handled the unloading and when the crane reached the limit of its sweep, loaded wagons were moved by horses owned by S Hawke, village greengrocer and carter, to the buffers. Mr Hawke's stables and cart shed were conveniently situated at the end of the railway company's warehousing in the Brixham Road (now converted into flats).

Motor traffic was steadily increasing and British Railways derived extra revenue from allowing motorists to park on the quayside in the marshalling area alongside the wagons, even when loading coal supplies. It is to be hoped the cars were already black! There was also a limited trade in gas coal for Dartmouth gasworks on Mayors Avenue. In 1931 the gas company had erected an overhead telpher coal conveyor, but unfortunately colliers could not lie alongside the Embankment as, even on a full tide, there was insufficient depth of water, so the coal was unloaded into RW&D's large barge *Goliath*, then towed over the river from Kingswear by one of the Lower Ferry *Hauley* tugs for discharge under the conveyor.

The Harbour Commission resurrected proposals that Dartmouth harbour could become an oil depot to fuel oil-burning ships in competition with Brixham, which had shown the foresight to establish itself as an oil port in the twenties, and could also offer further facilities to encourage yachtsmen to use the harbour. Unfortunately the first proposal was rendered unviable by the increase in the size, tonnage and draft of new shipping and the limited draft of Dartmouth harbour (not a problem in Brixham). But the RDYC applied for permission, which was granted, to erect a landing jetty in shallow water adjacent to the clubhouse to facilitate landing at all states of the tide. Another earlier scheme, to make the Dart a houseboat-river, was abandoned as just a few had availed themselves of this opportunity and had left and only the *Marguerite* remained. She had created many problems and there was some relief when the owner decided to move to Salcombe; there was no difficulty in obtaining volunteers to move her, with R Gatzais (port pilot), Jim and John Distin (shipbuilders), Major Bircham (harbour commissioner) and Dave Pillar all participating. The voyage had its problems as the boat left under tow by two launches belonging to Gatzais and the Distins; one of these broke down and Roy Gatzais was swept overboard and rescued by Dave Pillar. Finally *Marguerite* was secured in the Bag at Salcombe.

The country meanwhile was in mourning at the death of King George VI. Dartmouth had a close connection with the late king as he and his brother, the Duke of Windsor, were for a time cadets at BRNC and the King and Queen had...

Regatta 1952 At last this was a fair weather regatta and all yacht races were run, with entries up by 150 to nearly 500, the events being controlled from a committee boat. The athletics were transferred from Norton Park to Coronation Park which was largely restored to its pre-war condition. The Dartmouth Regatta Committee thanked the RDYC for running both days' racing and reported a small profit for the first time since the war.

There was considerable political activity nationwide as a general election had been called. This time the Conservative Party was returned and Winston Churchill was made Prime Minister again.

The naval college received several phone calls to the effect that a submarine periscope had been seen at several points in the harbour, raising fears that some foreign power was reconnoitring the area. It transpired that the vessel was a Royal Navy four-man X-craft attached to HMS *Gateshead* which was carrying out a 'harbour penetration exercise'.

1953
Ten years previously, on the unlucky thirteenth of February, four German fighter bombers swept in low beneath Dartmouth's harbour defences bringing death and destruction to the town, almost destroying the Butterwalk. Since then official bungling and bureaucracy had almost achieved what the bombers had failed to do, as the minimal temporary repairs were proving totally inadequate to withstand the ravages of time. Fortunately, in the hope of securing Government support and a grant, the seventy-two year old Society for the Protection of Ancient Buildings had been asked for a report on the building. It was even more fortunate that Bryan Hugh St John O'Neil, Britain's leading archaeologist and Chief Inspector of Ancient Buildings, was appointed to prepare the report, for before the war he had been in charge of the large scale restoration of Dartmouth Castle for the Ministry of Works, during which time he had developed a love for the town. Subsequently he had taken a personal interest in the Butterwalk's future. For the frontispiece of the report he used a picture of the Butterwalk's much-damaged façade. The report persuaded the Whitehall officials to sanction the first monetary grant in the country to restore a war-damaged building, the treasury making a grant of £10,000, and the War Damage Commission a further grant of £11,000. This left the town council, who had already expended £8,000 on temporary repairs, to raise the remaining £20,000

Top left: *The Grand Opening, April 17th 1954, after ten long years of procrastination and neglect of Dartmouth's principal architectural gem, the completely restored much-loved Butterwalk.*

DARTMOUTH MUSEUM

Top right and below: *The royal coat of arms over the fireplace in the King Charles Room. This spacious panelled room on the first floor, was for many years the* Merry Monarch *Café but is now Dartmouth's excellent museum.*

BRIAN LANGWORTHY

through loans spread over forty-five years. A leading architect, D G Martin, was appointed, drawings submitted and tenders sought, resulting in the contract being awarded to P Wilkins & Sons Ltd, and work commenced in May to restore the 318-year-old Butterwalk.

Then the *Chronicle* published some details (provided by the late Miss Henley) of a somewhat obscure Totnes painter Brockedon, son of a local ironmonger. His genius was recognized by Governor Holdsworth, who became his mentor and paid for him to receive tuition in Italy. On his return he produced a large oil painting of the 'Widow's Son', signed and dated 1787, which he presented to his benefactor. The work was so large that Governor Holdsworth in turn gave it to Dartmouth's St Saviours church where it was hung for all to admire. Miss Henley added a note that at one time the church cleaner was a partially blind man called 'Blind Tom', who when showing visitors around the church, insisted the figures in the picture were 'all Dartmouth people' in spite of the fact that the canvas was painted in Italy. Brokedon's real claim to fame was that he invented the indispensable lead for pencils we use today.

Since Miss Henley's the death in 1951, it appears that Percy Russell, antiquarian, had become the curator of the borough museum. He had coerced the Corporation to make available a modest area in the Newcomen Road library possibly because of restricted space in the Henley museum in Anzac Street. When the council acquired the old Methodist church, it was intended to house a library and a museum, but it opened only as a library. In these premises in June 1951, with Lady Waring and others, he created a replica 1850's room, and prominent residents lent valuable antiques, furniture and general exhibits. It was opened by the Mayor, councillors and the captain of the college. Thereafter Mr Russell encouraged the Corporation to allow the museum to relocate to the restored Butterwalk, taking up three rooms on the first floor, one of which contained the panelled King Charles II room which, for many years before the bombing, had been used as the Merry Monarch Café. The museum would lease the rooms to assist in financing the restoration and Mr Russell was closely involved in the work. Some years previously the Newcomen Society had proposed to the council the relocation of the museum to the Butterwalk.

In April Winston Churchill received a knighthood, and was made a Knight of the Garter. Queen Elizabeth and Prince Philip had the joy of launching the new royal yacht HMY *Britannia* which for the next forty-five years was to take their majesties to many parts of the world, and often to visit Dartmouth. Shortly afterwards, on 2 June, Queen Elizabeth was crowned in Westminster Abbey and the whole nation rejoiced with celebrations and street parties.

Signs of economic recovery in Dartmouth came when work started on the rebuilding of the Midland Bank (now HSBC Bank), which in 1943 had suffered a direct hit, killing the manager and an assistant, and the building with others had been demolished. The architect stated he had designed the new building to harmonize with the adjacent old Butterwalk (then being restored), and the work

P Stewart-Bam, Commodore RDYC (right) and Ross Llewellyn (left) with young club members during Junior Sailing Week at Waddeton Beach
RDYC

was to be carried out by R C Pillar & Son. Soon after, the same firm started on another phase of reconstruction on Eastmans, the butchers, on their bombed-out Duke Street premises. Both premises were to reopen in 1954.

Regatta 1953 This was an unsatisfactory event held in appalling weather. As the E Mark on course A was wrongly positioned by one-and-a-half miles, and as so many yachts could not find it, the next races were abandoned and the prize money added to the Saturday races. The gales on Saturday caused the Dragons and Torbay handicap Class B to retire. Regular winners since the regatta restarted were Miss A Hine-Haycock, Commander Morgan Giles, Mr & Mrs L Pritchard, D N Sanderson, Hugh Goodson, Captain T Wilton, Mr & Mrs Lewthwaite, Miss Simpson, and Miss Helen Vacher.

Finally the Korean War, almost forgotten on the other side of the world, ended in a rather unsettled way, but there was cause for some families to celebrate when loved ones were released from Chinese prisoner of war camps and 530 men disembarked at Southampton, including twenty-four men from the West Country, one of whom came from Dartmouth.

The Queen and Prince Phillip aboard the Royal Yacht Britannia *as seen through a surround of trees from the Royal Avenue Gardens.*
RICHARD WEBB

1954 On 1 January the *Chronicle* reached its centenary and published a celebratory edition to commemorate the founding of this provincial newspaper in 1854 by Robert Cranford.

In April, after ten years' of neglect and procrastination, the famous Butterwalk, finally restored to its former glory was officially opened by Lord Euston, vice chairman of the Society for the Protection of Ancient Buildings at a ceremony attended by Mayor and Corporation, Government officials, the architect, the builders and a large crowd of mainly local people. After the guests had departed, Percy Russell, museum curator, showed 142 members of the public around the excellent museum and there was high praise for the quality of the exhibits. These have since increased to form today's splendid collection of antiques, artefacts and ship models, many acquired by the late curator, Ralph Cawthorne, a man of many talents who possessed a knowledge of antiques, particularly maritime items, and was a superb modeller of ships. He fully utilised these talents to further the cause of Dartmouth's insufficiently patronised museum. The museum is run by volunteers who lease the premises and receive no grant aid, relying entirely on the entrance fee; a prime site, such as the Butterwalk, is vital. As space is at a premium and the Henley Museum is closed, an extension into the top floor in this council-owned listed building is urgently needed.

Mr Finch Ingram, local benefactor and entrepreneur, (left) with his son-in-law Lieutenant Colonel Richard Webb, co-founder of the Dartmouth & Kingswear Society in 1959, and his daughter Iris Webb, later president of the National Association of Flower Arrangement Societies.

<small>RICHARD WEBB</small>

Another happy event was a visit from the newly crowned Queen Elizabeth II and Prince Philip aboard HMY *Britannia*. A small armada of boats went out to see her and the escorting warships enter the harbour, but mist and haze restricted vision. Dartmouth and their royal guests enjoyed this short visit.

A real cause for celebration, particularly for the housewife, was the end of rationing after fourteen long years. There were parties where the hated ration books were torn up, thrown into the dustbin, and in some cases official bonfires were lit after the last rites were read!

Philips' yard, Noss, launched a new lightship *No. 17*, the twenty-fifth to be built in succession, and senior members of Trinity House were present at the ceremony.

Joy was short-lived, however, when it was learned that the British Transport Commission, owners of the railway ferry *The Mew*, was reviewing the viability of their forty-six-year-old cross-river service to Dartmouth. It claimed that *The Mew* had for some years been operating at a loss and it issued a new schedule of tolls, applicable from 1 March, doubling the passenger fare to three pence (3d, 1¹/₂p), and increasing other charges. Two months later it was announced that *The Mew* was to be scrapped and replaced with a much smaller vessel, the *Lady Elizabeth* on a six-month trial basis to asses profitability. She was later withdrawn and replaced by the two small passenger-only ferries *Humphrey Gilbert* and *Adrian Gilbert*. There was immediate reaction in the town, meetings were called and protests made to British Rail but all to no avail. On Friday 8 October the much-loved ugly duckling of the river made her last crossing. British Rail, like all nationalized industries, was bereft of soul and did not propose to do anything to mark forty-six years of service, so Dartmouth stepped in at the eleventh hour. The Mayor, council, prominent personalities and 500 townspeople made a final sentimental journey with *The Mew*. On return the borough band played 'Hearts of Oak' and the old ship, loved by all, cast off her pontoon moorings for the last time and sailed away with those intent on sharing her last voyage to the breakers at Plymouth. Her bell along with that of HMS *Dartmouth* now hangs in Dartmouth museum.

It was fortunate that this my concluding year was not only eventful but coincided with the return from abroad of the publisher of this volume and his parents, Lieutenant Colonel Richard Webb and his wife Iris, daughter of local entrepreneur and benefactor Finch Ingram, to reside at Warfleet. They soon became involved in local activities, Iris Webb founding the Dartmouth Flower Club, and later becoming president of the National Association of Flower Arrangement Societies, and Colonel Webb becoming president of the Dartmouth St John's Ambulance Brigade. He later initiated a protest against the demolition of the mellow high 1857 stone retaining walls to Warfleet House and against their replacement further back in poured concrete. This was done to widen the approach roads to Warfleet. There was public outrage at this desecration and a chance meeting with Christopher Milne led them to co-found with John Smith in 1959, the now influential Dartmouth & Kingswear Society which has since achieved so much to preserve the best and safeguard the general interests of the Dartmouth area.

Their son Richard won a scholarship to BRNC, but after working locally in Christopher Milne's Harbour Bookshop, he chose a literary career and moved to London to work in Fleet Street for Hulton Press, *Vogue* magazine, and Michael Joseph, the book publisher. But the West country called and he returned to Exeter to co-found Webb & Bower, and to publish 350 books with twenty national bestsellers including *The Country Diary of an Edwardian Lady* which achieved in the *Guinness Book of Records* the distinction of being the longest running number-one non-fiction bestseller of all time. However, a chance meeting with Gilly, former co-owner of Billy Budd's Bistro, Foss Street (now the Carved Angel Café) resulted in marriage and return to his hometown.

The author, who has loved Devon since his pre-war holidays with his Mancunian parents, Jack and Frances Collinson has now spent many happy years here, with his wife Kathleen, and dear daughter Donna. He has been a permanent Kingswear resident for over a quarter of a century.

So, after fifteen enjoyable years' researching this 'other Eden', and now that the eventful twentieth century has drawn to a close, it seems an opportune time for the author, in his eighty-second year, to join those hardy spirits aboard *The Mew* and sail off into the unknown, leaving to others the opportunity and pleasure of continuing the history of this 'demi-Paradise'.

Don Collinson, Kingswear, 2000

The final trip of the much loved forty-six year old The Mew *before she sailed off into the sunset for breaking up at Plymouth.*
DARTMOUTH MUSEUM

Postscript *1954-2054*

Seasoned travellers know that the success of any journey often depends on the choice of suitable reading matter, and in this instance, what could be a more appropriate companion than the 1954 centenary edition of the Dartmouth Chronicle, *celebrating its first hundred years of publication.*

It makes fascinating reading, relating events and highlighting people in the first edition, January 1854, and the editorial concentrates on forecasting what the town of Dartmouth would now be like. Therefore, the reader, with the benefit of time travel may like to assess the accuracy of those predictions, and ponder on what 'progress' (or lack of it) has been made since these words were written in 1954.

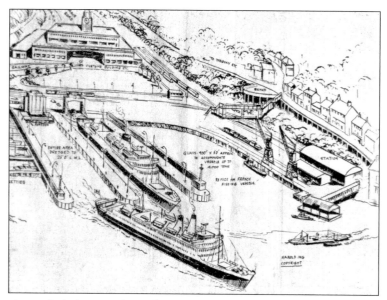

An artist's impression of Kingswear as a cross-channel ferry terminal. HAROLD ING

And the next 100 years?

The *Chronicle* this week is composed largely of features and photographs showing what has happened to Dartmouth in the last 100 years. It is a souvenir paper. But what is just as important is how appearances are going to alter in the next 100. What are the prospects.

It seems fairly certain that Dartmouth has reached the end of its decline. The Council and Harbour Commission are both well aware of the need for action and give their undivided attention to plans for restoration of full prosperity. The only stumbling block is finance.

Without doubt, by the time our next century is reached, that problem will have been overcome, and we shall have a deep water jetty. All are agreed it is essential. Perhaps Councillor Pillar will be able to see the fruition of his own special plan – a combined jetty, sun promenade and open-air bathing pool.

The gas works will have closed down. An eyesore though it undoubtedly is, it offers one of the very few industrial sites in Dartmouth, and so we shall find it a busy little factory, the elevator carrying over the road loads of coal or cement or other material.

The belt of light industry will be continued at Townstal, too, offering work on the spot to the many inhabitants of the estate, which by then will probably have pushed further out towards Totnes.

The estate itself will have changed beyond recognition. There will be more shops, churches, public houses, assembly halls, and amusements. The folk there have resolutely refused to let the area become a mere dormitory for Dartmouth. It needs a corporate life of its own.

In Dartmouth itself many of the fine old buildings in the town centre will have disappeared. It must be so if communications are to be improved, and 21st century motorists are not to be deterred from visiting the town by its impossibly narrow, excessively tortuous approaches.

Perhaps the main entrance of the future will cut across Market Square and through Foss Street. the new main road coming out in College Way will be fine for by-pass traffic, but the town by itself must be opened up for easier passage.

And what about the bridge? It is bound to come some time. The younger generation at least should live to see a great span at high level sweeping across the river, or a swing type at some point higher up. But in that case small passenger ferries may still be needed, and the boats will still be chugging their eternal way over the river.

With the rapid advance in aviation it is not too much to expect some provision will be made in Dartmouth, if only for helicopter traffic, and we might see them landing at Coronation Park, bringing their quota of visitors.

This prophecy is written with the next 100 years in mind. But must we wait? Some, at least, of these improvements could be brought about within the next few years.

APPENDIX I

DARTMOUTH'S RIVER STEAMBOATS

FLEET LIST 1827 to 1954

Since earliest times passengers and general goods traffic between Dartmouth, Totnes, and the villages between was maintained by a large fleet of passage boats, gaff- or lug-rigged ketches about 30 to 40 feet long, the numbers of which slowly decreased after the arrival of the following steamboat companies:

(A) 1856 – 1859	John Moody and Charles Seale Hayne
(B) 1856 – 1881	Gov Holdsworth/R Mortimer/W Froude
(C) 1859 – 1877	Dartmouth Steam Packet Co Ltd
(D) 1877 – 1904	Dartmouth & Torbay Steam Packet Co
(E) 1904/6 – 1976	(D) renamed River Dart Steamboat Co Ltd

Vessel	Built	Acq'd	Sold	Const		Tons/Lgth	Builder/Company
Paul Pry	1827	?	?	Wood	PS	23T/?	Chapel, Southampton/(?)
Dart	1836	1837	1841	Wood	PS	41T/67'	Bell, North Shields/(?)
Volante	1839	1847	1854	Wood	PS	19T/73'	Limehouse/(?)
Undine	1847	?	1864	Wood	PS	38T/90'	Thames Ironworks/ (?)
Royal Dartmouth	1856	1856	1881	Iron	PS	42T/85'	Scott Russell, London/ (B & D)
Louisa	1856	1856	1868	Iron/Wood	PS	35T/90'	Langley's, London/(A & C)
Mary	1851	1858	1859	Wood	PS	30T/95'	Glasgow/(A)
Pilot	1852	1858	1879	Iron	PS	100T/85'	Marshall, South Shields/(A & D)
Newcomen	1864	1864	1884	Iron	PS	47T/108'	Lewis & Stockwell/(C & D)
Eclair (cross-channel)	1865	1865	1868	Iron	PS	120T/180'	Kirkpatrick, Glasgow /(C)
Guide	1869	1869	1877	Wood	PS	104T/98'	Harvey, Hayle/(C & D)
Hauley	1877	1877	1898	Iron	SS	32T/62'	Harvey, Hayle/C & D)
Nimble	1878	1879	1910	Wood	SS	17T/58'	Brixham/(C & D)
Berry Castle	1880	1880	1917	Iron	PS	73T/108'	Polyblank, Kingswear/ C & D)
Dart	1883	1883	1893	Steel	SS	12T/54'	Davis, Abingdon/(C & D)
Dartmouth Castle	1885	1885	1907	Steel	PS	59T/100'	Harvey, Hayle/(C & D)
Totnes Castle	1894	1894	1912	Steel	PS	51T/79'	Philip, Dartmouth/(C & D)
Kingswear Castle	1904	1904	1924	Steel	PS	85T/108'	Cox, Falmouth/(D & E)
Dartmouth Castle	1907	1907	1947	Steel	PS	71T/100'	Cox, Falmouth/(E)
Compton Castle	1914	1914	1964	Steel	PS	97T/108'	Cox, Falmouth/(E)
Berry Castle	1921	1922	1947	Wood	MV	38T/60'	Philip, Dartmouth/(E)
Dittisham Castle	1921	1922	1940	Wood	MV	13T/39'	Philip, Dartmouth/(E)
Totnes Castle	1923	1923	1967	Wood	MV	91T/108'	Philip, Dartmouth/(E)
Kingswear Castle	1924	1924	1967	Steel	PS	94T/108'	Philip, Dartmouth/(E)
Clifton Castle	1926	1926	1942	Steel	MV	67T/70'	Philip, Dartmouth/(E)
Greenway Castle	1937	1937	1938	Wood	MV	17T/45'	Ferris & Blank, Dartmouth/(E)
Seymour Castle	1938	1938	1973	Wood	MV	37T60'	Ferris & Blank, Dartmouth/(E)
Torbay Prince	1947	1961	1964	Wood	MV	91T/81'	Blackmore, Bideford/(E)
Dartmouth Castle	1948	1948	1964	Steel	MV	81T/87'	Philip, Dartmouth/(E)
Berry Castle	1949	1961	1964	Steel	MV	50T/67'	Philip, Dartmouth/(E)

PS = Paddle Steamer   **SS = Screw Steamer**   **MV = Motor Vessel**

Footnote Only two paddle-steamers from this list survive, the *Compton Castle* and the *Kingswear Castle*, (details below), along with five motor vessels, *Clifton Castle, Seymour Castle, Dartmouth Castle, Berry Castle* and *Torbay Prince*.

In 1976 the River Dart Steamboat Co Ltd was restructured as the River Dart Boat & Leisure Co Ltd.

Compton Castle (1914) This was withdrawn in 1962, refurbished and sold as a museum and café at Squares' Quay, Kingsbridge, once appearing in the 'Onedin Line'. In 1978 she was sold for restoration in Looe, for return to the Dart to resume service, a commendable but unfulfilled desire. She was sold in 1982, her engines removed to a museum, and was basically stripped and restructured as a floating restaurant at Lemon Quay, Truro, where she remains (2000).

Kingswear Castle (1924) She was withdrawn in 1965 and purchased by the Paddle Steamer Preservation Society. In 1967 she was chartered to an Isle of Wight marina, later being withdrawn in 1971 to the society's headquarters on the River Medway. Volunteers raised funds and spent twelve years restoring her to her former glory running a service on the Medway and the Thames.

APPENDIX II

DARTMOUTH'S THREE FERRIES

1829 to 1954

From earliest times the geographical position of Kittery Point, near the sea, semi-sheltered and close to the opposite shore, ensured the establishment of a rowing ferry and flat-bottomed horse-float to serve the needs of travellers. By 1828 a second crossing became a necessity to link the new toll roads on both sides of the river. Plans to bridge the Dart at Dittisham by suspension bridge, the forerunner of many later schemes, were defeated in the House of Lords due to the efforts of Edward Elton, owner of Greenway. The engineer James Meadows Rendel solved the problem with a novel design, a floating bridge, to run from Sandquay to Noss Point, and the following schedule lists all ferries thereafter abbreviated thus: Lower Ferry – (L);   Higher Ferry – (H);   Railway Ferry – (R).

1829	A meeting is convened at the Castle Inn, Dartmouth, to consider a proposal to bridge the Dart by a steam-driven chain ferry.	(H)
1830	A company is formed, Parliamentary approval gained, orders placed and work commenced.	(H)
1831	*Floating Bridge* No. 1 arrives from I Blackburn, Plymouth; roads and landings are constructed, and a grand opening is held on 19 August.	(H)
1832	Financial problems arise, in particular a difficulty with a £60 per annum compensation to be paid to Mr Luttrell, Lower Ferry owner for loss of Royal Mail trade.	(H&L)
1835	To save costs the steam engine is replaced by horse-driven traction machinery.	(H)
1855	The *Floating Bridge* No. 1 sinks at night at her moorings at Sandquay during a fierce storm, fortunately without loss of life.	(H)
1856	Sir H P Seale, owner, is forced after legal action to provide a new *Floating Bridge* No. 2, built by W Kelly, Sandquay.	(H)
1857	Sir H P Seale accepts £2,000 and a seat on the board of the new Dartmouth & Torbay Railway Co to ensure his cooperation.	(H&R)
1864	The Railway Company, new owner of Kingswear's Plume of Feathers Inn and Lower Ferry, leases the ferry to Tom Avis.	(L)
1865	Mr Avis is provided with a two-horse-float; the Railway Company initiates a cross-river passenger service with the steamer *Perseverance*.	(L&R)
1866	Mr Avis purchases new rowing ferry boats and a 30ft steam launch *Pioneer* to operate the new two-horse-float.	(L)
1867	After thirty-three years of horse traction the *Floating Bridge* No. 2 reverts to steam propulsion.	(H)
1869	After only four years' service the railway ferry *Perseverance* is replaced by the new steam ferry *Dolphin*.	(R)
1872	Mr Avis buys a further steam launch *Picnic* to assist with the horse-float and for general public hire.	(L)
1873	Sir H P Seale sells his Mount Boone Estate, shipyards, Floating Bridge Inn and *Floating Bridge* No. 2 to Raleigh Estates.	(H)
1874	The *Floating Bridge* No. 2, dilapidated and now eighteen years old, is after short periods of work laid up for two years.	(H)
1876	A new *Floating Bridge* No. 3 arrives from Willoughbys, Plymouth, of approved design and able to make the crossing in three minutes.	(H)
1877	Mr Avis gives up his Lower Ferry lease after eleven years; John and Adam Casey of Kingswear take it over.	(L)
1878	They acquire two launches *Forester* and *Blanche*; the SDR repairs the old float and provides a new second float.	(L)
1894	Raleigh Estates orders another new improved *Floating Bridge* No. 4 from Philips to replace the 1876 *Floating Bridge* No 3.	(H)
1897	Adam Casey retires; John Casey's son Thomas stands in as crew as and when required.	(L)
1900	The *Dolphin* goes for a complete overhaul which includes improvements for passengers' comfort, chiefly a glazed flat-roofed deck saloon quickly named by locals 'the cucumber frame'.	(R)
1901	William Casey retires and young Tom Casey takes command, supported by Frederick Charles Heal who later becomes a partner; the GWR then replaces the old 1865 float with a new one from Philips.	(L)
1902	The ageing *Dolphin* receives beauty treatment for the impending visit of King Edward VII to lay the foundation stone of the new Royal Naval College, and for two four-minute trips the *Dolphin* has the honour of flying the royal standard while on the bridge Admiral Sir Frederick Collinson and Captain Thorne pilot the royal visitors across the Dart.	(R)
1907	The GWR replaces the 1876 float with a new one from Philips costing £365.	(L)
1908	The paddle-steamer *Dolphin*, after forty years' service, is sold to Appledore for scrap, and a new larger screw-driven

ferry, *The Mew*, from Cox's, Falmouth, arrives. She is capable of carrying 547 passengers, 231 more than the old *Dolphin*. Raleigh Estates abandons the *Floating Bridge* No. 4 and substitutes only a small rowing boat.   (R&H)

1909   Tom Casey orders from Philips a new launch *Hauley* to relieve the ageing launches *Blanche* and *Forester*.   (L)

1912   The *Floating Bridge* No. 4, after four years abandoned on the mud at Sandquay, is offered for sale and the business was purchased by John Williams, Devonport, who orders from Roger & Son, Plymouth, a new *Floating Bridge* No. 5.
(H)

1914   War is declared and staffing becomes a problem, particularly with the rowing ferries; Tom Casey acquires a 26ft launch, *Edna*, and orders a new launch from Rogers & Son, Falmouth, called *Relief*, which replaces the old rowing ferries after centuries of service.
(L)

1917   *Relief* fails to live up to her name and is withdrawn as no steersman can be found.   (L)

1918   The war ends and men slowly come home, gradually enabling normal service to be resumed on all three ferries.
(L,H&R)

1920   Mr Williams, owner of *Floating Bridge* No. 5, offers the *Floating Bridge*, slipways and approach roads for sale; Philips, now established at Simpson, Strickland & Co Ltd works at Noss, purchase all by private treaty and promptly build *Floating Bridge* No. 6.
(H)

1924   The GWR is by now paying the Lower Ferry considerable sums to transport its growing fleet of vehicles on its own ferry, so it experiments by running first a small vehicle down the pontoon and onto *The Mew*, then a purpose-built postal van. It withdraws *The Mew* and commissions Philips to strengthen her decks and remove the rear saloon to accommodate five or six vehicles, modifying both pontoons and gantries. This is the first time that passengers and vehicles have been transported together.
(R)

1925   Casey & Heal's lease expires and the GWR refuses to renew it; thus the Lower Ferry closes after centuries of service, though Casey runs a twelve-seater launch *I'll Try* from Longford Steps for ten months. The closure causes consternation in the town: the *Chronicle* relates that *The Mew* would have to carry among the passengers the farm animals, previously carried on the horse ferry. There is a vigorous campaign for its reopening. After some discussion the ferry rights, two floats and use of the slips are offered by the GWR to Dartmouth Council for £100 and a nominal fee of £5 per annum. This is accepted and tenders are invited for a service to start in the following year. This is awarded to new lessees Peters & Heseltine, Kingswear.   (L)

1926   The service restarts under the control of Mr Peters, the working member of the partnership, using Casey's 1909 tug *Hauley* and the council's old wooden floats.
(L)

1928   Vehicle traffic continues to increase; *Hauley* and the antiquated floats prove inadequate and a programme of replacement is instigated. The Corporation orders a new larger wooden float, carrying eight cars, which is quickly nicknamed 'Big Jumbo' and proves difficult to handle with the old *Hauley*.   (L)

1929   Mr Peters orders a new larger and more powerful tug named *Hauley I* from Percy Mitchell, Portmellon, and a new passenger launch *Perseverance* to replace Casey's old 1915 launch *Relief*.   (L)

1932   A second new tug *Hauley II* is ordered from Mr Mitchell, but Mr Peters has begun to extend his business interests into towage and running passenger launch trips from Torquay to Dartmouth and Dittisham, and also orders a 72ft passenger launch, the *Torbay Belle*. At the same time he is in negotiation with General Estates Co Ltd, London, to dispose of his Lower Ferry lease. In July he informs the council of his intentions and offers it the remaining portion of his lease for the exorbitant sum of £12,000, reduced to £8,000, which the council refuses. It agrees to the transfer of the lease.
(L)

1933   The new lessees order a third tug *Hauley III* from Portmellon while agreeing with the council to increase charges and replace the old worn out 1907 wooden float with a new larger steel float, which they would purchase and retain. The old float is given them for secondary use and disposal (the remains lie in Waterhead Creek).
(L)

1935   Traffic has by now so increased that they purchase a second steel float, the two wooden floats being used as reserves. Then in June the Admiralty yacht *Enchantress* entering harbour collides with the Lower Ferry (fortunately with no passengers or cars aboard the float) which sinks. As the tow ropes part the crewman jumps to safety aboard the tug.
(L)

1936   A new passenger launch *Reliance* from Lavers' Southtown yard is put on the Lower Ferry service.   (L)

1940   The railway ferry *The Mew* steams flat out for Dover to assist in the Dunkirk evacuation, but on arrival is declared unsuitable, and returns slowly to Dartmouth.
(R)

1942   Three years' war reduce manpower and all three services to a minimum and the Corporation has to loan a man to assist.
(H L & R)

1945   The war is over, and with men coming home the three ferries slowly return to normal pre-war service.(H L & R)

1949   Rumour proves correct and on 25 March, General Estates Ltd, Southampton, relinquishes its lease after fifteen years' service of running the Lower Ferry, which reverts back to the owner, the Corporation, which purchases the *Hauley* tugs and floats and appoints a Ferry Committee to resume the service.
(L)

1950   A new passenger launch, the *Newcomen*, is delivered from Blackmore's, Bideford, to replace the ageing *Perseverance* on the Lower Ferry service.
(L)

1954   After forty-six years the ageing but much loved railway ferry *The Mew* is withdrawn for scrapping at Plymouth, to the sorrow of Dartmouth people; she is replaced for a six month trial period by a much smaller vessel, the *Lady Elizabeth*, which is soon withdrawn and replaced by the passenger-only launches *Humphrey Gilbert* and *Adrian Gilbert*.
(R)

DARTMOUTH'S COALING TRADE

1850 to 1951

1850   Small steamers begin to call to replenish bunkers from local house-coal merchants.
1852   Captain Moody calls and recognizes the harbour's potential as a coaling station.
1855   He returns and buys Charles Vincent's shore-based house-coal business to bunker calling steamers.
1856   He overreaches his resources and sells out to his under-manager William Ashford Jnr.
1862   William Ashford Jnr decides to concentrate on his timber business and sells to R L Hingston.
1870   James Armerson buys hulk *Marinous* as a bunkering hulk, but she breaks loose and is wrecked.
1871   R L Hingston buys the wrecked barque *Happy* and converts her into a standing floating coal hulk.
1876   Powell Duffryn Colliers creates the firm G H Collins & Co and stations the hulk *Monarch* in the harbour.
1878   R L Hingston, to compete, contracts with a colliery to bunker its Nixon's Navigation Coals.
1880   Fox, Sons & Co, Plymouth, agent for Cwmaman Coal Co, stations a large hulk in the harbour.
1881   Bellamy & Co, agent for Dowlais Steam & Iron Co, also moors a large hulk in the harbour.
1882   R L Hingston buys a second larger wreck, *Prodomo*, and converts her into a coal hulk to station in the harbour.
1883   G H Collins & Co buys out Bellamy & Co to establish a second bunkering depot at Portland.
1884   Trade begins to centre on Portland, and Dartmouth starts to lose business.
1885   Thomas Wilton from North Shields joins Cwmaman Coal Co as agent.
1888   Jasper Bartlett of Dartmouth buys R L Hingston's business and forms the Channel Coaling Co.
1889   Whiteway & Ball, of Torquay, develops the house- and gas-coal trade over Kingswear jetties.
1891   Thomas Wilton leaves Cwmaman Coal Co and forms a partnership with coaling factor R D Renwick of Torquay.
1892   Renwick & Wilton's trade is mainly house-coals over Kingswear jetties.
1894   Cwmaman Coal Co withdraws; Fox, Sons & Co becomes its coaling and shipping agents.
1896   Renwick & Wilton buys the wrecked barque *Narwaal*, converts her and enters the bunkering business.
1890-
1900   Dartmouth's bunkering average for the decade is 65,119 tons per annum.
1901   The Harbour Commission, forty years the domain of the local landed gentry, is restructured and becomes the power base of successful businessmen, a cartel composed of the heads of the three local coaling companies.
1902   Forward, agent for the Mersey Steamship Co, chooses Dartmouth as the port of departure for its line of steamships to Morocco and negotiates with the GWR a coal-loading shute with sidings at Hoodown Point to bunker its ships in the harbour by barge with rail-freighted coal.
1903   Renwick, Wilton & Co reverses its policy of using chartered vessels and purchases outright the colliers that previously supplied the company.
1905   It ceases bunkering to concentrate on supplying its own colliers' gas- and house-coal locally over the Kingswear quays. Forward ceases coaling its liners from the Hoodown Point jetty to bunker direct by collier.
1907   Forward again reverses its policy and applies direct to the Harbour Commission for permission to moor a large hulk in the harbour. This move, resisted by the established coaling companies, is approved as Forward threatens to withdraw its line unless the request is granted.
1908   As feared, shortly after its hulk *Stratford* arrives, Forward creates the Dartmouth Coaling Co to serve, not only its own liners, but also other coaling steamships. By autumn financial problems force it to sell the liners to the Union Castle Line, but it retains the coaling company.
1909   The Commission receives a request from Denaby & Cadaby (Main) Colliery Ltd for permission to station a hulk in the harbour.
1910   The request is fiercely resisted by all the coaling companies, and is refused. Mr Wilton, the town council representative on the Commission, votes contrary to council wishes and incurs the anger of the council, lumpers and townspeople as the company decides to establish a depot in Brixham, thus creating a rival bunkering port barely five miles distant.
1911   Mr Wilton, sole owner of Renwick, Wilton & Co, forms the Wilton Steam Ship Co to enter the time-chartering business, to serve his own and other companies and orders (as with Renwick's, the first of several) a purpose-built collier. The Dartmouth Coaling Co is absorbed by Evans, Thomas & Radcliffe, Cardiff, which also acquires G H Collins and Channel Coaling Cos which, though they continue trading under their old names, are now one concern.
1913   Mr A H Bridson, chairman of the Commission for the last thirteen years, resigns after several disagreements with Mr Wilton. Mr Jasper Bartlett (chairman, Channel Coaling Co) takes the chair.
1914   War is declared and the conflict soon reduces trade and the workforce, while Mr Wilton is elected Mayor, a position he holds with merit for the duration of the war.

1917 The shortage of manpower becomes acute, and mechanization is introduced, to the unions' discomfort: wooden pontoons surmounted by mechanical grabs.

1918 Victory. Strikes become commonplace and the Brixham depot creates severe competition.

1919 The Admiralty returns Wilton's two surviving colliers, the SS *Torquay* and SS *Paignton* and the tug *Dartmothian*, which are sold away, and the Wilton Steam Ship Co is placed in voluntary liquidation

1921 The town council, resentful from earlier humiliation, determines to increase its strength on the Harbour Commission and submits a Parliamentary bill which improves its representation by 50 per cent.

1922 Due to depression, shipping is laid up and bunkering depleted. The coaling factors demand a cut in lumpers' wages and an end to the restrictive working practices gained in the war years. This is resisted by the T & GWU and a strike is called. Meanwhile Evans & Reed Steam Coal Co Ltd, Cardiff, owner since 1911 of Dartmouth's three bunkering firms, takes over the nearby Brixham bunkering business of Denaby & Cadaby (Main) Colliery Co Ltd, (established 1911) and creates a new company, the Torbay & Brixham Coaling Co Ltd.

1923 After ten months and severe hardship amongst the lumpers, a compromise is agreed, resulting in lower wages and revision of working terms.

1924 Sir T Wilton, in semi-retirement, forms with two sons the T & C Wilton Steamship Co Ltd and orders a new collier for trade over the Kingswear quay.

1925 Trade revives and for the first time in four years there are no ships laid up in the main harbour. However, many coal-burning ships are scrapped and new vessels are oil-fuelled. This results in a further decline in the port's staple trade of bunkering.

1926 The power of the growing trade unions is evident in disputes with the Government over coaling returns and a General Strike is called. Most employees return in a week or so, but 1,127,000 miners remain on strike for eight months, achieving little. Meanwhile coaling, the lifeblood of the harbour, virtually ceases. Bunkering reduced to minimum, there is great hardship for the lumpers, many existing soley on the soup kitchens.

1928 Trade slowly returns and Mr Wilton orders another collier, the SS *Newton Abbot*, and the coaling factors begin replacing their twenty-year-old standing hulks.

1929 This is the end of an era, with the demise of three giants of the coaling trade, first Sir T Wilton, then Jasper Bartlett, then George Henry Collins, all founders of Dartmouth's staple trade, bunkering.

1930 The T & C Wilton Shipping Co orders another collier, the SS *Bovey Tracey*, but trade is faltering, and shipping is returning to lay up above Noss.

1931 After fifty years' campaigning by the coaling companies, new quayside facilities are opened: an extended wharf, greater draft, and two travelling electric cranes on fixed tracks along the quays.

1935 The long lines of shipping laid up above Noss begin to diminish. The Government is now making a payment to encourage shipowners to replace old and worn-out vessels as foreign shipping numbers are overtaking British.

1936 Two mechanical grabs sink, and because of declining business, one is broken up.

1938 The threat of impending war causes the withdrawal of several laid-up vessels for overhaul, and the local MP, Mr Williams of Greenway, petitions the Government that 'regulations and restrictions' were prejudicial to British Coal and are driving vessels abroad, and the Harbour Commission issues 12,000 leaflets extolling the benefits of Dartmouth harbour.

1939 War is declared, and all shipping pressed into service. The shipyards are busy building new vessels, mostly oil-fired, to replace those lost to U-boats.

1941 Six German bombers cause death and destruction to the BRNC and Philips' shipyard, sinking the collier *Fernwood* and the floating grab.

1946 The war over, and with merchant shipping decimated, the outlook for Dartmouth's bunkering trade is ominous. However, the collier trade over Kingswear quays with gas-coal for Dartmouth and Hollacombe gasworks and house-coal for the local district and Torquay resumes, with deliveries from twenty-six colliers within the year, rising to a maximum in 1955 of 77 shiploads. Sadly the trade ends in 1963.

1950 The standing hulk *Juno* leaves, towed by a tug for the breakers' yard, but meets an honourable end by sinking *en route*.

1951 The two remaining standing hulks *Dagny* and *Sorkness* leave for the same fate, thus closing Dartmouth's coaling industry.

Footnote After 100 years Dartmouth's bunkering trade finally closed, and as the lives and times of the founding owners have been recorded, it is fitting to include a mention of a Dartmouth man who, for the last twenty years, dominated the local waterfront, Richard Leslie Dennis. At his death in the mid 1950s he held the following positions: chairman of Dartmouth Harbour Commission and Dartmouth Steam Laundry, managing director of River Dart Steamboat Co, George Henry Collins & Co, Channel Coaling Co, Dartmouth Coaling Co, Torbay & Brixham Coaling Co, and director of Evans & Reed Investment Co, Vol-Crepe Co and numerous other associated collieries.

APPENDIX IV

RAILWAY TO KINGSWEAR

1853 to 1954

THE DARTMOUTH & TORBAY, SOUTH DEVON, GREAT WESTERN RAILWAYS, AND BRITISH RAIL

Dartmouth, birthplace of steam power, deserved a railway, and hopes rose as the country's rail network crept ever nearer, reaching Exeter (1844), Newton Abbot (1846), Totnes (1847) and Torquay (1848). In 1853 Lord Courtenay, John Belfield, Governor Arthur Holdsworth and others drew up plans for the Dartmouth, Torbay & South Devon Railway, which failed through lack of finance. In 1856 the young energetic Charles Seale Hayne and seventy-seven other gentlemen convened a meeting in the Guildhall to promote rail communication to Dartmouth, with the following results:

1856 A committee is appointed to ascertain the most economic route to Dartmouth, via Totnes or via Torquay, the latter being chosen. The Dartmouth & Torbay Railway is formed (with Charles Seale Hayne as chairman), an engineer appointed (I K Brunel), and a prospectus issued for a railway, seven-and-a-half miles long from Torre to Maypool or Noss, costing £120,000.

1857 Royal Assent is received, Smith & Knight appointed contractors, preliminary surveys completed and the line set out to Paignton.

1858 After the ceremony of cutting the first sod at Torre, work proceeds on track laying and on the tunnel at Livermead, but delay and increased legislation costs occur due to landowners' demanding exorbitant prices.

1859 Paignton celebrates the opening of the first three miles of track, which includes viaduct, tunnel, and twenty bridges with a 'Paignton pudding' (weighing 2,100lb).

1860 Work continues with costs escalating, resulting in the submission of a Deviation Bill for extra finance and termination of the line at Greenway, but this meets fierce opposition from the landowner Mr Harvey.

1861 Brixham Road (Churston) is reached amidst further celebrations; the line now totals five-and-a-half miles, with two major viaducts, but celebrations are marred by news of the failure of the Deviation Bill. Two years of stagnation follow.

1862 Royal Assent is received for a bill to raise a further £70,000 to complete the line to Hoodown, and for powers to lease the line to the South Devon Railway. New contractors Blinkhorn & Atkinson are appointed to recommence work.

1863 Board of Trade grants a Provisional Order to appoint the Dartmouth Harbour Commission to build wharfs, warehouses, jetties and harbour works, with the authority to borrow £14,000, make by-laws, raise tolls and so on, and to transfer or lease all or part to the railway company. Work continues on the tunnel, stone and two wooden viaducts, foreshore blasting, embanking and finally the crossing of Waterhead Creek to a resited station in Kingswear.

1864 At last Kingswear terminus opens, with a temporary platform and booking office, thus completing the last two-and-a-half miles from Churston. A special train, the 'Lion', brings Charles Seale Hayne, directors and invited guests to celebrations in Kingswear and Dartmouth.

1865 The line is two-and-a-half years late and costs £130,000 over estimate. Another contractor, Call & Pethick, Plymouth completes the station, Blinkhorn & Atkinson the dockside facilities, lighthouse and Daymark; the railway ferry *Perseverance*, overdue and over estimate, arrives too late for the celebrations.

1866 Financial stringency forces the Dartmouth & Torbay Railway Co to accept an offer of amalgamation with the South Devon Railway Co, which leases the line for ten years, Charles Seale Hayne being given a seat on the board. He then forms the Dartmouth & Kingswear Hotel Co and negotiates from the railway a seventy-five-year lease on Kingswear's old Plume of Feathers Inn adjacent to the station. He converts the inn into the Dart Yacht Club Hotel, a quality four-storey hotel to accommodate passengers from the railway and from his newly arrived cross-channel paddle steamer *Eclair*.

1868 Unfortunately the cross-channel service proves uneconomic and the PS *Eclair* is sold away to Bristol owners.

1869 After only four years, the railway company's converted cross-river ferry *Perseverance* is constantly breaking down or under repair and is replaced by a new two-bowed ferry, *Dolphin*.

1871 Trade improves, for after fifteen years Dartmouth is once again chosen as a mail station by George Payne, who has formed the Cape & Natal Steamship Co.

1872 Gloom prevails as the service encounters financial problems, but fortunately the Donald Currie Line agrees to continue the Cape & Colonies service.

1876   The South Devon Railway Co in turn after ten years, leases the line to the Great Western Railway Co for 999 years. The harbour's increasing bunkering trade encourages the national coal group, Powel Duffryn Co Ltd to form G H Collins & Co and station a large floating hulk in the harbour. The hotel company reverts to private ownership.

1889   After twenty-three years Dartmouth's old pontoon with its floating booking office is replaced by a new pontoon and a quality-built station ashore, the only station in Britain with no track.

1891   Once again after twenty years Dartmouth loses its status as a mailing port when the Post Office diverts the service to Southampton, depriving the railway and port of some of its revenue.

1892   To standardize with the nationwide system the GWR continues its policy of converting from broad to narrow gauge, and with a selected team of men, the transformation of the line to Kingswear is completed in the remarkably short period of a few days.

1899   Part of Waterhead Creek is filled in to accommodate extra sidings and, after the change to narrow gauge, the terminus is further upgraded with a new signal box, wider-roofed platforms, weighbridge, cranes, overhead bridge and so on.

1900   Turn-of-the-century records illustrate the growth of the gas- and house-coal seaborne trade over the Kingswear quays from 1,300 tons in 1881 to 84,166 tons in 1897 bringing increased railway usage. Further infilling of Waterhead Creek enables the old engine shed turntable (23ft 8in) to be replaced by one 55ft 8in diameter, thus eliminating the need for heavy trains arriving at Newton Abbot to change to a smaller engine to proceed to Kingswear.

1901   Further infilling of Waterhead Creek allows more sidings and the extension of the passenger platform by 66ft.

1902   The construction at Hoodown Point of sidings and a coal shute enables Forward's new line of steamers to Morocco to bunker in the harbour with rail-freighted coal from barges.

1908   A new water tank is provided to replace the original 1864 tank.

1919   Work commences to move the line that bisected Philips' works, and crossed the two Noss Creeks on wooden viaducts erected in 1863 by R P Brereton, by re-routeing it behind the works and the creeks.

1924   After four years the deviation is declared open and the first train crosses, while the 1865 wooden engine shed in Kingswear station, too small for the current engines, is closed.

1925   The GWR makes a virtual gift of their Lower Ferry and slips to Dartmouth Town Council.

1926   Work commences at Hoodown Point on demolishing Brereton's 1863 wooden single-track viaduct over Waterhead Creek, and replacing it with a double-track steel and concrete structure, thus enabling the GWR's largest engines (such as the *Torbay Express*), to cross. Also the 1900, 55ft 8in turntable is replaced with a 66ft turntable.

1929   The island platform at Kingswear station is lengthened to 850ft which necessitates extensive new track layout, signalling alterations, further partial infilling of Waterhead Creek for additional sidings, and the demolition of the disused 1864 engine shed. Also at the Noss shipbuilding works, a ground frame and sidings are installed giving access to all parts of the works.

1930   A contract is placed with Industrial Constructions Ltd, London, for extensive work at Kingswear Quay. The wooden-piled 1869 Éclair Pier and Quay is demolished and a new 360ft-long piled reinforced concrete quay built 10ft further out into the river, to give two berths with increased draft. Three of the four old steam- and the one hand-crane are replaced by two 3-ton elevated mobile cranes on fixed 7ft-wide quayside track.

1932   The new dockside facilities are a great asset, resulting in increased coaling imports, particularly from vessels belonging to the T & C Wilton Steamship Co Ltd. The line then settles to a period of stability until war is declared in September 1939.

1939   Passenger traffic rapidly diminishes, as men join the services and manpower becomes a problem, while freight decreases due to the U-boat menace and colliers being requested by the Admiralty.

1941   A jetty is constructed adjacent to the Hoodown sidings to facilitate the refuelling and arming of British and Free French motor torpedo flotillas.

1942   An air raid by six German bombers causes heavy damage and casualties to the BRNC and Philips' shipyard, but the main line remains open.

1946   The war over, rail and seaborne services resume, and holiday traffic returns with up to fourteen trains per day arriving at Kingswear station.

1949   In August the Labour Government Transport Bill receives Royal Assent and the big four railway companies are nationalized under the title British Rail resulting in a period of reappraisal and the closure of many branch lines. The Kingswear line survives, but is reduced to no more than a basic railway.

Footnote As private motor car ownership increased, so did rail closure notices and in February 1972 a closure notice was served on the Kingswear line. Fortunately a group of railway enthusiasts forms the Dart Valley Railway Company and purchased the line for £250,000 reinstating limited services. In 1981 it was restructured as the Dartmouth & Torbay Railway Co, running a regular service of steam trains in the summer months and a limited number in winter. Thus the birthplace of the father of steam propulsion, Thomas Newcomen, still maintains its proud link with steam.

APPENDIX V

THE EARLS OF DARTMOUTH

1648 to Present Day

Virtue rejoices in trial

The family tree starts in 1343 with Thomas Legge, Sheriff and Lord Mayor of London from 1345 to 1354. He married Elizabeth Beauchamp, daughter of Thomas Earl of Warwick, an ancestor of Warwick the Kingmaker who led the rebellion against King Edward IV. He was followed by Simon, his son Thomas and then William (a popular family name), whose eldest son moved to Ireland. He was succeeded by Edward, who had six sons and seven daughters, and the first-born, William, who returned at the request of his godfather, Henry Danvers, Earl of Danby to serve as a volunteer under Gustavus Adolphus of Sweden and later under Maurice, Prince of Orange, in Holland. He then returned to England to hold high office under King Charles I. In 1647 he was wounded at Naseby and held in Coventry jail, from whence he escaped in his wife's clothing. He died in 1672 and was succeeded by his son.

Admiral George Legge, 1st Lord Dartmouth, 1648–1691, This oil painting was given in 1914 to the college by William Heneage Legge, 6th Earl of Dartmouth, associate of Dartmouth College, Hanover, USA.

KEITH FRANKS, BRNC

George Legge, 1st Baron Dartmouth, 1648-1691

He found favour in the court of King James II, being made Master of Ordnance and admiral of the fleet that bombarded Tangier, and he was created Baron Dartmouth. In 1687 he was ordered to intercept William of Orange who was bound for Dartmouth, but he failed, and William was forced to land at Brixham because of bad weather. The Baron was impeached for treason and imprisoned in the Tower, where he died and was succeeded by his son.

William, 2nd Baron and 1st Earl of Dartmouth 1672-1750

He found favour at the court of Queen Anne, and was made a Secretary of State and later a Lord Justice of England. He then became Viscount Lewisham of County Kent and the first Earl of Dartmouth. He was succeeded by his grandson.

William, 2nd Earl of Dartmouth 1731-1801

He was appointed Secretary of the Colonies and Head of the Board of Trade and Plantations by King George III, and was president of an independent trust formed to allocate funds raised to educate the Indian tribes in the expanding American colonies. These colonies were administered by Governors who were expected to further the Anglican faith but still retain the delicate balance that existed between London and the colonists, who were mainly 'heterodox and dissenters' who had left the mother country to pursue their chosen form of religion (as had the Pilgrim Fathers). The Bishop of London, titular head of the church in North America, felt that a policy of Christianizing pagan Indians would help to reduce the opposition to the Anglican church in the colonies. This view was shared by John Wentworth, the Governor of New Hampshire, who thought that educating the Indians would help maintain royal authority in America. It was his responsibility to promote the expansion of settlement in the Connecticut River valley where there were huge tracts of unoccupied land. He favoured the establishment of a charity school and wrote 'it would produce the political advancement of his Majesty's colonies by reclaiming numerous people from their savage desultory enmity to an orderly, peaceful and happy subjection to the laws and advantages of his mild and equitable government'. Here he was fortunate, for the Rev Eleazor Wheelock of Lebanon had in 1754 started a charity school to teach Christianity to the Indians and spread the gospel among the tribes (though they often reverted to their old tribal ways on their return home). He had campaigned tirelessly for the right to establish a college, preferably with a Royal Charter, and himself as head of a small board of his choice, to limit Anglican representation. To this end he despatched his leading Indian pupil Samson Occur together with a Nonconformist minister, Nathaniel Whitaker, to England to raise funds for the education of American Indians. They amassed £12,000, which was passed to the Earl of Dartmouth's independent trust for administration. With exceptional political perception, and after campaigning in several states for support and a suitable location, he reached agreement after protracted negotiation with Governor Wentworth, subject to compromise about the numbers on the board and the training of white missionaries. Both parties realized that funding and political mileage would accrue if the college were to be named after the sponsor, the Earl of Dartmouth (who had made a substantial contribution), and so in 1769 a Royal Charter was granted by King George III.

The college was founded in the newly established township of Hanover (1765), which was situated on the plains of the upper valley adjacent to the Connecticut River, between the White Mountains of New Hampshire and the Green Mountains of Vermont. It started in 1770 in a small log cabin, ostensibly to educate the Indians, but it quickly became the domain of colonists and expanded rapidly. The main building, Dartmouth Hall, was damaged by fire in 1904 and replaced by the present handsome structure, built in colonial style. The college today is a major academic seat of learning, set in over 200 acres and composed of academic centres, halls and nine major libraries. It employs over 3,100 staff, offering 4,275 students a four-year degree course in various subjects. (Dartmouth in England has only about 6,000 inhabitants.) The 2nd Earl was succeeded by his eldest son.

George, 3rd Earl of Dartmouth 1755-1810
He had five sons and seven daughters, and was succeeded by his eldest son.

William, 4th Earl of Dartmouth 1784-1853
He had one surviving son by his first marriage, six sons and nine daughters by his second marriage.

William Walter, 5th Earl of Dartmouth 1823-1891
He had one son and four unmarried daughters.

William Heneage, 6th Earl of Dartmouth 1851-1936
He had two sons and two daughters, and Dartmouth College, USA, named after the second Earl, presented him with an honorary LL.D degree. He also presented the Royal Naval College, Dartmouth, with a full length portrait in oils of the first Baron Dartmouth, Admiral George Legge. He was succeeded by his elder son.

William, 7th Earl of Dartmouth 1881-1958
He had a son, who was killed at Alamein in October 1942, and five daughters. He was succeeded by his brother.

Humphrey, 8th Earl of Dartmouth 1888-1962
He had three sons and a daughter and cemented an overdue family relationship with Dartmouth by becoming a cadet in 1903 at the Royal Naval College aboard the old three-decker *Britannia*, in its last term before the college reopened in new premises ashore at Mount Boone. He participated in the Battle of Jutland.

Gerald Humphrey, 9th Earl of Dartmouth 1924-1997
He had three sons and a daughter by his marriage in 1948 to Raine McCorquodale (prominent in the old GLC). The marriage was dissolved in 1976 and she married Earl Spencer, becoming stepmother to the late Diana, Princess of Wales, who visited BRNC for the passing-out ceremony in 1997. The 9th Earl, and Raine, Countess of Dartmouth, were the principal guests at the Hanover celebrations to mark the 200th anniversary of the founding of Dartmouth College.

William, 10th Earl of Dartmouth 1949 –
Viscount Lewisham now carries on the long and honourable lineage of the family.

The late Diana, Princess of Wales, (stepdaughter of Raine, former Countess of Dartmouth) attending the college for the Lord High Admirals Divisions on the 6th April 1989, and accompanied by the commandant, Captain J R Shiffner RN, a lady-in-waiting and her minder. The Princess is about to partake in the beagle naming ceremony.

G THOMAS

APPENDIX VI

DARTMOUTH AND KINGSWEAR

PUBLIC HOUSES 1903 and 2000

DARTMOUTH

1903 (26)	Location	2000 (15)
Admiral Nelson Inn	Newcomen Road	Private property
Bell Inn	Newport Street	Private property
Britannia Inn	Clarence Hill	Private property
Commercial Union Inn	Victoria Road	Windjammer
Dartmouth Arms Inn	Lower Street	Dartmouth Arms Inn
Floating Bridge Inn	Coombe Road	Floating Bridge Inn
Globe Inn	Smith Street	Private property
George & Dragon Inn	Mayors Avenue	George & Dragon
Kings Arms Inn	Fairfax Place	Riversea Fashions
Lindsay Arms Inn	Lower Street	Private property
London Inn	Location unknown	Unknown
Marine Tavern	Lower Ferry Slip	Demolished
Market House Inn	Market Square	Market House Inn
Queens Hotel	Smith Street	Private property
Raleigh Hotel	South Embankment	Riversea Fashions
Royal Castle Hotel	New Quay	Royal Castle Hotel
Royal Oak Inn	Lower Street	Bayards Restaurant
Seale Arms Inn	Victoria Road	Seale Arms
Seven Stars Hotel	Smith Street	Seven Stars Inn
Ship in Dock Inn	Clarence Street	Ship in Dock Inn
Steam Packet Inn	Duke Street	Cundells
Town Arms Inn	Higher Street	Bombed 1942
Trafalgar Inn	Newcomen Road	Private property
Union Inn	Market Square	Dolphin Inn
Valentine Inn	Foss Street	Private property
Victoria Hotel	Victoria Road	Little Admiral Hotel
Private house	Higher Street	Cherub Inn
Philips' Shipyard	Sandquay	Dart Marina Hotel
Gentleman's residence	One Gun Point	Gunfield Hotel
Townstal Field	Britannia Avenue	Lord Nelson Inn

KINGSWEAR

1903 (4)	Location	2000 (3)
Rock Inn	Noss Point	Private property
Royal Dart Hotel	The Square	Royal Dart Hotel
Ship Inn	Higher Street	Ship Inn
Steam Packet Inn	Fore Street	Steam Packet Inn

ROYAL CASTLE HOTEL
"CHOSEN BY KINGS"
DARTMOUTH
ESTABLISHED 1580.   TELEPHONE: DARTMOUTH 25

BIBLIOGRAPHY

Appleby, H N, *Great Western Ports* William Lewis 1933
Archibald, E H H, *The Metal Fighting Ship (In the English Navy) 1860/1970* Blandford 1971
Baring-Gould, S, *A Book of the West, – Devon* Methuen 1899
Beckett, D, *Stephenson's Britain* David & Charles 1984
Clammer, R, & Kittridge, A, *Passenger Steamers of the River Dart* Twelveheads Press 1987
Clark, E F, *George Parker Bidder, The Calculating Boy* KSL Publications 1983
Coaling, D, *Steam Yachts* Batsford 1980
Davies, E L, & Grove, E J, *The Royal Naval College, Dartmouth* Gieves & Hawkes 1980
Davis, G, *Dartmouth Royal Regatta, 1834/1987* Harbour Books 1987
Drummond, M, *Salt Water Palaces* Debretts Peerage 1979
Farr, Graham, *West Country Paddle Steamers* T Stephenson & Son 1967
Freeman, Ray, *Dartmouth and its Neighbours* Phillimore & Co 1990
Gliddon, Gerald, *The Somme* Sutton 1991
Greenhill, Basil, *The Merchant Schooners,* Vols 1 & 2 Percival Marshall & Co 1951 & 1957
Gregory, R H, *The South Devon Railway* Oakwood Press 1982
Harris, Helen, *Industrial Archaeology of Dartmoor* David & Charles 1968
Haws, Duncan, *Merchant Fleets, Union, Castle, and Union Castle Lines* TCL Publications 1990
Henley, E P, & William, C H, *His Days and Ways* R Cranford & Son 1927
Holgate, M, *The Secret of the Babbacombe Murder* Peninsula Press 1925
Hunt, Cecil, *Gallant Little Campeador* Methuem & Co. Ltd
Lawson, T W, & Thompson, W M, Lawson, *History of the America's Cup* Boston Mass. 1902
Langley, M, & Small, E, *Estuary and River Ferries of South West England* Raine Research Publications 1984
Langley, M, & Small, E, *Lost Ships of the West Country* Stanford Maritime 1988
Larn, R, *Devon Shipwrecks* David & Charles 1974
Masefield, J, *Jim Davis* Wells Gardner Darton & Co 1900
Mitchell, Peter, *Boatbuilders Story* Kingston - Mevagissey
Norway, A H, *Highways and Byeways in Devon and Cornwall* Macmillan 1911
Norway, A H, *Parson Peter* John Murray 1910
Oppenheim, M M, *Maritime History of Devon* University of Exeter 1968
Philip & Son, *1858-1958, A Century of Progress* Philip & Son 1958
Phillips-Birt, D, *The History of Yachting* Elm Tree Books 1974
Pike, J, *Iron Horse to the Sea* Ex Libris Press 1987
Potts, C R, *1844-1988, The Newton Abbot to Kingswear Railway* Oakwood Press 1988
Potts, C R, *The Brixham Branc,* Oakwood Press 1986
Rees, Sir J F, *The Story of Milford* University of Wales Press 1974
Rogers, H K, *The Newcomen Engine in the West of England* Moonraker Press 1976
Rolt, L T C, *Thomas Newcomen* Landmark Publishing 1963
Rolt, L T C, *Isambard Kingdom Brunel* Longman 1957
Russell, J Scott, *Steam and Steam Navigation* Adam & Charles Black 1841
Russell, P, *Dartmouth* Friends of Dartmouth Museum Association 1950
Smith, E C, *History of Marine Engineering* Babcock & Wilcox 1937
Thomas, D St John, *The Great Western Railway* David & Charles 1986
Underhill, H A, *Sailing Ship Rigs and Rigging* Brown Son & Ferguson 1937

Other Sources

A Century on the River Dart, D Griffiths; *A Treatise on Steam Trawling,* and a *Short History of Brixham*, J Horsley; *Cannon of Dartmouth Castle*, A C Carpenter; *Dartmouth Harbour as a Station for Mail Packets*, A H Holdsworth; *Dartmouth Chronicle Editions since 1854*, South Hams Newspapers Ltd; *Minutes*, Dartmouth Harbour Commission; various Dartmouth Historical Research Group booklets; *Town Regalia*, Dartmouth Town Council; *Dunster Castle*, National Trust; *Felixstowe—100 years a Working Port*, R Malster; *Floating Bridge Papers*, K Perkins; *Kelly's Directories*; *Kingswear Castle*, Landmark Trust; Philip & Son *Yard Book*; *Minutes* Royal Dart Yacht Club ; *The Liwentaal Enigma*, B Marsh; *Transactions of the Devonshire Association*.

INDEX

References followed by *ill* indicate an illustration.

Cuff, R (town clerk) 220, 229
Currie, Donald, Castle Line 52, 54, 69, 73, 76, 82, 92*ill*
Curtis, Captain William H H 103

Daniel, Father 156
Dart Sailing Club 103, 138
Dart Yacht Club (later Royal) 25, 45*ill*, 46, 55
Dartmouth & Kingswear Hotel Company 18, 19*ill*, 44-45
Dartmouth & Kingswear Steam Laundry 72, 75*ill*, 78, 114, 124, 161
Dartmouth & Torbay Steam Packet Co 61, 65, 71, 73, 74, 85, 93, 117
Dartmouth Chronicle, The 2*ill*, 28*ill*, 29, 86
Dartmouth Coaling Company 123, 128, 129, 134, 137, 167
Dartmouth Harbour Bill 266
Dartmouth Harbour Improvement Bill 68, 69
Dartmouth Improvement Act 17
Dartmouth, Massachusetts 211-212
Dartmouth Mutual Marine Association 55
Dartmouth, Plymouth & Torbay Steamship Trading Co Ltd 52-53
Dartmouth Pottery 258
Dartmouth Rowing Club 103, 183*ill*, 203, 203*ill*, 204*ill*
Davies, Mr (property developer) 35, 43
Day, J J (town clerk) 174
DBSC (Dart Boat Sailing Club) 56, 68, 103
de Courcy Ireland, Rev 139, 154
Dean, Major 103
Denaby & Cadeby 128*ill*, 129, 133, 135, 168
Dennis, R L 154, 157, 163, 231, 234, 266, 269
Despard, Rev G P 29
DHC (Dartmouth Harbour Commission) 14, 18, 19*ill*, 30, 32, 39, 41, 57, 60, 67, 71, 73-74, 78, 80, 82, 84, 87, 90, 95, 103, 123, 137, 154, 156, 168, 170, 223, 253, 272
Dobson, Frank 121, 171
dogs 44, 56, 102*ill*, 125, 125*ill*, 130, 224, 257
Douglass, Sir James 65, 65*ill*, 136
Douglass, William 136
D'Oyly Carte, Lady 182, 183*ill*, 208
DSC (Dartmouth Sailing Club, now Dartmouth Yacht Club) 263*ill*, 266
DSPC (Dartmouth Steam Packet Company) 18, 19*ill*, 35, 41, 43, 46, 50, 61
Dudley, Captain 72

East India & London Shipping Company Ltd. 39
Eastlake, T L 57
elections: council 50, 67, 68, 69, 129, 174; Harbour Commission 117, 137; Parliamentary 32, 35, 188
electricity 107
Elliott, Sir George 57, 59
Embankment Scheme, North 68, 69, 71, 73, 74*ill*, 184, 185*ill*
Embankment Scheme, South 2*ill*, 38, 48*ill*, 64, 67, 68, 69, 71, 72, 74*ill*, 75, 82, 84, 188
Evans, Commander Charles E, RNVR 131*ill*, 134
Exeter Flying Post 22, 23, 29
Exeter and Plymouth Gazette 22

ferries: *Adrian Gilbert*, (Lower Ferry) 276; *Blanche*, (Lower Ferry steam launch) 62, 66, 81, 102*ill*, 126, 136; Dittisham 11, 173, 223, 257; *Dolphin*, (1869) 18, 19*ill*, 50, 50*ill*, 61bis, 103, 104, 105*ill*, 109, 110, 121, 122; *Edna*, (Lower Ferry steam launch) 143; Floating Bridge (1st) 10, 11, 11*ill*, 23, 30; Floating Bridge (2nd) 32, 41, 54bis, 55, 145*ill*; Floating Bridge (3rd) 60, 60*ill*, 91-92; Floating Bridge (4th) 89*ill*, 92, 95, 107, 131, 135; Floating Bridge (5th) 134*ill*, 135, 156, 163; Floating Bridge (6th) 166*ill*, 167; *Forester*, (Lower Ferry steam launch) 61, 66, 81, 126; *Hauley*, (R D S C screw tug) 61, 64, 76, 76*ill*, 87, 93; *Hauley I*, (Lower Ferry tug) 61, 125, 126*ill*, 187*ill*, 188; *Hauley II*, (Lower Ferry tug) 61, 208, 212, 272; *Humphrey Gilbert*, (Lower Ferry) 276; *I'll Try*, (passenger launch) 177; Kingswear 9, 11; *Lady Elizabeth*, (Lower Ferry) 276; Lower Ferry Floats 124*ill*, 143, 177, 187, 187*ill*, 188, 208, 219*ill*, 220, 223, 226, 254; *Mew*, (1908) 121*ill*, 122, 124*ill*, 156, 177, 182, 187, 193*ill*, 204, 208, 240, 259, 264, 268, 276, 277*ill*; *Newcomen*, (Lower Ferry launch) 264, 264*ill*; *Perseverance* (1865) 18, 41, 42, 43, 50, 51*ill*, 122; *Perseverance II* (1929) 188, 260, 263, 264; *Pioneer*, (Lower Ferry steam launch) 46, 102; *Reliance*, (Lower Ferry launch 1935) 223; *Reliance*, (Lower Ferry launch 1947) 254, 260, 264, 264*ill*; *Relief*, (Lower Ferry steam launch) 142*ill*, 143, *see also* harbour craft, river steamboats

Ferris, R 179-180
fire brigade 83, 85, 91, 116, 117*ill*, 143, 215, 254, 267*ill*, 268
fishing fleet 29, 58, 168
Forward, Sir Dudley 106, 115, 123
Foster, Rev Priestly 54
Fotheringham, Mr 61
Fountain Violet Country Club 17, 255
Fownes Rev Thomas 16
Fownes/Fownes Luttrells 11, 14, 15-16, 32, 34, 56-57*ill*
Freake, Lady 212, 213, 232
Freake, Sir Charles James 47, 70
Freake, Sir Thomas G, Bt 70, 81, 92, 92*ill*
Free French Forces 245, 245*ill*, 246, 246*ill*, 252*ill*
Froude, William 17, 38, 39, 41, 51, 52*ill*, 64, 95
Fulford, Mr (architect) 71

Gale, Thomas 11, 14, 18
Gallant's Bower 17, 40, 65, 107, 118, 138
gas coal trade 269*ill*, 270-271
Gibbs, Commander Valentine F, RN 159
Gibbs, Lieutenant Colonel 92
Golden Hind, (replica) 225*ill*, 226
Golden Hind, (Sea Rangers HQ) 259, 259*ill*
golf courses 107, 216, 217*ill*
Gooding, W H 263, 266
Goodson, Hugh L 183, 275
Goodson, Sir Alfred 154, 164, 212
Grave of the unknown, The, Arthur Howe Holdsworth 16-17, 118
Griffiths, Captain (harbourmaster) 256, 262

harbour craft: *Betsy Newton*, (Brixham lifeboat) 168; *British Hero*, (steam tug) 34; *Brothers*, (barge) 74; *Brownie*, (steam launch) 95; Caledonian Steam Towing Company 33; *Cam*, (dredger) 185*ill*, 202, 213*ill*; *Challenger*, (chartered tug) 122; *Dartmothian*, (50 GT tug) 143, 159, 160; *Goliath*, (barge) 222, 272; *Good Intent*, (pilot cutter) 208; *Guide* (steam tug) 50, 51, 61; *Gwendoline*, (pilot cutter) 85-86, 100, 102, 114; *Hamoaze*, (Devonport lighter) 40; *Howe*, (quarantine hulk) 94; *Kingswear*, (steam launch) 102; *Lady Alice*, (portable launch) 179-180, 179*ill*, 180*ill*; *l'Aure*, (French tug) 240; *Lily*, (steam tug) 59; *l'Isere*, (French tug) 240; *May*, (lifeboat) 74; *Mayfly*, (hospital ship) 85, 85*ill*, 116, 174; *Meroe II*, (D C Co launch) 208; *Millie*, (pilot cutter) 141; *Nimble*, (steam launch) 77*ill*, 87, 93, 102, 115*ill*, 142*ill*; *Northumberland*, (chartered tug) 107; *Pendennis*, (screw tug) 87; *Pilot*, (steam tug) 18, 19*ill*, 34, 35, 39, 44, 44*ill*, 65, 150*ill*; *Portwey*, (steam tug) 243, 254, 256, 256*ill*, 269; *Prospero*, (Devonport steam tug) 40; *Rose*, (pilot cutter) 100, 114, 141; *Saevar*, (tug) 266; *Scotia*, (Devonport steam tug) 50, 70; *Sensation*, (steam tug) 65; *Star of the Night*, (Philip's launch) 88; *Thistle*, (screw tug) 48; *Totnes*, (steam tug) 125, 130, 141; *Tradesman*, (chartered tug) 268*ill*, 269; *Venture*, (screw tug) 100, 107, 117, 118, 125, 135, 143, 143*ill*; *Verne*, (70 foot tug) 91; *Victor*, (screw tug) 112; *Viking*, (Brazilian tug) 117; *Vixen*, (small tug) 125; *Vulcan*, (small tug) 125; *Warrior*, (chartered tug) 107; *Water Lily*, (screw water tender) 61, 102, 116, 143, *see also* ferries, river steamboats
Harvey, Mr (owner of Greenway) 37, 38, 47, 69
Hayne, Charles Seale 15, 15*ill*, 17, 18, 19*ill*, 30, 32, 33, 33-34, 35, 36, 39, 42, 43, 44-45, 52, 53, 72, 73, 74, 78, 81, 84, 89, 109, 118, 145*ill*
Heinke, C J & Co (divers) 118
Henley, Miss Pamela 258, 263, 266, 274
Henn, Lieutenant and Mrs 26, 88, 108-109, 109*ill*, 111
Herbert, Sir T 35
Hill, Alfred Neil 136
Hillman, Dan 140, 140*ill*
Hine-Haycock, Archibald 16, 135, 178, 202, 213, 216
Hine-Haycock, Miss A 259, 271*ill*, 275
Hingston, Mr (Danish vice-consul) 52, 59, 60, 66, 69, 77
History of the America's Cup, W T Lawson and W M Thomson 26
History of Yachting, Douglas Phillips-Birt 25
Hockin, Mr Percy (town clerk) 64, 68, 70, 86, 108, 116, 174
Hodge, Father 259
Holdsworth, E W H 27, 100
Holdsworth, Governor Arthur Howe 10, 11, 12*ill*, 16, 17-18, 22, 23, 30, 32, 34, 35, 36*ill*, 37, 45, 97, 145*ill*, 274
Holdsworth, Rev Robert 16

ACKNOWLEDGEMENTS

A chance remark by Dartmouth estate agent Greg Singer initiated a sojourn that resulted in more than twenty happy retirement years in 'Arcadia', Kingswear's sunlit shoreline. Living on the eastern shore of the Dart valley, I became increasingly aware of the dearth of recorded history of the harbour and of Kingswear, which rekindled my boyhood interest in shipping, functional architecture and local history.

This led me to Dartmouth's excellent museum, mainly devoted to artefacts and photographic material, all professionally managed by the late Ralph and Frances Cawthorne, the present curator, Chris Ruddlestone and the museum committee, to whom I owe many thanks. This led on to the Kingsbridge offices of Mike Roberts, director and general manager of South Hams Newspapers Ltd which includes the *Dartmouth Chronicle* where, in a small dungeon-like room, rich in treasure, were most of the back volumes of the *Dartmouth Chronicle* since its founding by Robert Cranford in 1854.

The journals were in minuscule print and devoid of pictures, but contained superb quality records, the highest standard of journalism and grammar, and a wealth of detailed information relating to local affairs. No event was too small to be recorded - even the leaving of a committee room to answer the call of nature was reported! Thus began fifteen years' dedication to scouring the small print, staring at blurred microfilm, taking copious notes and poor quality photostats while ever searching for photographs, hopefully mainly unpublished. The research embraced related local subjects, the railway, higher, lower ferries, river steamboats, mail liners, Harbour Commission, coaling trade, major figures, mansions and Kingswear Church, resulting in this 100 year journal of the life and times of Dartmouth, Kingswear and surrounding district.

Surprisingly, the *Chronicle* contained little intrusive reporting, the lifeblood of today's tabloids. Amorous encounters were equally prevalent but affairs both sides of the sheets received no vitriolic reporting. The writer hopes that lack of titillation will not diminish the reader's enjoyment!

Thanks are due to the following, without whose support there would be no story. First and foremost are Jean and Neil Baxter who took my uncertain efforts on tape and computer, retyped and edited them into a format suitable for publication and enthusiastic support from my daughter Donna. The late Brigadier W Hine-Haycock gave initial encouragement, by letter, material, and photographs; support also came from the late John Horsley, founder curator of Brixham Museum. President Colin Harris, flag officers, staff and members past and present of the Royal Dart Yacht Club made available minutes and photographs of club pictures. Peter Batts contributed the late Group Captain Gordon Davis's research material. Thanks are due to the Dart Harbour & Navigation Authority for the use of their minutes books from 1863 onwards, and special thanks to ex-port pilot, Dave Griffiths and John Pike, ex-chief Torquay librarian, who gave helpful advice and numerous photographs, as did Cyril King, researcher and former draughtsman of Philip & Son Ltd; Kingswear's premier photographer Gordon Thomas provided many rare photographs while reproducing many more. Fate introduced me to Neil Wilton with a wealth of family papers, half models and numerous photographs. Assistance in the form of research, letters, deeds, articles and photographs came from the following: Daphne Hine-Haycock, Sally Pidsley, Eric Bovey, Mrs and the late Mr R Hawke, Alan Kittridge (River Dart Steamboats), E F Clark (G P Bidder), Leslie Jones (Milford Haven), Christopher and Robert Hill (Samuel Lake), Sue Thomas, W Rogers and A Bryant (Albert Liwentaal), Phyllis Casey and Roy Lovett (Tom Casey), Richard Porter, BRNC, Mrs Angela Hutchings, Professor Fred Harper Principal of Seale Hayne Agricultural College, Professor Jere R Daniell II of Dartmouth College, New Hampshire USA, Sir David Clayton (genealogy), historians Ray Freeman (Dartmouth's dedicated researcher) and the late Ivor Smart (committed Dartmouth and Newcomen researcher), K Perkins (James Meadows Rendall), D Blackhurst, P Westcott, Harold Hutchings, R Little, A Carpenter, Mike Holgate, Dr Janet Cusack, Dr Warner, Colin Smart, Judy Diss, Dob Shelley, Lt Cdr P Holden, Martin Taylor, Honiton Galleries, D Southwick, Sarah Taylor, Mrs M Fardon, Mrs A Widdecombe, Mrs S Holman, J Butt, P Rudling, D Graham, G Bush, A Gill, J Thorpe, D Gerrard, R Kelland, S Widdecombe, Major D Molloy, the late Ross Llewellyn, G Philip, Mrs Slocombe, Audrey Le Lievre, G Weatherly, Kingswear Church, Dartmouth Town Council and the Felixstowe Dock & Railway Co. Numerous photographs are used from the collections of the late R Tucker and R Jones.

Thank you also to the staff of Torquay and Dartmouth Libraries, the British Library, Westcountry Studies Library, the Museums at Brixham, Totnes, Torquay, Ilfracombe and National Maritime Museums, the Landmark and National Trusts, Hanover Town USA, Britannia Royal Naval College, *Sea Breezes, Ships Monthly, Yachting World*. And finally thanks to Richard Webb and his wife Gilly, for their encouragement and support.

I have made every effort to ascertain the copyright of material used in this book but where I have not had success or used material inadvertently, please could the copyright holder contact me so that full credit can be given in the next reprint.

Don Collinson